LAW REFORM IN EARLY MODERN ENGLAND

This book provides an illuminating commentary of law reform in the early modern era (1500–1740) and views the moves to improve law and legal institutions in the context of changing political and governmental environments.

Taking a fresh look at law reform over several centuries, it explores the efforts of the king and parliament, and the body of literature supporting law reform that emerged with the growth of print media, to assess the place of the well-known attempts of the revolutionary era in the context of earlier and later movements. Law reform is seen as a long term concern and a longer time frame is essential to understand the 1640–1660 reform measures.

The book considers two law reform movements: the moderate movement which had a lengthy history and whose chief supporters were the governmental and parliamentary elites, and which focused on improving existing law and legal institutions, and the radical reform movement, which was concentrated in the revolutionary decades and which sought to overthrow the common law, the legal profession and the existing system of courts. Informed by attention to the institutional difficulties in completing legislation, this highlights the need to examine particular parliaments.

Although lawyers have often been seen as the chief obstacles to law reform, this book emphasises their contributions – particularly their role in legislation and in reforming the corpus of legal materials – and highlights the previously ignored reform efforts of Lord Chancellors.

Law Reform in Early Modern England 1500–1740

Crown, Parliament and the Press

Barbara J Shapiro

•HART•

OXFORD • LONDON • NEW YORK • NEW DELHI • SYDNEY

HART PUBLISHING

Bloomsbury Publishing Plc

Kemp House, Chawley Park, Cumnor Hill, Oxford, OX2 9PH, UK

1385 Broadway, New York, NY 10018, USA

HART PUBLISHING, the Hart/Stag logo, BLOOMSBURY and the Diana logo are trademarks of Bloomsbury Publishing Plc

First published in Great Britain 2019

A catalogue record for this book is available from the British Library.

Library of Congress Cataloging-in-Publication data

Names: Shapiro, Barbara J, author. Title: Law reform in early modern England : crown, parliament and the press / Barbara J Shapiro.

Description: Oxford ; New York : Hart, 2019. | Includes bibliographical references and index.

Identifiers: LCCN 2019042183 (print) | LCCN 2019042184 (ebook) | ISBN 9781509934218 (hardback) | ISBN 9781509934225 (epub)

Subjects: LCSH: Law reform—England—History—16th century. | Law reform—England—History—17th century. | Law reform—England—History—18th century.

Classification: LCC KD612 .S53 2019 (print) | LCC KD612 (ebook) | DDC 340/.309420903—dc23

LC record available at https://lccn.loc.gov/2019042183

LC ebook record available at https://lccn.loc.gov/2019042184

ISBN: HB: 978-1-50993-421-8
ePDF: 978-1-50993-423-2
ePub: 978-1-50993-422-5

Typeset by Compuscript Ltd, Shannon
Printed and bound in Great Britain by TJ International Ltd, Padstow, Cornwall

To find out more about our authors and books visit www.hartpublishing.co.uk. Here you will find extracts, author information, details of forthcoming events and the option to sign up for our newsletters.

To the memory of Tom Schumann

ACKNOWLEDGEMENTS

This study has been a long time coming and many people have helped along the way. My work could never have completed without the assistance of a great many political and legal historians, most of whom I have never met outside of their books and articles. I must also thank Vicki Kahn, Paul Sniderman, Norma Landau and David Lieberman for helpful conversations. And, most of all to Martin Shapiro who has read the manuscript in its many shapes and forms over a long period of time. The book is dedicated to my brother, Thomas G Schumann.

I would also like to thank the librarians who have assisted me, especially those at the Huntington Library in San Marino, California. I, like most of those working on early modern English history, am deeply indebted to the compilers of EEBO (Early English Books Online) and ECCO (Eighteenth Century Collections Online). Their online existence has become essential for those working on early modern English history.

I am grateful to the publishers who have permitted me to use material from my recent, and not so recent, publications dealing with law reform. These include 'Law Reform in Seventeenth Century England', *American Journal of Legal History* 19 (1975) 280–512, 'Sir Francis Bacon and the Mid-Seventeenth Century Movement for Law Reform', 24 *American Journal of Legal History* (1980) 331–352 and 'The Restoration Chapter in the History of English Law Reform', *Law Humanities* 10 (2016) 313–58.

TABLE OF CONTENTS

1

Introduction

The term 'law reform' has been closely associated with the English politics of the period from 1640 to 1660 both in recent times and the period itself.[1] Certainly there was a very high volume of voices for various legal changes which, for their proponents, would have been reforms and for their opponents anything but. The press provided a new channel for these voices. Most strikingly for all the almost constant voices for a catalogue of changes, many of which continued for years on end, few changes in English legal institutions and processes were actually accomplished.

An explanation of this paradox readily comes to mind. If there were loud voices for change, there might have been such voices against change as well. Certainly this explanation seems to be sufficient for some of the sluggishness of change. We will examine opposition as well as change enthusiasms. However, the main thrust of my argument here is that the stasis that is more remarkable than the actual changes was not so much the result of opposition to 'reform' as of the institutional incapacity of Crown and Parliament to enact proposed changes. This incapacity is the major theme of what follows and will, I believe, be fully shown by a detailed examination of 'law reform.'

This book seeks a better understanding of law reform in the early modern era. It views law reform broadly and looks at a variety of efforts to improve English law and legal institutions in the context of changing forms of government and the pressing issues of the day. Unlike earlier studies, it looks at law reform interest and efforts over a long stretch of time, from the beginning of the reign of Henry VIII in 1509 to the mid-eighteenth century. It charts the effort of kings, parliaments and others to improve the law and legal institutions, and explores the body of literature supporting law reform that would emerge with the growth of printed media. It seeks to reassess the place of the well-known law reform efforts of the revolutionary era in the context of earlier and later efforts. Given that legal institutions are part of a governmental structure, it will examine the extent that Crown aims furthered or limited the success of law reform and how law reform efforts were affected by government instability.

[1] See, eg, Donald Veall, *The Popular Movement for Law Reform 1640–1660* (Oxford, Clarendon Press, 1970); Stuart Prall, *The Agitation of Law Reform during the Puritan Revolution* (The Hague, Martinus Nijhoff, 1966); *An Experimental Essay touching the Reformation of the Lawes of England* (London, 1648); Henry Parker, *Reformation in the Courts and Cases Testamentary* (London, 1650).

A key question for anyone studying law reform is what is to be counted as 'reform'. For the most part, historians dealing with the mid-seventeenth century have been inclined to praise as reforms those changes individuals or groups sought to make if they were developments that that modern observers would consider beneficial. I examine what sixteenth-, seventeenth- and eighteenth-century actors wished to change in their laws and their legal institutions, whether we like those changes or not. Therefore, I include efforts at making adultery a capital offence as well those aimed at ending capital punishment for theft. My study also includes proposals raising the property qualification for jurors as reforms. What counts as reform depends on the eye of the beholder. Those eyes not only differ between modern and early modern observers but also among the latter. Proposals praised by their proponents were often considered by others to be ill-informed, injudicious or even dangerous. I use the term 'law reform' to include not only what contemporaries wished to change in the common law and the statutes, but also their efforts to reduce the cost of litigation and improve the courts, the legal profession and the literature of the law.[2] Although political trials for treason and impeachment cannot themselves be considered reforms, comments made during the trials, and in the very considerable public discussion that followed, will be discussed if they include criticism or suggestions for change in the law or legal procedure.

'Change' too is a slippery concept. It can be used to mean a change offered by a conscious agent, such as a king, a Lord Chancellor, a member of parliament or an anonymous pamphleteer. However, a good deal of change that takes place in legal systems cannot be attributed to particular individuals. Some of these changes were noted by contemporaries, while others, less visible, were not. Some are easy to date, others are not. We do not know exactly when witnesses became part of the jury trial. There was no legislation that initiated or approved of their introduction.[3] Trial by battle was abolished only several centuries after it had become obsolete. The crime of witchcraft was abolished by legislation in 1734, but prosecutions had been few and far between for a long time before that. Should we consider the gradual change in prosecution to be a reform or should 1734 be considered the appropriate date? Many legal practices changed over time with no legislation to mark the changes. The decline of jury participation in civil trials, for example, suggests yet another problem. Some consider the reduced role of the jury to be a good thing and thus a 'reform', arguing that jurors were not competent enough to decide complex legal issues. Others opposed the change as an erosion of the jury trial. Responses to 'change' as well as to clearly initiated reform proposals depended on the outlook and interests of the commentator.

Still another kind of change that is difficult to place in the narrative of law reform is dramatic fluctuation in litigation rates and overall utilisation of

[2] See Joanna Innes, '"Reform" in English Public Life: the Fortunes of a Word' in Joanna Innes and Arthur Burns (eds), *Rethinking the Age of Reform: Britain 1780–1850* (Cambridge, Cambridge University Press, 2003) 71–97.

[3] Occasional use of witnesses can be found in fifteenth-century civil cases.

the courts. Did greater use of courts and lawyers increase the likelihood that they would be the subject of complaint and reform? Developments of this type no doubt helped to shape expressions of interest in law reform, though it is difficult to establish a causal connection.

For the most part, I will use 'reform' and particularly 'law reform' to suggest that some person or group criticised some aspect of the legal system and proposed remedies, including those that might or might not be in keeping with what modern observers would consider reform. Generally, I will refer to 'change' or 'changes' when ideas and legal practice changed without obvious advocates or agents. Both 'law reform' and 'change' are slippery terms, but both are part of our established vocabulary. My attention is focused on agents of change, that is, the Crown and its officials, parliament and the authors of publications favouring changes in the law or the legal system, but I also include changes that were less visible to contemporaries.

The opportunity to use the press varied over time due to the growth of printed media on the one hand and the efforts of early modern governments to control what was published on the other. We know a great deal about criticism of the law during periods when press control was least effective and opportunities for publication were greatest. The revolutionary decade witnessed a breakdown in the government's ability to control the press. The short-lived revolutionary governments continued press control measures, with greater and lesser success. Because the revolutionary-era law reform publications are so varied, counting these publications does not get us very far. It is difficult to weigh the significance of a single-page broadside as opposed to a lengthy, frequently reprinted work or a brief mention in a newsbook. It is even more difficult to determine how representative or how influential each voicing might have been. Reformers who used the press were more visible than those who did not. Judges, who initiated reform in their respective courts, for example, were unlikely to be noticed. Legislative proposals that became law were better known than those that failed.

Research on the history of law reform in England has been concentrated on two periods: the revolutionary era 1640–60 and the nineteenth century. Because there has been so little attention to law reform either before or after the revolutionary era, it has been difficult to get a sense of what were thought to be continuing problems and what kind of reform proposals were offered exactly when to alleviate or end them. I suggest that law reform in England was a long-term concern and that such a long-term study is necessary to understand the developments of the mid-seventeenth century. I will attempt to show that there were two law reform movements: one focused on improving existing law and legal institutions that had a lengthy history, and another, more radical one, concentrated in the revolutionary decades, which sought to overthrow existing law and courts and replace them with alternatives based on different visions of law and policy.

Past studies that focus on the seventeenth-century era of civil war and interregnum for the most part concentrate on the burst of law reform publications that emerged between 1640 and 1660. On the whole, this body of work has been sympathetic to the reforms, viewing them as moving in the right direction. Several suggest that they were 'before their time' and were defeated by greedy lawyers. Some have treated mid-century law reform as the work of 'the people'. Previous studies have been less interested in what reform measures had been aired earlier or continued to be offered in the post-revolutionary decades. The earlier studies by Robert Brown, R Robinson, Goldwin Smith, Mary Cotterell and GB Nourse,[4] as well as later ones by Christopher Hill, Stuart Prall and Donald Veall, Wilfrid Prest, Desmond Brown and the unfortunately unpublished work of CR Niehous were largely in this vein.[5] Most recently there has been more specialised work on Quaker and Leveller contributions.[6] Unsurprisingly, the Restoration and the eighteenth century have largely been ignored.[7]

A second scholarly tradition, that of parliamentary historians engaged in the history of particular parliaments, has also given attention to law reform. For the Henrician period, there are Stanford Lehmberg's volumes on the parliaments of Henry VIII and Geoffrey Elton's extensive work on parliamentary and administrative pursuit of changes during the sixteenth century[8] David Dean's study of Elizabeth's Parliament devoted an entire chapter to law reform. Several of the parliamentary studies of the early Stuart period have also included material on law reform. Among these are TL Moir's study of the 1614 Parliament, and Robert Zaller's study of the Parliament of 1621. Mid-seventeenth-century parliaments have been well served by David Underdown and by Blair Worden, who has an insightful

[4] R Robinson, 'Anticipations under the Commonwealth of Changes in the Law' in JH Wigmore, E Freund and WE Mikell (eds), *Select Essays in Anglo-American Legal History* (Boston, Little Brown, 1907–08) 467 ff; Goldwin Smith, 'The Reform of the Laws of England, 1640–1660' (1941) 10 *University of Toronto Quarterly* 469; GB Nourse, 'Law Reform under the Commonwealth and Protectorate' (1959) 75 *Law Quarterly Review* 512; Robert Brown, 'The Law of England during the Period of the Commonwealth' (1931) 6 *Indiana Law Journal* 359; Mary Cotterell, 'Interregnum Law Reform, The Hale Commission of 1652' (1958) 83 *English Historical Review* 689.

[5] Stuart Prall, 'The Mid-seventeenth Century Movement for Law Reform' (1980) 25 *American Journal of Legal History* 332; Barbara Shapiro, 'Law Reform in Seventeenth Century England' (1975) 19 *American Journal of Legal History* 280; Veall (n 1); Wilfrid Prest, 'Law Reform and Legal Education in Interregnum England' (2002) 75 *Historical Research* 112; Wilfrid Prest, 'William Lambarde, Elizabethan Law Reform, and Early Stuart Politics' (1995) 34 *Journal of British Studies* 464; Robert Zaller, 'The Debate on Capital Punishment during the English Revolution' (1987) 31 *American Journal of Legal History* 126; Desmond Brown, 'Abortive Attempts to Codify English Criminal Law' (1992) 11 *Parliamentary History* 1; CR Niehaus, 'The Issue of Law Reform in the Revolution 1640–60' (PhD dissertation, Harvard University, 1957). Niehaus gives some attention to the pre-1640 period.

[6] R Michael Rogers, 'Quakers and the Law in Revolutionary England' (1987) 22 *Canadian Journal of History* 149; Ann Hughes, 'Gerrard Winstanley, News Culture and Law Reform in the Early 1650s' (2014) 36 *Prose Studies* 63.

[7] But see Barbara Shapiro, 'The Restoration Chapter in English Law Reform' (2016) 10 *Law and Humanities* 31; Wilfrid Prest, 'Law Reform in Eighteenth Century England' in Peter Birks (ed), *Life of the Law* (Proceedings of the 10th British Legal History Conference, Oxford, Oxford University Press, 1991) 113–23.

[8] Stanford Lehmberg, *The Reformation Parliament, 1529–36* (Cambridge, Cambridge University Press, 1970); Stanford Lehmberg, *The Later Parliaments of Henry VIII, 1536–1547* (Cambridge, Cambridge University Press, 1977); GR Elton, 'Tudor Government: The Points of Contact: Parliament' (1974) 24 *Transactions of the Royal Historical Society* 183; GR Elton, 'Parliament in the

chapter on the law reform of the Rump Parliament.[9] There is also the older work on the Barebones Parliament.[10] While these historians explore the law reform interests of the particular parliament or parliaments studied, they typically ignore the law reform measures of the periods that preceded or followed them. The history of law reform therefore requires connecting the dots between various parliaments. One of the emphases of this study will be parliament's continuing involvement with reform legislation.

Lack of attention to Restoration and eighteenth-century law reform can partly be attributed to traditional divisions of scholarly labour. Few historians of the revolutionary era have been interested in the Restoration and beyond. It is almost as if the seventeenth century ended for them in 1660. On the other hand, the concept of a long eighteenth century informs the work of many post-revolutionary historians. If one's research and mindset is shaped by an eighteenth century that begins in 1660 and marks the beginning of a new era, one is unlikely to examine earlier times. Continuities tend to be overlooked or minimised. Because the Restoration and the early eighteenth century are frequently depicted as reactionary, there has been little inclination to look for long-term continuities in the area of law reform. Yet another reason for the neglect of the length and breadth of law reform may be the eighteenth-century legal historian's focus on crime. We know a great deal more about crime than we do about other items of the law reform agenda.

Another reason for slighting pre-revolutionary efforts to improve the legal system is the long and dominant tradition of scholarly concern with constitutional conflicts between Crown and parliament.[11] The exclusion of religious legislation from the topic of law reform should also be rectified because such legislation had an enormous impact on the legal status of a great many people over a long period of time. While historians have given a great deal of attention to the difficulties of Roman Catholics and non-conforming Protestants, laws generated by such difficulties are not typically treated as a significant element of the legal system.

I will argue that there were two law reform movements: one that I label moderate and the other radical. I trace the moderate reform throughout the period under review, focusing on the efforts of Crown and parliament to improve the legal

Sixteenth Century; Frustrations and Fortune' (1979) 22 *Historical Journal* 255; GR Elton, *The Parliaments of Elizabeth 1559–1581* (Cambridge, Cambridge University Press, 1980); GR Elton, 'Reform by Statute' (1970) 50 *Proceedings of the British Academy* 177; GR Elton, 'English Law in the Sixteenth Century Reform in an Age of Change' in *Studies in Tudor and Stuart Politics and Government*, 4 vols (Cambridge, Cambridge University Press, 1983), vol III, 274–88.

[9] David L Dean, *Law-Making and Society in Late Elizabethan England: The Parliaments of Elizabeth 1584–1601* (Cambridge, Cambridge University Press, 996); TL Moir, *The Addled Parliament of 1614* (Oxford, Clarendon Press, 1958); Robert Zaller, *The Parliament of 1621* (Berkeley, University of California Press, 1971); David Underdown, *Pride's Purge: Politics in the English Revolution* (Oxford, Oxford University Press, 1971); Blair Worden, *The Rump Parliament 1648–1653* (Cambridge, Cambridge University Press, 1974).

[10] HA Glass, *The Barebone Parliament and the Religious Movements of the Seventeenth Century* (Oxford, Oxford University Press, 1899).

[11] While revisionists have emphasised harmony more than conflict, they have not been particularly interested in law reform.

system by reducing costs and delay, competing jurisdictions and what was felt to be 'corruption' in the system. I suggest that the moderate movement, which I trace from the sixteenth century until at least the mid-eighteenth century, was promoted first by the Crown and parliament, and then largely by parliament. I also discuss more radical efforts, voiced primarily during the revolutionary decades, to replace rather than reform existing law and legal institutions. The radical movement itself was not unified, being composed of political and religious individuals and groups with differing visions of a just society and good laws. Radical law reform rose and fell with the groups that supported it. It was promoted primarily by those who were not in the social and political elite and were unlikely to be members of parliament.

Organisation of the chapters that follow is chronological. My starting point is somewhat arbitrary since all periods exhibit some degree of dissatisfaction with law and the legal system. I begin with the reign of Henry VIII, which enjoyed a well-established set of legal institutions and then experienced major changes in those institutions. It focuses first on the efforts of Lord Chancellor Wolsey, then on the impact of the Reformation and the creation of new courts. The legal system looked quite different at the end of Henry's reign than it did at the beginning. The chapter also examines the reform measures introduced during the Edwardian and Marian periods. It is followed by a chapter on the lengthy Elizabethan period in which we can see the formation of a moderate reform agenda. It emphasises the role of the queen, her Lord Chancellors and the reform measures introduced in parliament. Chapter 4, which examines law reform under the early Stuarts, focuses on individual parliaments in order to illustrate how more immediate parliamentary issues affected the possibilities for completing law reform legislation. It also discusses the reform views of Sir Francis Bacon and Sir Edward Coke.

The revolutionary period is discussed in two chapters because of the rapid changes in government structure, the introduction of a second reform movement and the proliferation of printed commentary on law reform. Chapter 5 covers the period from the calling of the Long Parliament to the execution of Charles I. Chapter 6 covers law reform from the creation of the Commonwealth to the Restoration in 1660. Both chapters explore the difficulties experienced by revolutionary-era governments that stemmed from the competing claims of Crown and parliament to legal authority and the absence of a stable government that could claim the loyalty of most subjects. They also examine the problems that the ever-changing governments experienced with the judiciary and the legal profession.

The two revolutionary-era chapters are followed by one that examines law reform interest between the restoration of the monarchy in 1660 and the Revolution of 1688. It primarily deals with the efforts of the Cavalier Parliament to continue the tradition of moderate reform, the less well-known publications that supported law reform, the growing role of political parties, and the place of religion in shaping the legal system. Chapter 8 takes the narrative of law reform from the Revolution of 1688 to the mid-eighteenth century, focusing on parliament and several lesser-known reform publications.

The final chapter will attempt to draw conclusions about the two early modern reform agendas, with particular emphasis on the continuity of the moderate reform initiatives. It will also examine some of the unresolved or partially unresolved issues in the study of early modern law reform as well as the problems which are to be found in the study of most legal systems. It speculates on the nature of criticism of the law and law reform more generally in the hope that these speculations and unanswered questions will be of use to scholars concerned with law and law reform in other times and other places.

Each chapter follows roughly the same pattern. Chapters typically begin with an indication of the chief political and religious concerns of Crown and parliament so as to place law reform efforts in that context, drawing particular attention to the insufficiently recognised role of Lord Chancellors and Lord Keepers as spokesmen for reform. Parliamentary interest and activity in law reform are examined, as are parliament's institutional difficulties in completing legislation.

A good deal of each chapter is focused on specific areas of reform sought by parliament. These include reducing the costs and delays in litigation, and eliminating corruption in the legal process. They involved criticism of judges, lawyers and court officials as well as criticism of the common law courts, Chancery, the conciliar courts, the ecclesiastical courts and admiralty and the reform issues associated with the jurisdictional conflicts among them. Some chapters, but not all, consider issues of centralisation and decentralisation of legal administration in the context of law reform, noting the decay of local courts, the demand for new courts and issues relating to appeal. Most chapters also point out parliamentary concern with reforming juries and justices of the peace. Several also investigate the interest in and efforts taken to rationalise the common and statute law.

Although parliament was more focused on court reform than law reform, several types of law are highlighted. Most chapters consider parliamentary concern with religious law, criminal law, and laws relating to credit and debt, bankruptcy and moral behaviour, particularly adultery, sodomy, blasphemy and perjury. Although legislation on religious questions is not usually treated as a law reform topic, it is included because its changing provisions had such a substantial impact, especially on the legal lives of Roman Catholics and Protestant dissenters. For many, religion was probably the most important part of the law reform agenda.

Parliamentary interest in improving the execution of the criminal law is noted, as well as its concern with particular crimes. The disconnect between the harshness of the criminal law and the discretion exercised in its execution is considered in several chapters. Some changes in criminal punishments are linked to moving certain crimes from the ecclesiastical to the secular courts. Some, but not all, discuss interest in improving land law, that is, questions relating to tenure, leases, uses, statutes of limitation, fraudulent conveyances and land registration.

I will also refer to several of the more famous trials. Although trials, particularly political trials (and especially those for treason), do not easily fit under the rubric of reform, some of these elicited comments that sought reform in criminal procedure.

Publications dealing with law reform are given considerable attention in several chapters. Discussion is divided between polemical and professional writing. Polemical writing concentrated on attacks and defences of the common law, the courts and the legal profession, appropriate punishment for various crimes and the best way to reform individual items on the law reform agenda. Publications of legal professionals aimed at the reform of the corpus of legal materials. Although this large body of professional writing has not usually been associated with law reform, a good deal of it was designed to remedy the uncertainty and confusion that contemporaries, both lay and professional, associated with the law. The publications of Sir Francis Bacon, Sir Edward Coke and Sir Matthew Hale are discussed at some length.

However, several kinds of law will not be examined. Since judge-made law has such an important place in English legal history, my lack of attention to it requires some explanation. I have given it a reduced role in this study because defenders of the common law, both judges and lawyers, were committed to the ideology that judges merely informed their courts as to what the law was. They were to be interpreters not makers of law. While the view that the common law was unchanging was not accepted by the entire legal profession, it was nevertheless an important element in common legal thinking. Judges rarely admitted that they were agents of legal change, even though it was obvious to many that their decisions had changed the substance of the law. The myth of the unchanging common law thus underlined judicial reluctance to frame their decisions as reform. Judges then and now are reluctant to admit their law-making. Despite their widely held view that legislation often caused more damage than the abuses it was designed to correct, legal professionals openly participated in drafting and supporting change in the statutes.

This study also slights the constitutional conflicts traditionally at the centre of constitutional history. While tension and conflict between Crown and parliament certainly existed, and there were varying views of the appropriate sources of law and the role of Crown and parliament in law-making, such differences were largely, if not completely, absent in the debates over law reform. This study therefore includes little discussion of such familiar topics as purveyance and monopolies.

Before beginning my chronological march through English history from 1509 to 1740, I will provide a very brief sketch of major institutions in the legal system in existence at the beginning of the sixteenth century. It characterises the major courts that made up the legal system, beginning with the common law courts. While the common law was the dominant and most revered kind of law, it was not the only form of law. Its origins are to be found in feudal law and it dealt primarily with land tenure, inheritance and related topics. Initially its primary litigants were feudal lords, but other substantial landholders were soon added. Copyhold tenure and other lesser tenures were not initially litigated in the common law courts. The common law did not deal with all areas of law and for the most part did not move quickly into new areas of law. Because the common law was not a written law, it was open to charges of uncertainty and confusion. The language of the common law courts was Latin and Law French, a residue of the law's Anglo-French origins. Cases at common law were tried by local juries.

There were three common law courts: the Court of Common Pleas, King's Bench and the Exchequer. Although originally they were respectively to handle disputes between subjects, cases involving the monarch and royal revenue, the divisions were not rigidly adhered to and the business of the common law courts shifted from time to time. Legal culture was predominantly an oral culture absorbed by observation, osmosis and attendance at the Inns of Court, though manuscript yearbooks and writers such as Littleton also had a role in legal learning. Though the common law courts were considered the centrepiece of the English legal system, they were slow to respond to economic and other changes. Other institutions developed to fill these needs.

Chancery, a court of 'equity' rather than a court of 'law' also had a lengthy history. It, like the common law, developed from the king's duty to provide justice. The Lord Chancellor, as head of Chancery, was the keeper of the king's conscience and adjudicated matters not covered by the common law. Since these grew in number, the business of Chancery increased over time. Its legal procedure differed from that of the common law courts, relying on written depositions. Decisions were made by legally trained professionals rather than juries.

There were also ecclesiastical courts which, unlike the common law courts and Chancery, were not derived from the monarch. They operated at several levels arranged in hierarchical fashion, with final appeals to Rome. The law of these courts, which governed the behaviour of both clerics and laymen, was canon or church law. They adjudicated a wide variety of cases including disputes over tithes, wills and testaments, marriage and the many fees laymen owed the church. Regulating moral behaviour was also part of their jurisdiction. They dealt with cases involving adultery, sodomy, heresy and blasphemy, as well as defamation and perjury. The church courts administered punishments of several kinds, including fines and shaming rituals, but not capital punishment. The Court of High Commission, although not under the jurisdiction of the church, became an important court.

Composed of the king's most important advisors, the Privy Council performed judicial as well as administrative functions. It might take on issues that were unavailable in the common law courts as well as some that might have been litigated elsewhere. Over time, these functions became institutionalised in the Court of Star Chamber, the Court of Requests, the Council of the North, the Council of Wales and the Marches, and the Council of the West.

Local courts and local justice are less easy to characterise, since they consisted of a mélange of older hundred and county courts in various states of decay. Courts leet and baron were courts attached to particular manors. Justices of the peace appointed by the Crown performed both administrative and judicial functions. They were responsible for petty sessions in which they dealt with minor matters. At quarter sessions, several justices held jury trials for somewhat more serious offences. Some boroughs also had been given the right to hold courts.

The legal profession had several branches. There were the common lawyers, whose most-esteemed members were the sergeants at law who pleaded in the common law courts and from whose ranks judges were chosen. The distinctions between lawyers (today we would call them barristers) and attorneys and solicitors who served clients in their legal affairs but did not plead in court was not very clear; both were sometimes included under the rubric 'lawyers'. There were also lawyers trained in the civil and canon law who practised in the ecclesiastical courts, Chancery and Admiralty courts, none of which employed juries. Justices of the peace, that is, the local magistrates, were not legal professionals, although they exercised many judicial functions in their petty and quarter sessions.

Although one might draw a fairly simple diagram of these courts, it would be deceptive. The Crown's duty to provide justice meant that it was in some (although vague) sense the source of law. The courts had their origin in the Crown. But courts, and especially the common law courts, developed law and practices that the legal profession saw as separate from the Crown. The Crown had created these courts, which in turn created the common law, a law that claimed jurisdiction over the entire country. Over time, litigants came to prefer decisions of the common law judges over local justice because they were removed from the control of powerful local figures. The appointment and dismissal of the judges who sat in Westminster was in the hands of the Crown. When on the assize circuit, trying both civil and criminal cases before local juries, judges were agents of the Crown and the common law, bringing the common law to the counties of England.

Statute-making, the creation of new law or changes in the law, was the business of Crown and parliament. The Crown was a necessary component of statute-making and was often the source of legislative proposals. Parliament was not a regular part of government, coming into being intermittently at the will of the monarch. It was most often called when the monarch required financial support, normal revenues being insufficient to support war or other expensive endeavours.

Parliament, which was necessary for the approval of taxes, was also necessary for legislation. Monarchs might issue proclamations from time to time, but these did not have the status of law. Parliament was composed of two bodies, both entirely male: the House of Commons and the House of Lords. The elected House of Commons was largely composed of landed gentry and typically included a substantial contingent of lawyers. For part of the period, there was a considerable presence of privy councillors. The House of Lords was composed of hereditary noblemen, those ennobled by the Crown, bishops and heads of religious houses. Legislation required approval of both houses and the assent of the monarch. Parliament, like so many other English governmental institutions, performed judicial as well as legislative functions. It often decided individual cases by private legislation. Members of the upper house were tried by their peers in the House of Lords rather than in the regular courts.

The commonly invoked modern distinctions of executive, legislative and judicial branches do not serve us well in describing the early modern English governmental structure. Many, if not most, legal institutions combined judicial and administrative duties. What the appropriate roles were for the Crown, parliament and the courts was never very clear. Nor was the jurisdiction of particular courts. Jurisdictional boundaries were a frequent law reform topic.

2

The Early Tudors and Law Reform 1509–58

Best known for the Reformation and the vagaries of his many marriages, the reign of Henry VIII has not conventionally been considered an era of law reform, despite the dramatic changes in England's legal landscape. The most important of these were the rapid growth and expansion of Chancery, the development of the conciliar courts, the legal changes that accompanied the Reformation and the beginnings of a printed legal literature that would, over time, transform the nature of the legal profession. Some were the work of the Crown and its servants, some of the Crown and parliament jointly, and still others the efforts of lawyers and judges. This chapter examines these developments as well as Edwardian and Marian efforts at legal reform and the humanist contribution to law reform.

The nature and pace of legal reform was not uniform during the Henrician era. The impetus for reform during the first portion was largely the work of Cardinal Thomas Wolsey and centred on Chancery and the dramatic expansion of the conciliar courts. Initiated by the king's marital problems, it led to royal and parliament-inspired legislation that dramatically altered the legal position of the Crown in the church and made parliamentary legislation the vehicle for change in authorised religious belief and practice. New courts were created to implement collection of the king's expanding revenues stemming from the break with Rome and the dissolution of the monasteries. In addition to these two major changes, we can see the beginning of a parliamentary law reform agenda aimed at improving the existing law and courts, and the legal profession. This agenda would shape law reform efforts for many generations.

As any historian knows, rarely is there an obvious place to begin a historical narrative. Whatever date one chooses, the story always occurs in the context of an existing system of ideas and institutions. We therefore necessarily begin our examination of early modern law reform *en medias res* with a set of well-entrenched institutions and practices, that is, with an existing legal system that had grown over the centuries. Reform efforts were directed incrementally modifying this set of institutions and practices as well as initiating major changes. We focus largely on the Crown, parliaments and the courts. When referring to the Crown, we include the monarch's chief ministers and confidents as well as the monarch. Parliament was a necessary element in legislative change, yet it had no continued existence, typically being called when the Crown required financial support. Prorogation and adjournment, also at the will of the ruler, might come at any time, disrupting the completion of legislation. Law-making required a lengthy process: three readings in both the House of Commons and the House of Lords, committees to work out details and differences between the two houses, and the assent of the Crown. The legislative process was particularly difficult in periods when pressing matters absorbed much of parliament's attention. Most parliaments were successful in passing only a small part of their legislative agendas. Although in this and subsequent chapters the Crown and parliament are often treated separately, I do not wish to imply that they were usually in opposition. Legislative proposals often originated from government sources and might be drafted either by Crown officials or members of parliament. The Lord Chancellor was often an important promoter or participant in law reform, speaking to parliament on behalf of the Crown and presiding over the House of Lords. Judges might also be agents of reform in their respective courts. The common law judges' statements on law reform were often ambiguous or hesitant because the judges claimed to be interpreters of law rather than law-makers.

Henry VIII inherited an existing body of law and courts. The common law courts dealt with issues of the common law, mostly land and inheritance. Chancery, a court of equity, was dominated by the Lord Chancellor, typically a member of the clergy trusted by the monarch. Disputes at common law were tried by juries; Chancery cases were not. There were also hierarchically arranged ecclesiastical courts that dealt with cases related to heresy, marriage, tithes, wills and testaments, and moral infractions. These courts were the target of a good deal of anti-clerical sentiment and were sometimes in conflict with the common law courts. There were also local courts in varying states of decay, justices of the peace charged with administrative and judicial duties, manorial courts, and courts related to particular town corporations.

Together these entities made up the legal system, though by system we do not mean that they formed a rational arrangement. Rather, there are a number of legal institutions that sometimes overlapped and jostled with one another in various ways. Some had feudal or manorial origins, while others developed out of the king's duty to provide justice. The common law was by no means the only law. Canon law governed the ecclesiastical courts and was administered by civil and canon lawyers. Admiralty employed civil law and was staffed by civilians. The decrees of Chancery provided equitable decisions when remedies were unavailable in the common law courts. The Privy Council also decided some legal disputes, as did parliament. Statute law, made jointly by the king and parliament, was becoming increasingly important in making and changing law.[1]

There was also a body of criminal law, typically labeled pleas of the Crown, that dealt with treason and felonies, serious crimes that required the death penalty. Prosecution was largely in private hands, which meant that many crimes, both

[1] The Crown also issued proclamations, typically to enforce existing legislation. In 1539, legislation permitted proclamations to serve as law if no death penalty or forfeiture of goods was involved, and if consistent with existing law. This was repealed in 1547.

serious and non-serious, were not prosecuted. If perpetrators came to trial, they were tried by juries. Some first-time offenders evaded the death penalty by claiming benefit of clergy, a privilege once available only to clergymen. Benefit of clergy was being extended to male laymen who were able to read or recite a particular biblical passage. There were extremely harsh penalties for offences that are no longer considered heinous crimes. We will treat the proposals for change in the criminal law as reform, regardless of modern sensibilities.

Henry VIII inherited a relatively stable regime. Dynastic issues had become less prominent, though legal issues relating to royal succession, royal births and marriages were always present and could emerge in public discourse at any time.

Prior to the calling of the Reformation Parliament in 1529, the most important legal development was the changing structure of courts. Conciliar courts began to take up legal issues that the common law courts avoided or ignored. They also gave attention to situations that were thought to threaten peace and order. The Crown, the Privy Council and the Lord Chancellor were able to respond more rapidly than the common law courts to the changing social, economic and legal environment.

The year 1529 would mark a break in the very modest reforms earlier introduced by parliament and the beginning of a period of major statutory changes in the legal system. The numerous statutes relating to the break with Rome and the dissolution of the monasteries initiated a series of changes that would not only alter the religious landscape, but also would create new courts and a changed legal status of the monarch in relation to the church. Most of these changes were the result of the joint efforts of Crown and parliament. While the Reformation statutes have been well studied, they have not generally been discussed in the context of legal reform. Reform in religion came to mean reform by statute. Religious reform and legal reform may not have been the same, but statutes dealing with religious matters would have serious legal consequences for many English subjects. Legislative measures dealing with religion underline the fact that these alterations might be reforms for some and the opposite for others.

Openings of Parliament typically began with a speech by the king, or the Lord Chancellor, outlining the Crown's desires for the session. In 1529, and perhaps earlier, these addresses were likely to include encouragement to undertake law reform. In 1529 Lord Chancellor Thomas More told parliament that it should reform 'divers Laws that by Long Contyinuance of Time and Mutation of Things, were now grown insufficient and imperfect'.[2] Thomas Audley, Speaker of the House of Commons, also spoke of the laws as being 'very insufficient and imperfect', indicating that no laws had yet been 'made to reform the same'. In 1542, Audley's opening speech warned that the Laws needed to be made 'more vigorously taking away Superfluities'. '[M]any laws remain perfectly unknown, to the no small hurt of the republic.' Parliament should consider whether there was a need for

[2] *The Parliamentary and Constitutional History of England*, 24 vols (London, 1751–61), vol IV, 40. Mention of the 'divers new enormities sprung up' also appears in Hall's *Chronicle*.

'new laws' to curb 'new Vices.'[3] The opening speeches of many subsequent Lord Chancellors and Lord Keepers urged parliament to reform various aspects of the law. Their role as spokesmen for law reform has been largely ignored.

Crown and parliament were both engaged in law reform. Some reform impulses stemmed from governmental sources, while others originated in parliament. Because privy councillors and high officers of state were often members of the House of Lords or the House of Commons, it is frequently difficult to determine the origin of a particular measure; in 1517, there was an order 'for Reformation of misorders and other enormityes in the King's several courts.'[4]

I. The Common Law Courts and Chancery

We begin with the common law and the common law courts. Given the long and widely held belief that the common law did not change, reform in judge-made law was often disguised. Lawyers and judges were also reluctant to have parliament meddle with the common law through statutory change. However, the Crown and parliament were not reluctant to legislate about what they thought were abuses in the law courts. In 1510, a proclamation dealt with 'transferring Cases to Common Pleas and King's Bench to remedy the problems of times past.' Its aim was 'avoiding … the great vexations, costs and charges of his said subjects.'[5]

Chancery, an old well-established court, was modified substantially by Thomas Wolsey who, as Lord Chancellor, headed the court. It was a court of 'equity,' not 'law' and was to fill the gaps in the common law. It used a simpler procedure than the writs that initiated suits in the common law courts. Equitable jurisdiction increased rapidly during Wolsey's chancellorship. The number of suits that Chancery adjudicated expanded, providing remedies unavailable at common law. John Guy has documented the huge increase in property business, much of it at the expense of the Court of Common Pleas. Even common lawyers recognised the advantages for their clients in Chancery procedure which could provide arbitration and extra-legal compromises. As a result, parallel jurisdictions arose between the two courts and possible competition for business. The changes that gave

[3] *Parliamentary and Constitutional History*, IV, 175, 176; Stanford Lehmberg, *The Reformation Parliament: 1529–36* (Cambridge, Cambridge University Press, 1970) 131–32. Audley introduced several reform bills in 1539 and 1540. He proposed bills dealing with wills, jointures, marriage of minors, leases, unjust disseisin and protection for those who revealed murders or felonies, false jury verdicts and perjury. See Geoffrey Elton, *Reformation and Renewal: Thomas Cromwell and the Commonwealth* (New Haven, Yale University Press, 1973) 152.

[4] Quoted in JA Guy, *The Court of Star Chamber and its Records to the Reign of Elizabeth I* (London, Public Record Office, 1985) 6.

[5] Paul Hughes and James Larkin, *Tudor Royal Proclamations*, 3 vols (New Haven, Yale University Press, 1962), vol II, 264. It transferred cases pending before commissions of oyer and terminer to the King's Bench.

Chancery a larger share of legal business, unlike many reforms, were not the result of legislative intervention.

It was during this period that Thomas More and Christopher St Germain debated the nature and desirability of equity. St Germain, the defender of equity, recognised that overlaps between the common law and Chancery might lead to uncertainty and arbitrariness. There was never a clear line between the jurisdiction of 'law' and 'equity', and its absence meant that Chancery and the common law courts would often be at odds.[6] Chancery's rapid expansion altered the balance among the existing courts, enhancing Chancery's weight in the structure of courts. Additional changes took place when Thomas More replaced Wolsey as Lord Chancellor. More was not only the first non-cleric but also the first common lawyer to serve Chancery, a court which was characterised as 'keeper of 'the king's conscience'. Chancery, however, was moving from a generalised notion of conscience in the direction of specific relief measures, such as the injunction. When More was criticised for his use of injunctions, he defended them by showing 'both the number and causes of every one of them', saying that he was driven 'to that necessity for awarding out injunctions to relieve the people's injury'.[7] Yet, More was scrupulous about issuing injunctions and their numbers decreased during his tenure. More carried on the work of Wolsey.[8] Though there were tensions with the common law courts, their relations improved under More.[9] Under his leadership, Chancery jurisdiction continued to grow, offering new and more economical remedies than the now quite sluggish common law courts.

II. The Conciliar Courts

The growth and development of the conciliar courts, like that of Chancery, substantially altered the English legal system by offering new and expanded venues for adjudication. Like Chancery, the conciliar courts were to handle matters that could not be adjudicated in the common law courts. They were also to provide law and order where it was lacking. Like most courts, they were of Crown origin, outgrowths and expansions of the royal council's traditional role in deciding individual cases. As such cases began to take up too much time, the council hived off judicial functions. These evolved into the Court of Star Chamber, the Court of Requests and the Councils of the North, Wales and the Marches, and the West.

[6] JA Guy, 'The Development of Equitable Jurisdiction 1450–1550' in E Ives and AH Manchester (eds), *Law, Litigants and the Legal Profession* (London, Royal Historical Society, 1983) 80–88.

[7] More defended discretion, arguing that justices of courts that allowed discretion should 'mitigate and reform the rigour of the law themselves'. See William Roper, *The Life of Sir Thomas Moore, Knight* (Oxford, Early English Text Society, 1958) V, 197. See also Russell Osgood, 'Law in Sir Thomas More's *Utopia* as Compared to his Lord Chancellorships' (2006) I *Thomas More Studies* 176.

[8] Guy (n 4) 6.

[9] David Raack, 'A History of Injunctions in England before 1700' (1985) 61 *Indiana Law Journal* 571.

The Court of Star Chamber was an outgrowth of the royal council's long-standing practice of adjudicating cases without common law remedies. Shortly after the accession of Henry VIII, legislation authorised it to 'punish divers misdemeanors', including 'taking of money by juries … for reformation'.[10] It heard cases between private parties, but did not deal with treason or felonies. It dealt with problems of public order such as riot, rout and unlawful assembly. The Council in Star Chamber, given that label because it sat in a room with stars on the ceiling, soon became a separate court. Its procedure differed from that of the common law courts. Instead of a jury trial, it began with an English bill. Unlike the common law courts, which tried cases of felony, Star Chamber allowed counsel to both sides. It proceeded to punishment after hearing the examination of sworn witnesses. Fines rather than damages were awarded.

Again it was Thomas Wolsey who was the key figure in expanding Star Chamber. It quickly became a busy court attracting many litigants. Under Wolsey's direction, an increasing number of cases dealt with real property. Star Chamber also handed down decisions involving corrupt juries, perjury, defamation, forgery and fraud. As John Guy's study has shown, about three-quarters of the alleged violent acts tried there were fictitious, with riot or other offences being alleged to bring cases of land title into court. As the number of cases involving land expanded, the possibility of cases that ran parallel to those of the common law courts was created.[11] Wolsey not only expanded the number of cases but also gave a larger role to judges on the court. His efforts to enhance the opportunities for justice and to reduce abuses in the operation of the legal system were significant in making Star Chamber a popular and settled court.

Sir Thomas More and Thomas Audley, Wolsey's successors as Lord Chancellor, both common lawyers, continued his vision of Star Chamber, but were less arrogant and more knowledgeable about the law. When Thomas More became Lord Chancellor in 1529, he announced a plan to enact laws to prevent 'new Enormities … amongst the People'.[12] There was a new statute for Star Chamber that emphasised the need to combat perversions of public justice. However, More's influence, in Star Chamber and elsewhere, eroded as the king's divorce proceedings went forward. More's successor, Lord Keeper Sir Thomas Audley, was active and met daily with the court. Clear separation from the Privy Council occurred in 1536. The court became more concerned with corruption of sheriffs, justices of the peace and juries, but continued to be a popular court for civil litigation.[13]

Wolsey was also the key figure in remodelling the Court of Requests, another offshoot of the council. While the origin of the Court of Requests can be traced

[10] 3 Henry VIII c 1. The statute referred to the increase in murder, robberies and perjuries.

[11] John Guy, *The Cardinal's Court* (Hassocks, Harvester Press, 1977) 9, 13–17. See also Stanford Lehmberg, 'Star Chamber, 1485–1509' (1961) 21 *Huntington Library Quarterly* 189.

[12] Quoted in Guy (n 11) 132.

[13] ibid 57–58, 91, 115, 122–24, 132, 134, 136–38. Cromwell was active in supporting the court. The number of criminal cases increased under Edward VI, Mary I and Elizabeth I. See also Lehmberg (n 11).

back to the reign of Richard III, Wolsey energetically expanded its reach. It was a court for those unable to manage the high costs of the common law courts. Its procedures were similar to those of Chancery and, like other equity courts, its decisions were based on 'fairness'. It largely dealt with civil matters, but was not permitted to hear suits for land or forgiveness of debt. The court's low cost and rapid procedure made it attractive to litigants. It was particularly attractive for women who were treated more favourably than in the common law courts.[14] Although common lawyers became hostile to the Court of Requests as it encroached on their business, it remained popular until its demise during the Civil War era.

One of the continuing problems for England's rulers was the difficulty of governing and of providing justice in the more remote parts of the country. Some areas were not fully integrated into the legal system, dominated by powerful local magnates and so distant from Westminster that access to the central courts was costly and difficult. Scottish border problems and, most recently, hostility to the Reformation and the Pilgrimage of Grace uprising of 1536 further aggravated matters. Bringing the 'rule of law' to outlying areas of the country became essential to a unified state. Like Star Chamber and the Court of Requests, the Council of the North, the Council of Wales and the Marches, and the Council of the West were outgrowths of the royal council. Each of these courts was entrusted with administrative and judicial authority to bring about greater central control and justice.

The Council of the North had its origin in the late fifteenth century, but was re-established and greatly expanded in 1537, its new commission providing increased judicial and financial administrative functions. It dealt with both civil and criminal business, using common law procedures and juries for treason, murder and felony and the bill procedure of Star Chamber for other types of cases. Assizes were held less frequently in the North than elsewhere due to an insufficient number of the king's judges. In 1545, an order of the Privy Council redefined the Council's structure, emphasising 'the speedy and difficult administration of justice to be had between party and party'.[15]

Wales remained a problem. It was said in parliament that the Welsh 'continued and persevred … in commission of diverse and manifest thefts, murders and rebellions, willful burnings of houses' and other 'abominable malifacts'.[16]

[14] Requests took appeals from manor courts when disputes over the customary rights of widows were involved. See Tim Stretton, 'Women, Customs and Equity in the Court of Requests' in Jenny Kermode and Garthine Walker (eds), *Women, Crime and the Courts in Early Modern England* (Chapel Hill, University of North Carolina Press, 1994) 170–90. The court lost business when copyhold tenure became litigable in the common law courts.

[15] FW Brook, 'The Council of the North' in Joel Hurstfield (ed), *The Tudors* (London, Sidgwick & Jackson, 1973); Rachel Reid, *The King's Council in the North* (London, Longmans, 1921).

[16] Quoted in Lehmberg (n 3) 210, citing SP 1//84, fol. 131 PRO. Legislation also provided remedies against unjust Marcher lords, prohibited bringing weapons to court and gave increased authority to justices of the peace and gaol delivery in counties bordering on Wales. Courts were to be kept in 'sure and peaceable places'. A statute to punish jury perjury in Wales was passed in 1534–35; 26 Henry VIII c 4. Another dealt with murders and felons at sessions courts; 26 Henry VIII c 6.

Between 1534 and 1542, legislation incorporated Wales into the English legal system, providing it with assizes, justices of the peace and sheriffs. The Council of Wales was given two commissions: one for felonies and another to hear and determine by bill, witnesses and examination.[17] Law and justice were to be the same as in England, and English became the language of the law and the courts. Law and legal institutions were part of the state-building process.[18]

The Council of the West was created in 1539 to cover four western counties on the model of the Councils of the North and Wales. It was instituted because of the need 'for the spedye and yndifferent administration of Justice' and to protect the area from possible invasion. Although the body was reported to be 'very busy with suits', it lasted only a year, its demise probably related to the fall of Thomas Cromwell, who had favoured its creation.[19]

Ireland, like Wales, was to be brought under English control and governed by English law. In 1536, parliament, responding to rebellion there, asserted that Ireland belonged to England and claimed jurisdiction over the entire country, not just the Pale. Henry VIII added King of Ireland to his title in 1542. Subsequent rulers would attempt to anglicise its government and law. The English would try to bring Ireland under English control, sometimes by military means, sometimes under a Lord Deputy appointed by the Crown and sometimes by the imposition of English law and legal institutions.

These regional conciliar courts covered peripheral areas lacking adequate facilities for the administration of justice. They grew rapidly during the Henrician period, transforming the legal environment. Litigants flocked to the new courts, which provided roughly the same legal services as the centralised common law and central conciliar courts. They would later become less popular when the Crown's reputation for justice diminished and clashes with common lawyers increased. The judicial system of the Tudors was characterised by a variety of institutions that combined administrative and judicial functions. When that combination appeared less beneficial, the conciliar courts would be challenged.

The rise and fall of the conciliar courts provides an example of the slipperiness of the term 'reform'. At their outset, they were viewed as reforms, in that they provided justice where it was lacking or inadequate. But institutional developments regarded as reform in one period could and would become the objects of further reform during a later period. Courts instituted to provide increasingly impartial access to the law later came to be considered impediments to justice. By the time of their abolition by parliament, they were considered an abuse. Eventually the conciliar courts, both central and peripheral, were abolished by an angry parliament.

[17] 34 and 35 Henry VIII c 26.

[18] See SG Ellis, 'Tudor State Formation and the Shaping of the British Isles' in SG Ellis and Sarah Barger (eds), *Conquest and Union: Fashioning British State 1485–1725* (London, Longman, 1995) 40–63.

[19] JA Youings, 'The Council of the West' (1960) 10 *Transactions of the Royal Historical Society* 42, 43, 46; CAJ Skeel, 'The Council of the West' (1921) 4 *Transactions of the Royal Historical Society* 62.

III. Ecclesiastical Courts and the Reformation

There was nothing very new in the tension between the ecclesiastical and common law courts when Henry VIII became king. Anti-clericalism was evident in the growing humanist movement and in the Richard Hunne case, which revolved around issues of heresy and murder and the church's many financial charges and fees. Some reform efforts dealing with the church related to long-standing problems such as sanctuary and the payment of mortuary fees. Others stemmed from the more recent effort to dissolve Henry's marriage to Catherine of Aragon and the ensuing conflict with Rome over appeals.

Both prior to and after 1529, the Crown attempted to limit the reach of sanctuaries, which were largely exempt from law. The crime of heresy attracted more critical attention as religious beliefs diverged. After 1529, the pace of efforts to reform the ecclesiastical courts and ecclesiastical law speeded up. In 1532, a House of Common petition, the Supplication of the Ordinaries, listed a group of familiar complaints – the ecclesiastical courts' unjust use of *ex officio* proceedings, the 'subtle interrogatories which often trapped ignorant men in heresy trials', and the expenses and delays when laymen were cited to appear outside their own diocese. Excommunication for 'light causes' and excessive fees were also causes for complaint.[20] The Supplication resulted in four statutes. These were considered reforms by those who supported them. Convocations and many clerics did not consider them to be so.[21]

Statutes altered what was permissible to be believed and practised. Refusal to accept the royal supremacy of the church became a crime, a crime that ended the life of Lord Chancellor Thomas More. Each statute enacted to settle religious belief and behaviour would be seen by its proponents as reform in the right direction and by its opponents as unwelcome, irreligious and/or retrogressive. There would be many such contentious statutes throughout the early modern period.

Henry's attempt to gain an annulment of his marriage introduced major changes in the law and legal system. Although litigants in the ecclesiastical courts could no longer appeal to Rome, the structure of the courts was left largely intact, with jurisdiction over cases of marriage, wills and testaments, tithes and moral faults. The legal status of canon law soon came under scrutiny. Legislation brought the church under secular control. Henry became Supreme Head of the Church by a legislative act. Secular authorities gained authority over the church in England.

The dissolution of the monasteries also had a huge impact on England's legal law and legal institutions. When monastic land was sold or gifted to laymen, much

[20] Lehmberg (n 3) 140.

[21] Geoffrey Elton suggests that the last draft of the Supplication was prepared by the government. See Geoffrey Elton, 'The Commons Supplication of 1532' in *Tudor and Stuart Politics and Government* (Cambridge, Cambridge University Press, 1974). However, see also Lehmberg (n 3) 113, 140.

of it entered the land market. The expansion of that market filled the courts with cases involving land titles and fraudulent conveyances. The transfer of monastic lands to the laity would also engender litigation over tithes formerly paid to the clergy. Dissolution also changed the composition of parliament, removing the heads of monastic houses from the House of Lords. Although bishops would continue to sit in the upper house, the removal of many its clerical members would leave the upper house with less clerical influence.

Benefit of clergy, a privilege initially designed to keep the clergy under the jurisdiction of the ecclesiastical rather than the secular courts, was under attack. The privilege allowed first-time convicted clerics to escape the death penalty for felonies. It was gradually extended to literate laymen, increasing the number who might escape the death penalty. Parliament then began removing benefit of clergy from one felony after another. When parliament made moral crimes (such as sodomy) felonies, these crimes, once adjudicated in the ecclesiastical courts, came under the jurisdiction of the common law courts and became subject to the death penalty. Removal of the privilege resulted in a somewhat more secularised criminal regime.

IV. Reformation and the Courts

Geoffrey Elton, the noted historian of the Henrician period, has appropriately referred to the Henrician era as being engaged in a 'court-making industry', which he saw as a particular concern of Thomas Cromwell, who had become the king's chief minister after the fall of More. The first and most important of these was the Court of Augmentations that appears to have been developed by Lord Chancellor Audley, a close associate of Cromwell.[22] It was created to deal with the formerly church revenues. In 1540, the Court of First Fruits, another revenue court, took over the 'first fruits' and annates, a portion of the first year's income of those who received benefices. It also collected a tenth of the revenues of the benefice annually.[23] The year 1540 also saw the establishment of the Court of General Surveyors, which would later be merged with Augmentations and then Exchequer. The Court of Wards and Liveries, which was also given a statutory basis in 1540, handled the king's income from feudal dues. Lord Chancellor Audley had a major role in its formation as well.[24]

[22] Elton (n 3) 141–42; 27 Henry VIII c 27. See also WC Richardson, *History of the Court of Augmentations 1536–1554* (Baton Rouge, Louisiana State University Press, 1967). Charles Gray considered the Reformation to be 'the great historical event overhanging the law of jurisdiction'. See Charles Gray, 'Parliament, Liberty and the Law' in JH Hexter (ed), *Liberty and the Law* (Palo Alto, Stanford University Press, 1991) 170.

[23] 32 Henry VIII c 45. Value was established by the *Valor Ecclesiasticus*, a survey of the financial revenues of the church.

[24] Elton (n 3) 141–42.

V. Local Justice: Justices of the Peace and Juries

Justices of the peace, an essential part of the legal and administrative system, were vulnerable to criticism, as were sheriffs and other crown officials who were frequently 'hurt, maimed, slain, and murdered in and for the administration and execution' of official duties. A proclamation of 1538 designed to remedy this situation made such assaults punishable by death. If the officer was hurt or maimed, the perpetrator would lose all lands, goods and chattels, and would be perpetually imprisoned. If murder or death resulted, the death penalty would be inflicted. A similar proclamation was issued in 1547. Proclamations and legislation of this type would become a common feature of the early modern legal environment.[25]

While juries were a source of pride, and jury trials were contrasted favourably with non-jury civil law trials, they were the subject to a good deal of criticism throughout the early modern era.[26] In the reign of Henry VIII, juries were often accused of being partial rather than impartial and frequently influenced by the more powerful members of the community. They were accused of perjury, that is, of rendering knowingly false verdicts. Jurors were criticised for failing to meet the property qualification or, if qualified, for avoiding jury service. They were sometimes characterised as ignorant, incapable of understanding the case before them, and likely to be swayed by lawyers and judges.

Parliament's reform proposals focused on ensuring that the property qualifications were being met or on raising property qualifications because inflation had made old requirement too low. Proposals also emphasised the lack of jury impartiality.[27] The Solicitor General introduced a bill to increase fines on delinquent juries. Concern over jury perjury, which would continue throughout the early modern era, resulted in several Henrician statutes. Property qualifications for town and city dwellers were altered to reflect movables as well as real property. Sheriffs, who selected jurors, also came under criticism. There was successful legislation to punish sheriffs who chose 'biased and corrupt' jurors and 'jurors who reached untrue verdicts'.[28] The Crown, worried about verdicts given 'untrewlie against the King', prosecuted 'corrupt' juries in Star Chamber.[29]

[25] Hughes and Larkin (n 5) vol I, 262.

[26] For Thomas More's reservations about juries, see 'The Debellation of Salem and Bizance' in John Guy et al (eds), *The Complete Works of Thomas More* (New Haven, Yale University Press, 1988) vol X, 135. See also Anthony Musson, 'Lay Participation: The Paradox of the Jury' (2015) 3 *Comparative Legal History* 245.

[27] For a 1542 bill to ensure jury impartiality, see Lehmberg (n 3) 155, 358, 23; Henry VIII c 6 (1542). For a bill for impartial juries, see LJ I, 28, 29.

[28] 24 Henry VIII c 13 (1531) See also 35 Henry VIII c 6 (1542); 31 Henry VIII c 22. For jury perjury in Wales, see 26 Henry VIII c 4 (1534); 35 Henry VIII c 2.

[29] Star Chamber, Chancery and the ecclesiastical courts did not use juries.

VI. The Legal Profession

Lawyers have never had a good press and the Henrician era was no exception. Complaints abounded of their greed and of their fomenting unnecessary and vexatious lawsuits. Barratry – that is, stirring up unnecessary litigation – was a frequent charge. Thomas Cromwell urged 'some good ways may be considered and devised for restraint and utter extinction of the abuses of the lawyers of this realm'. He suggest lower salaries for 'men of the long robe' as well as reducing the number of attorneys 'in all the shires of this realm' who caused 'people of discretion great harm'.[30]

On the other hand, lawyers were playing an increasing role in government. They were important to the Crown, whose ministers and other government officials were more likely to be lawyers than clerics. Following the fall of Cardinal Wolsey, Thomas More, a common lawyer, became the first secular Lord Chancellor. Thomas Cromwell, whom Geoffrey Elton considers to have been responsible for most Henrician law reform,[31] and many others who served Henry at the time of the Reformation, were lawyers. They were a substantial group in the House of Commons and would remain so throughout the early modern period. Landholders and others sought their services.

Some reform proposals of the Henrician period were directed at courts, while others were directed at various bodies of law. The most prominent were land law, criminal law and, to a lesser degree, the laws relating to credit and debt.

VII. Land Law

Legal problems associated with the transfer of land had a lengthy history. Transfer of freehold land during the feudal period was demonstrated by livery of seisin, which involved transferring a clod of earth with witnesses to observe the transfer. As conveyance by deed and other devices became more common, uncertainty and opportunities for fraud increased. The landed classes adopted the use. A use, the forerunner of the trust, transferred land to a third party or group, which would handle the property as the landholder wished, while avoiding payments that would have been owed to the Crown. Needless to say, the Crown was hostile to the development. As early as 1529, Henry VIII sought to end uses so that he could collect the revenues gained through seisin. He tried and failed again due to resistance in the House of Commons. In 1536, the Statute of Uses, a compromise

[30] Quoted in Lehmberg (n 3) 220–21, citing Cottonian Ms, Titus B, fols 169v, 160. Cromwell received a petition complaining that the House of Commons was 'ruled by lawyers'; see Lehmberg (n 3) 213.

[31] Geoffrey Elton, 'English Law in the Sixteenth Century: Reform in an Age of Change' in *Studies in Tudor and Stuart Politics and Government*, 4 vols (Cambridge, Cambridge University Press, 1983), vol III, 280, 284–86.

between the interests of the Crown and landholders, became law. Litigation dealing with uses and later trusts was handled by Chancery, and seisin by the common law courts, adding significantly to the tension between the two. The Statute of Wills followed in 1540, giving landholders the ability to devise by will and thus greater control over who would inherit.[32]

Although proposals for land registration to prevent secret conveyances and other fraudulent practices are most often associated with mid-seventeenth-century reformers, registration proposals were explored during the Tudor period as well. A bill of 1529 would have required that the deeds of newly purchased lands be publicly read in the church in the parish of purchase and that a record be placed in the shire town. Yet another involved the 'enrollment of bargains and contracts of lands and tenements'. Royal officials would record all transactions, which would then be transmitted to Chancery and become searchable. Failure to record the transactions would render them void. A weakened version providing for enrolment at existing Westminster courts or by the justice of the peace became law, but was not enforced.[33] Schemes for land registration that would ensure greater certainty of titles to land and reduce fraud would be revived periodically throughout the early modern era. While the heritage of feudal law and ancient land tenures remained, the power of landholders over alienation was dramatically changed. If the Statutes of Uses, Wills and Enrollment of titles were the most important legislation relating to land law, parliament was also willing to discuss and legislate on other matters dealing with land.[34]

VIII. Crime and the Criminal Law

Crime is a problem for most legal systems. England was no exception and had, when Henry VIII assumed the throne, both laws and institutions in place to prevent offences and try malefactors. These did not produce the desired level of control. Crimes, designated as treasons, felonies or misdemeanours, were treated quite differently, with different punishments and often in different courts.

The definition of treason, a crime against the king, was frequently at issue during the Reformation. As was so often the case, changes in the law of treason were seen as reforms by those who sought them, but not by those who suffered

[32] 32 Henry VIII c 1. Wills had to be written and witnessed. There were additions to the Statute of Wills in 1542–43.

[33] Lehmberg (n 3) 238; See also W Jones, *The Tudor Commonwealth 1529–1559* (London, Althone, 1979) 209–11.

[34] Parliament considered or passed legislation concerning tenures in capite, statutes of limitations and prescription (CJ, I, 5, 6), uses upon fines and recoveries (CJ, I, 7; LJ, I, 338) and 'rents upon reserved leases'(CJ, I, 6). Others would have provided that demesne lands let in the future by 'copy of Court Roll for three lives' should be treated as customary lands (CJ, I, 13). A bill providing for 'enrollment of Deeds with Proclamations' for London was introduced but not passed (CJ, I, 4; LJ, I, 33). Holland adopted land registration in 1529.

from them. Changes were enacted several times during the Henrician period to enhance protection to the king. In 1534, it became treason to disavow the Act of Supremacy making the king Head of the Church or in words or writing to imagine or attempt bodily harm to the king, the queen or their heirs apparent.[35] It was also treason to declare the king a heretic or a tyrant. This legislation, probably initiated to end criticism of Anne Boleyn, was supported by a royal proclamation in 1536. It became treason to marry the king's children or other relatives without permission.[36]

Preventing and punishing crimes by the better execution of existing laws and the passage of new ones were pursued by both monarchs and parliament. Prosecution was difficult given the lack of a police force. The dominance of private prosecution created considerable inconvenience and expense for those who prosecuted. Although it is unclear how much lawlessness actually existed, proclamations and proposed legislation indicate that it was often thought to have reached new heights.[37] In 1511, a proclamation for enforcing the Statute of Winchester (1285) suggested that 'great decay and ruin of this his realm has continued many years by means of heinous murders, felonies, robberies, riots, unlawful assemblies'. It was therefore necessary to enforce statutes that 'have not been duly executed'. It was said that juries were failing to indict 'misdeeds' and that escapes and concealments of felonies were frequent. Bills were introduced to prevent and punish murder and other homicides[38] as well as crimes against property.[39] Proclamations were commonly employed to enforce existing law, and in 1539 legislation allowed proclamations to serve as law and to be obeyed as 'though an act of parliament'.[40]

As suggested earlier, benefit of clergy, which permitted first-time felony offenders to escape the death penalty if they could read or recite the 'neck verse', was under attack. A statute eliminating benefit of clergy for murder, rape, robbery, theft 'and all other mischievous deeds' was passed as early as 1489.[41] It was eliminated again in 1513 for murder and felonies 'of and upon malice prepensed'.[42] In 1530, it was modified to allow benefit of clergy a second time in cases of 'manslaughter by chance medley', but not for 'malice murder prepensed'. The next year it was removed for petty treason, murder and felony for those below the position of subdeacon. If benefit of clergy was initially introduced to ensure that clerics

[35] 26 Henry VIII c 13.

[36] Legislation for commissioners to try treason in Wales; 32 Henry VIII c 4. In 1541, legislation required cases of treason to be tried in the shire where the offence was committed; 33 Henry VIII c 23. For treason committed outside of England; see 35 Henry VIII c 2. The Henrician treason acts were repealed in 1547.

[37] Hughes and Larkin (n 5) vol II, 82.

[38] LJ, I, 12, 13; 1515; CJ, I, 31 (felons and murderers) 4 Henry VIII c 6; 22 Henry VIII c 2 (poisoning).

[39] LJ, I, 7 (1509).

[40] 31 Henry VIII c 8, repealed in 1547.

[41] 4 H VII c 13 1489.

[42] 4 Henry VIII c 2. See also 6 Henry VIII c 6.

would be tried in the ecclesiastical courts, statutes were increasingly motivated by a desire to eliminate avoidance of the death penalty by serious offenders. In 1533, those who refused to enter a plea could not claim benefit of clergy.[43] Reforming criminal law for this generation meant greater use of the death penalty.

There was a new statute covering the crime of poisoning.[44] Another provided that self-defence resulting in the death of thieves would no longer be penalised or result in the forfeiture of goods.[45] Another required convicted robbers to restore stolen property.[46]

England's first law against witchcraft, conjuring, sorcery and enchantments was enacted in 1542. The legislation, labelled 'for Reformation', made witchcraft a felony without benefit of clergy. Prior to the statute, witchcraft had been tried in the ecclesiastical courts, courts that could not administer the death penalty. Those accused of witchcraft would now be tried by lay jurors rather than by civil and canon lawyers.[47]

Legislation was proposed making sodomy a felony ineligible for benefit of clergy. It too would be tried in the secular rather than the ecclesiastical courts. The statute, supported by Cromwell and drafted by the judges, passed easily.[48] There were also statutes in 1529, 1535 and 1536 making embezzlement by servants a felony.[49] As servants became more like employees than members of the household, embezzlement became a growing problem and was not covered by older laws. New crimes required new legislation.

Perjury, the violation of an oath, especially in connection with trials, was an endemic problem for much of the early modern era. Perjury, like witchcraft, sodomy and other moral offences, had been under the jurisdiction of the ecclesiastical courts whose punishments for perjury were thought by many to be insufficiently severe. Reformers argued for harsher penalties, but not usually to make such acts felonies that would require the death penalty. The very first statute in Henry VIII's first parliament was aimed at curbing and punishing perjury.[50] Another, dealing with the perjury and punishment for 'untrue verdicts', became law in 1531.[51] Subornation of perjury, that is, persuading someone to commit perjury, became criminal in an Act of 1540. Most concern was directed at jury perjury, that is, rendering a false verdict, a crime coming to be handled by Star Chamber. Perjury by witnesses, who were becoming increasingly common in the

[43] 4 Henry VIII c 8.

[44] 21 Henry VIII c 9.

[45] 24 Henry VIII c 5.

[46] 21 Henry VIII c 11.

[47] 33 Henry VIII c 8.

[48] 25 Henry VIII c 6; Elton (n 3) 158, 158n. Similar legislation was passed under Elizabeth I. Prosecution for sodomy was rare, but remained a capital crime until 1861.

[49] 21 Henry VIII c 7; 27 Henry VIII c 17; 28 Henry VIII c 2. Embezzlement dealt with goods committed to servants in trust. Embezzlement was a statutory rather than a common law crime.

[50] 1 Henry VIII c 11; 23 Henry VIII c 3. In 1536, there was a bill to continue the statute of perjury; 28 Henry VIII c 9.

[51] 23 Henry VIII c 3. There was legislation to punish jury perjury in Wales; 26 Henry VIII c 4.

common law courts, did not become the subject of legislation until 1563. There was considerable discussion over the appropriate punishment for perjury throughout the early modern period with reform proposals ranging from monetary penalties to death. For most of the early modern period, perjury was treated as an offence against God, a violation of an oath rather than an offence against the state.[52]

Proclamations were issued in 1538 and again in 1547 making the assault of officers in pursuit of their duties punishable by death without benefit of clergy if the officers were killed.[53] The problem of assault on officers involved in keeping the peace 'to the subversion of all good civil orders' would continue long after the end of the Henrician era.[54] Informers, never popular, but viewed as a necessary part of law enforcement, were regulated in Henry's first parliament.[55]

Henry's reign also saw a never realised proposal for Conservators of the Common Weal, a body that would enforce the penal statutes and aid officers in apprehending offenders. The draft indicated that the laws were now printed 'in our maternal English Tongue', but were not well enforced. The drafter wrote: 'Better it were they had never been made, unless they should be put in due and perfect execution.' To enforce the penal laws, salaried officials would act as public prosecutors replacing the use of informers. Pleas and entries were to be in English and trial by juries at the assizes. Conservators would have discretion to use 'the rigour and extremjytie' required by the statutes or to use discretion to assess 'reasonable fynes'.[56]

Another concern was sanctuaries, enclaves exempt from secular law. Royal authorities often sought to reduce or end the number of criminals escaping to sanctuaries to avoid criminal sanctions by avoiding the reach of the secular courts. The move to end sanctuaries was also part of a more general concern with reducing exemptions from the law. Abolition of sanctuaries would also reduce the ability of debtors to escape creditors as well as reduce the 'liberties' or special legal exemptions of certain areas. A House of Lords resolution called for the 'utter destruction' of sanctuaries.[57] A sanctuary statute was passed in 1514 and would be followed by several more.[58] By 1540, sanctuary had been abolished for most serious crimes.

Problems related to credit and debt more generally were also addressed. Some debtors were too poor to pay what they owed, while others evaded payment

[52] See Barbara J Shapiro, 'Oaths, Credibility and the Legal Process in Early Modern England' (2013) 6 *Law and Humanities* 145 (Part I); (2013) 7 *Law and Humanities* 19 (Part II).

[53] The legislation was repealed during Edward's reign. See Hughes and Larkin (n 5) vol I, 262–63, 404.

[54] In 1532, there was legislation requiring towns to build or maintain jails and for justices of the peace to collect taxes to provide jails in non-corporate areas. 23 Henry VIII c 2; Lehmberg (n 3) 155.

[55] 1 Henry VIII c 4.

[56] Elton (n 3) 126–27, 131, 139, 141–42. The origin of the proposal is unclear. See TFT Plucknett, 'Some Proposed Legislation of Henry VIII' (1930) 19 *Transactions of the Royal Historical Society* 19.

[57] LJ, I, 254.

[58] 21 Henry VIII c 23; 22 Henry VIII c 4; 23; Henry VIII c 14; 27 Henry VIII c 19; 32 Henry VIII c 12. The preamble of the 1540 legislation referred to 'idle and evil-disposed persons' whose 'great and sundry and detestable murders, robbers [and] other great and heinous offenses'.

by imprisonment. The position of creditors was strengthened by a statute allowing them to control a debtor's lands until the obligation was satisfied.[59] In 1542, the first of many bankruptcy laws was passed, which allowed the Chancellor to imprison the bankrupt and take the property in question to pay the debt. Subsequent parliaments would continue to wrestle with the problems of both poor and wealthy imprisoned debtors.

The legal landscape looked very different at the end of the reign. While there was relatively little change in the common law courts, they now had more rivals. Chancery had become more important in meeting the country's changing needs. There were now several new and expanded conciliar courts, most noteworthy being the Court of Star Chamber and the Councils for Wales and the North. Efforts had been made to enforce the law, especially in the more distant areas, and sanctuaries had been substantially reduced. The Reformation had altered the ecclesiastical structure, reducing its legal reach. The Crown and parliament had jointly become the agent of changes to religious doctrine and practice. New financial courts were created to handle issues stemming from the break with the church in Rome and the dissolution of the monasteries. Tensions between the Crown and major landholders were reduced by the Statutes of Uses and the Statute of Wills. Experiments in land registration were being explored. The most noteworthy developments in the area of criminal law were the elimination of benefit of clergy from several felonies and a shift of several crimes from the ecclesiastical to the secular courts.

IX. Edward VI

Although the reigns of Edward VI and Mary I are most often discussed in the context of religious and theological conflict, these monarchs and their parliaments were not devoid of interest in improving the legal system. Although early in Edward's reign the focus was on repealing Henrician heresy and treason legislation and then the passage of the 1549 and 1552 Protestant prayer books, the young king was committed to continuing the Henrician project of a compilation of laws. Legislation was introduced to reduce 'superfluous and tedious statutes'.[60] Edward's political diary in 1550 indicates that shortly after the prorogation of parliament, the 'Master of Requests and certain other lawyers were appointed to make a short table of the laws and acts that were not wholly unprofitable and to present it to the Council board'.[61] The king's *Discourse on the Reform of Abuses in Church and State* proclaimed: 'hereafter, when time shall serve, the superfluous and tedious statutes

[59] 23 Henry VIII c 6; 34 and 35 Henry VIII c 4. See Lehmberg (n 3) 155, 358.

[60] CJ, I, 44.

[61] WK Jordan (ed), *The Chronicle and Political Papers of King Edward VI* (London, Allen & Unwin, 1966) 43–44, 115; Stephen Alford, *Kingship and Politics in the Reign of Edward VI* (Cambridge, Cambridge University Press, 2000).

were brought into one sum together and made more plain and short, to the intent that men might better understand them, which I think shall much help to advance the profit of the commonwealth'. Edward was also critical of the slack execution of the laws and the lawyers and judges who had 'much offended in corruption and bribery'.[62]

Judging from the amount of legislation introduced in Edwardian parliaments, there was substantial reform interest, though bills were frequently recorded so briefly that it is not possible to determine more than the topic of concern. Late in 1547, a bill for 'Reformation of diverse Laws and Process in the laws of the Realm' and for 'reformation of the Common Laws of the Realm' was introduced in the House of Commons.[63] This may or may not have been the same as the bill for 'The new Book for Reformation in the Laws of the Realm' approved by the House of Commons in March 1548. The bill was sent to the upper house, but nothing more was heard of it.[64] The bill 'for Process and Orders in the Common Laws' in January 1549 may have been a related proposal.[65] In 1552, a commission was appointed to investigate the Henrician revenue courts for corruption and inefficiency.

Legislation calling for 'the Erection of New Court of Chancery commonly to be called the Court of Chancery for Ecclesiastical and Civil Causes' was considered by the upper house, but got no further than the committee stage.[66] Legislation concerning jurisdiction of the bishops and other ecclesiastical courts was discussed,[67] as was the ecclesiastical jurisdiction of the House of Lords.[68] Attention was also given to county courts.[69]

Spearheaded by Archbishop Thomas Cranmer, work on the codification of the ecclesiastical law continued. A mixed commission of clerics and laymen was created by parliament and ordered to gather, order and compile the canons.[70] Revision would again be considered during the reign of Elizabeth I.

The legal profession received attention from both Crown and parliament. A proclamation was issued regulating who might practise in various courts.[71] Legislation was introduced in 1551 for 'Reformation of the Abuses and Deceitful

[62] Jordan (n 61) 164, 166. The king was also personally involved with the commission to execute the penal laws and oversee the courts.

[63] CJ, I, 2, 50.

[64] CJ, I, 6, 8, 10.

[65] LJ, I, 351, 352.

[66] CJ, I, 4, 5, 7. It is not clear how this proposal would have altered Chancery and the existing ecclesiastical courts. See Michael Graves, *The House of the Lords in the Parliaments of Edward VI and Mary* (Cambridge, Cambridge University Press, 1981).

[67] 7 Edw VI c 2; LJ, I, 299, 201, 334, 336, 359, 367, 369, 371.

[68] LJ, I, 299, 201, 334, 336, 359, 367, 369, 371.

[69] CJ, I, 41; LJ, 303; 1 Edw VI c 7; 2 and 3 Edw VI c 25.

[70] 3 and 4 Edw VI c 11. Drafts were considered by a group of theologians, civil lawyers, common lawyers and prominent Protestant refugee clerics. See Diarmaid MacCulloch, *Thomas Cranmer* (New Haven, Yale University Press, 1996) 327, 501, 503; Jasper Ridley, *Thomas Cranmer* (Oxford, Oxford University Press, 1962) 330–34, 533–34. Legislation dealing with marriage pre-contracts, jointure and dower was also introduced; CJ, I, 7, 8; LJ, I, 295, 316, 319, 354.

[71] Hughes and Larkin (n 5) vol I, 409. A proclamation of 1547 repeated a Henrician proclamation on maiming and killing royal officers; Hughes and Larkin (n 5) vol I, 404.

Practice of Undersheriff, Attorneys, and Officers of the Courts of the Common Law'. Legislation forbidding the sale of court and other public offices and the corruption and excessive fees associated with it became law in 1551. Despite the efforts of this and later parliaments to curb or end the practice, the sale of court and other offices continued throughout the early modern period and beyond.[72]

The most significant legislation was the establishment of Protestantism. The Acts of Uniformity of 1549 and 1555 introduced a legally established Protestant church. Legislation provided a new book of common prayer and outlined punitive measures for failing to comply with its use.[73]

Henrician treason legislation was replaced and all of the new Henrician felonies were abolished. Punishment for treasonable 'words' became less harsh and 'two sufficient and lawful witnesses' or confession became necessary for conviction. Saying that the king was not the Supreme Head of the Church became a misdemeanour for a first offence, felony for a second and treason for a third.[74]

Parliamentary interest in crime was largely devoted to the more efficient prosecution of murderers, felons and their accessories.[75] New statutes were enacted to ensure that those involved in another's death should not profit from it[76] and that those robbers who committed robbery in one jurisdiction and fled to another could be prosecuted.[77] There were attempts to eliminate benefit of clergy for house robbers, horse thieves and other offenders.[78] Earlier legislation removing benefit of clergy for the most egregious crimes would be repeated and extended by later parliaments. A bill dealing with 'trial in Criminal Causes' was introduced and legislation making sodomy a felony was passed.[79] The failure of law reform bills was not unusual given that 65 per cent of all Edwardian bills failed.[80]

Not all interest in altering the law originated from parliament and the Crown. When agrarian change pitted aristocratic and gentry landholders against tenants, the conflict might result in destructive peasant uprisings that included demands for better protection of tenant rights. During Kett's Rebellion in 1549, dissatisfaction with aristocratic local courts resulted in rebel demands for equal justice in the royal courts. Landholding conflicts fit into the narrative of English law reform. From one point of view, the increasing agricultural productivity made possible by

[72] 5 and 6 Edward VI c 16. See Koenraad Swart, *Sale of Public Offices in the Seventeenth Century* (Utrecht, Martinus Nijhoff, 1970) 112–27.

[73] 2 and 3 Edw VI c 1; 5 and 6 Edw VI c 1.

[74] 1 Edw VI c 12 modified in 5 and 6 Edw VI c 2, when two witnesses were required to confront the accused in his or her presence. The two witness rule was required in canon and civil law. See Lamar Hill, 'The Two Witness Rule in English Treason Trials' (1968) 12 *American Journal of Legal History* 95.

[75] CJ, I, 2, 9, 14; LJ, I, 322, 361, 362, 371; 2 and 3 Edw VI c 24; 3 and 4 Edw VI; 5 and 6 Edw VI c 9; 5 and 6 Edw VI, c 10; 5 and 6 Edw VI c 9, c 10; also 5 and 6 Edw VI c 10.

[76] CJ, I, 14; LJ, I, 361, 362, 371.

[77] CJ I, 1, 10, 14, 21, 22 23, 29, 322; LJ, I, 354, 361, 362, 371, 429; and 6 Edw VI c 10.

[78] CJ I, 10, 17; LJ, I, 354, 399, 401, 404, 417, 418, 429; 2 and 3 Edw VI c 33 (no benefit of clergy or sanctuary for stealing horses); 2 and 3 Edw VI c 24 (murder and felons); 1 Edw VI c 33 (horse stealing).

[79] 2 and 3 Edw VI c 17 (sodomy).

[80] Michael AR Graves, *The Tudor Parliaments: Crown, Lords and Commons, 1485–1603* (London, Longman, 1985) 86.

aggressive aristocratic and gentry enclosers may be seen as a positive development; from another, enclosure, particularly of common land, might be considered as a grievance needing reform. Should legal efforts to prevent enclosure be considered reformist? Economic change resulting in changes to the legal position of tenants, like many 'reform' issues, depends on the vantage point of the viewers.[81]

X. The Reign of Queen Mary

Although Mary I was deeply engrossed with the problems of reuniting the English church with Rome, reversing the secularisation of monastic land, marriage to Phillip II of Spain and Wyatt's Rebellion, Marian parliaments did not turn away from law reform.[82] The reign began on a reformist note in October 1553 when the House of Commons heard 'arguments for Reformation of the Laws'.[83] Two years later, a bill provided that certain persons should 'peruse the penal laws for Reformation' and to bring in penal laws 'in short Form'.[84] Concern with reducing the number of penal laws and putting them into a more rational form would be heard repeatedly during the early modern era; it was not a uniquely mid-seventeenth-century reform issue.

The courts, legal procedures and substantive law received attention as well. Several measures sought modifications in the land law. Legislation confirmed title to former church lands. There was a bill limiting prescription.[85] Others dealt with uses and the security of land.[86] The lack of secure titles to land would be addressed by this and later parliaments. There was another act for uniting, dissolving or dismantling several of Henry VIII's revenue courts,[87] as well as bills dealing with the Court of Wards.[88] The financial courts created in the wake of the Reformation were modified. Both the Court of Augmentations and the Court of First Fruits and Tenths were merged with the Court of Exchequer, though Mary hoped to return clerical income to Rome.[89]

Treason legislation was again rewritten.[90] Attention was directed at the better apprehension of criminals and at providing harsher punishments for some offences. In 1554, there was successful legislation for 'Revealing of Murtherers

[81] Andy Wood, *The 1549 Rebellions and the Making of Early Modern England* (Cambridge, Cambridge University Press, 2007) 156–57, 160–63; Jane Whittle, 'Lords and Tenants in Kett's Rebellion, 1549' (2010) 207 *Past and Present* 3.

[82] For Marian parliaments, see Graves (n 80) 99–114.

[83] CJ, I, 27.

[84] CJ, I, 42, 44.

[85] 1 Mary c 5.

[86] CJ, I, 12, 27, 42, 43.

[87] CJ, I, 31, 32.

[88] CJ, I, 32.

[89] 2 and 3 Philip and Mary c 4.

[90] 1 and 2 Philip and Mary c 11, c 12.

and Thieves' and for excluding accessories to murder and other felonies from benefit of clergy.[91] Although it is hard to imagine what might have been harsher than the then current law, a bill to provide 'a more grievous punishment for murder' was proposed.[92] There was legislation dealing with the purchase of stolen horses and the unlawful abduction of 'any young maide or Women childe'.[93] Some attention was also given to the crime of counterfeit coining.[94] The Henrician sodomy legislation was repealed and the offence returned to the ecclesiastical courts. Legislation regularising the justices of the peace role in pre-trial process became law, with the Marian bail statute of 1554 requiring the justices to examine prisoners before granting bail. A statute of 1555 required the justices to examine and record the testimony of witnesses in felony and manslaughter cases.[95] It is likely that these statutes contributed to more uniform pre-trial practice.

Despite the religious and political turbulence of the Edwardian and Marian years and the brevity of their reigns, concern with reforming the law and the courts was a significant feature of these reigns and should not be omitted from the history of English legal reform.

XI. Renaissance Humanism and Law Reform

Humanists, who were at the forefront of intellectual developments in the sixteenth century, were often engaged in a critical examination of the English economy, its law and its legal institutions. The lauded humanist lawyer Thomas More, who became a leading government servant and eventually Lord Chancellor, led the way. His *Utopia* was both a scathing attack on the English legal system and a model for an ideal legal regime. More's critique centred on the English legal profession and the criminal law. Capital punishment for theft is characterised as self-defeating because it encouraged thieves to kill their victims. Utopians censured those nations with 'an infinite number of laws and interpretations' and viewed it as 'highly unjust to bind men by laws that are too numerous to be read, and are too obscure to be readily understood'. Laws must be few, simple to understand and widely publicised. Lawyers were unnecessary. Utopian litigants argued their own causes.[96] The abolition of the legal profession, reform of the punishment for theft and advocacy

[91] 2 and 3 Philip and Mary c 10; 4 and 5 Philip and Mary c 4.

[92] CJ, I, 39, 41–3, 44, 48; LJ I, 197–8. 535; 4 and 5 Philip and Mary c 4. Benefit of clergy was removed for accessories in murder and other felonies.

[93] 2 and 3 Philip and Mary c 7; 4 and 5 Philip and Mary c 8 (abduction).

[94] 1 and 2 Mary c 11 (seditious words); 1 and 2 Mary c 3.

[95] John Langbein, *Prosecuting Crime in the Renaissance: England, Germany, France* (Cambridge, MA, Harvard University Press, 1974) 55–63, 111, 119. Langbein suggests that the bail statute originated with the Crown and that the justices' role in collecting evidence had a prosecutorial function. However, depositions were not presented to jurors.

[96] Thomas More, *Utopia*, H Ogden (ed) (Princeton, Princeton University Press, 1949) 60–61. First published in Latin in 1516. English translations appeared in 1551, 1556, 1597, 1624, 1639 and 1685.

of severe punishment for adulterers would find an echo in the proposals of radical reformers of the mid-seventeenth century.[97] Despite the radical transformation of the legal system depicted in Utopia, More, in the same work, in the voice of the respected Cardinal Morton, supported modest, experimental, incremental changes in English law. Morton, who had served both as Archbishop of Canterbury and Lord Chancellor, became More's spokesman for a moderate approach to incremental law reform.

The Commonwealthmen, humanist scholars devoted to public policy and the improvement of society, concerned themselves with remedying the defects of English law. Uncertainty of the law was a common theme. Richard Morison suggested that the laws 'that nowe be unwritten, might be written, that now lye dispersed and uncerteyn, myght be gathered together and made certain; [and] reduced into the Latin tongue'.[98] Morison was confident that codification would do much to end the confusion, delay and expense of legal proceedings.[99]

However, codification or reduction of the laws was not a uniquely English concern and similar effort could be found in Charles V's penal code of 1532 as well as in Castile, the Netherlands and other Spanish kingdoms. French kings encouraged codification and reform to reduce the number, duration and costs of lawsuits resulting from contradictory customs in various provinces.

Thomas Starkey, a humanist in the circle of Thomas Cromwell who thought that the common law had 'no stable ground', favoured either the 'reduction' of the law to make it more easily accessible or its replacement by the civil law. He found the 'the Judgments of years [the yearbooks] be infinite and full of much controversy, and beside that, of small authority', due to judicial freedom of interpretation. He emphasised the uncertainty of the law, its delays and its subtleties caused by clever common lawyers, and deplored the multiplicity of suits and use of lawsuits to vex enemies. The character Pole in Starkey's *Dialogue* suggests that the laws were too many and too diverse, and wished 'that all those laws should be brought into small number, and be written also in our mother tongue, or else put into Latin'. Most cases should remain in the counties. He believed that there were too many lawyers and that the profession should be limited to gentlemen.[100]

Sir Thomas Elyot's widely read *The Boke Named the Governor* (1531) criticised the barbarity of law French that served 'no commoditie or necessary purpose' except for lawyers. He too thought the law should be written in a clearer and

[97] Adulterers would be enslaved for a first offence and executed for a second.

[98] Morison, quoted in J McConica, *English Humanists and Reformation Politics under Henry VIII and Edward VI* (Oxford, Clarendon Press, 1966) 185. See also Geoffrey Elton, 'Reform by Statute; Thomas Starkey's Dialogue and Thomas Cromwell's Policy' (1970) 54 *Proceedings of the British Academy* 177.

[99] W Gordon Zeeveld refers to a Morison manuscript, 'A discourse touching the Reformation of the Laws of England'.

[100] Thomas Starkey, *A Dialogue between Reginald Pole and Thomas Lupset*, TF Mayer (ed), Camden Fourth Series, vol 37 (London, Office of the Royal Historical Society, 1989) 80–82, 126–27, 131; Elton (n 98) 177, 178–80; JH Baker, 'English Law and the Renaissance' (1985) 44 *Cambridge Law Journal* 46.

more elegant style, in English, Latin or good French.[101] St Germain's *Doctor and Student* suggested that English was necessary to reach a wider audience.[102] The desirability of replacing law French in legal proceedings would be debated for many decades, though the suggestion of Latin as a replacement for law French would disappear.

A 'good reasonable common law' in English was also supported by John Rastell, a humanist lawyer in the circle of Thomas More. Rastell, also a compiler and printer of law books, sent proposals to Cromwell for improving the common law and Chancery. These included reforms in pleading in the common law courts, the use of injunctions and witnesses in Chancery, and a reduction of fees in all courts.[103] Rastell was responsible for one of the earliest collection of printed statutes.

XII. Printing and Law Reform

Since the groundbreaking work of Elizabeth Eisenstein on the role of printing in early modern culture, legal scholars have considered its importance for the law and legal profession.[104] Although oral transmission and manuscript materials continued to be important, students of law and legal professionals increasingly came to rely on printed texts. These included yearbooks and law reports, statutes, surveys of the law and legal authorities on particular topics. Legal printing began during the reign of Henry VII and, over time, more and more legal learning would

[101] Sir Thomas Elyot, *The Boke Named the Governour*, Donald Rule (ed) (New York, Garland, 1992) 66–68, 70. Elyot had considerable legal experience, having been a clerk for the assizes for the Western circuit. He was also immersed in the work of Star Chamber. See Guy (n 4) 11, 13.

[102] JH Baker, 'The Three Languages of the Common Law' (1997–98) 43 *McGill Law Journal* 5.

[103] Lehmberg (n 3) 218.

[104] Elizabeth Eisenstein, *The Printing Press as an Agent of Change*, 2 vols (Cambridge, Cambridge University Press, 1973–79). Most scholars agree on the importance of printing, but differ on the continuing importance of memory, the oral tradition of learning, and legal manuscripts. See David Ibbetson, 'Legal Printing and Legal Doctrine' (2000) 5 *Irish Jurist* 345; Ian Williams, '"He Credetted More the printed Booke": Common Lawyers' Receptivity to Print, c 1550–1640' (2011) 28 *Law and History Review* 39; Ian Williams, 'Common Law Scholarship and the Written Word' in Lorna Hutson (ed), *The Oxford History of Law and Literature* (Oxford, Oxford University Press, 2017) 61–79; Katherine F Pantzer, 'Printing the English Statutes 1484–1640: Some Historical Implications' in *Books and Society in History* (New York, Bowker Pub Co, 1983) 69–114; JH Baker, 'The Books of the Common Law' in Lotte Hellinga and JB Trapp (eds), *The Cambridge History of the Book in Britain 1400–1577* (Cambridge, Cambridge University Press, 1999), vol III, 411–32, who suggests printing narrowed the canon of legal literature (at 432); Richard Ross, 'The Memorial Culture of Early Modern English Lawyers: Memory as Keyword, Shelter and Identity 1560–1640' (1998) 10 *Yale Journal of Law and Humanities* 229; Richard Ross, 'The Commoning of the Common Law: The Renaissance Debate over Printing English Law' (1998) 10 *University of Pennsylvania Law Review* 323; Sebastian Sobecki, *Unwritten Verities: The Making of England's Vernacular Culture 1463–1549* (Notre Dame, IN, University of Notre Dame Press, 2014); Edith Henderson, 'Legal Literature and the Impact of Printing on the English Legal Profession' (1975) 68 *Law Library Journal* 288.

be transmitted in printed form. The process was an incremental one, with lawyers making use of both manuscripts and printed books. Printing of legal materials coincided with the humanist call for simplification, codification and the replacement of law French.[105]

The printing of legal material should be included in the narrative of early modern English law reform because much of it was inspired by the desire to make the law more certain, more comprehensible and more available. Legal publications were often self-consciously offered as improvements for a law often characterised as impenetrable, disorderly and uncertain.[106] Some legal publications appeared in law French, some were translated into English, and some were printed in English from the outset.

The first type was the yearbooks and their abridgements. These were volumes of old case reports which existed previously in manuscript form, typically without record of the decisions taken or reasons given.[107] Next were reports consisting of collections of more recent cases in law French, typically the personal notes of judges and others. The reports, which would remain in law French longer than most legal material, were often confusing and did not conform to any agreed-upon format. Abridgements and digests of cases had become common in the 1450s and were soon being printed. *Le Graunde Abridgment*, which has been characterised as 'the book that made the common law', was an alphabetically arranged digest of nearly 14,000 cases from the yearbooks.[108]

There were overviews of the law, sometimes labelled 'institutions', that provided the principles of the common law. Richard Taverner's *Institutions or principle grounds of the laws of England*, a publication of this type, was characterised by the author as 'very profitable for all sortes of people to knowe'.[109] The older *La Natura Brevium*, which had at least nine English printings before Elizabeth I's reign, was largely being replaced with Anthony Fitzherbert's *La novel natura brevium*, a work that remained in continuous use until the nineteenth century.

[105] For the role of humanists in printing legal material, see David Hartley, *The law Emprynted and Englysshed: The Printing Press as an Agent of Change in Law and Legal Culture, 1575–1642* (Oxford, Hart Publishing, 2015); Baker (n 104).

[106] Although intended to provide greater certainty, printing sometimes exposed confusion and lack of clarity. The commercial motives of printers were also important. For the printing of statutes, see Geoffrey Elton, 'The Sessional Printing of the Statutes 1484–1547' in *Studies in Tudor and Stuart Politics and Government*, 4 vols (Cambridge, Cambridge University Press, 1983), vol III, 92–109.

[107] Yearbooks, which were printed until 1535, included a miscellany of judicial comment, opinion and dissents. See LW Abbott, *Law Reporting in England 1485–1585* (London, University of London, Legal Series, 1973) 14, 23. Early reports overlapped with the yearbooks.

[108] HJ Graham and JW Hechel, 'The Book that Made the Common Law: The First Printing of Fitzherbert's La Graunde Abridgement, 1514–16' (1957) 5 *Law Library Journal* 100. There were also printed editions of writs and the forms of action.

[109] *Institutions in the Laws of England or the principall Grounds of the Laws and Statutes of England.* There were editions in 1542, 1543, 1544, 1545 and 1555; Richard Taverner, *Institutions or the principal laws and customs et estatutes of England* (London, 1540 and 1556).

Printing new statutes after each session of parliament began during the reign of Henry VII, and continued during the reign of Henry VIII. Statutes were promulgated publicly and distributed to towns, cities, quarter sessions, markets and fairs.[110] After 1512, promulgation changed to printed broadsides. Rastell, the humanist printer and himself a compiler of statutes, indicated in 1519 that the king was determined to have statutes in English, so that 'the People of the Realm might soon have the knowledge of the statutes and ordinances'.[111] The statutes of Henry VIII often included elaborate preambles explaining, supporting and justifying them.

There were also collections and abridgments of the statutes. William Rastell produced a frequently reprinted collection with an abridgement and tables.[112] He suggested that the laws 'should be written in such a manner and so openly published and declared that the people might without any difficulty have the knowledge' of them.[113]

Some volumes covered particular legal topics, perhaps the most important being Littleton's *Tenures*. English translations began in 1528; there were at least 15 English printings by 1557. John Rastell was responsible for the first English printing of Littleton. By the mid-sixteenth century, diagrams were added to facilitate understanding. Several works dealing with criminal law appeared. John Rastell's *Tabula libri assurarum et placitorum corone* of 1514 attempted to provide simpler methods of organization and Justice William Staunford's *Les plees del coron* (1557) promised to make the material more accessible by dividing it into tables and commonplaces and by having the cases 'appear under certain principles, rules and grounds'.[114] There is no doubt that many legal authors, editors and printers aimed at making the law easier to understand and access.

Printed handbooks providing information on the duties of justices of the peace and the legal materials necessary for justices of the peace to perform those duties were a significant addition. Anthony Fitzherbert's *The boke of justices of peas*, first printed in 1505 and reissued 11 times by 1538, was translated into English in 1538. It had eight printings before Elizabeth I's reign. This kind of handbook or manual included material on the justices' judicial obligations in petty and quarter sessions, as well as in a wide range of economic and social regulations.

[110] See Howard J Graham, '"Our Tong Maternell Marvellously Amendeyd and Augmented": The First Englishing and Printing of the Medieval Statutes at Large 1530–1533' (1995–96) 13 *UCLA Law Review* 58.

[111] John D Cowley, *A Bibliography of Abridgements, Digests, and Dictionaries of English Lawe* (London, Selden Society, 1932) 94.

[112] *Abbreviamenum statutorum* (1499). Abridgements of the statutes were printed in English in 1531, 1533, 1534, 1538 and 1542; Howard Graham, 'The Rastells and the Printed English Law Book of the Renaissance' (1954) 47 *Law Library Journal* 6.

[113] Quoted in Sobecki (n 104) *Unwritten Verities* 137.

[114] William Staunford, *Les plees del coron* (London, 1557), Preface. There were editions in 1557, 1560, 1567, 1574, 1583 and 1607.

Their many printings no doubt helped to make the administration of many statutes more uniform.[115]

Fitzherbert's *Diuersite de court[es] et lour iurisdiction*, which first appeared in 1538, had nine printings before the death of Henry VIII. John Rastell's legal dictionary *Exposiciones termeninorum legum anglorum*, which provided the terms of the law in English and law French, first appeared in 1523. Expressing his reform intentions, Rastell referred to 'certain obscure and dark terms concerning the lawes of this realm', emphasised the need for 'good order', thought the law was being 'kept secretly in the knowledge of a few persons and from the knowledge of the great multitude may rather be called a trap and a net to bring people to vexation and trouble than a good order to bring them to peace and quietness'.[116] His dictionary, which continued in print for several centuries, was designed to help bring about the desired peace and quiet.

Over the decades between the beginning of the reign of Henry VIII and the death of Mary I, only a few publications focused generally on the law. St Germain's *Doctor and Student*, which examined the nature of equity, was first published in Latin in 1528. It appeared in English in 1530, 1531, 1532 and again in 1550. Sir John Fortescue's *De laudibus legum Angliae* provided support for the English-style monarchy and praised the common law, comparing its procedure positively with that of the civil law. Written in the 1470s, Fortescue's laudatory treatment of the law was printed in Latin in 1545. More's idealised image of an alternate England became available in English in 1551 and was printed again in 1556.

Unlike those of the mid-seventeenth century and later reformers, these criticisms of the law and proposals for reform were not typically addressed to parliament. An exception was Henry Brinkelow's *The Complaint of Roderyck More*, a catalogue of complaints that characterised lawyers as motivated by greed and judges by partiality. He proposed that both should be paid salaries out of royal revenues. Lawyers who pleaded for money should be punished with the loss of their right hand and be permanently forbidden from pleading in court. Brinkelow also complained of the innumerable, crafty subtleties of the law as well as lawsuits that were prolonged from year to year. He recommended that the courts of the Marshalsea and Augmentations be reformed, and abuses in the common law courts and Chancery ended.[117]

The printing of legal texts existed side by side with manuscript sources and the oral transmission of law that emanated from the courts and the Inns of Court. The Inns, the centre of legal education and legal culture, were beginning to attract

[115] Anthony Fitzherbert, *The Boke of Justices of Peace* was printed with additions and corrections frequently after 1506. There were also guide books for constables.

[116] Proem 1527 ed. See Sebastian Sobecki, '"Certain Obscure and Dark Terms": John Rastell and the First English Law Lexicon' in Philip Bossier (ed), *Dynamic Translations in the European Law* (Rome, Vecchiarelli, 2010) 73–84.

[117] Printed in 1542, 1548, 1560, 1562 and 1640.

laymen who never planned a legal career as well as those headed for the profession of law. Living among law students and lawyers allowed young gentlemen to absorb a smattering of legal knowledge and imbibe respect and admiration for the common law. Over time, the orality of legal culture would begin to decline as knowledge of the law became increasingly available in printed form.

Although the Henrician, Edwardian and Marian eras, with the exception of printing of religious texts, did not see much in the way of writing and publication on law reform directed at the public at large, print had become of increasing importance. Statutes and abridgements to the statutes were printed and a canon of legal texts expanded greatly.[118] The transformation of legal materials available to the legal profession and to some extent to literate laymen would, over a century, fundamentally change the nature of the legal profession and legal learning.

XIII. Conclusion

Looking over the first half of the sixteenth century, several developments are to be noted. Both Crown and parliament were actively engaged in law reform. The development of the conciliar courts and the expansion of Chancery provided new remedies for old and new legal problems. Star Chamber could correct a variety of legal abuses uncorrectable in the common law courts and attracted a large number of litigants, many of whom used the court to avoid the complexities of the common law. Star Chamber and the additional other conciliar courts altered the structure of the courts, and some would, in the future, increase the conflict among the various courts for jurisdiction over certain types of remedies. Jurisdictional rivalries also contributed to the relative importance of the common law courts. The common law courts would have a smaller share of the law business.[119] A diagram of the English courts would look quite different in 1547 from that in 1509.

The Reformation changed the legal system in a number of ways. It ended ecclesiastical appeals to Rome, allowing the church in England to develop without Roman control and supervision. Laws on religious doctrine and practice would be in the largely secular hands of Crown and parliament. Parliament became the necessary venue for determining the established religion of England. Clerical power eroded in the House of Lords, which was essential to law-making. Crown officials were increasingly more likely to be lawyers than clerics, and the Lord Chancellor and Chancery became more secularised. The dissolution of the monasteries threw an enormous amount of land on the market, leading to a myriad of transactions that

[118] Anthony Fitzherbert's *The New Book of Justice of the Peace*, and William Staunford's *Les plees del coron* were reprinted. Both the *Natura brevium* and Fitzherbert's *La novel natura brevium* were published, as was Richard Taverner's *Institutions and principall grounds*, a summary of land law.

[119] See JH Baker, *An Introduction to Legal History*, 3rd edn (London, Butterworths, 2002) 43; NG Jones, 'The Bill of Middlesex and the Chancery, 1556–1608' (2002) 22 *Journal of Law and History* 4.

in turn resulted in confusion and increased the possibilities for fraud in land titles and transactions. Buyers and sellers, tenants and landlords became engaged in an increasing number of transactions that engendered the need for lawyers and other legal professionals, drawing more attention to the legal system and its defects. The Reformation and its aftermath also resulted in the creation of several new courts. The religious upheavals during the reigns of Henry VIII, Edward VI and Mary I make it clear that conflicting views of religion would occupy a substantial part of the legislative agenda.

Law reform during this period was largely sought by the Crown, Crown officials, humanist intellectuals and members of parliament. There was as yet no readily available outlet for law reform sentiment among the population at large, and we know relatively little about the extent of their satisfaction or dissatisfaction with the existing legal environment. Law reform during the reigns of Elizabeth I and the early Stuarts would take place within a set of legal institutions that were in place by the end of Henry VIII's reign.

3

The Elizabethan Era 1558–1603

The reign of Elizabeth I, like that of Henry VIII, allows us to examine law reform over a lengthy period of time, in this instance a period when a Protestant regime was put in place by the joint efforts of Crown and parliament. It was a period fraught with challenges over the succession, the newly established church and prayer book, and domestic and foreign efforts to topple the regime. The broad outlines of the legal system were not challenged. The reform efforts of both Crown and parliament to modify legal practices were modest efforts to make the system work better. This chapter focuses on Crown interest in law reform and parliamentary efforts to reform the courts and certain areas of law. The last portion of the chapter highlights the efforts of the legal profession to improve the organisation and rational treatment of the law in law reports, abridgements, statutes and other legal material. Although such efforts are not typically considered as part of law reform, they constitute a significant part of the early modern reforming agenda.

I. The Crown and Law Reform

Because Crown interest in law reform has been largely neglected by historians, we begin with a focus on government efforts to move parliament in the direction of reform. Although we know relatively little directly about the queen's interest, her Lord Chancellors and Lord Keepers promoted law reform when they spoke to the parliament on her behalf. If Elizabeth was not the primary impulse behind their recommendations, she must have approved them. Despite the many pressing issues before Elizabeth and her parliaments, law reform was a prominent theme of the Lord Chancellors and Lord Keepers who addressed parliament at its openings. Typically these speeches presented reform as the desire of the monarch.

At the opening of Elizabeth's first parliament in 1559, Lord Keeper Bacon informed parliament of its duty to 'reform and remove all enormities and mischiefs which could be harmful to the civil order or policies of the realm'. It must determine what is:

> [C]ontrary or hurtful to the commonwealth … for which no laws be yet provided; and whether the laws before this time made be sufficient to redress the enormities they were meant to remove, and whether any laws made but for a time be meet to be continued … or presently to cease; besides whether any laws to be severe, too sharp, or too

soft and gentle. To be short, you are to consider all other imperfections of laws made and all the wants of laws to be made, and thereupon to provide their meetest remedies respecting the nature and quality of the disorder and offense, the inclination and disposition of the people, and the manner of the time.[1]

During the queen's second parliament in 1563, Lord Keeper Nicholas Bacon, an eloquent speaker, a privy councillor and brother-in-law to William Cecil, advised the assembly to consider which laws were too harsh or too lenient. An excessive number of laws led to 'so many doubts that the subject is sometimes to seek how to observe them, and the counsellor how to give advice concerning them'.[2] In 1571 Lord Keeper Bacon again informed parliament that law reform was one of the Queen's aims. In 1575 this relentless advocate of reform drew up a plan to reduce the statutes.[3]

Law reform remained a prominent feature of the opening speeches of Elizabeth's later Lord Chancellors and Lord Keepers. Parliament responded positively to these overtures. Privy councillors who held seats in parliament helped to guide government policy. In 1584 Christopher Hatton, a royal favourite and member of the Privy Council, speaking on behalf of the queen, told members of parliament: 'And withal, that those of this House toward the Law would join together to their best endeavours to devise some good Laws to abridge and cut-off the long tedious courses and extreme chargeable Circuits and superfluous delays of Suits in Law.' Sir Simonds D'Ewes noted that the Solicitor General Egerton had also spoken of the excessive number of penal laws in force, 'very intolerable to the Subjects, neither possible to be kept, and yet not any put in Execution'. A committee was appointed to review the 'excessive number of penal laws in force … against the next sitting of this court … [and] thereupon proceed to some course of diminishing the great number of them'. Little, however, was accomplished during the 1584 session because of the 'shortness of the time and the sudden ending of the parliament'.[4]

Reform was again aired in 1592, when Nicholas Bacon's son, Francis Bacon, praised the queen for a 'course taken by her own direction for the repealing of all heavy and snared laws'.[5] Two years later, his masque presented at Gray's Inn Christmas revels elaborated on the theme, advising the masque ruler to 'purge out

[1] *Proceedings in the Parliaments of Elizabeth I, 1558–1582*, TE Hartley (ed), 3 vols (Leicester, Leicester University Press, 1981), vol I, 15, 35; Robert Tittler, *Nicholas Bacon, The Making of a Tudor Statesmen* (Athens, OH, Ohio University Press, 1975). Bacon was out of favour between 1563 and 1565.

[2] The same year, Cecil favoured regulation of lawyers' fees. See *Proceedings in the Parliaments of Elizabeth I* (n 1) vol I, 83.

[3] *Proceedings in the Parliaments of Elizabeth* (n 1) vol I, 317, 336; John Neale, *Elizabeth and Her Parliaments, 1559–1581* (London, Jonathan Cape, 1953) 239.

[4] Sir Simonds D'Ewes, *A Complete Journal of the Votes, Speeches, and Debates* (1693) 344, 345, 622, The committee included the privy councillors in the House, Solicitor General Egerton, the Recorder of London and members of the House. Hatton served as Lord Chancellor from 1587 to 1591.

[5] Francis Bacon, *The Works of Sir Francis Bacon*, James Spedding, B Ellis and David Heath (eds), 15 vols (London, 1857–1874), vol VIII, 130. Bacon was a member of parliament in 1581, 1584, 1585, 1588, 1592, 1597 and 1601.

multiplicitie of laws, clear the uncertainty of them, repeal those that are snaring and press the execution of those that are wholesome and necessary'. The masque prince is counselled to 'define the jurisdiction of your courts, and repress all causeless and vexatious suits'. He is also charged with punishing 'extortions and extortions of office, all corruption in trials and sentences of Judgment'.[6] Bacon emphasises the ruler as the impetus for law reform.

Crown interest was displayed again in 1593, when Lord Keeper Puckering's opening speech spoke of royal concern with abridging the laws. The laws were 'so many and great that they are fitly to be termed *elephantinae leges*'.[7] Sir Simonds D'Ewes, a member of parliament, noted his own 'great contentment in her Majesties Speeches the other day delivered by the Lord Keeper'. Cautiously, he indicated that reform 'was not to be done suddenly nor at one Parliament, nor scarce a whole year would suffice to purge the Statute-Book and lessen the Volumes of Laws, being so many of them'.[8] Francis Bacon expressed similar 'contentment' with her Majesty's speeches urging how fitting it was that 'abridgement were made of the laws and statutes of the realm … being so many in number that neither the common people can half practice them, nor the lawyer sufficiently understand them'.[9]

Speaking at Elizabeth's command in October 1597, Lord Keeper Thomas Egerton's opening speech again insisted that Parliament take up law reform: 'And whereas the number of Laws already made is very great, some of them being obsolete and worn out of use, others idle and vain, serving to no purpose; some again over-heavy and too severe for the offense, others too loose and slack for the faults they are to punish; and many so full of difficulty to be understood, that they cause many Controversies and much trouble to arise amongst the Subjects.' Parliament was to act where it found 'superfluity, to prune and cut off, where defect, to supply, and where ambiguity to explain, that they be not burdensome but profitable to the Common-Wealth'. Parliament quickly responded with a motion to abridge and reform 'the excessive number of superfluous and burthensome penal laws'. The motion was seconded by Bacon and committed to a group that included the privy councillors and all sergeants and lawyers in the House.[10]

The 1597 scenario was repeated in Elizabeth's last parliament of 1601, when the Lord Keeper advised that the 'laws in force might be revised and explained, and

[6] *Gesta Grayorum or the High and Mighty Prince: Henry Prince of Purpoole*, Desmond Bland (ed) (Liverpool, Liverpool University Press, 1968) 54. Bacon's *Maxims of the Law* recommended that the monarch 'enter into a general amendment of the state of your laws'; Bacon (n 5) vol VI, 88, 99–100, 110. He indicates that for many years, Elizabeth had planned 'a general amendment of the statutes of Laws And to reduce them to more brevity and certainty' (Bacon (n 5) vol VIII, 316). See Barbara Shapiro, 'Sir Francis Bacon and the Mid-seventeenth Century Movement for Law Reform' (1980) 24 *American Journal of Legal History* 331. Donald Veall considers both Bacon and Coke as 'prime movers' of law reform before 1640. See Donald Veall, *The Popular Movement for Law Reform* (Oxford, Oxford University Press, 1970) 65, 69–72.

[7] GB Harrison, *The Elizabethan Journals* 2 vols (Garden City, Doubleday Anchor, 1965) I, 161.

[8] D'Ewes (n 4) 473.

[9] Bacon (n 5) vol VIII, 204.

[10] D'Ewes (n 4) 524, 553.

no new Laws made'. The response was again positive, one member saying that the penal laws 'were like Thorns that did prick, but did yield no Fruit; … the necessity of time makes a necessity of alteration of Laws'. Commending the proceedings of former ages, he concluded with 'a desire of a committee'.[11] Bacon, a member of the committee, spoke in favour of the bill, saying: 'Time is the true Controuler of Laws and therefore there having been a great alteration of Time, since Repeal of a number of Laws; I know, and do assure myself there are many, more than I know, Laws both needless, and dangerous.' He recommended that every parliament appoint a committee to consider the continuance of statutes.[12]

However, reform and consolidation of the statutes proved to be more difficult and more time consuming than anticipated. The committee did not produce much. Yet, it is difficult to distinguish committees for rationalisation of the statutes from those appointed to work on continuing statutes, since both dealt with expiring and obsolete statutes. Both were instructed to 'perfect' and improve the statutes in addition to extending those requiring renewal.[13] Many statutes were enacted for a short period of time, often with the beginning of the next parliament, and would lapse if not continued. Thus, a lot of statutes needed review each session. The job of dealing with obsolete, conflicting and competing statutes could not often be accomplished in the brief time available to parliamentary committees before prorogation or dismissal.

II. Parliament and Law Reform

Although parliament was essential for changing and therefore reforming the law, legislation was not easily obtained. Elizabethan parliaments met only intermittently. During Elizabeth's reign of over four decades, parliament met only for the equivalent of three years. There was always uncertainty as to when parliaments might meet and when they might be interrupted by prorogation or ended by dismissal. These decisions were made by the Crown and were not taken with law reform as the highest consideration. Passage of legislation was rarely easy. Many bills languished or disappeared even if not opposed. The law-making process was laborious, requiring three readings in each house. Differences between the two houses, and often time-consuming consultation between them, diminished the likelihood that legislation would be completed. No legislation could be completed without royal assent.

[11] The committee included the privy councillors, the Master of Requests, Sir Edward Hoby, Sir Walter Raleigh and Francis Bacon. Lawyer Mr. Wiseman agreed that 'divers particular Laws … were now both needless to be performed, as also dangers to the Subject by reason of the Penalties'. D'Ewes (n 4) 622.

[12] Continuance statutes 1 Eliz I, c 18; 13 Eliz I c 25; 27 Eliz I, c 13; 31 Eliz I, c 11; 35 Eliz I, c 7; 39 Eliz I, c 18; 43 Eliz I, c 9.

[13] For continuance bills, see Chris Kyle. '"It Being Not Fit to Be without a Law"; Continuance Acts 1604–1648' (2000) 19 *Parliamentary History* 196. Continuance Acts were passed in 1571, 1584, 1585, 1585, 1589, 1593, 1597 and 1601. The titles of these acts included language of 'reviving, continuance,

The legal profession was well represented in both houses of parliament. Lawyers were enthusiastic participants in attempts at rationalising statutes and reducing their number as well as other reform work. In the lower house, lawyers played a role in drafting bills and were frequent speakers on behalf or against proposed legislation. The House of Lords had the judges close at hand and often consulted with them. The presence of privy councillors in parliament was significant in presenting Crown views there.

Early parliaments focused on establishing the church and concerns about the succession and the queen's marriage. Later parliaments were preoccupied with domestic and foreign threats to the regime, or contentious economic and political issues such as monopolies. Law reform was a continuing presence on the parliamentary agenda, but not a predominant one. Passage rates were low, as they were for bills on most topics.[14]

The legal environment changed a great deal during Elizabeth's lengthy reign. Beginning in about 1580, there was an enormous growth in the amount of litigation, an increase that lasted for several decades. A far greater number of cases thus had to be handled by courts that did not expand much to accommodate the increased business.[15] There was greater pressure on the courts and ever-longer delays. Participation in litigation now engaged a large part of the population, not just the social and political elites.[16] Debt and credit had become a part of daily life. Problems associated with the myriad of large and small transactions led to numerous disagreements, many of which resulted in litigation.[17]

The legal profession was also changing. There were simply an insufficient number of lawyers to accommodate the growing demand for legal services. Not only did the number of lawyers (barristers) grow, but so did the number of attorneys who, while not permitted to plead in the central courts, were increasingly

explanation and perfecting of diverse Statutes'. It is not known whether the committees consulted one another or the extent to which their membership overlapped.

[14] About 29 per cent of the acts passed between 1559 and 1581 were for a limited time; from 1581 to 1601, it was about 32 per cent. See Geoffrey Elton, *The Parliaments of England, 1559–81* (Cambridge, Cambridge University Press, 1986) 134. Elton estimates that 514 bills were introduced in the first seven sessions of Elizabeth's reign. A total of 144 public bills became law; thirty-four passed both houses, but did not have the royal assent. See Geoffrey Elton, 'Parliament in the Sixteenth Century' in *Studies in Tudor and Stuart Politics and Government*, 4 vols (Cambridge, Cambridge University Press, 1983), vol III, 161–62.

[15] Between 1490 and 1640, cases in the Courts of King's Bench and Common Pleas rose from 2,100 to 29,000 (cases in last stages). See John H Baker, *Introduction to Legal History*, 3rd edn (London, Butterworths, 1990) 216–17.

[16] Christopher Brooks, *Lawyers, Litigation and English Society since 1450* (London, Hambledon, 1998); Christopher Brooks, 'Litigation, Participation and Agency in Seventeenth and Eighteenth Century England' in David Lemming (ed) *The British and Their Law in the Eighteenth Century* (Woodford, Boydell Press, 2005). For discussion of the increase in litigation and use of the courts in connection with state formation, see S Hindle, *The State and Social Change in Early Modern England 1550–1640* (Woodford, Boydell, 2000); M Braddick, *State Formation in Early Modern England 1550–1700* (Cambridge, Cambridge University Press, 2000).

[17] See Craig Muldrew, *The Economy of Obligation: The Culture of Credit and Social Relations in Early Modern England* (Basingstoke, Macmillan, 1998).

consulting with clients during the first phase of lawsuits. Although the line between barristers and attorneys, and attorneys and solicitors remained somewhat blurred, it was increasingly recognised. Barristers who pleaded in court were the more respected upper portion of the profession, while attorneys were typically of lower social status. They were viewed as less learned, but able to handle the endless pretrial work. Barristers were educated at the Inns of Court, while attorneys were not.[18] And despite the fact that some barristers also practised as attorneys, the culture of the Inns provided a social and educational milieu that distinguished the lawyers from the attorneys. The Inns of Court of Court expanded during the Elizabethan era, in part because of the growing demand for lawyers and in part because many of the sons of gentlemen without any intention of becoming legal professionals attended and absorbed the common law values and culture of the Inns.[19] Attorneys and solicitors were often vilified.

Although criticism of the legal profession was a perennial feature of the English legal environment, the expansion of the profession and litigation appears to have been accompanied by a substantial increase in criticism.[20] The changing legal environment meant that Elizabeth's later parliaments became more conscious of the problems of the legal system and more attuned to the possibility of reforming what were considered its abuses.[21]

III. Parliament, the Courts and Legal Institutions

We first look to parliamentary efforts to reform the courts, the legal profession and key legal institutions such as juries, grand juries and justices of the peace. Jurisdictional conflicts among the courts were endemic. Courts jostled against one another as each strove to maintain or expand their business. Conflicts were often couched in the language of reform, with one or another court characterised as improperly encroaching on the jurisdiction of others. Common lawyers, whose voices were often heard in parliament, were particularly active in protecting the

[18] See Christopher Brooks, *Pettifoggers and the Vipers of the Commonwealth: The Lower Branch of the Legal Profession in Early Modern England* (Cambridge, Cambridge University Press, 1986); Christopher Brooks, 'Common Lawyers in England 1558–1642' in Wilfred Prest (ed), *Lawyers in Early Modern England and America* (London, Longmans, 1981) 42–61.

[19] Wilfrid Prest, *The Inns of Court under Elizabeth and the Early Stuarts, 1590–1640* (London, Longmans, 1972).

[20] See Edward Gieskes, *Representing the Professions: Administration, Law, and Theater in Early Modern England* (Newark, University of Delaware Press, 1996); EF Tucker, *Intruder into Eden: Representations of the Common Lawyer in English Literature, 1350–1650* (Columbia, SC, Camden House, 1984); Jessica Winston, 'Legal Satire and the Legal Profession in the 1590s' in Lorna Hutson (ed), *Oxford Handbook of English Law and Literature* (Oxford, Oxford University Press, 2017) 121–47; Wilfrid Prest, *Rise of the Barristers* (Oxford, Oxford University Press, 1984).

[21] Geoffrey Elton, *Parliaments of England 1559–91* (Cambridge, Cambridge University Press, 1986) 277, 281; David Dean, *Lawmaking and Society in Late Elizabethan England: The Parliament of England, 1584–1601* (Cambridge, Cambridge University Press, 1990).

jurisdiction of the common law courts against the ecclesiastical courts and the High Commission. Jurisdictional conflicts also took place within the common law courts as well as with Chancery and other non-common law courts. King's Bench, for example, developed the Bill of Middlesex, a legal fiction allowing it to gain a great deal of business at the expense of Common Pleas. Litigants found it far less expensive to use King's Bench in a variety of cases. King's Bench business increased tenfold between 1560 and 1640.[22]

Parliamentary attention was also focused on reforming the high costs and lengthy delays in reaching judgments, that is, on improving the legal environment for litigants and on improving the operation of the courts in the face of rapid growth in litigation and consequent overcrowding. Some legislative efforts were couched in general terms, though most addressed the failings of particular courts. A good deal of attention was given to correcting the errors of particular courts in particular cases due to the lack of a recognised system of appeals.[23]

IV. The Courts

Tension between the ecclesiastical and common law courts had grown more intense as the Reformation unfolded. The most common criticisms of the ecclesiastical courts related to tithes, probate, high fees, and excessive use of excommunication and penance. Criticism was aired in scholarly tracts, polemical pamphlets and petitions to parliament. The most potent weapon of the common law courts in disputes with the church courts proved to be writs of prohibition that prevented the completion of cases in the ecclesiastical courts on the grounds that they were not within their jurisdiction. Complaints in the 1584 Parliament led to Archbishop John Whitgift's regulation of fees in 1585 and 1587. Fees were stabilised for about 40 years.[24] Over time, jurisdiction over adultery, perjury, witchcraft, usury and bigamy would be transferred to or shared with the common law courts.

The development of High Commission, which represented the authority of the Crown in ecclesiastical matters, became contentious. While the Commission itself was not new to the Elizabethan scene, scrutiny increased as it evolved into a court.

[22] John H Baker, *An Introduction to Legal History* (London, Butterworths, 2000) 43. See also NG Jones, 'The Bill of Middlesex and the Chancery 1556–1608' (2001) 22 *Journal of Legal History* 1.

[23] One of the very few was a bill for reforming abuses of officers and process in the Court of Exchequer. It had three readings in the upper house before disappearing: LJ, II, 254, 256, 261. There was also a bill concerned with the 'expedition of Justice in Causes of Demurrers and Pleadings'. The preamble of another bill called 'for Redress of erroneous Judgmentes in the Courte commonly called the Kinges Benche'. See Dean (n 21) 211–12. Dean also suggests that redefining the Exchequer Chamber to hear appeals from Queen's Bench and Common Pleas was 'argueably the most important of the several statutes reforming the law in these parliaments on law reform' (at 212–13). For Dean on parliamentary law reform in the latter part of Elizabeth's reign, see Dean (n 21) 188–216.

[24] RB Outhwaite, *The Rise and Fall of the English Ecclesiastical Courts 1599–1860* (Cambridge, Cambridge University Press, 2006) 67, 69, 73–75. See also Richard H Helmholtz, 'Writs of Prohibition and Ecclesiastical Sanctions in the English Courts Christian' (1975) 60 *Minnesota Law Review* 1011.

By 1580, it was recognised as a court. Composed of canon lawyers, bishops and laymen, and headed by Archbishop Whitgift, it was particularly disliked by the common lawyers and Puritans for its use of the *ex officio* oath and its vigorous anti-Puritan policies. Although its procedure resembled that of the council and Star Chamber, it was attacked for its similarities to the Roman Inquisition.[25] Since the Commission was an extension of Elizabeth's authority, she resented it being the subject of parliamentary intervention.[26] High Commission would be a focus of reform until its abolition.

Star Chamber, a popular court that greatly expanded during the Elizabethan era, was not the subject of parliamentary inquiry or legislation. Cases were judged by privy councillors and common law judges. It had a wide jurisdiction in civil and criminal cases not adjudicated by the common law courts. These included riot, sedition, conspiracy, perjury and subornation of perjury.[27] It also expanded its role in cases of fraud, forgery and extortion. The court was eagerly sought by litigants, who often alleged riot, forced entry or assault as a means of getting property cases into the court. Some cases were initiated as parallel litigation in other courts in order to harass opponents. Nevertheless, its later notorious reputation should not be allowed to obscure its high reputation in the Elizabethan period. Coke thought it to be 'the most honorable court (our Parliament excepted) that is in the Christian world, in respect of the judges of the court, and of their Honourable proceeding according to their just jurisdiction'. Lambarde and Francis Bacon expressed similar views of the court's importance.[28]

There continued to be efforts to better integrate peripheral areas into the legal system. Although the process in Wales had been nearly completed, lawlessness remained a problem. In 1566 there were bills calling for accused felons in Wales to be tried at Great Sessions and for establishing justices of the peace. In 1576 judges were added to the circuits.[29]

The Council of the North, which over time had come to deal with civil and criminal cases using common law and English bill procedures, was altered to better

[25] It could fine and punish, but could not employ torture or the death penalty. For a defence, see Richard Cosin, *An apologie for sundrie proceedings by jurisdiction ecclesiasticall of late times by some challenged* (London, 1591).

[26] D'Ewes (n 4) 158, 468; Roland Usher, *The Rise and Fall of High Commission* (Oxford, Oxford University Press, 1913).

[27] See TG Barnes, 'Star Chamber Litigation and Their Counsel, 1596–1641' in JH Baker (ed), *Legal Records and the Historian* (London, Royal Historical Society, 1978) 7–28; TG Barnes, 'Star Chamber Mythology' (1961) 5 *American Journal of Legal History* 1. Cases were often sent to arbitration by local gentry and justices of the peace. See John Guy, *The Court of Star Chamber and its Records in the Reign of Elizabeth I* (London, HMSO, 1985) 48, 56, 57.

[28] Sir Edward Coke, *Fourth Part of the Institutes* (1644; I used the 1797 edn) 17; Bacon (n 5) vol V, 94–95, 97, 98.See also William Lambarde, *Archeion, or a discourse upon the High Courts of Justice in England* (London, 1591) 175–77.

[29] 18 Eliz I c 8. For avoiding frivolous suits in Welsh courts, see 43 Eliz I c 6. In 1584 there was a bill to reform errors in civil and common laws in Wales and Counties Palatine; HL, I, 354, 364, 372. See Penry Williams, *The Council in the Marches of Wales under Elizabeth* (Cardiff, University of Wales Press, 1958).

integrate the northern counties into the English administrative system. Northern turbulence became rebellion in 1569 when Catholic aristocrats attempted to restore Catholicism and replace Elizabeth with Mary, the Roman Catholic Queen of Scots. After the rebellion was put down, Protestant control of the Council was established. The 'great age of the Council' began with the Lord Presidency of Lord Huntington and lasted until his death.[30] The court could punish with fines, the pillory, the wearing of papers or imprisonment. Common lawyers remained suspicious of its jurisdiction, and in 1598 legislation was introduced to forbid the Council from staying proceedings of any superior court at Westminster.[31] Lawlessness remained an issue. In 1591 an act for Cumberland was passed to prevent the many 'incursions … robberies and burning and spoiling of towns, villages and houses, that [were] forced to pay blackmail'.

The English continued to impose the common law and English legal institutions on Ireland. The Courts of King's Bench, Common Pleas and Exchequer sat in Dublin. Circuit courts, justices of the peace and juries had also been introduced. A Star Chamber-like court was established in 1571, which, like its counterpart in England, was initially popular. Parliament and the government used legislation to reform Irish law and its legal institutions. During the latter part of Elizabeth's reign, a series of rebellions meant that war was often part of the Irish legal environment.[32] The imposition of English law and legal institutions was successful in Wales, but not in Ireland.

Admiralty was attacked in parliament by the common lawyers, mostly over jurisdictional issues. There was legislation concerning appeals in civil and maritime cases in 1563 and 1566.[33] In 1575 a royal commission examined competing jurisdictional claims of the common law courts and Admiralty over bills of exchange, insurance and writs of prohibition issued by the common law courts.[34] Although it would continue to arouse the suspicion of common lawyers, Admiralty offered advantages to merchants. The civil law it employed enabled it to make use of a summary procedure that was quicker than common law proceedings, especially in cases involving overseas parties. Tensions heightened in the 1580s and would become even more intense in the early decades of the seventeenth century.

Parliament's concern with the legal profession was focused on its lower ranks, that is, on solicitors and attorneys. A speaker who offered a bill to 'suppress the Multitude of Common Solicitors' referred to the 'Lewd Abuses of Prolling

[30] FW Brooks, 'The Council of the North' in Joel Hurstfield (ed), *The Tudors* (London, Sidgwick & Jackson, 1973) 194.

[31] RR Reid, *The King's Council of the North* (London, Longmans, 1921) 343, 350.

[32] See Nicholas Canny, *Making Ireland British, 1570–1650* (Oxford, Oxford University Press, 2003); Nicholas Canny, *The Elizabethan Conquest of Ireland: A Pattern Established, 1565–76* (Hassocks, Harvester Press, 1975).

[33] 8 Eliz I c 5, 1566; 13 Eliz I c 5. For a proposal to avoid long delays in maritime cases, see CJ, I, 77. See also Lionel Laing, 'Historical Origins of Admiralty Jurisdiction' (1946) 45 *Michigan Law Review* 163.

[34] CJ, I, 77. There was conflict over merchant contracts and commercial actions that were land-based.

Solicitors and their great Multitude; who set Dissention between Man and Man, like a Snake cut in pieces, crawl together and joine themselves against, to stir up evil Spirits of Dissention'.[35] It was not an unusual criticism. There was a failed bill in 1571 to limit lawyers' fees and the excessive number of attorneys. In 1581 complaints about the multiplicity of lawyers and their 'evil doings' led to efforts to restrict Bench attorneys and increase their qualifications. Characterising them as 'Vipers of the Commonwealth', Egerton in 1601 called for a bill to limit the number of solicitors.[36]

Juries, grand juries and justices of the peace, institutions that performed essential roles in the legal system, were the subject of some criticism in Elizabethan parliaments, though not the subject of much legislation. An unsuccessful bill of 1571 criticised sheriffs for failing to pick the 'better sort' of jurors instead of 'men of weak judgment and very mean estate whose education have not made them fit for service'.[37] Legislation to return 'more able and more sufficient jurors' did pass in 1585, becoming one of many sixteenth- and seventeenth-century acts directed at eliminating unqualified and partisan jurors. Jurors were also criticised for refusing to convict defendants despite the evidence.[38]

William Lambarde, an acute observer of the courts, expressed similar concern over the unwillingness of grand jurors to present offenders. Their reluctance to 'cut off treasons, murders, witchcraft, rapes and other felonies' was dangerous and resulted in lawlessness. Lambarde accused grand jurors of arrogating to themselves decisions of guilt and innocence that belonged to the trial jury and of making decisions of equity, mercy and pardon that belonged to others. According to Lambarde, grand jurors favoured friends and their betters, and sought vengeance against enemies. He suggests that everyone complained of these defects, though they had 'ready, easy and speedy justice' at their fingertips. Continued grand jury failure to indict, he warned, would lead the government to make use of non-jury proceedings such as Star Chamber.[39]

The justices of the peace, with responsibility for administering 'stacks of statutes' and adjudicating cases in petty and quarter sessions, came in for a modest amount of reform interest. It has been estimated that these magistrates had to deal with some 300 statutes by the end of the century. Chosen largely from the county gentry, the unpaid office was sought primarily for its prestige, but involved major

[35] D'Ewes (n 4) 631; Hayward Townshend, *Historicall Collections or, An Exact Account of the Proceedings of the Last Four Parliaments of Q. Elizabeth* (London, 1680) 210. See also Brooks, *Pettifoggers and Vipers of the Commonwealth* (n 18).

[36] Quoted in Brooks (n 18) 135.

[37] CJ, I, 34.

[38] 27 Eliz I c 6.

[39] Wilfrid Prest, 'William Lambarde, Elizabethan Law Reform and Early Stuart Politics' (1995) 34 *Journal of British Studies* 464. Lambarde's comments appear in his posthumously published *The Just Lawyer* (London, 1631); *Courts of Justice Corrected and amended. Or the Corrupt Lawyer* (London, 1642). See also W Dunkel, *William Lambarde, Elizabethan Jurist* (New Brunswick, NJ, Rutgers University Press, 1965).

commitments of time and energy if it was to function adequately. The justices were often accused of corruption. One critic depicted them as dispensing 'with a whole dozen of penal statutes' for 'half a dozen chickens'.[40] In 1571 Nicholas Bacon criticised them for negligence and for improperly leading and swaying juries.[41] In 1575 the Privy Council referred to their 'enormities, absurdities and mischiefs.[42]

V. Legislating Law Reform

Parliament's reform concerns extended beyond courts, the legal profession and legal institutions to particular areas of law. Legislative efforts were primarily concerned with the statutes and their execution, and did not often deal with the substance of the common law. Since the Reformation, reform in the religious sphere required legislative action. Though such measures are typically treated under the rubric of religious rather than law reform, they not only determined the legality of the religious establishment, but prescribed penal sanctions for those who did not obey the prescribed legal requirements. Those who disobeyed became enmeshed in a variety of courts and legal proceedings.[43]

Lawful efforts to alter the established religion and church necessarily centred on parliament. The first and most important religious measures were those that ended the previous legislatively prescribed Roman Catholic religious regime and established the Elizabethan church on a Protestant foundation. The Act of Supremacy determined the legal status of the queen within the church, and the Act of Uniformity established the Protestant church, its liturgy and prayer book. Those refusing to attend church and or to comply with the Act's provisions were subject to punishment. Clerical refusal to abide by the prescribed practices such as kneeling or refusing to wear the prescribed vestments were subject to punishment or dismissal. Laymen who failed to conform by refusing to attend church services were subject to fines.

Those dissatisfied with the religious settlement necessarily sought reform from parliament. In 1572 it received two 'admonitions', the first requesting parliament to 'rightly reform' the church and the second proposing repeal of certain statutes and an enhanced role of the parish in selecting ministers. In 1587 the Puritan 'bill and the book' was directed at voiding all the laws in force regarding ecclesiastical government, including the Book of Common Prayer. Protestant Separatists were not tolerated and several were executed. Cranmer's earlier efforts to reform and revise the canons were completed. However, the resulting *Reformatio legum*

[40] GB Harrison (ed), *Elizabethan Journals*, 2 vols (New York, Doubleday, 1965), vol II, 294–95.

[41] *Proceedings in the Parliaments of Elizabeth I* (n 1) vol I, 317, 336; JE Neale, *Elizabeth and Her Parliaments, 1559–1581* (New York, Norton & Company, 1958).

[42] Bertram Osborne, *Justices of the Peace, 1361–1848* (Shaftsbury, Dorset, Sedghill Press, 1960) 37.

[43] For a discussion of parliamentary law reform during the latter part of Elizabeth's reign, see Dean (n 21) 188–216.

ecclesiasticarum, printed in 1571, was not approved by the queen, probably because the revised canons were viewed as critical of the Elizabethan church.[44]

While both Protestants and Roman Catholics dissenters were subject to penalties, the latter experienced much harsher ones, especially as parliament responded to Roman Catholic plots to assassinate the queen and replace her with a Catholic monarch. It was becoming difficult to distinguish Catholicism from treason after 1570 when a papal bull declared the queen a heretic and encouraged disobedience to her government. Legislation in 1580 and 1593 provided harsh punishments for Popish recusants, Jesuits and seminary priests. A significant number of Roman Catholic clerics lost their lives. Religious affiliation and practice were enmeshed in the legal system, and punitive measures against dissidents were part of the business of the courts and the justices of the peace. Anti-Catholic legislation was part of English law. Religious reform was deeply embedded in the legal system, and religious reform meant changes in the law.

Elizabethans of all classes were involved in giving and receiving credit. Nearly all families at one time or another were entangled in credit arrangements. All those from the smallest farmers and merchants to the gentry and aristocrats, who often owed large sums borrowed for elaborate building and improvement projects, were enmeshed in the laws respecting debt. Problems relating to credit and debt became particularly pressing when economic conditions were difficult and when there were acute shortages of coin.[45] Inability or disinclination to pay what was owed was embedded in legal arrangements that might imprison debtors both large and small. The gaols that housed poor, indebted prisoners imposed horrible conditions, while wealthy debtors paid their keepers for comfortable living conditions. The system meant that poor debtors, who were unable to work, could not pay their debts and that wealthy ones could live comfortably and avoid paying. Creditors, both large and small, often went unpaid. A number of bills attempted to regulate and reform legal provisions relating to credit and debt and to bankruptcy, a legal procedure limited to merchants.[46] There was a bill for denying sanctuary for debtors and, in 1566, a bill to compel the payment of debts.[47] There were bills against 'double payment of Debts upon Shop Books'[48] and to void fraudulent gifts, bargains and alienations made to deceive creditors. They included punishment of bankrupts,[49] who typically were viewed with suspicion. Although one bill that dealt with 'cozening bankrupts' was ordered not to be read, bankruptcy legislation was successful in 1571. Compared to later parliaments, Elizabethan legislators paid little attention to the plight of those imprisoned for debt.

[44] D'Ewes (n 4) 540; Norman Jones, 'An Elizabethan Bill for the Reformation of Ecclesiastical Law' (1985) 4 *Parliamentary History* 171.

[45] See Muldrew (n 17) passim.

[46] Louis Leventhal, 'The Early History of English Bankruptcy' (1919) 67 *University of Pennsylvania Law Review* 1.

[47] CJ, I, 71, 73, 78, 79.

[48] D'Ewes (n 4) 661.

[49] CJ, I, 79; LJ, I, 624, 630, 634.

Given the attempted assassinations, succession plots, the Northern Rebellion and the papal bull declaring Elizabeth a heretic and absolving her subjects from obedience to her, it was felt necessary to alter the laws of treason. In 1571 there were additions to include treasonous words and bringing in or possessing papal bulls, and in 1585 to make the entry of Jesuits and seminary priests treason.[50] While modern commentators are unlikely to view such legislation as reform, for Elizabethan Protestants, they were very necessary ones. There was also legislation to punish seditious words and rumours.[51] Clipping and counterfeiting coins remained treasons punishable by death, but corruption of blood and loss of dower were eliminated to protect the families of the convicted.[52]

Benefit of clergy continued to be removed from felonious offenders for rape and burglary,[53] and in 1597 for robbing houses in daytime when no one was present. There were bills to eliminate it for pick purses and cut purses, crimes of particular concern to urban dwellers.[54] However, a bill abolishing benefit of clergy for house burning was rejected in 1589. Legislation to prevent servants robbing their masters and punishing embezzlement was passed in 1563 and 1588.[55] A bill was introduced in the upper house that provided that those convicted of manslaughter would not forfeit land, tenements or goods.[56] The queen refused assent to a proposal for summary corporal punishment for the theft of grain, orchard theft and wood stealing, but robberies of that kind became specifically unlawful in 1601.[57] There were several legislative efforts to reduce the theft of horses, cattle and sheep. Horse theft was a particular problem because of the ease of selling them in markets. One act required registration of horsesellers with market officials.[58] Game laws, of benefit to landholders, covering the unlawful taking of fish, deer and hawks, were also enacted.[59] There was an unsuccessful effort to deny clergy for stealing women in 1593 that proved successful in 1597–98, as well as a bill for preventing clandestine marriage.[60]

Witchcraft, which was once under the purview of the ecclesiastical courts, became a felony without benefit of clergy in 1562. Capital punishment was to be inflicted only when witchcraft caused death. If no death occurred, lesser penalties such as imprisonment were to be inflicted.[61] The statute, which modified the Henrician legislation, was part of the shift from the ecclesiastical to the

[50] 13 Eliz I c 1 and 2; 27 Eliz I c 2.

[51] 11 Eliz I c 6; 23 Eliz I c 2.

[52] 18 Eliz I c 1; 5 Eliz I c 11; 4 Eliz c 3. The corruption of the blood provision was repeated in the treason act of 1649.

[53] 14 Eliz I c 7; 8 Eliz I c 4; 18 Eliz I c 7. These tended to be repetitions of earlier legislation.

[54] LJ, I, 631; CJ I, 704–05; 39 Eliz I c 15.

[55] 5 Eliz I c 10; 31 Eliz I c 4. There had been similar legislation earlier.

[56] LJ, I, 630.

[57] 43 Eliz I c 7. See LJ, II, 158, 160–63, 211–12, 215; D'Ewes (n 5) 181, 384.

[58] Dean (n 21) 189–91.

[59] 5 Eliz I c 9.

[60] See Dean (n 21) 190–91.

[61] 5 Eliz I c 16, 1562. For Ireland, see 28 Eliz I c 2. A witchcraft act was passed in Scotland in 1563.

secular courts. Common law judges and juries would try witchcraft cases.[62] Juries may have been more willing to send witches to their deaths.[63] Star Chamber and the ecclesiastical courts would continue to hear perjury cases. Additional legislation to prevent perjury and subornation of perjury was enacted by Elizabeth's last parliament.[64]

Frauds were a source of major concern. There was successful legislation dealing with 'misemployment of Lands, Goods, and Stocks of Money given to Charitable uses',[65] frauds in the administration of intestate goods,[66] fraudulent assurances by traders[67] and fraudulent 'evidences and Writings'.[68] There were also bills dealing with fraudulent gifts and conveyances,[69] and false deeds and wills.[70] Fraudulent practices related to land and other transactions would be a continuing concern of later parliamentary reformers.

Given the span of Elizabeth's reign and Puritan concerns about moral discipline, parliament gave relatively little attention to reforming morality. There were bills to prevent 'usual and common swearing', profaneness and drunkenness.[71] An anti-sodomy statute passed,[72] but an act in 1601 to suppress adultery did not. In the latter instance, worry about ecclesiastical judges making decisions on the inheritances of laymen resulted in the House of Commons giving the bill 'a Great No' and 'Away with it'.[73]

Informers, employed to increase prosecution and conviction under various penal statutes, played a significant role in a legal system lacking police. Despite considerable reliance on informers, there were fears that they were responsible for bogus prosecutions and false testimony for financial gain. Legislative proposals emphasised reform of their 'abuses', not their elimination. There were bills to

[62] Michael D Gordon argues that the statute was not innovative and was intended to revive penalties for existing crimes. The ecclesiastical courts and Star Chamber had punished perjury before 1563 and continued to do so afterwards. The law was continued in 13 Eliz I c 25 and made perpetual in 29 Eliz I c 5. If no oath was involved, it was not perjury. See Michael D Gordon, 'The Invention of the Common Law Crime: Perjury and the Elizabethan Courts' (1980) 24 *American Journal of Legal History* 145.

[63] A large proportion of those accused, accusing and witnessing were women. There were low conviction rates at the assizes. See Jim Sharpe, 'Women, Witchcraft and the Legal Process' in Jennifer Kermode and Garthine Walker (eds), *Women, Crime and the Courts in Early Modern England* (Chapel Hill, University of North Carolina Press, 1944) 106–24.

[64] 43 Eliz I c 5; 5 Eliz I c 9.

[65] 43 Eliz I c 4. For charitable trusts, see 39 Eliz I c 6.

[66] 43 Eliz I c 8.

[67] 27 Eliz I c 4; 29 Eliz I c 3.

[68] 5 Eliz I c 14. In 1576, 18 Eliz I c 4 dealt with fraudulent conveyances by rebels in the north. For fraud concerning jeofails, see 18 Eliz I c 14. The House of Lords passed and sent to the House of Commons a bill to 'reform Deceits and Frauds in Auditors and their Clerks'; LJ, II, 256, 261. There were bills to prevent fraudulent conveyances in 1584–85, 1587 and 1601.

[69] CJ I, 84, 89; 13 Eliz I c 5.

[70] CJ, I, 65; LJ, I, 598.

[71] LJ, I, 601; LJ I, 254, 262; CJ, I, 78, LJ, I, 601.

[72] 5 Eliz I c 17. Henrician legislation transferred sodomy to the secular courts. It was returned to the ecclesiastical courts under Mary I. Sodomy cases were rare.

[73] D'Ewes (n 4) 641.

redress disorders in 1584, 1585 and 1589. Reliance on informers who were given monetary incentives to spur prosecution would continue in a variety forms for much of the early modern era.

Several bills were developed to prevent or minimise the delays in lawsuits or to discourage vexatious suits. Although the House of Lords sought a measure providing better execution of 'certain Statutes and for the Reformation of certain Disorders used in the law',[74] other proposals were more specific. In 1566 there was a bill to avoid 'wrongful Vexations upon the Writ of Latitat', a legal device allowing certain trials to be heard in King's Bench.[75] Another allowed defendants to recover their costs if 'wrongly vexed'.[76] In 1566 the House of Lords considered a bill to confirm fines and recoveries even if there were default of the original writ.[77] The House of Commons considered delays in real actions in 1566.[78] In 1585 there was an act to expedite justice in cases of demurrers and pleading.[79]

Because there was no regular method of appeal except by writ of error, review of erroneous or unfair judgments was difficult and often impossible. A number of legislative reform measures were introduced. In 1581 legislation was enacted to reform errors in fines and recoveries.[80] An act of 1585 sought to redress erroneous judgments in Queen's Bench. In 1589 another dealt with writs of error in Queen's Bench and Exchequer. The absence of a settled mechanism for appeals would continue to plague dissatisfied litigants and enflame the common lawyers who saw Chancery intervention as preventing execution of their judgments. Litigants and lawyers dissatisfied with common law court decisions often took the opportunity to seek more satisfying judgments in other courts.

A significant change in the operation of the courts occurred in 1563, when courts of record were empowered to compel the attendance of witnesses. Although witnesses had already become common in jury trials, the legislation signalled that witnesses had become a general regular feature in English trials.

Despite the many recommendations of Elizabeth's Lord Chancellors and Keepers, not all parliaments were equally concerned with law reform. Reform interest and activity became somewhat stronger during the latter part of her reign as litigation levels and court delays increased. Elizabeth's last parliament again saw bills to 'avoid trifling and frivolous suits' in the Westminster courts, to reduce unnecessary 'expenses in suits of law'[81] and to end 'unnecessary delays in Execution upon judgments' in cases of debt.[82]

[74] LJ, I, 629.
[75] LJ, I, 645, 647, 649, 660, 661.
[76] 8 Eliz I c 2.
[77] LJ, I, 632, 662, 667; See also LJ, I, 629, 630, 631.
[78] CJ, I, 79.
[79] 27 Eliz I c 5.
[80] 23 Eliz I c 3.
[81] LJ, II, 248, 350, 261.
[82] LJ, II, 257.

VI. Internal Court Reform

Although we emphasize Crown and legislatively sponsored reform, court reform was also initiated by judges. Lord Chancellors and Keepers issued orders eliminating abuses in Chancery in 1583 and 1584, and Egerton, Master of the Rolls in 1593 and Lord Keeper in 1594, tried to modernise the court on several occasions. In 1596 he attempted to clarify court procedure in order to prevent frivolous suits and lengthy proceedings. Two years later, he attempted to speed up proceedings.[83]

Despite the repeated reform orders, Chancery abuses were not easily corrected. Although Chancery grew in procedural subtlety and formality during the second half of the sixteenth century, it also experienced increased pressure from the growing number of litigants and accusations of excessive fees, long delays and capricious decision-making. However much it was criticised, Chancery had an important place in the legal system, dealing with fraud and fair play, trusts, uses, charities. It also dealt with taking undue advantage when the enforcement of legal rights was unavailable or being subverted, specific performance of contracts and agreements, fulfilment of duties and obligations and providing relief under conditions of mistake, ignorance and accident. Its jurisdictional boundaries were unclear and it was not infrequently involved in jurisdictional disputes with the ecclesiastical and common law courts.[84]

The Lord Chief Justice of Common Pleas, emphasising the judicial role in correcting faults in his court, issued orders dealing with officers, court clerks and attorneys.[85] In 1597 Lord Keeper Egerton, in his capacity as President of the Court of Star Chamber, issued 'Orders for reformation of the dilatory proceedings' in 'her Majesties most honorable Court of Starr Chamber'.[86] Judges were not unsympathetic to court reform, though their efforts did not stem criticism or result in long-term results.

Given the number of courts, many of whose jurisdiction was ill-defined or overlapping with that of other courts, each court attempted to defend or enhance what it viewed as its own territory. Tithes and wills, traditionally under the jurisdiction of the ecclesiastical courts, often involved property, which was traditionally under the jurisdiction of the common law courts. When Chancery attempted to correct erroneous or unfair decisions of the common law and other courts, those

[83] William Jones, The *Elizabethan Court of Chancery* (Oxford, Oxford University Press, 1967) 50–52, 61, 62, 79, 84, 85–87.

[84] Jones, *Elizabethan Chancery*, 99, 343–78, 392–93, 407, 420–24.

[85] *The Ancient and Modern … describing past and present practice of King's Bench and Common Pleas* (London, 1674) To the Reader, 42, 69. The volume was designed to show 'what course the Reverend Judges have taken at all times to reform the Causes of Each Court'.

[86] Star Chamber was particularly active in safeguarding the procedural rights of defendants and prosecutors during Egerton's presidency (1596–1617); see Barnes 'Star Chamber Mythology' (n 27) 6n. During Elizabeth's reign, the Court of Exchequer developed an equity side that would overlap with that of Chancery.

courts rejected interference with their judgments. Chancery used the injunction and the common law courts prohibitions to their advantage. Common lawyers were watchful and jealous of the jurisdiction of Chancery, the ecclesiastical courts, and the Councils of Wales and the North. Litigants and lawyers went from court to court to delay judgment or to find a court more sympathetic to their cause. Whenever possible, courts defended their jurisdiction and argued that the offending courts must be reined in. Common lawyers were aggressive in characterising non-common law courts as offenders and aggrandisers in need of reform. Such jurisdictional conflicts were endemic and would continue to plague the English legal system for many generations.

Jurisdictional issues also arose among the common law courts. King's Bench, by means of a legal fiction, was able to assert jurisdiction over cases traditionally adjudicated in Common Pleas, therefore increasing its business at the expense of another common law court. There was also a substantial change in the status of the barons of the Exchequer when, in 1579, they were given the same rank and dignity as other common law judges.[87] The changing status of the Exchequer barons may have stemmed from the pressure of increased litigation that required more judges and/or from the decreased distinction between exchequer and civil cases.

VII. Law Reform and the Publication of Legal Texts

Although efforts to improve the state of professional legal texts have not usually been considered law reform, they should be recognised as serious efforts of the legal profession to improve the condition of English law. Lawyers and non-lawyers complained of the confusing and disorderly state of the common law, conflicting judicial opinions, and confusion as to what statutes were actually in force.

Printed legal texts continued to proliferate, and lawyers and judges became increasingly dependent on them. Older texts were reprinted, often with additions and corrections to bring them up to date, and new ones printed. Most fell into a set of legal genres; yearbooks and case reports, often, but not always, the work of judges, abridgments of those reports, statute books and their abridgments, and overviews of the common law sometimes entitled Institutes or Institutions. There were also efforts to 'methodise' the law, that is, to make it more understandable, more manageable and more easily retrievable, as well as publications devoted to particular areas of law and handbooks for justices of the peace.[88]

Yearbooks and case reports were the essential tools of lawyers and judges. Law reports, typically compiled for private use, were anything but uniform in substance

[87] From that time onwards, they were to be selected from the sergeants at law and went on circuit, as did the other judges. See Edward Foss, *Judges of England*, 9 vols (London, Longmans, 1848–164), vol V, 409.

[88] See John H Baker, 'English Law Books and legal Publishing' in J Barnard and DF McKenzie (eds), *The Cambridge History of the Book in Britain 1557–1695*, 4 vols (Cambridge, Cambridge University Press, 2002), vol IV, 474.

or presentation. Judges, lawyers and law students recorded for themselves what they found useful or noteworthy. Some were prepared for publication, but many were not. Judicial reports were typically published posthumously, so authors had no opportunity to revise or correct them. While print made the reports far more accessible, it also exposed conflicting judicial opinions that undermined the certainty of the law. Providing reasons for their legal judgments was not routine for judges. Although reports had no official status, by the end of the century, judicial decisions might carry considerable weight. The doctrine of precedent had not yet emerged, but the increased availability of reports contributed to the evolution of common law from the common learning of lawyers and judges to case law.[89]

Older yearbooks and reports, typically in law French, continued to circulate or were updated. James Dyers' appeared in 1585, 1592 and 1601.[90] Edmund Plowden's *Les Commentaries on les reports*, printed seven times during the Elizabethan period, points to the growing appetite for and increasing reliance on printed reports. His *Commentaries*, less procedurally oriented than the yearbooks, emphasised that memory was 'unfaithful and slippery'. Reporters must simplify by extracting 'the pure only, and to leave the refuse'.[91]

Sir Edward Coke shared the view that 'the common learning' of lawyers was 'in our books' and 'our book cases are the best proof what the law is'.[92] If the recorded cases were the 'best proof' of the law, recording must be improved. Coke's 12 volumes of *Reports*, which quickly became essential texts, were designed to reform the state of law reporting. Coke condemned the 'want of a true and certain Report' and denounced 'the case that hath been adjudged standing upon the racket of many runaway Reports (especially of such as understand not the state of the Question'. All too often, law reports were 'disordered and disjointed' and the right reason and rule of the judges 'utterly mistaken', leading to 'many absurd and strange opinions … fathered on grave & reverend Judges, many times with the multitude, & sometimes with the learned' who were either 'beguile[d]' or 'bedevil[d]' by 'their conceits and judgments'. Coke also highlighted the importance of writing and printing. Without written and published yearbooks, 'the opinions, censures and judgments' of judges would have been 'long since wasted

[89] DJ Ibbetson, 'Report and Record in Early Modern Common Law' in Nain Wijffels (ed), *Case Law in the Making*, 2 vols (Berlin, Duncker & Humblot, 1997), vol I, 56–50, 63–65. By the 1590s, Coke had probably decided to print his reports (at 59). See also Charles M Gray, 'Parliament, Liberty and the Law' in JH Hexter (ed), *Parliament and Liberty from the Reign of Elizabeth to the English Civil War* (Palo Alto, Stanford University Press, 1992) 157–60; W Bryson, 'Equity Reports and Records in Early Modern England' in Nain Wijffels (ed), *Case Law in the Making*, 2 vols (Berlin, Duncker & Humblot, 1997), vol I, 69–82.

[90] James Dyer, *Cy ensuont ascuns novel cases* (London, 1585). His reports included extra-judicial discussions of the judges. See LW Abbott, *Law Reporting in England 1485–1660* (London, University of London Legal Series, 1973) 156, 157, 174, 190, 196.

[91] Edmund Plowden, *Les commentaries et les reports* (London, 1581) Preface.

[92] Edward Coke, *Les reports de Edward Coke* (London, 1601) *Praefatio ad lectorum*. Abridgements in English appeared in 1650, 1651, 1656, 1657, 1658, 1666 and 1680.

and worn away with the worm of oblivion'. Without them, the certainty of the law would have been lost. Coke emphasised the fallibility of 'slippery memory' and the 'wandering and masterless Reports'.[93] Law reporting must be both reformed and printed.

Despite his critique, Coke praised the judges whose opinions he reported. These were now collected 'for the help of their memories who heard them, and perfectly knew them, for the instruction of others who knew them not, but imperfect heard of them, and lately, for the common good (for that is my chief purpose) in quieting & establishing of the possessions of many in these general cases, wherein there hath been such variety of opinions'.[94] Rather than following a method of his own devising, he would 'follow the form that the Learned shall allowe of'. Though Coke considered his reports to be an improvement over earlier reports, he nevertheless advised that one should not neglect 'the oulde Books of years, reported in former ages, for assuredly out of the old fields must spring and grow the new corne'.[95] His *Third part of the Reports* (1602) again railed against reports containing 'obscure and misprinted' cases. He also objected to judge-compiled reports, referring to an allegedly earlier practice when kings appointed 'discreet and learned professors of the Law' to report the 'judgments and opinions … as well for resolving of such doubts and questions therein'. If the earlier practice was revived, judges might 'speak with one mouth' providing much-needed certainty. Coke is adamant that judges must include 'all the reasons and causes of their judgments'. He also recommended that reports be digested into several volumes to provide 'coherence and concordance'.[96] He also favoured reform of legal argumentation, recommending return to an older-style correcting current practice that included too many lengthy arguments and citation of cases and authorities.

Coke characterised his reports as being 'in the nature of commentaries, either for the better apprehending of the true construction of certain general Acts of Parliament with certain principal points never expounded before, or for the better understanding of the True sense and reason of the Judgments and resolutions formerly reported, or for resolution of such doubts are therein remained undecided'.[97] They would avoid 'Obscurity, Ambiguity, Jeopardy, Novelty and Prolixity'.[98]

Although Coke famously wrote of the dangers of legal innovation, he did not reject all reform. While innovation in some laws was dangerous, the 'alteration of

[93] Coke, *The First part of the Institutes*, Preface.
[94] Coke, *First Report*, Preface.
[95] ibid.
[96] Coke, *Third Part of the Reports*, Preface.
[97] ibid.
[98] Coke, *Seventh Part of the Reports*, Preface. Coke praised the reports of James Dyer, the 'exquisite and elaborate Commentaries' of Master Plowden and 'the two great abridgements' of Fitzherbert and Brooke. Coke, *Third Part*, Preface.

others' might be accomplished with 'lesse peril'. When undertaking reform of laws and courts, it was necessary 'to foresee that a proportional remedy be applied', so that when 'curing … defects past', the alterations cause no 'more dangerous effects' in the future. Coke was highly critical of statutory changes to the common law. 'Multiple infinite troubles, questions, suits and difficulties' had resulted from the introduction of uses that were once unknown to the common law. 'New-found perpetuities' were a 'monstrous brood carved out of mere invention and never known to the ancient sage of the Law'. However, digesting the common law 'into method' had little appeal. 'Expounding the law should rest solely with the judges and sages of the realm' and, in cases of 'greatest difficulty and importance', with parliament.[99]

Coke, like Bacon, King James and many members of parliament, supported reform of the penal statutes. Like so many reformers, he favoured 'one plainer and perspicuous law divided to articles, so as every subject may know what acts be in force, what repealed … what branches and parts abridged, what enlarged'. While reform of the statutes, which had been commanded by the king, was worthy of 'singular commendation', Coke did not think that the same could be done for the common law.[100] Nor was he pleased with critics of the law who 'daily … impune' the laws.[101]

Given the length and complexity of law reports, abridgements had become a mainstay of Elizabethan lawyers. Older abridgments continued to be used, those of Fitzherbert, Stratham and Brooke being especially admired. Plowden's *Abridgement de tout les cases* (1597) proved a welcome addition.[102] 'Tables', sometimes similar to a modern table of contents, were often added to further summarise the law.[103] However, Coke and other leading lawyers were suspicion of the overuse of abridgements, feeling that they were all too likely to be used instead of the reports they abridged. Abridgments caused 'confused judgments' and poor 'deliverie or utterance'.[104]

[99] Coke, *Tenth Part of the Reports*, Preface; Coke, *Fourth Part of the Reports*, Preface to the Reader. Coke, *Third Part of the Reports*, Preface. In 1628 Coke indicated 'never yet was any fundamental law shaken but infinite trouble ensued'. *See Commons Debates, 1628*, 3 vols (New Haven, Yale University Press, 1977–83), vol III, 95.

[100] Coke, *Fourth Part of the Reports*, Preface.

[101] Coke, *Third Part of the Reports*, Preface.

[102] Sir William Staunford recommended a digest of the common law based on Sir Anthony Fitzherbert's *Abridgement* to clarify the principles of the common law; Anthony Fitzherbert, *La Graunde Abridgement*. There were Elizabethan printings in 1565, 1573 1576 and 1577. Sir Robert Brooke's, *The Graunde Abridgment* had several Elizabethan printings; William Rastell, *La Table or Summary of notable things in Fitzherbert's Abridgement* (London, 1565). See David J Harvey, *The Law Emprynted and Englished: The Printing Press as an Agent of Change in Law and Legal Culture 1575–1642* (Oxford, Hart Publishing, 2015) 155. Plowden's *Abridgement des tout les cases* was issued in 1597 and 1607. Richard Totell held the monopoly for law book printing from 1553 to 1593. For Elizabethan law reports, see LW Abbott, *Law Reporting in England 1535–1585* (London, Athlone, 1973) 150–239.

[103] Thomas Ashe provided 'tables' for both Dyer's and Coke's reports.

[104] Coke, *Fourth Part of the Reports*, Preface.

Littleton's *Tenures*, appearing repeatedly in both law French and English, must have been one of the (if not the) most purchased legal text. Another elementary guide to land law, John Perkins' *A Profitable Booke*, appeared in 1567. Guides to pleas of the Crown, both old and new, were available.[105] Despite its Latin title, Ferdinado Pulton's *De pace regis et regni* was written in English 'open to all the persons that are willing to read'.[106]

Surveys of the principles of the common law were becoming more readily available. Fitzherbert's often reprinted *La Novel natura brevium* explained that law, like all arts and sciences, had 'rules and Foundations' and that maxims were 'very necessary for those who well understood the laws'. They were the 'fundamentals on which the law depends'. The anonymous *Institutions or Principall grounds of the Laws and Statutes of England*, which had been popular since its first printing, had three Elizabethan printings.[107]

Francis Bacon's *Collection of some Principal Rules and Maxims of the Common Law*, written but not printed during his lifetime, was his effort to state the principles of the law and it make it more comprehensible. Bacon, who applauded the queen's plans for 'a general amendment of the state of [the] laws' and for reducing 'them to more brevity and certainty', characterises his maxims as an effort to collect the 'rules and grounds dispersed throughout the body of the same laws'. They would help decide doubts, eliminate 'unprofitable subtlety', create a 'more sound' sense of the law and aid in the 'amendment' of 'some measure of the very nature and complexity of the whole law'. His preferred method was to put these rules and grounds in the form of aphorisms.[108]

Rastell's *Exposition of the terms of the Laws of England*, reissued in 1563 with a new preface, emphasised the need for uniformity and publicity. 'If kept to knowledge of a few', law became a 'trap' and a 'net to bring people to Vexation and trouble'. Its nine printings between 1563 and 1605 suggest that this was an important vehicle for dispersing knowledge of the law.[109]

Although the statutes were becoming available in several formats, complaints were frequently voiced about the uncertainty over which were currently in force and which were obsolete, conflicting or repealed. New statutes were printed after each parliamentary session and older statutes from the reigns of Henry VIII, Edward VI and Mary I reprinted.[110] Statutes were to be openly declared every leet

[105] Published in 1557. There were additional printings in 1569, 1579 and 1583.

[106] Ferdinando Pulton, *De pace regis et regni* (London, 1609). Bracton was printed in 1569.

[107] Anthony Fitzherbert, *La novel natura brevium* (1552). There were also a number of other volumes entitled *Natura Brevium*. Another older *Institutions or principle Grounds and Statutes of the Lawes of England*, 'very profitable for all sortes of people to know', had six printings during Elizabeth's reign. John Perkins' *A Profitable Book … treating of the Laws of England*, which provided the basics of land law, had 13 printings during her reign.

[108] Bacon (n 5) vol VIII, 316, 320.

[109] It was issued eight times between 1607 and 1641.

[110] About 50 copies of each public act were printed. See Katherine Pantzer, 'Printing the English Statutes 1489–1649: Some Historical Implications' in Kenneth Carpenter (ed), *Books and Society in History* (New York, RR Bowker, 1983) 69–114.

and law day, and once a term in the common law courts and Chancery. There were also collections of the statutes. Those of William Rastell and Christopher Barker were printed regularly. Rastell's *A Collection of all the Statutes* attempted to make the statutes more accessible by excluding various legal expressions, most preambles and unnecessary and overlapping portions of the statute.[111]

Abridgments of the statutes were also available. In 1562 a proclamation announced that an abridgement of a group of mostly regulatory statutes was needed because of the 'mane enormities', 'negligence of officers' and 'resumption of offendours', that were 'dayle encreasing'. It referred to the need for 'reformation'. The preamble of *An Abridgment of all the Penal Statutes* was printed in 1581 by the authority of Parliament 'so each will know the laws'. Pulton's *Abstract of all the Penal Statutes*, first published in 1577, also emphasised his 'intent that everyone which desired to know may read and thereby perceive the cause and contents' of the law. Like many other reform-minded lawyers, Pulton commented on the confusing state of the statutes, some partially repealed, that made understanding the law so difficult. The law should be 'plaine and easy' to understand. He hoped that others would reduce the confused number of our laws into 'some perfect method'.[112] Lawyers may have been suspicious of tampering with the common law, but were not averse to clarifying the statutes.

Given the barrage of complaints about the state of both the common law and the statutes, it is not surprising that Pulton and others favoured 'methods' for making them more orderly, more rational and easier to understanding. Ramist and other 'methods' attracted the attention of many intellectuals during the Elizabethan era, and several writers attempted to apply them to legal materials. Among them was Abraham Fraunce, a lawyer and poet who proposed using Ramist logic to improve the law, now contained 'in vast volumes confusedly scattered and utterly undigested', written in 'hotchpot French' and resulting in difficult-to-use reports. Ramist logic could provide a 'more orderly explication of the laws'. Presentation of the laws should be general, with 'mitigation and detractions' left to the 'conscience and discretion' of learned judges. Like many influenced by Ramus, Fraunce adopted visual schemes that organised material in a diagrammatic form.[113]

William Fulbecke also recommended 'methodising' as a solution to the 'ocean of reports' and 'perplexed confusion of opinions'. Laws should be 'plain and manifest to all', not 'obscured', as they were currently 'with difficult cases, shadowed in conceited terms, and as it were, covered with cloudes and wrapped in darkness'. There was 'nothing in the law, which may not be reduced into some universall

[111] See also William Rastell, *A collection in English of the statutes now in force* (1565, 1566, 1572, 1574, 1579, 1583, 1588, 1594, 1595); Christopher Barker, *A Collection in English, of all the statutes now in force, from Magna Carta to the third year of Elizabeth's reign* (1583).

[112] *Abstract of all the Penal Statutes* (London, 1577). It also appeared in 1587, 1588 and 1591.

[113] Abraham Fraunce, *The Lawyer's Logicke* (London, 1588) Preface. Fraunce's volume was closer to a handbook of logic or dialectic than one of law.

theorie'. Fulbecke recommended an 'artificial analysis', which began with general rules and principles, then divided 'the whole into partes' and then subdivided the parts 'into parcells'. This method of division and subdivision would provide 'a constant and coherence of the entire thing' and its parts. Fulbecke also favoured putting the law 'in Tables' for easier access.[114]

Printed handbooks for justices of the peace became more readily available. Fitzherbert's was updated and enlarged by Richard Crompton, but continued to be printed in law French. It would be replaced by William Lambarde's *Eirenarcha*, which had six printings by the end of the century. Lambarde, who referred to the 'stacks of statutes' that the magistrates must implement, also aimed to give 'some light of Order and Method to the manifold' materials needed by the justices.[115]

The search for better ways of organising and presenting what was widely recognised as a disorderly and often incomprehensible body of legal material was the aim of numerous legal authors, many of whom characterised their work as providing an improved model.

Some older and some newer works dealing with the law were also becoming more available. More's *Utopia* was first translated into English in 1551 and was printed again in 1597. Sir John Fortescue's *De Laudibus legum Anglorum*, the famous 'learned commentary of the politque lawes of England', was issued in English in 1567, 1573 and 1599. John Cowell's *The pandects of the law of nations* (1602) helped readers to compare civil and common law. Christopher St Germain's *Doctor and Student* had several printings. Thomas Smith's *De Republica Anglorum*, sometimes published under the title *The Commonwealth of England*, described the government, legal institutions and legal procedures at considerable length. Smith characterised parliament as able to abrogate old laws and make new ones, and alter the rights and possessions of private individuals. It circulated in manuscript before becoming available in print in 1583.[116]

Religious publications of all kinds addressed legal issues relating to the legal basis of the church establishment, its liturgy, practices and doctrine. Although there were too many to mention, one cannot avoid taking note of Richard Hooker's majestic *The Laws of Ecclesiastical Polity*, a work that sought to answer Puritan claims that Scripture alone prescribed the nature of church government and that the English church was corrupted because it had not eliminated elements of Roman Catholic practice. Hooker identified various types of law and justified the legislatively established church.

[114] William Fulbecke, *A Direction or Preparative to the study of the Laws* (London, 1600). Fulbecke rejected the Ramist method and, unlike Ramus, did not seek the certainty of mathematical demonstration. He praised the legal work of Sir William Stanford, saying with respect to 'Method' that it 'may be a law to the writers of the law which shall succeed him'.

[115] William Lambarde, *Eirenarcha, or the office of the justices of peace* (London, 1581), dedicatory preface. Abridgements of the statutes were issued to the justices in 1561–62.

[116] It was issued again in 1584, 1589 and 1594. There were 11 English editions before 1640.

VIII. Conclusion

The over 40-year reign of Elizabeth I saw a good deal of criticism of the law, the courts and the legal profession. Laws dealing with religious doctrine, policy and polity were contested in and out of parliament, with those proposing changes claiming the mantle of reformer. As jurisdictional issues became more intense, common lawyers characterised their positions as reform against the aggrandisement or incursion of ecclesiastical, equity and conciliar courts. Parliament was active in trying to reform the long delays and high costs of litigation with a series of modest reforms aimed at making the legal system work better. There was some attention to crime, but no substantial change, except in the area of treason and witchcraft. Attention was given to reducing the invocation of benefit of clergy by first-time offenders. However, no voices were to be heard favouring a transformation of the legal system or legal profession. Law reform meant moderate reform. This was a period in which the Crown, and its Lord Chancellors and Lord Keepers, actively supported reform legislation. So did many lawyers, though protective of their status and income. Nathaniel and then Francis Bacon became voices for reform in parliament, and Coke supported similar modest and cautious reform. Reform of the statutes garnered the greatest support.

One area of very active reform was performed by the legal profession itself, which was engaged in efforts to improve the reports and abridgments and to apply new techniques such as Ramist methodising. Looking back over the Elizabethan period, we can see that complaints about abuses increased with the rapid growth of litigation and the resulting increased public engagement with lawyers and courts. The complaints did not lead to much change, but there was more awareness of defects in how the legal system worked. High costs and long delays were common complaints and jurisdictional tensions and conflicts made solutions more difficult.

Although not usually considered in connection with law reform, legal publication was the most successful part of Elizabethan law reform. Lawyers, who were so often seen as opposing law reform, were actively engaged in reforming the materials of the law. Such efforts would become part of the Jacobean reform agenda as well. Reforms sought during the Elizabethan era were roughly of the same type as in earlier reigns. Jacobean reformers would follow this pattern.

4

The Early Stuarts 1603–40

Historians have traditionally focused on the constitutional issues and conflicts of the early Stuart period and have, with the exception of historians of parliament, rarely paid much attention to law reform efforts. These efforts are therefore relatively unknown and their continuity with earlier law reform has gone unnoticed.[1] This chapter begins with James I's involvement with law reform. It is followed by a chronological treatment of Jacobean parliaments and will attempt to demonstrate that the failures of law reform measures were determined, as much or more by the difficulties in completing legislation and the fate of particular parliaments than by support or opposition to reform. The chapter concludes with law reform interest expressed in public and private media, and reform motives expressed in the growing number of publications produced primarily for the legal profession.

I. James I and Law Reform

Although James I, like most English rulers, called parliaments when he was most in need of financial support, he also encouraged parliament to pursue law reform. The king's first speech to parliament stressed execution of the law more than reform, noting the dangers of legislating without sufficient leisure to 'wisely deliberate' and the need to be 'warie about proposing novelties'. 'The life and strength of the Law' did not consist in 'heaping up infinite and confused numbers of Laws, but in the right interpretation and good execution of good and wholesome Laws'. In 1606 James emphasised defects in the laws requiring remedies, while at the same time assuring parliament that 'the grounds of the Common Law of England are the best of any Law in the world'. He criticised 'obscuritie in some points of this our written Law, and the want of fulnesse in others, the variations of Cases and mens curiosities breeding every day new questions and to the practice of bad' answers that tied later judges to the 'unjust and partial' opinions of earlier ones. He looked to parliament for the 'clearing and the sweeping off the rust' of the laws, not

[1] Donald Veall briefly discusses pre-revolutionary developments in *The Popular Movement for Law Reform 1640–1660* (Oxford, Oxford University Press, 1970).

their abolition.[2] His proposals were presented as moderate and cautious. Though 'corrupt judges' might lead to unjust laws, it was 'better' to have 'a certain Law with some spots in it' than to live with uncertainty. Like Bacon, he was concerned with the presentation of legal materials and recommended that 'all the approved Cases' be 'set down and allowed by Parliament for standing Lawes in all time to come'.[3] James expressed concern with improving juries in a proclamation of 1607. Juries were an 'excellent institution' if jurors were men 'of such qualities, credit, [and] understanding, as are worthy to be trusted with so great a charge'. But 'time and abuse' had led sheriffs and bailiffs to exempt 'many of the ablest and fittest persons', making jurors too often 'simple', 'ignorant' and unable to understand difficult cases. The remedy was 'gentlemen' of the 'best quality.[4]

The king's proposal for a 'perfect Union of Laws and Persons' between England and Scotland provided the opportunity for 'amending and polishing' English laws as well as for removing 'hostile' or 'conflicting laws'.[5] James denied any 'great antipathy' between the laws and customs of England and Scotland, arguing that Scotland did not have its own common law and that the civil law was only used there when Scots law was defective. Reconciling the statutes and eliminating conflicting laws was therefore the 'principal work' at hand.[6] James' interest in rationalising the laws may have stemmed from familiarity with Scotland's Elizabethan-era commissions for codifying the law and the statutes[7] and/or with Bacon's reform proposals.

When, in 1610, it became clear that a union of laws was not going to succeed, the king issued a proclamation for remedying the 'multiplicity and doubtful interpretation' of some statutes and others 'worn out with time'. He indicated that those statutes had been reviewed and that he had asked the Privy Council to select 'discreet persons learned in the Law' to collect the statutes now actually in force and to 'digest them into some orderly Method'.[8] After review by the judges, they would be sent to parliament. The proclamation confirms James' commitment to law reform.

Speaking to parliament in March 1610, James again underlined both the need for law reform and his commitment to the common law. While 'no law' could

[2] James VI and I, *Political Writings*, Johann Sommerville (ed) (Cambridge, Cambridge University Press, 1994) 161, 162, 163.

[3] ibid 161–62.

[4] All persons who had freeholds were to be returned to serve as jurors. See James Larkin and Paul Hughes, *Stuart Royal Proclamations*, 3 vols (New Haven, Yale University Press, 1964–69), vol I, 168.

[5] ibid vol 164, 167, 174–75.

[6] ibid 172–74. See also *Parliamentary Diary of Robert Bowyer 1606–1607*, DH Willson (ed) (Minneapolis, University of Minnesota Press, 1931), 256n, 259.

[7] There were proposals for codification of the laws in Scotland from the fifteenth century. Litigation in Scotland was increasingly likely to involve statutes. A commission to work on the statutes was formed in 1566 and some work was done in the 1570s. There were also commissions in 1628 and 1633. During his time as King of Scotland, James VI had wanted the poor to have access to the judicial system; Julian Goodare, *The Government of Scotland 1560–1625* (Oxford, Oxford University Press, 2004) 74, 78, 79, 81, 82, 162, 250.

[8] James I (n 2) 183, 186–87.

provide 'better or more advantages for a King', several 'things in the common law' should be 'purged & cleared'. It should be written in our 'vulgar Language' instead of a 'corrupt language' understood only by lawyers. He faulted the law for having no 'settled Text', being grounded either in 'old Customes, or else upon the Reports and Cases of Judges'. The people should not have to depend 'upon the bare opinions of Judges, and uncertain Reports'. Parliament should therefore set down both the 'exposition of the Law' and the reports of cases 'fit to serve for Law in all times hereafter'. Both reports and statutes should be 'maturely reviewed, and reconciled' and 'contarieties … scraped out of our Bookes'. Penal laws no longer 'agree[ing] with the condition of our time, might likewise be left out of our books'. This 'worthy work' of 'reformation' deserved parliament's attention.[9] Lord Chancellor Ellesmere, speaking to the House of Lords, also recommended that judges be appointed to review the penal statutes and suggest which should be repealed. A list of 'snaring' statutes was evidently compiled, but no further action seems to have been taken.[10] Ellesmere, like many lawyers and laymen, thought that the 'Incertentye of Judicature' should 'be reformed and reduced to more certainty'.[11] If judges didn't know the ancient law, they could neither know nor follow the statute only 'follow their noses and grope at in the dark'.[12]

II. Parliament 1603–10

James I's first parliament met off and on in five sessions between 1604 and 1610. The narrative of this parliament typically emphasises both Crown efforts to obtain a union with Scotland and increase financial support, and parliament's efforts to reduce feudal obligations, end purveyance (the right to obtain goods at reduced rates), clarify the legal status of proclamations, patents and monopolies, and strengthen the enforcement of laws affecting Roman Catholics and Puritan dissenters. Despite conflict between Crown and parliament on some of these matters, the two could work in tandem on law reform.

Parliament had a broader reform agenda than the Crown. While it shared James' concerns about uncertainty in the law and the confused state of the statutes, it also voiced discontent with the high costs and long delays in the courts, jurisdictional rivalries, defects of the legal profession and shortcomings in the

[9] ibid 186–87.

[10] Elizabeth R Foster (ed), *Proceedings in Parliament 1610* (New Haven, Yale University Press, 1966), vol I, 9, 160; SR Gardiner, *Parliamentary Debates in 1610*, 2 vols (Camden Society, 1862), first ser LCCCI, 8n.

[11] Thomas Egerton, Memorials, mss in Huntington Library; see Louis A Knafla, *Law and Politics of Jacobean England: The Trials of Lord Chancellor Ellesmere* (Cambridge, Cambridge University Press, 1977).

[12] He also produced the first treatise on statutory interpretation. In other instances, interpretation should follow the intent of the legislators.

laws relating to debt and crime. These problems had been on the reform agenda of Elizabethan parliaments and would continue to occupy parliament's attention throughout the early modern period.

The first major item taken up was the king's proposal for uniting the laws of England and Scotland. Although many MPs viewed this as a threat to the common law, Sir Edwin Sandys saw the occasion as an opportunity to review the English laws not currently in 'high repute' and suggested a commission to prepare a perfect union.[13] In 1607 Sandys favoured a proposal for reviewing and reducing statutes 'to more order and certainty'.[14] John Doddridge, a respected lawyer, recommended reform because 'old statutes are obscure and the reason is, for that we are so far removed from the times wherein they were made'.[15] In the course of discussing conflicting laws, parliament addressed the question of whether or not English defence witnesses in felony cases should be able to testify under oath as they did in civil cases. One member argued that 'if civil litigants may have sworn witnesses then those on trial for their lives certainly should'.[16]

Most law reform issues discussed in James' first parliament fell into the categories of courts and court procedure and the legal profession. There was a bill for restraining frivolous suits[17] and one to prevent extortion renamed 'An Act for the Better Execution of Justice'. The latter was engrossed after 'much argument pro and contro' and passed in the lower house.[18] The bill dealing with process and pleading in the Court of Exchequer passed and was sent to the House of Lords.[19] There was a bill to prevent overcharging by stewards of courts leet and baron[20] as well as a 'much disputed' bill 'for a Court of Merchants within London, for matters only concerning Merchandizing'.[21] Parliament also attempted to reform the Court of Marshalsea, which a 1607 petition characterised as having 'transgressed

[13] Wallace Notestein, *The House of Commons 1604–1610* (New Haven, Yale University Press, 1971) 219, 242, 246, 247.

[14] *Parliamentary Diary of Robert Bowyer* (n 6) 256n, 259.

[15] ER Foster, *Proceedings in Parliament, 1610*, II, 207.

[16] Sandys also favoured counsel for defendants in capital crimes. There was discussion about whether defence witnesses in treason and felony should or should not be permitted, and whether they should be permitted to testify under oath. See *Parliamentary Diary of Robert Bowyer* (n 6) 10–19, 303–04, 307n, 326, 328–29, 333–34, 350–53, 360–61. See also Barbara J Shapiro, 'Oaths, Credibility and the Legal Process in Early Modern England, Part I' (2013) 6 *Law and Humanities* 145, 155–56. In 1607 a proclamation indicated that jurors were to discern and credit testimony according to their 'conscience and understanding'; see Larkin and Hughes (n 4) 16. The treason trials of Sir Walter Raleigh raised questions about the number of witnesses required and whether they were required to present evidence face to face. Coke, the prosecutor, labelled Raleigh a 'viper, the 'rankest traitor in all England, a 'monster' with 'an English face but a Spanish heart'.

[17] CJ, I, 161, 174, 182.

[18] CJ, I, 179.

[19] CJ, I, 184.

[20] CJ, II, 301, 305, 312. It received a third reading. A bill to improve the records of courts and leet and baron was rejected due to some 'notable Mischief' in the bill; CJ, I, 162.

[21] Some suggested French and Scots models. The bill was rejected after its first reading; CJ, I, 165, 190.

all … bounds and limits'.[22] And in 1610 there was a bill to 'ease in pleadings against troublesome and contentious suits'.[23]

Jurisdictional struggles between the common law and non-common law courts continued, with Chancery coming in for particular attention in 1603 and 1606.[24] Admiralty's jurisdiction over commercial cases was debated, with Sir Edward Coke, as might be expected, trying to limit its jurisdiction over both land and sea merchant contracts.[25] Common lawyers expressed hostility to the civil law that governed Admiralty procedure, framing their proposals as reform measures. Defenders of Admiralty emphasised the need for law consistent with the needs of foreign trade.

There were disputes over impositions, that is, duties on trade, and the customs duties that provided non parliamentary financial support for the Crown. In Bates' case of 1606, the court sided with the Crown on the legality of customs duties, casting the judiciary into the middle of a political conflict. Shortly after the case was decided one MP noted that the judges and their judgments sometimes 'parted … and that the opinions of three or four judges … must needs come short of the wisdom of Parliament'.[26] Judicial opinions on controversial issues, and especially those that questioned the legality of various Crown financial devices, were beginning to intersect with reform sentiment.

Religious issues concerned with the law and courts were much in play. As early as the 1603 Millinery Petition, Puritans complained of excommunication for trifles, unreasonable fees in the ecclesiastical courts and the *ex officio* oath in High Commission. Sir Edwin Sandys compared High Commission to the Inquisition.[27] The king ordered the judges to discuss High Commission with the Privy Council and Lord Chancellor Ellesmere. In 1609 Ellesmere tried to settle differences at a conference. At one point, James indicated he would reform High Commission by limiting its jurisdiction to spiritual causes.[28] High Commission would remain

[22] CJ, I, 207, 277, 278, 282, 285, 287, 290, 291, 301, 310; Douglas Greene, 'The Court of the Marshalsea in Late Tudor and Stuart England' (1976) 20 *American Journal of Legal History* 269, 276, 277. The court's name was later changed to the Court of the Verge and then the Palace Court.

[23] *Parliamentary Diary of Robert Bowyer* (n 6) vol I, 272.

[24] CJ, I, 33

[25] George F Steckley, 'Merchants and the Admiralty Court during the English Revolution' (1978) 22 *American Journal of Legal History* 137.

[26] Quoted in Andrew Thrush, *The House of Commons 1604–1629*, 3 vols (Cambridge, Cambridge University Press, 2010), vol I, 178–79.

[27] Roland Usher, *The Rise and Fall of the High Commission* (Oxford, Oxford University Press, 1913) 611, 698. Martin Ingram considers the accusations exaggerated, finding little excessive delay, extortionate fees or frequent use of excommunication. See Martin Ingram, *Church Courts: Sex and Marriage in England 1570–1640* (Cambridge, Cambridge University Press, 2017) 63, 64, 65, 74–75.

[28] New letters patent were issued in 1611. Between 1611 and 1641, High Commission functioned primarily as a court of law. Most suits were party suits; only about 20 per cent were *ex officio* cases. *Ex officio* cases were typically initiated by petitions of poor individuals. Most cases involved matrimonial issues or offences of the clergy; RG Usher, *The Rise and Fall of High Commission* 236, 257, 260, 263. High Commission courts were established in Scotland in 1610.

the subject of reform until its abolition. There were bills 'granting of Prohibitions and Consultations in spiritual Cause' and 'for the Reformation of Abuses in Ecclesiastical Courts and Causes'.[29]

The problems generated by Roman Catholicism, especially following the Gunpowder Plot, led to changes in the laws relating to Catholics. Recusants could no longer practise law or medicine, fines for non-attendance at Church of England services were increased, and it became treason to obey the authority of the pope rather than the king.[30] The recusancy laws and other legislation dealing with Roman Catholics would remain a parliamentary concern for generations.

The 'Multitudes and Misdemeanors of Attorneys and Solicitors' again received attention. In this instance it specifically mentioned that it was not directed against 'just and honest sergeants and councellors-at-law'.[31] Typically, complaints focused more on the lower part of the profession.

Legislation was introduced to relieve indebted prisoners, 'for Recovery of small Debts and for relief of Poor Debtors in London',[32] as well as another to make the 'lands, tenements and heritments' of all debtors payable to their creditors at their death.[33] There was also a bill 'for better Relief of the Creditors against such as shall become Bankrupts'.[34] An attempt to reduce fraud in land transactions, a concern of many early modern parliaments, led parliament to again consider the registration of judgments 'that may impeach purchasers or farmers of lands'.[35]

Criminal penalties received attention. There were bills to eliminate benefit of clergy for manslaughter, as well as for cattle, sheep and horse theft.[36] Bigamy became a felony[37] and stabbing became a felony without benefit of clergy if the injured party died.[38] The witchcraft law was broadened in 1604 and, like its Elizabethan predecessor, removed the crime from the jurisdiction of the ecclesiastical courts.[39] Bills for better execution of the penal statutes and for reformation of the continuing abuses by informers were also introduced.[40]

Most of the reform proposals in James' parliaments were similar to those of earlier proposals. None would have caused a major change in the legal system. Yet the differences between Crown and parliament were frequently troublesome. In 1610 parliament foundered over its inability to reach agreement on the Great

[29] CJ, I, 243, 249, 255.
[30] 3 Jac 1 c 4.
[31] 3 Jac I c 7. There were efforts to regulate attorneys in 1580, 1589, 1601, 1610, 1625 and 1629.
[32] CJ, I, 187, 217; 3 Jac 1 c 14.
[33] CJ, I, 214.
[34] CJ, I, 239; LJ, II, 325; 2 Jac I c 15.
[35] CJ, I, 522.
[36] CJ, I, 148, 162, 181, 189, 202, 206, 233, 235, 244.
[37] I Jac I c 11.
[38] I Jac I c 8.
[39] 2 Jac 1 c 12. The legislation had the support of the judges. Trials would be held at the assizes.
[40] CJ, I, 161, 335, 229. There was debate on a bill for better execution of justice and for oppressive criminal offences in the northern parts of England. LJ, II, 616, 619, 631, 641, 645.

Contract, which would have provided a steady annual Crown income in exchange for elimination of feudal dues, purveyance and the Court of Wards. No legislation was passed during the final session of James I's first parliament.

III. The Addled Parliament

The Addled Parliament of 1614, called by the king for financial assistance, again devoted considerable attention to law reform. Legislation was offered by both the Privy Council and members of parliament.[41] A substantial number of law reform bills were introduced, though parliament again ended abruptly without any completed legislation.

Courts, and especially Chancery, were again the subject of reform. There were familiar complaints that Chancery judgments, made by a single judge's conscience, might be capricious, leaving litigants and lawyers without predictable expectations. John Selden famously said that 'Equity is a roguish thing, by law we have a measure … Equity is according to the conscience' of the Chancellor and, as that is 'larger or narrower so … is equity' as if 'they should make the standard for measure we … call a foot, to be the Chancellor's foot; what an uncertain measure would this be; one Chancellor has a long foot', another a short foot and a third an 'indifferent foot'. 'Tis the same thing in the chancellor's conscience.'[42] Although Chancery was to dispense equity and required discretion, this discretion often seemed capricious and arbitrary, making it difficult to anticipate Chancery rulings. The proposal for reforming Chancery and limiting the powers of the Lord Chancellor was introduced just as Parliament received the message of dissolution. The issue of whether courts might review the judgments of other courts and whether parliament also possessed this power was aired. It was even rumoured that 'there is an Act of Parliament … to reverse the judgments of other courts'. The lack of clarity as to who might review judgments of the common law courts and the judgments of Chancery remained unresolved.[43]

There were Crown and parliament bills requiring that fees in all courts be 'manifested' and for 'reformation of the excessive Fees taken by practisers of the common and civil law, their clerks and clerks of the court'.[44] Bills were also introduced to prevent and punish 'Abuses in procuring Process and Supersedeas for the

[41] See Thomas Moir, *The Addled Parliament of 1614* (Oxford, Oxford University Press, 1958) 200–04. The House of Commons consisted of about 19 per cent lawyers in 1614; Thrush (n 26) vol I, 173–77.

[42] John Selden, *Table Talk*, 3rd edn (London, 1716) 37. See also Dennis Klinck, *Conscience, Equity and the Court of Chancery in Early Modern England* (Farnham, Ashgate, 2010).

[43] CJ, I, 505; CJ, I, 270, 271, 276. Chancery was the place for litigants to go to for specific relief, for discovery of documents or for obtaining party testimony. It handled trusts, mortgages, multi-party or multi-issue disputes.

[44] CJ, I, 489. See also Moir (n 41) 203.

Peace and good behavior, out of his Majesty's Courts at Westminster', which were said to be 'a Great Vexation'.[45] Additional legislation was proposed for 'restitution of Possession, to be granted in certain cases upon Entries with Force, or holding with Force', as well as an 'Act for peace of king's subjects after Judgment by them at the common Law' and a statute of limitations.[46]

The ecclesiastical courts came under scrutiny. There were again bills to curb excessive excommunication for small offences and against the *ex officio* oath.[47] A House of Lords bill for 'avoiding suits and questions touching wills of land' was committed, but was reported as having 'so great Imperfection both in Matter and Form' that 'their Lordships thought fit' to 'sleep [and] be no further proceeded'.[48] Legislation was also offered to alter the laws in Wales[49] and for preserving records of sessions of the peace.[50]

Parliament again saw proposals to remedy the ever-troubling matters of debt. A bill for the recovery of small debts was introduced and debated. Opponents worried that cases would be tried by those without 'skill or Judgment in Law', that is, by juries.[51] 'An Act for the Discovery of fraudulent practices of Bankrupts and for the Relief of Creditors against Bankrupts' was introduced but 'dashed'.[52] Legislation was introduced again to make estates of the attainted liable for the payments of their just and true debts.[53]

Francis Bacon, now Solicitor General, introduced a bill calling for the appointment of commissioners to 'review the state of penal laws, to the end that such as are obsolete and snaring may be repealed, and such as are fit to continue and concern matter may be reduced respectively into one clear form of law'.[54] Bacon and others would repeat this proposal many times. The task was a difficult one, not least because about 25 per cent of all early seventeenth-century acts were enacted for a limited time, making for frequent repetition of the same or similar legislation. Many expiring statutes were continued, but not all.[55]

The Addled Parliament was dissolved before legislation of any kind was passed. It would be eight years before Parliament met again. Failure to pass any legislation had occurred in 1610 and 1614, and yet again in 1621. Failure to implement

[45] CJ, I, 474, 489.

[46] CJ, I, 505. Moir located a list of bills 'to be propounded, not yet consulted upon', which included suppression of liberties, fees of sergeants, counsellors at law and their clerks, limiting the number of attorneys, Sabbath abuses and preserving records of the sessions of the peace; Moir (n 41) 201–03.

[47] CJ, I, 465, 503.

[48] LJ, II, 695.

[49] Moir (n 41) 210.

[50] CJ, I, 496, 503; Moir (n 41) 203.

[51] CJ, I, 474, 490.

[52] CJ, I, 481, 496; CJ, I, 409, 470.

[53] CJ, I, 461, 470.

[54] CJ, I, 470. The Crown also offered bill for declaring the 'just ancient fees of Course'; Moir (n 41) 202–04.

[55] CJ, I, 520. See Chris Kyle, '"It Being Not Fit to Bee without a Law": Expiring Laws, Continuance Acts, 1604–1641' (2000) 19 *Parliamentary History* 199.

reform in 1614 can be attributed to the uncertainty of dissolution that might occur when Crown demands were thwarted. Many of the lost proposals of 1614 would be reintroduced in later parliaments. Although opposition to reform bills was often blamed on lawyer hostility, reform measures were typically drafted by common lawyers.

IV. 1615–20

Crown concern with law reform continued during the lengthy period between parliaments, with Francis Bacon as its chief spokesman within the government. His 1614 'Memorial touching the Review of Penal Laws and Amendment of the Common Laws', written for the king, suggested a cooperative reform effort modelled on something like Henry VIII's commission to reform canon law. Bacon, always insistent on parliamentary approval, recommended commissioners named by parliament to present their completed work to parliament. He recommended a major overhaul of the existing corpus of legal literature, a project that would occupy him for the remainder of his life. The project required revision of the yearbooks and law reports. The latter, though improved by Coke, nevertheless required a thorough reorganisation. Law reporting should no longer be in the hands of judges. The common law must be reduced 'to a course or digest of Books of competent volumes' and their 'nature and content rectified'.[56] The statute law, with its numerous 'ensnaring penal laws', must be reduced in number, 'the obsolete weeded out' and penalties modified. Bacon reported that the work, initiated on his 'motion' and at the Crown's direction, had already been advanced by a group of lawyers in preparation for the next parliament.[57] In the same year, the Privy Council presented a reform programme to the king that included Bacon's law reform proposals.[58]

On becoming a member of the Privy Council in 1616, Bacon sent the king another memorandum elaborating on his plan for reforming the corpus of legal writing. His proposals emphasised the need for a better legal dictionary, institutes, an introductory survey and better organisation of the statutes. Drawing attention to the moderateness of his intent, he insisted that he did not wish to alter the 'matter of the law', but only the 'manner of their registry, expression, and tradition: so that it giveth them rather light than any new nature'. He insisted: 'I dare not

[56] Francis Bacon *The Works of Francis Bacon*, James Spedding, Robert Ellis and Douglas Heath (eds) (London, Longman, 1861–79), vol XIII, 71.

[57] ibid vol XII, 60, 62, 65, 67–69; vol XIII, 71. See also *Commons Debates, 1621*, Wallace Notestein, Frances Relf and Harley Simpson (eds), 7 vols (New Haven, Yale University Press, 1935), vol II, 44, 47–48, 64–65, 72; Kyle (n 55) 195–210.

[58] Menna Prestwich, *Cranfield: Politics and Profit under the Stuarts: The Career of Lionel Cranfield* (Oxford, Clarendon Press, 1966) 119.

advise to cast the law into a new mould.'[59] Casting the law into a new mould would become the aim of radical reformers of a later generation.

The jurisdictional conflicts between Coke and Lord Chancellor Ellesmere continued during the interval between parliaments, with prohibitions, injunctions and harsh words flying back and forth between the common law courts and Chancery and other courts. Coke, Chief Justice of the King's Bench between 1613 and 1616, was determined to curb the jurisdiction of the non-common law courts, especially Chancery. Coke and Ellesmere battled over the finality of judgments at common law, the enlargement of Chancery jurisdiction and the improper use of injunctions and prohibitions.[60] A royal commission headed by Bacon was appointed to determine whether any statutes prevented Chancery from acting after a judgment at law. Ellesmere did not object to Chancery reform and during his tenure attempted reforms in his court, believing: 'It would be a great quietnesse to ye subjects and a good means to voide such needless trouble and expenses, if the Jurisdiction of the Courts, were conteyned with some known, certain and Reasonable Bounds and Limits.' Ellesmere also favoured revision of the statutes to keep them relevant to the times and supported repeal of those that were superfluous and insufficient.[61]

The jurisdictional battles of the period present something of a problem for the historian. From the common lawyer's point of view, Chancery was overreaching, expanding its jurisdiction and thwarting legitimate decisions of the common law courts. Chancery therefore needed reform. Chancery and its supporters saw the matter differently, emphasising its role in providing remedies unavailable at common law, arguing that prohibitions prevented Chancery from performing its functions and insisting that Chancery provided a much-needed remedy for unjust common law court decisions. It is thus unclear whether these jurisdictional battles should be treated as rival courts seeking to protect and expand their respective jurisdictions and business or whether one or the other camp was entitled to the title of reformer. Should Coke, the common lawyer, be seen as the reformer? Or should Lord Chancellors Ellesmere or Bacon be entitled to wear the mantle of reform? As a court of equity, Chancery was in an awkward position. If it developed fixed rules as some wished, it would become too law-like, which would reduce its flexibility. If it had no known rules, it would become too arbitrary and capricious. Its institutional dilemma was to be able to provide equity when needed, but also provide some predictability to litigants and their lawyers.

Shortly before becoming Lord Chancellor in 1617, Bacon announced his reform agenda for Chancery. It included containing its jurisdiction, reducing unnecessary

[59] Bacon (n 56) vol XIII, 64–67; vol VI, 67, 71.

[60] David W Raack, 'A History of Injunctions in England before 1700' (1986) 61 *Indiana Law Journal* 575. Coke used the writ *of habeas corpus* to release parties imprisoned for disregarding injunctions.

[61] ibid 576, 578, 579; Knafla (n 11) 62, 82, 86; see also 273, 274, 277. Ellesmere's 'Memorials for the Judicature' referred to defects in writs and forms of action, the fees of sergeants and attorneys, corruption and lack of expertise in the legal profession; Knafla (n 11) 107–10.

delays, eliminating 'needless charge and expense', and reducing the number of injunctions. Bacon emphasised Chancery rule-making as a necessary reform. Bacon's 1617 Ordinances, one of several efforts at making Chancery decisions less discretionary and more predictable, were, like those of earlier Lord Chancellors, difficult to enforce.[62]

Perhaps with Coke in mind, whom he would shortly dismiss, the king, in a speech to the judges in Star Chamber in 1616, insisted that the common law courts, like others, 'ought to keepe their owne limits and boundes'. 'Too many prohibitions' allowed litigants to 'go from court to Court', resulting in 'great delay of Justice' and 'causes endless'. He vindicated Chancery from charges of 'misconceipt and contempt'. Only the king could correct appeals from Chancery. Although James reiterated he had no wish to alter the common law, he pointed to 'diverse things' requiring 'reformation'. He wished to purge the law of 'Incertaintie and Noueltie', indicating that remedies were 'properly … done in Parliament by advice of the Judges'. However, the judges themselves had introduced 'corrruptions … by the Niceties that are used'. When issuing judgments 'never heard of before', they became 'Law-givers, and not Law-tellers'. Judges were 'interpretours of Law', not 'makers of Law'. The king also drew attention to the judges' role in supervising the justices of the peace, too many of whom were being either 'idle Slowbellies given to a life of ease and delight' or 'busie-bodies' who made 'justice to serve for a shadow to Faction' or helped their kindred or friends.[63]

Nor was the project of rationalising the statutes forgotten in the interval between parliaments. Finch reported that a parliamentary committee worked 10 hours a day during the summer of 1620 reviewing all the laws in force on a variety of subjects in readiness for the next session of parliament.

V. The Parliaments of 1621 and 1624

The Parliaments of 1621 and 1624, the height of pre-civil war law reform, are treated together in order to show that the fate of legislation, reform or otherwise, was more often the result of unexpected prorogation or dissolution than hostility from within parliament. Although both parliaments offered roughly the same law reform measures, their outcomes were dramatically different. Many of the reform bills of 1614 were reintroduced in 1621. Some were reintroduced in 1624 and were successful. Although the composition and leadership of the 1624 Parliament was

[62] Bacon (n 56) vol XIII, 189. The *Chancery Ordinance made by the Right Honourable Sir Francis Bacon … For the better and more regular Administration of Justice in the Chancery* was printed in 1618 and again in 1642.

[63] James I (n 2) 204, 210, 211–12, 213, 214, 217, 220, 221–22. The king praised Danish law, where the 'very Law-Booke it selfe is their only Judge' and its legal proceedings were conducted without lawyers. 'Happy were all kingdoms' if they could follow the Denmark's example (at 212).

little changed, it proved more harmonious than its predecessor. It also had the advantage of the already drafted and debated bills of 1621 being ready at the beginning of its session, avoiding the lengthy period needed to draft and amend bills and work out differences between the houses.[64] Coke, no longer a judge and now a member of parliament, drafted and promoted many of the reform measures of 1621 and 1624.[65] Lionel Cranfield, Master of the Court of Wards, was also a proponent of law reform.

Although reluctant to call parliament after the failure of the Addled Parliament, in 1621 James was again in need of supply. Although parliamentary attention centred on monopolies, foreign affairs, the proposed marriage between Prince Charles and a Spanish infanta, and Roman Catholic issues, it again launched a series of measures to reform the courts, their fees and judges, and some areas of law. Clashes with the Crown over parliament's claims to freedom of speech, especially on foreign policy, led to parliament's Protestation. James, insisting parliament had no right to debate foreign policy, tore the offending Protestation out of the journals of the House of Commons. Parliament was shocked when it was informed it would be adjourned in seven days. Although the upper house successfully petitioned for more time and was offered a few additional days, the House of Commons preferred to pass no bills rather than just a few. No legislative measures of any kind became law between 1610 and 1624.[66]

Reform was in the air in 1621. Bacon's opening speech as Lord Chancellor urged the king 'to go on with reformation of your courts of justice … which your Parliament has entered into'.[67] However, Bacon's impeachment a few months later lost him a parliamentary platform to promote law reform. James' opening speech spoke of the need for 'just and faithful judges' and promised 'to remedy any judge found faulty'. He also suggested that the 'many new crimes and abuses that do daily creep unto this kingdom' should be remedied by Parliament.[68]

Both the 1621 and 1624 Parliaments began with a committee to meet weekly to examine 'every Court of Justice, Ecclesiastical or Temporal'. Headed by Coke in 1621 and Sir Robert Phelips in 1624, the committees were 'to hear and consider

[64] Robert Zaller suggests that Bacon's preparation for the Parliament of 1621 was inadequate and that the committee system was breaking down due to too much work. See Robert Zaller, *The Parliament of 1621: A Study in Constitutional Conflict* (Berkeley, University of California Press, 1971) 24–25, 125. Conrad Russell suggests that there were too many bills and that the parliament could not agree on their order. See Conrad Russell, *Parliament and English Politics 1621–1629* (Oxford, Oxford University Press, 1979) 42.

[65] See Stephen D White, *Sir Edward Coke and 'The Grievances of the Commonwealth' 1621–1628* (Chapel Hill, University of North Carolina Press, 1979) 27–85.

[66] Zaller (n 64) 135. In 1621, nine bills passed both houses, 20 were sent up, and four passed, but were not sent up. A total of 29 were committed and 43 were read once. The two most important in 1624 were the Act against Monopoly and the Act for Discovery for Repressing Popish Recusants, the latter a re-enactment of the 1606 statute that itself was largely a re-enactment of 1581.

[67] Bacon (n 56) vol XIII, 289.

[68] *The House of Commons 1604–1629*, Andrew Thrush and John Ferris (eds), 6 vols (Cambridge, Cambridge University Press for the History of Parliament Trust, 2010), vol II, 1, 21

of all Complaints, which shall be made unto them, of any Court of Justice' and draw bills to redress abuses.[69] Bills were drafted dealing with several courts, central and local, and their fees, procedures, judges and clerks. Lionel Cranfield, Master of the Court of Wards, urged that if anything in the Court of Wards 'or any other court' was 'burthensome to the Subject', it should have 'a Course taken to help it'.[70] Phelips claimed that 'onely the judges of the Common Lawe have stoode untainted'. Judicial corruption was a common theme in 1621 and 1624.[71]

Although most courts were scrutinised for abuses, Chancery received the most attention. Star Chamber, surprisingly, received none. A variety of bills were introduced, some dealing with particular courts and some with courts more generally. There were five bills dealing with court fees in 1621.[72] Spurred on by the animosity of the common lawyers and the belief that its abuses were pervasive, several bills were introduced in 1621 and 1624 to remedy the delays, high costs and lack of certainty and finality in Chancery. There was controversy over Chancery bills of conformity, in which creditors were to accept less than was owed and not sue debtors.[73] A bill treating reversing judgments of courts of equity was considered, but did not pass in 1621. Bills that would have subordinated Chancery to the common law courts would have substantially reduced the role of equity. The act 'for the Reversing of Decrees in Courts of Equity on Just Cause' would have required hearing of such cases by three common law judges and the Chancery judges, giving common law judges veto power over Chancery decrees.[74]

Concern over corruption in Chancery proceedings led to investigations of its judge. As a result, Lord Chancellor Bacon was impeached in 1621. Charges of bribery and corruption present something of a problem for the student of reform. Since most court officials, including judges, received little or no salary, gifts of money and goods of material value were expected when service was given. Like tips in modern restaurants, they were considered both obligatory, in the sense of being part of the service, and voluntary. Are tips bribes, in the sense of expecting special service? Those who held offices typically had purchased them or received them from patrons with the expectation that they would be used to generate income for the office-holder. Payments and gifts were thus built into the system. Bacon admitted he had accepted gifts, but insisted that they had not influenced his judicial decisions.

[69] CJ, I, 514, 525, 572, 573, 578, 650.

[70] CJ, I, 151, 514; *Commons Debates, 1621* (n 57) vol II, 44,154; vol IV, 274.

[71] ibid vol V, 181.

[72] Zaller (n 64) 94.

[73] *Commons Debates, 1621* (n 57) vol II, 222; vol IV, 153–54; vol V, 549–50; vol VI, 63. The City of London petitioned against bills of conformity that some thought to be the cause of the trade depression. Both the king and Coke opposed the bills of conformity; White (n 65) 61. It has also been suggested that Parliament was less anxious for Chancery reform in 1624. See *The House of Commons 1504–1629* (n 68) vol III, 584. The bill to limit certain Chancery suits was not revived in 1624.

[74] Zaller (n 64) 96–97. Zaller suggests that the House of Commons' reforms consisted of a restatement of Bacon's Orders in Chancery (at 95).

The Court of Wards also came under attack in 1621 and 1624. There were jurisdictional conflicts between the Court of Wards and Chancery. It was suggested that both courts 'had done wronge' and that the abuses of both should be reformed.[75] The ecclesiastical courts and High Commission were also reviewed, though the 1621 bill dealing with proving wills and procuring administrations received only a single reading.[76] A committee investigating the Prerogative Court of Canterbury resulted in charges against its judge, Sir John Bennet.

Legislation to prevent transfer of suits from quarter sessions to Westminster was enacted, which Coke argued would help prevent 'the Multiplication of Suits'. The question of whether the parliament could overturn the judgments of the Court of Requests and the Court of the Exchequer would be aired in 1624 and again in 1628. In 1624, 1625 and 1626 there were bills to overturn the judgments of King's Bench. None of the bills was successful.[77] 'An Act for Limitation of Actions and For Avoiding suits in Law', also designed to reduce the number of suits, was introduced in 1621 and became law in 1624. In 1621 there had been debate as to whether such legislation would help or harm landholders, whether it would multiply rather than reduce lawsuits and whether a 20-year limit was sufficient.[78] Another law 'for the general quietness of the subject against all pretences of concealments' confirmed the titles of subject's land held in possession for 60 years that had once been in the possession of the king. It too had been introduced in 1621 and became law in 1624.[79] Legislation on jeofails, that is, preventing mistakes or oversights in pleading, was introduced in 1621 and became law in 1624.[80] The bill dealing with the fees of court officers was not revived in 1624. In 1621 parliament considered enlarging and making perpetual an act to make pleading easier for those engaged in contentious suits against justices of the peace and other officers. This became law in 1624.[81] Legislation was again introduced to address the problem of 'insufficient' jurors.[82]

Both Crown and parliament had rationalisation of the statutes on their agenda. In 1621 it was reported that Sir Henry Finch and William Noy, both associates of Bacon, 'by the Direction of the King, and the Lords of Counsel, by Advice of the now Lord Chancellor, Treasurer and Lord Hubbard, took, much Pains in surveying the Statutes … That they found almost 400 fit to be repealed as being Snares to us'. A second committee, which included Coke and other lawyers, including

[75] *The Common Debates, 1621*, Wallace Notestein, Frances Relf and Hartley Simpson (eds) (New Haven, Yale University Press, 1935), vol V, 48–49.

[76] CJ, I, 539.

[77] *The House of Commons 1604–1629* (n 68) vol III, 584; Thrush (n 26) 35.

[78] 21 Jac 1 c 16 (statute of limitations); LJ, III, 252, 266, 363, 403, 404; *Commons Debates, 1621* (n 57) vol II, 64–65; vol IV, 431; vol V, 45; vol I, 606. There were bills for process of peace and good behaviour in 1621 and 1624.

[79] 21 Jac I c 2.

[80] 21 Jac I c 13. There had been intermittent statutes on the subject since the reign of Edward III.

[81] 21 Jac I c 12. This extended an earlier act.

[82] CJ, I, 582.

Noy, Finch and William Hakewill, assisted the first committee. It was to 'draw all the Statutes, concerning One Matter, into one or more plain and perfect Law; and to consider which are fit to be repealed, which expired, which in force, which fit to be continued'. Finch believed that 'their Labours were extant'.[83] Hakewill's bill, which introduced 80 redundant statutes for repeal, has been called 'one of the most ambitious programs for the repeal of obsolete laws which had been undertaken'.[84] Except where they foresaw reduction of their income, lawyers were not hostile to reform, and took the lead in 1621 and 1624. The king remained sympathetic to rationalisation and urged the House of Commons to repeal obsolete laws.

Attention again turned to problems relating to credit and debt in 1621 and 1624. We have noted the difference of opinion over Chancery's bills of conformity. The Crown, the Privy Council and Chancery favoured composition with creditors, the extension of time for payment and arbitration. Those opposed wished debts to be paid in full. Various bills adjusting creditor–debtor relations were introduced in 1621 and became law in 1624.[85] A bill for recovery of small debts and duties in London was also introduced in 1621.[86]

While parliament was not especially interested in reforming the criminal code, legislation in 1624 abolished capital punishment for women convicted of small felonies. Previously only men had been eligible to claim benefit of clergy.[87] There was also legislation requiring the death penalty for women who delivered illegitimate children found dead, unless they could prove the child was stillborn. Infanticide was gradually shifted from the ecclesiastical to the common law courts. When such transfer occurred, penalties typically became harsher because the ecclesiastical courts could not inflict the death penalty.[88] The infanticide statute provides an example of how long it might take for bills to become law, earlier bills having been introduced in 1606–07 and 1610.[89] The treatment of informers was

[83] CJ, I, 519, 320; *Commons Debates, 1621* (n 57) vol II, 72, Coke also thought that 'One plain and perspicuous law divided into articles, so as every subject may know what acts be in force'; *The Fourth Part of the Reports of Sir Edward Coke*, J Thomas and J Fraser (eds), 6 vols (London, 1826), vol II, v, ix. Noy, a supporter of law reform in the 1620s, became Attorney General under Charles I and supported ship money. A total of 61 acts were continued, 69 were repealed and two were revived. Kyle characterised the continuance statutes a 'sweeping law measure' that 'made an effective start to rewriting the statutes'; Kyle (n 55) 205; 21 Jac I c 28.

[84] Prestwich (n 58) 317, 317n.

[85] LJ, III, 342, 388; 1 Jac I c 19.

[86] CJ, I, 521, 526, 577, 586, 596, 703; *Commons Debates, 1621* (n 57) vol VII, 36, 174, 175, 182.

[87] 21 Jac I c 6; LJ, III, 274. The bill failed in 1621, but was successful in 1624. See Garthine Walker, 'Women, Theft and the World of Stolen Goods' in Jennifer Kermode and Garthine Walker (eds), *Women, Crime and the Courts in Early Modern England* (Chapel Hill, University of North Carolina Press, 1994).

[88] 21 Jac I c 27. The transition of infanticide to the civil courts was already apparent by the Elizabethan period. See Keith Wrightson, 'Infanticide in Earlier Seventeenth Century England' (1975) 5 *Local Population Studies* 10; Laura Gowring, 'Secret Births and Infanticide in Seventeenth Century England' (1997) 156 *Past and Present* 87.

[89] There was discussion as to whether the export of wool should be a felony and a bill to exempt the gentry from the servile punishment of whipping; CJ, 135, 136, 182; LJ, III, 174, 175, 182.

the subject of several Elizabethan and Jacobean reform efforts, and was again the subject of legislative reform in 1621 and 1624.

Parliamentary discussion of abolition of the long obsolete trial by battle in 1624 indicates how the process by which a given practice or law became obsolete might be very gradual, the date of parliamentary legislation marking its final formalisation.[90]

As we have seen, investigation of abuses in the courts expanded to judges of those courts and resulted in the impeachments of Lord Chancellor Bacon and Lionel Cranfield, Master of the Court of Wards. Ironically, these were the two most important proponents of law reform. The first major use of the impeachment process in this period which required accusation by the lower house and trial by the House of Lords was directed at the hated monopolist Sir Giles Mompesson. It was then employed to bring down Bacon and Cranfield. Bacon's impeachment, according to Sir Edward Sandys, was a sign 'of sickness in all Courts' and 'Cause for a new Day'.[91] John Chamberlain reported on the 'tempest' falling on Bacon, 'against whome there come in daylie more petitions and accusations than they can overcome, wherein his owne friends are made special instruments against him'.[92] Bacon not only lost the office of Lord Chancellor but also his opportunities to promote law reform in parliament and the Privy Council.[93]

The revival of impeachment may be considered a reform insofar as it provided a legal instrument to bring high officials to answer for their illegal actions. However, it also provided a legal instrument to pursue officials whose policies and practices were disliked, becoming an instrument to intimidate and punish political enemies whether or not they were guilty of a crime. Whatever the status of impeachment in the reform narrative, it constituted a significant development in parliament's role in the legal system.[94]

However, not all legal change resulted from parliamentary action. The growth of transportation of convicted criminals reduced the number of executions and, over time, substantially altered the way in which the criminal justice system functioned. There were, of course, judicial opinions that altered the substance of the law.

[90] LJ, 272, 274; CJ, II, 92, 101. The last case is thought to have taken place in the Elizabethan period. Sir Thomas Smith in 1583 noted that it was obsolete, but it remained in force. Parliament considered abolition on several occasions, but this did not occur until the nineteenth century.

[91] CJ, I, 584.

[92] John Chamberlain, *Letters*, NE McClure (ed), 2 vols (Philadelphia, American Philosophical Society, 1939), vol II, 354. When Bacon was examined by the committee for courts of justice, the question arose as to whether those who testified against him should or should not testify under oath; Zaller (n 64) 78–81. See also Linda L Peck, *Court Patronage and Corruption in Early Stuart England* (London, Unwin-Hyman, 1990).

[93] There were bills against selling judicial places in the Parliament of 1621, 1625 and 1626. See William Prest, 'Judicial Corruption in Early Modern England' (1991) 133 *Past and Present* 68.

[94] See Colin Tite, *Impeachment and Parliamentary Judicature in Early Stuart England* (London, Athlone, 1974); Allen Horstman, 'The Parliament of 1621 Revisited: The Beginnings of Impeachment', in Buchanan Sharp and Mark Fissel (eds), *Law and Authority in Early Modern England* (Newark, University of Delaware Press, 2007) 77–105. Medieval parliaments also used impeachments.

These changes were frequently unobserved due to their often incremental nature as well as judicial reluctance to admit that judges engaged in legal innovation.

Another insufficiently noticed legal development was the rapid growth of the judicial powers of the House of Lords. As James S Hart has shown, other than its role in criminal impeachments, this development was largely invisible, unmarked by legislation or proclamation. Hart also examines the re-emergence of the House of Lords as a court for private litigation, its role in providing legal remedies and its appellate function. He attributes these developments to the pressure of public discontent with the available venues for legal remedy and to parliament's failure to provide for the needs of a growing population and an increasingly complex economy. Beginning in 1621, the upper house began receiving large numbers of petitions from private individuals dealing mostly with ordinary cases of debt, inheritance of property, contracts and domestic disputes. Some were cases of first instance. Others were appeals or review of proceedings or decisions of other courts. Part of the problem leading to the increased judicial activity of the upper house was the lack of regular appeals procedures. Appeals from the common law courts could only be initiated by the not very effective writ of error, and there was no regular appeal mechanism from the prerogative and equity courts. Jurisdictional conflicts resulted from the efforts of Chancery to review decisions of the common law courts. Most courts were unable to handle the growing caseloads caused by the spurt in litigation and the growing complexity of transactions of all types. Hart suggests that the House of Lords' entry into the judicial arena was a response to the incredible overload of other courts, as well as a response to the privy council's gradual withdrawal from private litigation. The House of Lords began to intercede in jurisdictional disputes and review Chancery proceedings and decrees on a regular basis. Committees appointed to handle each case took legal advice from the judges. The judicial role of the House of Lords was a significant addition to the legal system that received little attention at the time or subsequently.[95]

Parliament's investigation of court abuses, the revival of impeachment and the development of a judicial role for the House of Lords brought the relationship between parliament and the courts into question. At issue were parliament's role in investigating and controlling Crown judicial officials and parliament's authority to limit the jurisdiction of the courts. John Selden and Edward Alford, for example, argued that parliament might examine judicial actions, but judges could not meddle with the business of parliament. Cranfield thought otherwise, responding that parliament could investigate abuses of the courts, but could not alter their jurisdiction, because that could only be done by the king. Historian of parliament Andrew Thrush notes that parliament was unable to make the judiciary subservient

[95] See James S Hart, *Justice upon Petition: The House of Lords and the Reformation of Justice, 1621–1675* (New York, HarperCollins, 1991) 2–3, 15–16, 18–19, 23, 30–34, 36. See also Jess Flemion, 'Slow Process, Due Process and the High Court of Parliament: A Reinterpretation of the Revival of Judicature in the House of Lords in the 1620s' (1974) 12 *Historical Journal* 3. Petitioning the House of Lords had become a regular way of redress against a decree of an inferior court by the third parliament of Charles I; Zaller (n 64) 215n.

or to put the jurisdiction of the courts under parliamentary control.[96] Later parliaments, however, would move much further in these directions, abolishing several major courts, impeaching judges and Crown officials, and making claims to appoint and dismiss judges.

The reforms sought in 1621 and achieved in 1624 did not seek major alterations in the law or the legal profession; rather, they were to make existing legal institutions function better for those who used them. Although the Crown was a participant in reform efforts, especially before 1621, reformation of the laws and the legal system was becoming became primarily the province of parliament.

VI. Charles I 1625–40

Although typically absent from accounts of law reform, the reign of Charles I deserves a place in the law reform narrative. The Parliaments of 1625 and 1626 were called by the king to obtain funds for war. Although not at the top of the parliamentary agenda, both parliaments devoted considerable attention to law reform.[97] These efforts' most striking feature was similarity to the reform agenda of earlier parliaments. In 1625 a House of Commons committee for courts of justice composed of the whole house was ordered to meet weekly.[98] There was a bill to limit time of actions to prevent delays caused by removing suits from inferior courts to Westminster. Legislation was again proposed forbidding the sale of judicial offices and bribery, in this instance linked to charges against the Duke of Buckingham for buying and selling judicial places.[99] Both the Court of Wards and the equity courts received attention, and common lawyers continued to criticise Chancery injunctions. A House of Commons committee was appointed to draft measures to correct erroneous decrees and orders in the courts of equity.[100] Although the Court of Requests heard about as many suits as Chancery, it was Chancery that bore the brunt of criticism. Sir Julius Caesar, Master of the Rolls, developed orders redressing Chancery errors, overly long written procedures and other abuses.[101]

[96] *The House of Commons 1604–1629* (n 68) vol I, 34, 35, 36; Zaller (n 64) 215. In 1621 there was an attempt to shift the appointment of justices of the peace from the Lord Chancellor to four common law judges; Zaller (n 64) 100–01.

[97] There was little Crown preparation for the Parliaments of 1625, 1626, and 1638. See David Harris Willson, *The Privy Councilors in the House of Commons 1604–1629* (Minneapolis, University of Minnesota Press, 1940) 9.

[98] CJ, I, 618, 838, 888. Coke became a less active supporter of law reform. See White (n 65) 221. There were committees for courts of justice in 1621, 1624, 1628, 1626 and 1628–29.

[99] CJ, I, 810, 822, 829, 848, 888; *Proceedings in Parliament, 1625*, Maija Jansson and Wlliam Bidwell (eds) (New Haven, Yale University Press, 1987) 258, 269, 385; Wilfred Prest, 'Judicial Corruption in Early Modern England' (1991) 133 *Past and Present*, 74, 75.

[100] CJ, I, 820, 843; *Proceedings in Parliament, 1625* (n 99) 228, 303, 308.

[101] A 1625 Caesar manuscript noted the king's promise 'for the lessening of the fees in every Court of Westminster Hall'. See John Campbell, *The Lives of the Lord Chancellors and Keepers of the Great Seal of England*, 10 vols (London, John Murray, 1868), vol II, 557, 558.

Although the Court of Requests did not draw the attention of Parliament, it was fiercely attacked by Sir Edward Coke and the common lawyers. Requests handled a variety of cases including civil petitions from the poor, marriage contracts and settlements and wage disputes between servants and apprentices and their masters. It served women litigants. Its low cost and rapid procedure expanded its business at the expense of the common law. The Court of Requests had injunctive powers and clashed with the common law courts.

Church courts were scrutinised, and legislation was again introduced to curb citations and end excessive excommunication.[102] Attacks on High Commission, especially by Puritans and common lawyers, became more intense. The clerk of parliament was ordered to bring in a bill dealing with the *ex officio* oath.[103]

When denial of habeas corpus and the unjust detainment of men in prison were discussed, a committee resolved that there should be no imprisonment by the king or the Privy Council without the cause being stated. The House of Lords, perhaps in connection with impeachments of the previous reign, considered allowing defendants who were members of parliament in the House of Commons to have counsel and copies of all depositions.[104] Treason and felony defendants in the common law courts did not have these privileges. Bills in the areas of crime and debt were again offered. Bills limiting benefit of clergy in some cases and preventing invocation of benefit of clergy a second time were introduced and rejected. There were bills dealing with petty larceny, adultery and fornication, and Sabbath abuses, as well as an anti-clerical measure preventing the clergy from serving as justices of the peace.[105]

The life of the 1625 Parliament was short; that of the Parliament of 1626 was somewhat longer, but it was dissolved when the impeachment of Buckingham became a serious possibility. Few measures of any kind became law and no law reform legislation was completed in 1625 or 1626. Charles then turned to non-parliamentary methods of raising revenue. Forced loans resulted in refusals to pay, which in turn led to trials that gained much public attention.[106] Judicial refusal to hold on the legality of the loans led the king to accuse the judges of 'great Insolence'. Judges were increasingly in the political spotlight for corruption and their legal opinions.

Reluctantly, Charles called parliament again in 1628. Instead of focusing on providing war finance as the king wished, it focused on Catholic and Arminian

[102] CJ, I, 833, 839, 882; *Proceedings in Parliament, 1626*, William Bidwell and Maija Jonson (eds) (New Haven, Yale University Press, 1991), vol I, 296, 600. In 1625 12 per cent of the house of Commons were lawyers; Thrush (n 26) 173–77.

[103] CJ, I, 624 820, 878. See RH Helmholtz (ed), *The Privilege against Self-Incrimination* (Chicago, University of Chicago Press, 1997).

[104] LJ, III, 418; *Proceedings in Parliament, 1625* (n 99) 269.

[105] *Proceedings in Parliament, 1625* (n 99) 210, 221–23, 228, 245, 269, 359, 411, 414; CJ I, 800, 810, 830, 865; LJ, III, 567, 569, 575.

[106] See Richard Cust, *The Forced Loan and English Politics 1626–1628* (Oxford, Oxford University Press, 1987).

issues and the Petition of Right, a document outlining Crown abuses such as forced loans, arbitrary imprisonment, billeting of soldiers and martial law. Though the law reform agenda we have been describing was diverted by the debates over the Petition of Right, it was not entirely neglected. A committee for courts of justice met weekly.[107] Another concerned itself with the Court of Wards.[108] There were bills forbidding the purchase of judicial places, limiting citations issued by the ecclesiastical courts[109] and removing border counties from the jurisdiction of the Council in the Marches.[110] The Crown presented bills for the regulation of attorneys and for listing lawyers' fees.[111] Bills for reformation of prisoners committed to the common gaol[112] and for punishment for adultery and fornication got as far as the committee stage.[113] Legislation was introduced again to disable clergymen from serving as justices of the peace.[114] A committee composed entirely of lawyers produced a bill involving expiring and continuing laws, an episode in Parliament's long-term project of rationalising the statutes.[115] The parliament that ended in 1629, the last for many years, was a tumultuous one, and at its end the king complained that the House of Commons had extended its privileges by 'setting up general committees for religion, for courts of justice, for trade, and the like, a course never heard of until late'.[116] Law reform, which earlier had been the joint work of Crown and parliament, was shifting to parliament.

Although there would be no parliaments for 11 years, royal intentions can perhaps be inferred from the policies carried out by Sir Thomas Wentworth, later Lord Strafford, who sought to implement the king's vision of absolutist rule when serving as Lord President of the North and then Lord Deputy in Ireland. As Lord Deputy, Strafford combined a heavy-handed administration with the implementation of several reforms sought by parliament. He spearheaded efforts to expedite and reduce the cost of litigation, reduce and regulate fees, keep litigants from bringing small cases to Dublin, improve debt procedures and prevent the manipulation

[107] The committee concentrated on individual petitions; CJ I, 921; *Commons Debates for 1629*, Wallace Notestein and Frances Helen Relf (eds) (Minneapolis, University of Minnesota Press, 1921) 48. See also Thomas Fuller, *Ephemerides Parliamentaria, or, A Faithful Register of the Transactions in Parliament* (London, 1654).

[108] CJ I, 899; *Commons Debates for 1629* (n 107) 178.

[109] CJ, I, 889.

[110] CJ, I, 889, 920, 926, 921, 926; *Commons Debates, 1628*, RC Johnson (ed), 3 vols (New Haven, Yale University Press, 1977), vol III, 452; Diary of Sir Richard Grosvenor in *Commons Debates for 1629* (n 107) 190; LJ, III, 763 831; Thrush and Ferris, *The House of Commons 1604–1629*, III, 593.

[111] Conrad Russell, *Parliament and English Politics*, 395. A proclamation of 1627 referred to a commission 'lately granted to enquire of new offices erected and new fees exacted in courts of justice' (London, 1627).

[112] LJ, III, 743, 831.

[113] CJ, I, 880, 899 922 20.

[114] CJ, I, 899, 921, 922, 925, 926; LJ, I, 21.

[115] CJ, I, 880 833, 639; Kyle (n 55) 202.

[116] SR Gardiner, *The Constitutional Documents of the Puritan Revolution, 1628–1660* (Oxford, Clarendon Press, 1899) 26–27.

of juries.[117] This kind of reform could be supported both by absolutists and their most vocal critics.

Dissatisfaction with the prerogative courts mounted. Star Chamber, for many years a popular court, now 'raised a deep distaste in the hearts of many people'.[118] It handled cases involving real and fictional instances of riot and assault, and was the primary venue for adjudicating cases involving fraud, forgery and perjury. Consternation mounted among common lawyers as their clients initiated parallel suits in Star Chamber. During the 1630s, Star Chamber became the venue for enforcing proclamations. Physical mutilations meted out to Burton, Bastwick and Prynne for seditious libel were greeted with opprobrium by their Puritan supporters. It should be pointed out that while Star Chamber procedure differed from that of the common law courts, it implemented the common and statute law, especially the law dealing with misdemeanours. Its typical punishments were imprisonment and fines, the latter often remitted or mitigated. It could not employ the death penalty. It also provided protections unavailable in the common law courts, including the right to counsel and the right of defence witnesses to testify under oath.[119]

The Council of the North was a popular and convenient court with a large civil and criminal business. Coke, with some exaggeration, suggested that it handled 6,000 cases a year. Unlike the period of leadership under Lord Huntington during Elizabeth I's reign, it had become riddled with factional politics during the reign of the early Stuarts.[120] High Commission, long a subject of criticism, became even more unpopular under Archbishop Laud's direction. Writs of prohibition had often been issued against High Commission, and Coke and his fellow common lawyers claimed that it overstepped its jurisdiction. Like Star Chamber, most High

[117] During the reign of James I, the Lord Deputy established English central courts, quarter sessions and assizes. In 1607 there were three judges each in King's Bench, Common Pleas and Exchequer. The English courts in Ireland can be considered successful if one uses the number of people using the courts. John McCavitt, '"Good Planets in their Several Spheares"; The Establishment of Assize Courts in Ireland' (1993) 24 *Irish Jurist* 249, 250. Strafford controlled the Court of Castle Chamber and used the Court of Wards to extract revenue for the crown. Castle Chamber was similar to Star Chamber, handling cases of riot, extortion, perjury and conspiracy. Hugh Kearney, *Strafford in Ireland 1633–41* (Manchester, Manchester University Press, 1959) 69–70, 73 75, 81–82. English officials dominated these courts; see Nicholas Canny, *Making Ireland British, 1580–1650* (Oxford, Oxford University Press, 2001) 301–03.

[118] *The House of Commons 1604–1629* (n 68) vol III, 594. In 1633 the Privy Council ordered Coke's law reports and his treatise on Littleton to be purged of erroneous opinions. See Bulstrode Whitelocke, *Memorials of the English Affairs 1625–60*, 4 vols (Oxford, 1853), vol I, 75–76.

[119] Between 1603 and 1625, over half of the 2,228 actions brought to Star Chamber made reference to other suits. See Thomas Barnes, 'Star Chamber Litigants, and Their Counsel 1596–1641' in John H Baker (ed), *Legal Records and the Historians* (London, Royal Historical Society, 1978) 7, 10. The Star Chamber decree of 1637 expanded licensing requirements; see David J Harvey, *The Law Emprynted and Englished: The Printing Press as an Agent of Change in Law and Legal Culture 1575–1642* (Oxford, Hart Publishing, 2015) 261–71. See also John Kenyon, *The Stuart Constitution, 1603–1688* (Cambridge, Cambridge University Press, 1986) 224; Thomas Barnes, 'Star Chamber Mythology (1961) 5 *American Journal of Legal History* 1.

[120] FW Brooks, 'The Council of the North' in Joel Hurstfield (ed), *The Tudors* (London, Sidgwick & Jackson, 1973) 186–87.

Commission cases involved private litigants.[121] Admiralty jurisdiction, often in conflict with the common law courts over merchant contracts, was the subject of a royal commission investigation in 1632. The result was a victory for Admiralty, but conflict between common law and Admiralty courts continued.

Crown efforts to increase its financial resources without parliamentary approval resulted in a heated conflict over the legality of ship money. Resistance to the levy led to a widely publicised trial that ended with a legal victory for the Crown. Both the decision and the fact that judges on assize had complied with Crown demands encouraging the collection of ship money increased the politicisation of the judiciary still further. The terms of judicial tenure were becoming a more significant issue. When the Long Parliament met, several judges would be charged with treason for their opinions.

VII. Publications and Debate 1603–40

It is not possible to say how widely parliament's law reform agenda was shared or even how well it was known to a broader public. Parliamentary debates were not to be discussed outside parliament. The reforms we have been describing were those promoted by a parliament that desired a cheaper and more effective version of the current legal system. While non-parliamentary comment was not often recorded, a few examples can be found in private letters and a sprinkling of publications.

In a letter of 1621, John Chamberlain reported on parliament's concern with bribery and extortion in matters of justice, noting the 'tempest' that had 'fallen upon my Lord Chancellor'. In 1624 he had no 'great good opinion' of the law's 'dilatory' courses'. The law had 'become a protection for cousening and bad debtors' rather than 'relief for the honest subject', and lawsuits had become 'tedious and chargeable'. A tenant could no longer be sure of 'what he hath, or when he shall have it'. Things had 'growne much out of order within these fowre or five yeares over that they were wont to be'.[122]

An influential member of parliament, Fulke Greville, Lord Brooke, supported law reform. The laws must be ordered and 'set down so cleerly as each man' could understand them and expressed in ordinary language, preferably in the form of aphorisms. It was necessary to reform the 'strange variety' of process and trials, and the law's 'foreign accents' that were responsible for 'obscuring sence, and multiplying doubt'. Brooke worried about the corruption of justice and judges and the greed of pleaders. Citing the example of the French provincial courts, Brooke suggests the need for better courts in England's remoter provinces.[123]

[121] Only 20 per cent were initiated by the Commission. See Kenyon (n 119) 178.

[122] Chamberlain (n 92) vol III, 354, 564.

[123] Fulke Greville, 'Of Laws' in Alexander Grosart (ed), *Works in Verse and Prose*, 4 vols (New York, AMS Press, 1966), vol I, 99, 100, 103–05; *The Remains of Sir Fulke Greville* (London, 1670) 71–75, 78.

The Present State of England, a popular chorography or description of England by William Carey, reiterated the usual complaints, among them the 'inconveniences' of suits over 'every trifling Action for Gain' that all too often required litigants to spend three times the value of what they sued for. Legal counsellors with 'venal voices' made suits 'very tedious, and more costly', and existing remedies for excessive fees had 'no good Effect'. Unnecessarily lengthy bills in the English courts were 'full of Matter impertinent'. Carey claimed to have seen a 40-page bill, 'which, copied out, was brought to six Sheets'. Chancery interrogatories were often 'vain and Frivolous', and there were too many Chancery clerks. Carey, writing in 1627, noted that the latest parliament intended to reform these and other 'great' grievances.[124]

Robert Burton's widely read and frequently reprinted *Anatomy of Melancholy* criticised the treatment of bankrupts and creditors, worried about the frequency of perjury and false witnessing, and urged that persistent thieves should be hanged or sentenced to slavery in galleys and mines. He attacked contentious lawsuits, the wrangling of lawyers and their excessive number. Judges were prone to bribery and altered and misconstrued laws.[125]

The popular genre of 'characters', short, often satirical, descriptions of various types of people and professions, reinforced the stereotype of the bad lawyer as greedy, fomenting lawsuits, and manipulating words and language to obfuscate. Nor were lawyers treated kindly in the drama.

One of the few printed publications supporting review of the penal laws, the Westminster courts and the court of 'arbitrary discretion' was the *Advertisements of 1610–11*, whose author condemned abuses in issuing prohibitions and expressed anxiety that proclamations might become law. The *Advertisements* also referred to House of Commons debate over limiting wardships, reform of patents and purveyance, publication of court fees and rationalisation of the penal laws.[126]

Further evidence is also found in Sir John Davies' 1615 defence of the common law. Rejecting the charge of 'uncertainty in the reason and judgements of the law', Davies insisted that English law was more certain 'than of any other human Law in the world'. To the commonly heard charge of costly and unnecessary delays, he responded that clients and solicitors were responsible for many 'bad and dishonest causes'. Law French was defended on the grounds that 'the proper and peculiar phrase of the Common Law cannot be so well express[ed], nor any case in law be so succinctly, sensibly, withal so fully reported, as in this speech'. Law French was easily learned, perhaps in as little as 10 days. 'Vulgar imputations cast upon the Law and Lawyers' were 'easily cleared'. While critics complained of solicitors who

[124] Walter Carey, *The Present State of England* (1627), in *Harleian Miscellany, A Collection of Rare, Curious and Entertaining Pamphlets and Tracts*, 8 vols (London, 1744–46), vol II, 201, 203–04.

[125] Robert Burton, *Anatomy of Melancholy*. There were editions in 1621, 1624, 1632 and 1638. I used the edition of 1800, 2 vols, vol I, 49–50, 72. See also John Day, *Law Trickes* (London, 1608), in which lawyers are treated as avaricious vultures.

[126] 'Advertisements' (1610–11) in *Somers Tracts* (London, 1746), vol II, 146, 155, 164.

drew their causes to 'an extraordinary length', the 'truth' of the matter was that the fault lay in the 'stomacke or malice' of clients who spent 'all they are worth' to defeat their adversaries and continued suits even against the advice of their counsellors. Responding to the charge of too many lawsuits, Davies argued that complex and flourishing societies necessarily generated more lawsuits than simple ones. '[V]ulgar errors' attributed uncertainty to the rules of law, and 'prevarication or corruption' to the legal profession.[127]

Although law reform appears to have figured relatively little in the private correspondence or printed media of the period, it was a particularly fruitful time for the legal profession's efforts to better organise legal material for the legal profession. Such publications not only had a profound effect on the practice of the law, but a substantial number were also consciously reformist in attempting to make English law more accessible and more comprehensible. The goal was pursued in a number of directions. These included rationalising and abridging the statutes, reporting and abridging law cases, constructing overviews of the legal system, 'methodising' the law and providing new dictionaries of legal terms. Some of these publications made their reforming goals clear, while others did not, but all sought to improve the presentation and ordering of law.

Memory was gradually becoming a less important resource for lawyers as the number of printed yearbooks and law reports grew. Law was ceasing to consist primarily of the collective memory of judges and lawyers, and citing of cases was becoming a more common practice.[128] Eleven volumes of Coke's reports became available beginning in 1600. In 1610 there was a bill for 'reforming the Year Books and the courts of Common Law and the Establishing of Reporters and others Remedying of the incertainty of Laws'.[129]

Francis Bacon tirelessly proposed reforming, restructuring and rationalising legal materials.[130] His *Advancement of Learning* brought law reform to the attention of the public. Reform, he insisted, should be undertaken by 'statesmen', not philosophers or lawyers, the former being prone to make 'imaginary commonwealth[s]', the latter overly focused on 'received law … not what ought to be the law'. Only those with 'wisdom of the laws' should determine 'the causes and remedies' of the laws' 'doubtfulness' and 'uncertainty'. Knowledgeable reformers must consider how the laws are 'to be penned and delivered, whether in texts or in acts, brief or large, with preambles, or without', as well as 'how they are to be pruned and reformed from time to time, and what is the best means to keep them

[127] Sir John Davies, *Le Primer Report des Cases (Irish Reports)* (Dublin, 1615; London, 1628; I used the 1680 edn) Dedicatory letter to Lord Chancellor Ellesmere, unpaginated.

[128] Ian Williams, '"He Creditted More the Printed Book": Common Lawyers' Receptivity to Print c 1550–1640' (2010) 28 *Law and History Review* 39. See also Richard Ross, 'The Memorial Culture of Early Modern English Lawyers, 1560–1640' (1998) 10 *Yale Journal of Law and Humanities* 229.

[129] Notestein (n 13) 54.

[130] For Bacon and law reform, see Barbara J Shapiro, 'Sir Francis Bacon and the Mid-seventeenth Century Movement for Law Reform' (1980 24 *American Journal of Legal History* 331; Daniel Coquillette, *Francis Bacon* (Palo Alto, Stanford University Press, 1992).

from being too vast in volumes, or too full of multiplicity and crossness'. They must decide whether laws should be 'pressed' 'rigorously or tenderly, how they were 'to be mitigated by equity and good conscience, and whether discretion and strict law are to be mingled in the same courts'. How the practice, profession and erudition of law should be censured and governed must be determined as well.[131]

Bacon's most extended treatment of law reform appeared in his post-impeachment *Augmentis Scientarum* (1623). As earlier, he focused on the causes and remedies for uncertainty. Obscurity was caused by 'an excessive accumulation of laws' and from 'ambiguity … in the drawing of them; or from negligent and ill-ordered methods of interpreting law; or lastly, from a contradiction and inconsistency of judgments'. Since the laws had grown 'voluminous' and 'confused', it might be necessary 'to remodel them entirely, and reduce them to a sound and manageable body'. Obsolete legal materials should be excised. 'Let the most approved antinomies' be received, and 'the rest omitted'. Repetitive legal rules must be 'erased' and the 'one which is the most perfect among them be retained'. 'Wordy and too prolix' laws should be 'compressed and abridged'. When complete, a new digest must be confirmed by the legislative power … lest, under pretense of digesting old laws, new laws be secretly imposed'.[132]

Since judicial decisions were the 'anchors of laws', better law reporting was essential, 'especially if they be doubtful and contain some difficulty or novelty'. Judgments must be recorded 'word for word' and the 'reasons which judges allege for their judgments' included. Reports would then be 'digested in chronological order' rather than by 'method' and 'titles' to provide a 'kind of history or narrative of the laws'. Unlike current practice, judges should not be permitted to 'meddle' with the reports. Reporters should be salaried officials selected 'from the most learned counsel'.[133]

No authorities were to be considered 'authentic' or 'at least let them [be] sparingly accepted'. The 'enormous multitude of authors' caused 'confusion in the laws, perplexity in judges, and proceedings of infinite length'. The large number also forced lawyers to take refuge in abridgments. While abridgements made men 'ready to practice', they also produced 'idlers in the science' of law. However, they were acceptable if used to 'facilitate the recollection of the law, but not to teach it'.[134]

'Auxiliary' volumes were necessary as well. These included 'institutes' arranged 'in a clear and perspicuous order' to introduce novices to the 'higher' parts of private law and a dictionary to explain the meaning of legal terms.[135] A 'good and careful treatise on the rules of law' was also necessary. Rules or maxims 'gathered from the harmony of laws and decided cases' should be presented in the form of

[131] Bacon (n 56) vol XIII, 60–64. See also vol VII, 314–17; vol XIV, 289, 354, 360–61.

[132] Bacon (n 56) vol V, 98, 100, 101.

[133] As earlier, Bacon thought Coke's *Reports* an improvement, but nevertheless too full of Coke's own views. See ibid vol V, 104; vol XIII, 262–68.

[134] ibid vol V, 104.

[135] ibid vol V, 104; vol X, 70.

'distinct and disjoined aphorisms' that left ample opportunity for discussion.[136] Bacon had himself collected maxims of this type, published posthumously as *Maxims of the Law.*[137]

Bacon also commented on legal procedure and the courts. He sought a middle way between the 'too prolix and formal' methods of the English and the 'too informal and summary' proceedings of the Scots. Many problems were due to the litigious who made use of the law's complicated procedures to multiply and delay lawsuits. Like Davies, Bacon thought excessive levels of litigation owed more to litigants than to the legal profession.[138]

Bacon had little to say about the common law courts, but was highly critical of the ecclesiastical courts[139] and the Court of Wards.[140] Star Chamber and Chancery should provide relief when the law was 'deficient'. Though necessary to supply gaps in the law, these courts must 'entirely confine themselves to monstrous and extraordinary cases, and not encroach upon the ordinary jurisdiction'.[141] Decrees with their reasons must be given in full and open court. Decisions in both courts were to be made by groups of judges. Bacon, an experienced common lawyer as well as a Chancery judge, thought it necessary to retain the distinction between law and equity. If mixed, 'discretion' would 'in the end supersede the law'.[142]

Bacon had more to say about a Star Chamber-like court, which, like Chancery, was to 'abate the rigor of the law and to supply its defects'. It should be forbidden from making decrees contrary to statute and could exercise no jurisdiction where common law remedies were available. Equity courts must not be permitted to 'swell and overflow, so as, under colour of mitigating the rigour of the law, to break its strength and relax its sinews by drawing everything to be a matter of discretion'.[143]

Bacon had a good deal to say about the judiciary. He recommended frequent consultation between kings, statesmen and judges because 'just laws and true

[136] ibid vol VII, 320, 321.

[137] *Maxims of the Law* was published in 1630, 1636 and 1639. Another auxiliary text would consist of a 'survey of the antiquities', that is, those 'writings on laws and judgments' that preceded the body of law. Purged of customary fables, the most useful of these should be collected into a single volume. See Bacon (n 56) vol V, 104. Bacon's overhaul of the entire corpus of the law also included 'Summaries' that arranged the law 'under titles and heads' to 'reduce to order what is dispersed in the law, and abridge what is difficult and prolix'. Bacon's final auxiliary volume was a collection of the various forms of pleading to aid practitioners and to help disclose the 'oracles and mysteries of laws'. Bacon (n 56) vol V, 104, 106, 107, 108.

[138] Bacon (n 56) vol XI, 64, 496, 497, 509; vol VII, 314, 315, 316.

[139] He opposed excommunication for minor offences and the improper use of the *ex officio* oath, whose use in the church courts were 'contrary to the laws and customs' of England. Tithes, legacies and administrations should be removed from the jurisdiction of the ecclesiastical courts, leaving them with matrimonial cases, accusations against ministers, simony, heresy and blasphemy. See Francis Bacon, 'Certain Considerations Touching the Better Pacification and Edification of the Church of England' in Bacon (n 56) vol X, 1090.

[140] Bacon (n 56) vol XI, 284–98.

[141] ibid vol V, 94–95.

[142] ibid vol V, 95. The Star Chamber-like court would have the authority to punish new offences and to increase punishment in older ones in 'heinous and enormous' but not capital cases.

[143] ibid vol V, 95, 97, 98.

policy' were inseparable, being 'like the spirits and sinews ... one moves with the others'.[144] Bacon's publications, more than any others, proposed and publicised law reform in the early Stuart era.

Many legal publications had a stated reformist intent. The *Abuses and Remedies of the High Court of Chancery* by George Norburie, published from within the Chancery establishment, noted the 'grievous complaints' discussed in James' first parliament where high fees of the Master of Chancery were 'held a grievance to the commonwealth not to be endured'. However, Chancery had introduced many 'good orders', some lately published by Lord Chancellor Bacon. Reformation of how references were handled by the Master of the Rolls had effected 'more than the parliament could bring to pass'. Nevertheless, 'unless the cause be taken away', the efforts of parliament and Crown would be useless and complaints would continue to 'fill the whole kingdom with combustion'.[145]

Among the items needing correction were the 'strange of authority of the court beyond its limits in matters of judicature', the 'impunity of litigious persons', dilatory proceedings, unnecessary offices, and the excessive fees of clerks and court officers. It could not be denied that 'the boundless power of the chancery' was the cause of many 'clamours against the lord chancellor'. Yet Norburie thought it difficult to condemn a Lord Chancellor for transgressing written laws or instructions because the Chancellor judged 'according to his conscience, and to the best of his understanding and knowledge'. Currently, 'hardly three out of ten' Chancery suits had 'any colour or shadow of just complaint'. Delays were blamed on exaggerated claims and the excessive motions of lawyers. When in doubt, Norburie advised Chancery judges not to look to precedent, but instead to act 'according to the rules of a good consciences, guided by the word of God, and upon certain knowledge of the lawes of the realm agreeable therein'.[146] His comment underlines the period's uncertainty about the extent to which Chancery should operate by rules, precedent or the varying consciences of individual Lord Chancellors.

The much-criticised ecclesiastical courts were described, explained and defended in Thomas Ridley's *A View of the Civile and Ecclesiastical Law*. Suggesting that these laws were insufficiently known, Ridley, a member of High Commission, recognised that there were legitimate grievances that could be 'amended'. Writing at a time when some feared that the civil law endangered the common law, Ridley argued for retention of both the civil and ecclesiastical law.[147]

[144] ibid vol V, 509–10. The essay 'Of Judicature' summarises Bacon's views on judicial impartiality, judicial corruption and the role that judges might play in reforming the legal system. Like most common lawyers, he believed that judges were 'to interpret law and not to make law or give law'; ibid vol V, 506–07.

[145] Printed in Francis Hargraves, *A Collection of Tracts Relative to the Law of England* (London, 1787) 428–29. Norburie, one of Chancery's six clerks, had assisted a parliamentary committee investigating Chancery. His volume was presented to Lord Keeper Williams.

[146] ibid 44.

[147] Thomas Ridley, *A View of the Civile and Ecclesiastical Law* (London, 1607) Preface to James I; issued again in 1634, 1637 and 1639.

There were several approaches to reforming and reshaping the materials of the law, some in keeping with Bacon's scheme, others not. Several legal works focused on providing a new or better 'method'. William Fulbecke's *A Direction or Preparative to the Study of the Law*, reprinted in 1620, was followed by John Dodderidge's *Lawyer's Light* in 1629. Dodderidge employed 'method' and logic to 'purge' English law 'from the great confusion, tedious and superfluous iterations' of the reports. He would reduce 'every title of the Law particularly to a Methode, and so consequently, the whole body thereof into a perfect shape'.[148] Fitzherbert's *La Novel Natural Brevium*, which provided rules of the common law, was reissued in 1609, 1616 and 1635, and continued to be an invaluable aid for lawyers. Thomas Powell's 1623 *Attournies Academy* outlined the manner of proceedings in a wide range of courts.

Printed collections of statutes and abridgements of statutes continued to grow in number and importance.[149] Ferdinando Pulton produced *A Kalender, or table comprehending the effect of all the statutes* beginning in 1606. His *De pace Regis et regni*, despite its Latin title, was written in English so that ordinary persons would have knowledge of the 'criminall and capitall' laws. His *Abstract of all the Penal Statutes*, first issued in 1577, classified the statutes under headings and emphasised his 'intent that everyone which desireth to know may read and thereby perceive the cause and contents' of the law.[150]

There were legal dictionaries and comparisons of English and civil law. The older *Exposition of the terms of the laws* had at least eight printings between 1603 and 1640. John Cowell's *Interpreter* (1607), a much-used and widely admired legal dictionary, compared the terms of the common and civil laws. However, its favourable view of the royal prerogative led Coke and others to urge Cowell's prosecution. There was also William Fulbecke's *A Parallel conference of the civil law, the canon law, and the common law of the realm* (1601).[151]

Books designed to give an overview of the law and the legal system, sometimes called Institutes, were becoming more available, often in English. Sir Henry Finch's well-respected *Law, a discourse in four Books* (1627) adopted a Ramist methodising mode.[152] Finch's earlier *Nomotechnia*, written in law French, was designed 'to form into one body, in harmonious order, the damaged and fragmented parts of the law of our country'. His clarification would make use of precise definition and

[148] John Doddridge, *The English Lawyer: Describing a method of the managing of the laws of this land* (London, 1631) 191, 240, 243–45, 260. The 1629 edition was entitled *The Lawyers Light*.

[149] Ferdinando Pulton, *A Collection of sundrie statutes* (London, 1618); Rastell's *A Collection in English of the Statutes* appeared in 1608, 1611 and 1612.

[150] Ferdinando Pulton, *Abstract of all the Penal Statutes* (London, 1577). Pulton's *De pace Regis et regni* appeared in 1609, 1610, 1615, and 1623. See also William Staunford, *Les plees del coron*, an Elizabethan work reprinted in 1607.

[151] See also William Fulbecke, *A Second Part of the Parallel* (London, 1602).

[152] Henry Finch, *Law, or, a discourse* (London, 1627) was the basis of the later summaries by William Noy, Edmund Wingate and Michael Hawke's *Grounds of the Law of England* (1657). For Cowell and Finch, see David Siepp, 'The Structure of English Common Law in the Seventeenth Century' in WM Gordon and TD Fergus (eds), *Legal History in the Making* (London, Hambledon, 1991) 61–83.

division into categories, placing each individual item in its proper place.[153] Another effort to make the law more understandable was John Cowell's *Institutiones Juris Anglicanae*, which had four early seventeenth-century printings and was translated into English and printed at the order of parliament in 1651. Cowell characterised it as a digest or method 'useful for all gentlemen who are studious and desire to understand the customs of this nation'.[154] William Lambarde's posthumously published *Archeion, A Description of the High Courts of Justice in England* provided a brief description of courts.[155]

Sir Edward Coke's *Institutes of the Laws of England*, the most influential work of this kind, announced its reformist aims. Coke designed it to overcome the 'difficulties and darkness both of the matter and terms and words of the action'.[156] He defended writing in English.[157] *The First Part of the Institutes*, a commentary on Littleton, dealt with the law of real property. Published in 1628, 1629 and 1630, it was digested into 'alphabeticall order and method'. *The Second Part* was an exposition of the statutes. *The Third Part*, which covered the criminal law and pleas of the Crown, showed little interest in changing criminal law or criminal procedure. However, Coke did suggest that denying the oath to witnesses in felony trials could not be found in the statutes, ancient authors, cases or records.[158] His comment suggests that the prohibition may have been challenged. He also thought that many statutes were unclear, 'repealed' or 'expired', and 'many treasons, felonies and other crimes' were no longer 'warrantable by law at this day'.[159]

The Fourth Part of the Institutes described the courts of justice, 'together as it were, in one map, or table (which hitherto were never yet done)', so that the complex jurisdictions of the courts could be 'distinctly understood and observed'. Wishing to provide remedies for conflicting jurisdictions, he collected 'materials towards the raising of this great and honorable building'. Coke attributed excessive litigation to the dispersal of monastic and chantry property, 'swarms of informers', the 'multitude of attorneys' and to peace and plenty. The last was characterised as the 'nurse of suits'.[160]

[153] He would 'first divide the law into classes (genera)' and 'then distinguish certain branches of these … sift the properties appertaining to each one individually, and encompass all with reliable, appropriate and all-embracing rules'. He would 'describe general matters generally and once for all', allotting 'particular items to individual groups, each in its own place'. These would be illustrated with 'clear, precise and appropriate' examples'. Everything would contain 'the unequivocal truth, everything having a natural and consistent relationship with everything else'. See Henry Finch, *Nomotechnnia* (London, 1613) iv–v.

[154] *Institutes of the Lawes of England digested into a method* (London, 1651).There were at least six printings *of Institutions or, Principall grounds of the Laws and Statutes of England* between 1604 and 1625.

[155] William Lambarde, *Archeion, A Description of the HIgh Courts of Justice in England* (London, 1635) Lambarde criticised entangling laws, delays, vexatious lawyers and unfair judges, and had a favourable view of Star Chamber (at 85–86, 89–90).

[156] Sir Edward Coke, *The Third Part of the Institutes* (London, 1644), Proem.

[157] ibid.

[158] ibid 79.

[159] ibid Proem.

[160] Coke (n 83) 75.

Despite the reforming elements of his *Reports* and the *Institutes*, Coke did not favour change in the common law, 'for that which hath been refined and perfected by all the wisest men in former succession of ages and proved and approved by continual experience to be good and profitable for the commonwealth cannot without hazard and danger be altered or changed'.[161] He preferred judicial interpretation to statute-making because the former clarified, but did not alter the laws. He was sympathetic to some legislative reform, but was anxious about statutory encroachments on the common law, which could cause 'infinite troubles, questions, suits and difficulties'.[162]

The justicing manuals designed to make the law more accessible for justices of the peace continued to find an ample audience. Lambarde's had several early seventeenth-century printings, but was being replaced by Michael Dalton's *The Country Justice*, which would serve justices of the peace for the rest of the seventeenth century and beyond. Like so many legal writers, Dalton's aims were to 'digest' the material 'into some order and method', to 'let things down plainly and briefe' and to assist the justices in 'redressing of the abuses and defects' in the performance of their duties.[163] The justicing manuals were an important channel for communicating legal information to laymen on many aspects of the law.

VIII. Conclusion

Reform interests were strong, especially between 1603 and 1624, with James and Bacon being the most powerful spokesmen. Bacon was a champion of law reform in parliament, in private advice to James and in publications for non-legal audiences. Parliament engaged in continuing efforts to reform the courts and their legal proceedings in order to make the existing system quicker and less expensive. All courts were subject to reform attention, but Chancery and the ecclesiastical courts received the most. Until the 1630s, Star Chamber was not part of the reform agenda. The legislative agenda was quite clear, but the legislature did not prove to be an effective means of introducing reform. While the Crown and parliament frequently differed on issues of royal finance, foreign policy and the extent of the royal prerogative, reform of the legal system was not a major area of contention.

Public interest can be heard, but was not very evident in the print media. Bacon's ventures into print, addressed to non-lawyers, were the most prominent. Equally, if not more important, was the development of a professional literature, much of which was motivated by reform impulses. Although a good many lawyers

[161] Edward Coke, *Reports*, (eds) EJ Thomas, JF Fraser 1826 ed. Preface, v, vi.

[162] Coke (n 83) Preface.

[163] Michael Dalton, *The Country Justice* (London, 1618). There were five editions before the Civil War, three between 1643 and 1656, and seven between 1661 and 1700.

may have insisted that the content of the law was not to be altered, there was a good deal of consensus that it needed to become more accessible and understandable.

Early Stuart law reform was part of a lengthy tradition, extending back at least as far as the reign of Henry VIII, which continued unbroken during the reigns of Edward VI, Mary I and Elizabeth I. However, the Jacobean period constituted the high point in that tradition. Much was accomplished in 1624, but it was not the kind of reform that was meant to be transformative. It was concerned primarily with improving the operation of the existing courts and quite consciously left the substance of the common law untouched.

Despite the many difficulties in completing legislation, the journals of both houses of parliament testify to substantial concern for improving the legal system. Law reform was part of the legislative agenda in every parliament of James I and Charles I. The legislative process in the early seventeenth century was not favourable to the completion of legislation on any topic. In the Elizabethan and Jacobean periods, similar reform measures were introduced and reintroduced, less because of opposition than because parliaments were in session only sporadically. Law reform was never at the top of parliament's agenda, but it was a feature of most pre-Civil War parliaments. The absence of parliament between 1629 and 1640 obscures the continuity between the reform agenda of the early Stuarts and the early years of the Long Parliament. Many of the law reform issues that came under the scrutiny of the parliamentary reformers before 1640 would be taken up again during the revolutionary era. Moderate law reform would continue during the next two decades, but it would be challenged by more vocal and revolutionary rivals.

5

The Civil War and Parliamentary Rule 1640–49

The 11-year hiatus of Parliament that ended in 1640 ushered in a period of political and constitutional upheaval resulting in major changes in the legal system. The prerogative courts were dismantled and traditional notions of treason challenged as Parliament attempted to impeach the king's most trusted advisors and judges. The collapse of the censorship regime and the huge expansion of press output that followed resulted in a huge increase in the public's knowledge of parliamentary business, knowledge that in the past had been severely limited. There were new channels for disseminating commentary on law. News writers now covered domestic as well as foreign news. A new audience centred in London and its environs was now able to enter and respond to the discourse on law reform. This chapter will give attention to the changing conditions for litigation and the possibilities for law reform before and during the Civil War era.

I. The Short Parliament

The outbreak of war with Scotland, and the king's need for financial resources to defeat the Scots, precipitated the calling of the Short Parliament in 1640. Parliamentary leaders insisted on remedying grievances before granting the king supply. Despite concern with matters of religion, the legality of ship money and parliamentary privileges, law reform was on parliament's agenda. A committee for courts of justice was appointed, soon to be followed by discussion of the 'denial of Justice in the Courts of Westminster to the subjects prejudice'. Members of the House of Commons were requested to bring in bills from earlier parliaments.[1] There were bills to deal with 'trifling suits' and for 'avoiding of causeless Suits and Ease in just Suits, at Common Law'.[2] A bill calling 'for reformation of abuses in Ecclesiastical Courts' again condemned improper use of excommunication, penance, accusation by accusers 'not to be known' and oaths 'contrary

[1] CJ, II, 3, 12, 13, 17; Historical Manuscripts Commission, Salisbury, XXII, 310.
[2] CJ, II, 3, 16, 1.

to lawes humane and divine'.[3] The Edwardian *Reformatio legum ecclesiasticarum* was reissued in 1640. There was a bill to deal with problems associated with the administration of wills, and complaints of fees in High Commission as well as an anti-clerical measure forbidding certain clergymen from serving as justices of the peace.[4] Legislation was also introduced for 'avoiding suits at Lawe'.[5] Parliament, however, was dismissed after three weeks with nothing accomplished. Law reform could not take place without a functioning legislative body.

II. The Long Parliament

Parliament met again in November 1640 as the king's need for financial support for the war in Scotland continued to mount. Almost immediately after the opening of parliament, a House of Commons committee of the whole for courts of justice was established and ordered to meet weekly.[6] Abuses in the ecclesiastical courts and arbitrary proceedings in the courts were included in John Pym's 7 November list of grievances.[7] Only a month later, the Grand Remonstrance, a list of over 200 grievances, included demands for regulating the courts of justice and for 'abridging both the delays and charges of lawsuits'. It alleged that Star Chamber and High Commission were 'forges of misery, oppression and violence'.[8] Committees were appointed to deal with 'obstructions in Courts of Justice', judges, ship money, Star Chamber, High Commission and 'undue proceedings at the Council Table'.[9] Shortly afterwards, the upper house appointed a committee to examine 'all Abuses in Matters of Imprisonment, and also examine all other Abuses in Courts of Justice'.[10] In 1642 the House resolved that 'the buying and selling of judicial places' and other offices in courts of justice was a 'cause of the evils of this kingdom'.[11] Lower house committees were appointed to deal with the Court of Wards and the Earl Marshall's Court.[12] There were bills in 1641, 1644 and 1648 to make punishment

[3] *The Short Parliament; Diary of Sir Thomas Aston*, Judith Maltby (ed) (London, Camden 4th Series, 1988) 66–67, 87, 110–11; *Proceedings of the Short Parliament of 1640*, W Coates and E Cope (eds) (London, Royal Historical Society, 1979) 234–35.

[4] CJ, II, 13, 16, 17.

[5] Aston, *Diary*, 118. The bill had a single reading.

[6] Maija Jannson (ed), *Proceedings in the Opening Session of the Long Parliament: House of Commons*, 6 vols (Rochester, University of Rochester Press, 2000), vol I, 19. 40.

[7] John Kenyon, *The Stuart Constitution* (Cambridge, Cambridge University Press, 1966) 204–05. Pym referred to the 'corruption of Judges, Star Chamber, Council table [and] the king'. See *Proceedings of the Short Parliament of 1640* (n 3) 234–35.

[8] Kenyon (n 7) 216; RR Reid, *The King's Council in the North* (Wakefield, England, 1975). The Root and Branch Petition attacked abuses in the ecclesiastical courts.

[9] Kenyon (n 7) 216; CJ, III, 254.

[10] LJ, IV, 98.

[11] CJ, I, 264, 594, 810, 820; II, 438. The upper house considered a bill making giving 'money for Places of Judicature a felony'; LJ, IV, 139.

[12] CJ, II, 87, 89.

for adultery harsher.[13] Legislation requiring the death penalty for blasphemy was passed in 1648. Clearly, law reform was on the agenda from the time that the Long Parliament assembled.

Bills also dealt with the problems of poor imprisoned debtors. Sir Simonds D'Ewes thought the system to be flawed but improvable, it being unchristian that the poor unable to pay their debts should 'starve and rot in Prison'. The English, he thought, might consider the Dutch practice of putting the poor to work to discharge their debt.[14] Debt reform was one of the few types of law in which reformers looked at Dutch, Danish or French law exemplars.

There was concern over abuses in the ecclesiastical courts, and legislation was again considered for preventing clergymen from serving as justices of the peace.[15] A House of Lords committee proposed reforming penal statutes with the purpose of eliminating obsolete laws. In 1641 the House of Lords requested the king to change judicial patents to *quam se bene gesserint*.[16] Legislation was introduced to avoid 'the infinite number of small and trifling suits commenced in the courts of Westminster'.[17]

A list of grievances sent to the king in April 1642 included sale of judicial positions and offices in the courts of justice. Another denounced 'all excessive Fees' and 'unnecessary Delays', and demanded that 'the Proceedings of Justice' be made 'more easy, certain, than of late they have been'.[18] The Nineteen Propositions sent to the king in June included provisions that judges hold their offices on terms of good behaviour, and that the appointment of chief judges and other high offices of the Crown require the approbation of both houses.[19] Parliamentary approval of judicial appointments would have been a major innovation. Concern over expiring statutes, a serious problem if parliament were to be again unexpectedly dissolved, resulted in a Triennial Act clause requiring that if parliament were dissolved, expiring acts would remain in force until the next parliament. Parliament was necessary for legislation, reform or otherwise.

The House of Lords reassumed its juridical activities, functioning as a venue for appeals and a variety of other cases. It was inundated with petitions relating to prosecutions for nonconformity, deprivations of ecclesiastical livings and income, arbitrary imprisonment and the corrupt sale of government offices.[20] It was aided in its judicial functions by the judges.

[13] RB Outhwaite, *Clandestine Marriage in England 1500–1860* (London, Hambledon, 1995) 9. See also Keith Thomas, 'The Puritans and Adultery, The Act of 1650 Reconsidered' in Donald Pennington and Keith Thomas (eds), *Puritans and Revolutionaries* (Oxford, Clarendon Press, 1978) 257–82.

[14] CJ, II, 128; Sears McGee, *An Industrious Man: The Worlds of Sir Simonds D'Ewes* (Palo Alto, Stanford University Press, 2015) 348. In 1645 it was suggested that there were about 8,000 imprisoned for debt; see Louis Leventhal, 'The Early History of Bankruptcy' (1919) 18 *University of Pennsylvania Law Review* 1.

[15] CJ II, 79, 94, 99, 102, 18, 67; *Proceedings in the Opening Sessions of the Long Parliament*, Maija Jansson (ed), 8 vols (Rochester, NY, University of Rochester Press, 2000–07), vol I, 391, 399.

[16] LJ, IV, 130, 159.

[17] CJ, II, 121. It had one reading.

[18] LJ, IV, 690, 691; V, 96, 68.

[19] Kenyon (n 8) 245.

[20] LJ, IV, 69, 87, 93.

III. The Courts

The legal system was transformed when the prerogative or conciliar courts, a major part of the English court system, were dismantled. Star Chamber, praised by both Bacon and Coke just two decades earlier, had been a popular court frequently sought by suiters, who preferred it to the common law courts. Coke had characterised it as 'the most honorable court (our Parliament excepted) that is in the Christian world, in respect of the judges of the court, and of their Honourable proceeding according to their just jurisdiction and the ancient and just orders of the Court'.[21] For many decades, it had handled cases involving fraud, conspiracy, extortion, forgery, riot, counterfeiting, perjury and corrupt juries that acquitted contrary to the evidence.[22] It also handled cases involving real property when plaintiffs alleged riot as a means of getting their cases to Star Chamber, a practice that resulted in the ire of the common lawyers.

Attitudes towards Star Chamber changed during the 1630s. The harsh physical punishments given to Puritans Henry Burton, John Bastwick and William Prynne for seditious libel and its role in enforcing proclamations no doubt played a part in the shift in the public's view.[23] Though many common lawyers practised in Star Chamber, they became the court's most vociferous opponents.[24] Shortly after the Long Parliament met, a House of Commons committee was appointed to consider Star Chamber. Sir Simonds D'Ewes, a member of the committee, charged that 'the irregularities of the Court had been so extreme as there could be no moderating of them'.[25] According to Lord Andevers, the court 'has grown a Monster'. Its 'arbitrary judgments' destroy the common law.[26] Star Chamber and 'all courts of like jurisdiction' had 'of late Times assumed unto itself a power to intermeddle in civil cause and matters of private interest between party and party, and have adventured to determine of the estates and liberties of the subject, contrary to the law of the land … by which great and manifold mischiefs and inconveniences have arisen'.[27] Hostility was no doubt also related to the growing dissatisfaction with the king, his policies and his advisors. Since many of the judges in Star Chamber were members of Charles' Privy Council, it should not be surprising that hostility was directed at Star Chamber. Its role in the enforcement of the unpopular collection of ship money was a particular irritant.

[21] Edward Coke, *Fourth Part of the Institutes of the laws of England* (1644; I used the 1797 edn.) 650.

[22] Charles Hamilton, 'Stars of the Court of the Star Chamber, 1630–41' (1939) 21 *Transactions of the Royal Historical Society* 11.

[23] Thomas Barnes, 'Star Chamber Mythology' (1961) 5 *American Journal of Legal History* 1. Only 19 of the 236 sentences between 1640 and 1641 involved corporal punishment, and few of these aroused public interest. Most Star Chamber cases never came to trial.

[24] See RP Alford, 'The Star Chamber and the Regulation of the Legal Profession, 1570–1640' (2011) 51 *American Journal of Legal History* 639.

[25] CJ, II, 44.

[26] Lord Andevers, *Two Speeches* (London, 1641) 3–4.

[27] 16 Car I c 10; *An Act for regulating of the Privie Councell, and for taking away the court, commonly called, The Star-Chamber* (London, 1640).

However much vilified, Star Chamber had offered greater protections to defendants than had the common law courts. Star Chamber defendants had the right to counsel as well as the right to call witnesses who testified under oath.[28] Decrees regulating the press, once issued by Star Chamber, now became a matter for parliament, which would be no less committed than the Crown to regulation.

Legislation ended the judicial activities of the Privy Council as well as Star Chamber abolishing the Council of the North, the Council in the Marches of Wales, the Court of the Duchy of Lancaster and the Court of the County Palatine of Chester, all of which combined the exercise of conciliar and common law. Cases previously litigated in those courts would now be litigated in the 'ordinary courts of justice and by the ordinary course of the law'.[29] The common law courts prevailed over their competitors.

High Commission was also abolished. For some decades, and especially under the influence of Archbishop William Laud, its actions hit the Puritan clergy particularly hard, inflicting clerical deprivations, fines and imprisonment without bail. Particularly disliked were summons issued on the basis of suspicion, examination under oath without specific charges and the *ex officio* oath.[30] The legislation abolishing High Commission cited the 'insufferable wrong and oppression of the King's subjects' when the Commission used its powers to 'fine and imprison … and exercise other authority not belonging to the ecclesiastical Jurisdiction'. The legislation forbade self-accusation in all courts and proclaimed 'no new courts shall be erected within England or Wales with similar power, jurisdiction or authority'.[31] However, the ecclesiastical courts, which were not prerogative courts were not dissolved.

The Court of Requests, rarely mentioned in parliament, also disappeared, though it was not formally dissolved. This equity court, which was popular because of its low costs, exercised jurisdiction disliked by the common lawyers and had been subject to numerous prohibitions.[32]

Chancery remained largely unscathed. Francis Bacon's reforming ordinances were published in 1642. The dissolution of Star Chamber, High Commission and other prerogative courts signalled a victory of the common law courts over their rivals and an end to much, though by no means all, of the jurisdictional conflicts that had plagued the legal system for so many years.

[28] Barnes (n 23) 1, 9. Star Chamber cases were handled more easily and flexibly than in the common law courts. Star Chamber adapted civil law type remedies to various criminal offences. See Thomas Barnes, 'Star Chamber and the Sophistication of Criminal Law' [1977] *Criminal Law Review* 316; John F Acevedo, 'The Ideological Origins of the Right to Counsel' (2006) 68 *South Carolina Law Review* 87.

[29] Kenyon (n 8) 225. The Council of Wales and the Marches was reinstated in 1660 and abolished again in 1689.

[30] About 80 per cent of its cases were brought by private litigants against inadequate clergy. By the 1630s, many marriage cases were litigated there. ibid 178–79.

[31] 16 Car I c 11. Later, there would be a grand jury petition to re-establish the Court at York. Some common lawyers admitted that it was convenient, less expensive, less troublesome and met a real need. See Reid (n 8) 450.

[32] CJ, II, 8. Its records end in 1642. Courts of request were sometimes called courts of conscience.

IV. Impeachment

Parliament, which had ended the judicial careers of Bacon and Cranfield by impeachment, now attempted to employ that procedure to bring down the king's chief advisors, Thomas Wentworth, now Lord Strafford, and Archbishop Laud. The charges against them would no longer be bribery or corruption resulting in fines and loss of office, but treason, which carried the death penalty. Strafford was charged with bringing in arbitrary and tyrannical government and attempting to overthrow the laws of England and Ireland, as well as for some of his actions as Lord Deputy of Ireland and Lord President of the Council of the North. Among the many complaints was the accusation of drawing cases to York instead of Westminster.[33] The proceedings and the arguments were circulated widely. Parliamentary speeches, some of which were published, both justified and condemned the charges. Lucius Cary, Lord Falkland, called Strafford a source of the nation's miseries. Oliver St John, an ally of John Hamden and John Pym, justified condemning Strafford on the basis of the doctrine *salus populi*, the welfare of the people.[34]

When it turned out to be difficult to prove the charge of treason, it was argued that, though individually Stafford's acts did not constitute treason, together they constituted 'cumulative treason', a previously unknown concept.[35] Finding it impossible to convict Strafford of a known crime, parliament revived the act of attainder to condemn him to death. Attainder was a legislative act declaring the accused guilty without the need for the standard of proof required in a judicial proceeding. When George Digby, Earl of Bristol, initially a supporter of the impeachment charge, spoke against attainder, arguing that it was illegal to convict someone for something that had not been illegal at the time the acts were done, his speech was burnt on the order of the House of Commons. Before long, it was being reported that some people 'began to be divided in opinion' because Strafford's misdemeanours, 'though ever so many and so great, could not be put together to make one Treason'.[36] Whatever the legality of the charge, the bill of attainder passed both houses and the king agreed to Strafford's execution.

The trial and execution were widely publicised. It was reported that 'everything sells that comes in print under his name … either in favor of him or against him'.[37]

[33] Reid (n 8) 435.

[34] *A Complete Collection of State Trials*, T Howell (ed) (London, Longmans, 1802–28), vol III, 1476, 92; Oliver St John, *An Argument of Law concerning the Bill of Attainder of High Treason of Thomas Earle of Strafford* (London, 1641). See also *The Speech or Declaration of John Pym … of the Charge of High Treason against Thomas, Earle of Strafford* (London, 1641).

[35] See Conrad Russell, 'The Theory of Treason in the Trial of Strafford' (1965) 80 *English Historical Review* 30; Alan Orr, *Treason and the State: Law, Politics and Ideology in the English Civil War* (Cambridge, Cambridge University Press, 2002); Adele Hast, 'State Treason Trials during the Puritan Revolution, 1640–1660' (1972) 15 *Historical Journal* 37.

[36] Quoted in David Cressy, *England on Edge, Crisis and Revolution, 1640–1642* (Oxford, Oxford University Press, 2006) 296.

[37] Quoted in ibid 296.

Over 100 publications dealt with the trial. Strafford's denial of the charge of cumulative treason was printed several times and there were at least seven editions of his scaffold speech.[38] Treason trials of prominent figures received far more press attention in print than did abuses in the law or the law courts.

The use of impeachment and bills of attainder raises the question of whether these legislative instruments should be viewed as reformist measures or as parliamentary usurpation and/or evasion of the law of treason. Finding a legal basis for eliminating those whom the government considered enemies would prove difficult for successive revolutionary-era governments, several of which turned to special courts or parliament to prosecute their enemies.

Parliament also attempted to use impeachment proceedings to bring down Laud, the much reviled Archbishop of Canterbury. Laud was charged with expanding and usurping clerical jurisdiction and 'traitorously seeking to subvert the fundamental laws and government of the Kingdom'. He was found guilty of the facts with which he was charged, but these were not found to constitute treason 'by any known and established law of the land'.[39] Parliament again turned to an act of attainder, which simply declared Laud guilty. His trial, like that of Strafford, was widely publicised, eliciting nearly 100 publications. If one uses the number of publications as a gauge, there was far greater public interest and knowledge of the trials of Strafford and Laud than for dismantling the prerogative courts.

Parliament also moved to impeach the judges responsible for the ship money decision. They too were accused of having 'traitorously and wickedly endeavored to subvert the fundamental laws and established government'. Denzil Hollis spoke of their 'perfidiousness', 'their failure to be guardians and interpreters of the laws and their 'accursed glosses' that made the text 'speak another language and another sense than ever our ancestors … intended'.[40] Another said that the judges were 'the authors of all our oppressions in giving wrong judgments contrary to their oaths'. Still another said: 'Let the common law destroy them that would have destroyed it.' 'Take away' both 'the judgments and judges together'.[41]

Since few ship money judges remained alive, parliament focused on Sir John Finch, widely believed to have been responsible for the decision supporting the legality of ship money. Finch was charged with conspiracy to produce arbitrary and tyrannical government, threatening jurors and influencing the king against parliament. Lord Falkland, whose speech against the Lord Keeper was printed, condemned the extra-legal judgments of the judges as well as the argument

[38] ibid 296, 296n; A Cromartie, 'The Printing of Parliamentary Speeches November 1640–July 1642' (1990) 33 *Historical Journal* 23. The earlier trials of Raleigh and Essex were also accompanied by numerous printed accounts.

[39] Orr (n 35) 115; *State Trials*, vol IV, 598. Proceedings moved slowly and Laud was not executed until 1645.

[40] Speech of Denzil Hollis, in WJ Jones, *Politics and the Bench: The Judges and the Origins of the English Civil War* (London, Allen & Unwin, 1971) 214; LJ, IV, 303 *The Accusation and Impeachment of John Lord Finch, Keeper of the Great Seal* (London, 1640).

[41] Quoted in Jones (n 40) 141; see also 199–200, 215.

from 'necessity' in the ship money case.[42] Sir Robert Berkeley, a justice of King's Bench also accused of treason, was convicted only of crimes and misdemeanours. However, the action against Berkeley was said to have 'struck a great terror in the rest of his brethren then sitting in Westminster Hall'.[43] Several judges, including Finch, fled the country. He was imprisoned until his escape to The Hague at the time of the execution of King Charles. By October 1642, every King's Bench judge was either with the king or in prison.

The trials highlighted the issue of the judicial tenure. Should judges be appointed *quamdiu se bene gesserint*, that is, during good behaviour, rather than during the king's pleasure, a standard allowing the king to dismiss judges at any time for any reason?[44] The Nineteen Propositions had included the provision that all judges were to hold their places *quamdiu se bene gesserint*. The trials also raised questions about punishment for judicial opinions, what constituted judicial misconduct and who should determine its punishment.

Clearly, normal legal channels were bypassed or stretched in the trials of Strafford, Laud and the judges. For many, they constituted reform; for others, they were a travesty of justice. Revolutions typically involve removal of the chief power holders of one political regime and replacing them with more congenial ones. Therefore, the actions taken against Strafford, Laud and the judges might be considered a natural or necessary logical step in the revolutionary process. Parliament, however, did not consider itself to be revolutionary and frequently employed a rhetoric of restoration when it adopted novel measures.

By 1642, major changes in England's legal structure had taken place. The prerogative courts had been dismantled and those persons thought responsible for leading the king towards destructive policies had been removed. Parliament exhibited an extraordinary consensus on these measures, and the king reluctantly acceded to them. However, things changed dramatically when the king and some members of parliament left London. Royal assent to legislation became difficult, if not impossible. Parliament attempted to negotiate a settlement with the Crown, a difficult task given Charles' slipperiness and the growing military pressure on settlement terms. The army now became a political force and would have a major impact on the movement for law reform.

Faced with the task of creating a non-episcopal, established church, parliament established the Assembly of Divines. Presbyterians favoured a clerically dominated system with no religious toleration. Yielding to pressure from its Presbyterian Scots allies, parliament initially leaned in a Presbyterian direction. Independents wished to give greater authority to individual congregations and typically supported some degree of toleration for the religious sects that were emerging. The religious

[42] *Lord Faulkland, his learned speech in Parliament … touching the judges and the Lord Keeper* (London, 1641) 3–5, 9. For the charges against Berkeley, see 199–208; Bulstrode Whitelocke, *Memorials of the English Affairs*, 4 vols (Oxford, 1853), vol I, 112, 113, 115, 117.

[43] Jones (n 40) 141, 142.

[44] LJ, IV, 132.

spectrum quickly became more complex as new religious groups emerged, many of which favoured a broad religious toleration, separation of church and state, and a quite radical approach to law reform. Parliament had little time, and perhaps little inclination, to energetically pursue a law reform agenda in 1642.

New issues relating to law and the courts soon emerged. Some related to the operation of the courts, others to the questionable legality of legislation without royal assent. Trained to respect and support the law, lawyers and judges found themselves in a difficult position. Many faced decisions about whether they should support parliament's or the Crown's views of legality. Although lawyers continued to draft bills and speak for or against the legality of proposed parliamentary measures, the legal profession was uncomfortable with parliament's claims to govern and legislate without the king.[45] Half of the 12 judges sided with the Crown, the other half with parliament, and those who accepted judicial appointments from parliament often did so with reservations. No earlier parliament had ever appointed judges.

A somewhat similar issue developed when both king and parliament asserted authority over the militia.[46] In 1641 parliament ordered the judges to publicise a resolution of the House of Commons that the king's commission of array was against the liberty and property of the subject. It would not be long before parliament would claim to possess all the king's governmental functions. The king attempted to continue governing, first from York and then from Oxford. He 'resolved to maintain and govern by the laws, and not by arbitrary power' and issued the standard instructions to judges leaving for assize in July 1641.[47]

Both king and parliament claimed the authority to supervise the courts and judicial proceedings. Charles was anxious to keep the courts open and the circuits functioning. Judges sympathetic to the king and many members of the House of Lords found their way to Oxford when the king summoned the courts there. The common law courts and the assizes continued to function for a while, but by 1643 the legal system was no longer operating. Several quarter sessions were interrupted or suspended. The courts were part of what Anthony Fletcher has characterised as a 'creeping paralysis' of the machinery of government.[48]

[45] The House of Commons contained 75 barrister MPs, 42 of whom would side with parliament; Douglas Brunton and DH Pennington, *Members of the Long Parliament* (Hamden, CT, Archon Books, 1968) 5.

[46] See John Marsh, *An Argument or Debate in Law: of the Great Question concerning the Militia* (London, 1642).

[47] In May, the Lord Keeper sent the Great Seal to the king at York.

[48] Anthony Fletcher, *Reform in the Provinces: The Government of Stuart England* (New Haven, Yale University Press, 1986). There were no quarter sessions held in Warwickshire in 1643, 1644 or 1645. Petty sessions continued to function in most areas (at 96, 124). Probate courts operated in London and Oxford, the former being far busier. See CJ Kitching, 'Probate during the Civil War and Interregnum, Part I' (1976) 5 *Journal of the Society of Archivists* 283. The Prerogative Court of Canterbury continued to exist, but its counterpart at York declined. See also Stephen Black, 'The Courts and Judges of Westminster Hall during the Great Rebellion, 1640–1660' (1986) 7 *Journal of Legal History* 23, 24–26, 39.

Early in 1643, parliament passed an ordinance forbidding removal of the law term to Oxford. Another put off the assizes because 'public justice … cannot be expected to be administered in a just and indifferent way' when judges are awed by military power. From January 1644 onwards, there were additional ordinances to prevent the adjournment of the law terms to Oxford. Officers in the courts of justice were commanded to take the Covenant. Persons bringing royalist messages to the Westminster judges were to be treated as spies and tried by martial law. In 1644 Charles was still issuing proclamations removing King's Bench and Exchequer to Oxford. No circuits appear to have been held between 1643 and 1646. After almost two years of vacancy, Chancery reopened in January 1644 in Westminster, sealing over 500 writs on the first day.[49]

Competition between king and parliament for control and operation of the legal system continued until Oxford surrendered to the parliamentary army. By early 1646, it was parliament not the king who was ordering the judges to go on circuit. August Bulstrode Whitelocke reported that 'the judges rode in some counties, and held the assizes, to the rejoicing of the people'.[50]

Reconstituting the judiciary was not easy. For a considerable period, there was an insufficient number of judges to operate the Westminster courts. The courts and the Inns of Court were barely functioning and would no longer function as the centre of legal culture. Litigation came to a standstill. In 1645 an ordinance disabled judges who had deserted their places. Another provided for the appointment of new judges. Though the Westminster courts and the circuits revived following parliament's victories, there was uncertainty over whether parliament could lawfully appoint new judges. How cases previously adjudicated by the abolished prerogative courts should be handled also contributed to legal uncertainty.[51]

There were also ambiguities concerning the Great Seal, which was necessary for both the authentication of many legal acts and for the original writs necessary to begin cases in the common law courts. When the Seal, which had been sent to the king, came into parliament's possession, it was broken in the presence of both Houses of Parliament. A new Great Seal was made in November of 1643 and commissioners were appointed to carry out its functions. In 1645 the commissioners were charged with selecting new judges who would then need the approval of both Houses of Parliament. Parliament asserted that it, not the king, had the right to appoint judges.[52]

[49] LJ, V, 568, 627; VI, 301–02, 390, 403; III, 163, 372; John Campbell, *Lives of the Lord Chancellors and Keepers*, 8 vols (London, John Murray 1845–69), vol III, 22.

[50] LJ, VIII, 163, 372; Whitelocke (n 42) vol II, 64. The assizes were busy in 1648 (vol II, 273, 278, 286, 287).

[51] LJ, X, 570; Black (n 48) 30–35. In 1645 Whitelocke reported a proposal to fully salary judges: Whitelocke (n 42) vol I, 519.

[52] CJ, VI, 227; LJ, VI, 301–02; VII, 570.

V. Parliament and Law Reform 1643–48

The years 1643 to 1648 saw little in the way of law reform as parliament was preoccupied with pressing military, financial and administrative matters, as well as with its complicated dealings with the king. The Court of Wards was abolished in 1646, ending the feudal obligations of many landholders. Some attention was given to clarifying Admiralty jurisdiction.[53] Justices of the peace now had to pass a political test. Only 'such as are very well affected to the Service of Parliament' would be permitted to serve. When the appeals jurisdiction of the House of Lords was contested, the lower house drafted an ordinance to restrain upper house jurisdiction in civil and criminal cases.[54]

In 1646 there was an ordinance to prevent clandestine marriage without parental consent. Committees were established for probating wills, to receive complaints about fees in Chancery and other equity courts, and regulating Chancery. A commission enabled the Master of the Rolls and the judges to hear and determine cases in Chancery. Chancery was firmly instructed not to proceed in 'any case determinable at law'.[55] In 1648 there were ordinances excluding benefit of clergy for various offences and punishing blasphemy.[56]

Parliament continued to exert control over the press, with varying degrees of success. Independents and the army attempted to undermine Presbyterian licensing of printed books and newsbooks. Ordinances designed to regulate printing and to prevent the publication of scandalous pamphlets were passed in 1643 and 1647. Parliament was determined to establish control over the press.[57]

There was an intense debate over tithes. The religious sects were vociferous in seeking abolition, believing them to be contrary to the Gospel.[58] Most ordained ministers, Anglican, Presbyterian and Independent, supported tithes as a means of supporting the ministry. Tithes were also defended by holders of 'impropriated' tithes – tithes held by laymen who had purchased monastic land. Printed petitions and tracts were also offered. Parliament was committed to maintaining tithes. Beginning in 1644, there were ordinances decreeing that tithes were to be

[53] LJ, IV, 150, 152; LJ, VII, 183; LJ, IX, 186–87, 240–41; CJ, V, 504, 523, 629. The Admiralty ordinance of 1648, largely a restatement of the 1633 agreement, was renewed four times. In 1647 there was a petition to take away Admiralty 'root and branch'. See George F Steckley, 'Merchants and the Admiralty Court during the English Revolution' (1978) 22 *American Journal of Legal History* 154, 158–60, 164, 167, 169, 171.

[54] CJ, V, 317, 374. See William Prynne, *A Plea for the Lords* (London, 1648).

[55] Whitelocke (n 42) vol II, 72, 77, 78–79.

[56] Charles Firth and R Rait, *Acts and Ordinances of the Interregnum 1642–1660*, 4 vols (London, Her Majesty's Stationery Office, 1911), vol III, 17.

[57] See Jason Peacey, *Politics and Pamphleteers during the English Civil Wars and Interregnum* (Aldershot, Ashgate, 2004) 149–55, 165–72.

[58] See *The husbandman's plea against tithes* (London, 1647); *The Country's plea against tithes* (London, 1646). The author attempted to prove this by 'God's Word and moral reason'.

'paid according to the Laws and Customs of this realm'.[59] There were additional ordinances in 1645 and 1648 requiring their payment.[60] Abolition of tithes was obviously a reform in the eyes of those who proposed it, yet it was anything but in the eyes of ordained ministers and those who supported an established church. Reform was in the eye of the beholder.

The abolition of episcopacy in 1646 had a substantial impact on parliament and the courts. Bishops were removed from the House of Lords, and the ecclesiastical courts, for centuries a feature of England's legal system, ceased to function. What institution or institutions would absorb jurisdiction over marriage, divorce, wills and testaments, tithes, defamation and moral offences? When parliament turned to legislate on what had formerly been ecclesiastical crimes, it was free to require the death penalty. Bills were introduced in 1644, 1647 and 1648 dealing with incest, adultery, fornication and drunkenness.[61] A 1648 ordinance dealt with blasphemy and heresy.[62] However, the transfer of ecclesiastical jurisdiction to alternative venues continued, and in 1653 legislation provided for a probate court covering the whole country.

VI. Radical Law Reform 1640–48

Major changes on the law reform front occurred in 1642, when a second, more radical movement emerged. I use the term 'radical' here to suggest a major departure from the then current legal regime, a different vision of a desirable legal regime and a willingness to jettison a considerable portions or even the whole of the current regime.[63] I use 'moderate' to indicate reformers who wished to introduce improvements in the existing system. Those supporting the parliamentary or

[59] Some tracts offered alternate ways of supporting the clergy. See Sir Henry Spelman, *The Larger Treatise Concerning Tithes* (London, 1647); Sir Henry Spelman, *An Answer to a question concerning the settlement or abolition of Tithes* (London 1646)). *The Ordinance for Tythes Dismounted* (London, 1645) contrasted honest 'mechanic Preachers', 'Coblers' and 'Tinkers' with a university educated ministry with their 'black cassoks' and 'lily-white hands'. Scripture determined that tithes were illegitimate (at 11, 23–25). Martin Bowne, *Tithes re-mounted and advanced by the Word of God* (London, 1646); *Certain desires for the settlement and improving of ministers means* (London, 1646).

[60] LJ, IX, 360; CJ, III, 511, 566; Firth and Rait (n 56) vol I, 567; Margaret James, 'The Political Importance of the Tithes Controversy in the English Revolution, 1640–1660' (1941) 26 *History* 1.

[61] LJ, VI, 724; CJ, V, 523, 724; Firth and Rait (n 56) vol III, 17.

[62] CJ, V, 184,188, 320; Firth and Rait (n 56) vol III, 17. Whitelocke spoke against the harshness of the ordinance: Whitelocke (n 42) vol II, 306.

[63] For discussion of the term 'radical', see JC Davis, 'Radicalism in a Traditional Society: The Evolution of Radical Thought in the English Commonwealth 1649–1660' (1982) 3 *History of Political Thought* 93; Conal Condren, *The Language of Politics in Seventeenth Century England* (London, Macmillan, 1994); Glen Burgess and Matthew Festenstein, *English Radicalism 1550–1850* (Cambridge, Cambridge University Press, 2002). For anti-Normanism, see Christopher Hill, 'The Norman Yoke' in *Puritanism and Revolution: Studies in the Interpretation of the English Revolution of the Seventeenth Century* (London, Mercury Books, 1962) 50–122; JGA Pocock, *The Ancient Constitution and the Feudal Law: A Reissue with a Retrospect* (Cambridge, Cambridge University Press, 1987); Janelle Greenberg, *The Radical Face of the Ancient Constitution: St Edward's 'Law' in Early Modern England* (Cambridge, Cambridge

Crown measures are treated as moderates. There were now two law reform movements.

Radical law reformers fell into three overlapping groups: the Levellers, the fast-growing religious sects and the New Model Army. Most of those who favoured radical reform were outside parliament, while most supporters of law reform in parliament fell into the moderate camp. Moderate reformers focused on the expense and delays in the courts, and did not have a transformative vision of the English polity or society.

VII. The Levellers

Leveller supporters wished for a far more egalitarian society than then existed. The franchise would be greatly expanded to come fairly close to universal male suffrage, and there would be equality before the law with no special privileges for the aristocracy.[64]

Anti-Normanism was at the heart of many Leveller law reform proposals. Levellers believed that the Norman Conquest of 1066 had brought with it tyrant kings, feudal tenures, the common law and the legal profession, and they had no use for any of them. Instead of the highly centralised Westminster-dominated courts that ensured legal uniformity across England, they favoured local courts in every hundred that would end 'all differences arising in that hundred'.[65] Controversies should be ended by two, three or 12 men of the neighbourhood 'as they were' before the introduction of common lawyers and judges. Their vision was feared by those who denounced 'cantonisation' of law. Levellers looked back to the pre-Norman, Saxon polity for inspiration, a polity that featured local courts and brief trials conducted in English, not law French. The law would be brief, so that all suits 'may be more clear and certain in the issues, and not so tedious nor chargeable in the proceedings as now'.[66] Levellers contributed substantially to the anti-lawyer sentiment that was becoming increasingly strident. They attacked lawyers for their greed, for their inclination to encourage long delays and for keeping legal costs high. Lawyers were 'locusts' who swarmed 'over the land, devouring, and impoverishing' all.[67]

Perhaps because of the many legal difficulties and frequent imprisonment of their leader John Lilburne, the Levellers emphasised reforming criminal procedure.

University Press, 2001); J Sommerville, 'Ancient Constitution Reassessed' in Malcolm Smuts (ed), *The Stuart Court and Europe, Essays in Politics and Political Change* (Cambridge, Cambridge, University Press, 1996).

[64] Unlike the Diggers or True Levellers, the Levellers did not support the abolition of private property. See GE Aylmer (ed), *The Levellers in the English Revolution* (Ithaca, Cornell University Press, 1975).

[65] *Regall Tyrannie Discovered* (London, 1647) 25. Members of the legal profession tended to see continuity rather than a sharp break. See Pocock (n 63).

[66] *The Humble Petition to Parliament*, September 1648, in Kenyon (n 8) 307.

[67] Aylmer (n 64) 60.

They favoured legal counsel for criminal defendants and the two-witness rule in felony cases. There should be protections against self-incrimination and no one should be questioned or 'punished for doing of that against which no law hath been provided'. All trials should be jury trials.[68]

Punishments should be proportioned to offences 'so that men's lives and estates might not be forfeited upon trivial and slight occasions'.[69] There should be no capital punishment 'but upon … weighty and considerable causes'.[70] The Levellers were also advocates for ending imprisonment for debt and proposed that real property be eligible for payment of debt. They were also steady supporters of religious toleration and opponents of tithes.[71]

Levellers were innovative in their abundant use of petitions, often very long ones. Their leaders, and particularly Lilburne, also employed print venues liberally to bring Leveller views to the public, particularly to the Londoners and lower ranks of the army where they found supporters.[72] 'The Remonstrance of many thousands of free people of England' (September 1649) was reported to have had 98,000 signatures. News books also helped circulate Leveller views, and so did the wearing of green ribbons to indicate support.

In 1647 and 1648, when Levellers attempted to influence parliament and the army, they incurred the ire of both. Parliament was sympathetic neither to their egalitarian views nor to their law reform proposals. When Leveller ideas began to penetrate the army's lower ranks, army grandees, such as Oliver Cromwell and Henry Ireton, sought to reduce their influence. A Leveller mutiny in 1649 was crushed and virtually ended the movement. Lilburne, who was banished in 1652, drifted into Quaker circles. The Leveller reform programme envisioned a simpler, more egalitarian society rather than the more complex market-oriented society that was developing in England. While moderates and others valued continuity in laws and institutions, Levellers were among the groups who emphasised the need for a sharp break from the then current law and current legal institutions.

The Diggers or True Levellers were a far smaller, shorter-lived and more radical group led by Gerrard Winstanley. Aside from the abolition of private property, the Digger position differed little from some of the other religious sects that were developing during this period. Driven largely by a religious vision, Winstanley and a few followers took over common land for cultivation.[73] Like the Levellers,

[68] *Humble Petition* (n 66) 307.

[69] ibid 322.

[70] The Large Petition of March 1647. The Second Agreement included capital punishment for 'forceful destruction' of the Agreement. See *Leveller Manifestos of the Puritan Revolution*, Donald Wolf (ed) (New York, Thomas Nelson, 1944) 140, 240, 302.

[71] *Mercurius Populi*, 11 November 1647. However, see RB Seaberg, 'The Norman Conquest and the Argument from Continuity' (1981) 24 *Historical Journal* 791.

[72] Philip Baker suggests the Levellers were influenced by London's participatory civic culture in 'London's Liberty in Chains Discovered: The Levellers, the Civic Past and Popular Protest in Civil War London' (2013) 76 *Huntington Library Quarterly* 559.

[73] Winstanley believed if large landholders were relieved of their feudal obligations to the king, the common people should not have to make comparable payments to lords of the manor. Gerard Winstanley, *Appeal to the House of Commons* (1649) in GH Sabine (ed), *Works* (Ithaca, Cornell University

Diggers believed that the Norman Conquest had brought with it the common law and the common lawyers who had made English laws into 'yoaks and manacles'. The law enslaved the poor and made the earth, which should have been the common treasury of all, private. What remained of the Norman Yoke should be 'thrown down and plucked up'. 'There shall be no Tyrant Kings, Lords of Manors, tything Priests, oppressing Lawyers, exacting Landlords.' The 'Righteous Law shall be the Rule for everyone, and the judge of all men'. Everything must be reformed. Parliament should not just 'put new wine in old bottles'. 'As the government must be new, so must the laws'.[74]

Unlike the Levellers, Winstanley would have abolished juries. Judges, elected for a single year, would not be permitted to interpret the laws. Disputes were to be handled locally and litigants were, if possible, to settle their differences without legal professionals. Lawyers came under special criticism as they 'under pretense of justice, administer the will of the Conquerors'.[75] Anyone who took money for legal services should be condemned to death. The common law should be replaced with a well-publicised 'short and pithy' code. The death penalty would be abolished for theft, but retained for treason, rape, buying and selling, and for administration of the law.[76] Most of these ideas were shared with the Levellers. The Diggers, who were active during the late 1640s and early 1650s, had no support in parliament. Although suppressed in 1650, their tracts continued to appear. Despite their small numbers, the Diggers produced a substantial number of reform tracts and pamphlets.

A considerably larger but more amorphous force favouring radical changes in the English legal system is to be found in the growing number of religious sects. Their conception of the nature of the church led them to be strong supporters of religious toleration and enemies of tithes and an established church. Because only those who had had the appropriate religious experience were eligible to become members of the church, a church established by parliament that included both the saved and non-saved was unacceptable. The state should exert no coercive power over religious belief and practice. Scripture played a huge role in their conception of law, though various sects differed over the extent to which Scripture should determine English law. Some favoured the complete replacement of then current law, while others felt that it should conform to Scripture as much as possible. Since Scripture demanded restitution, most opposed capital punishment for theft and insisted on the two-witness rule for conviction of capital crimes on the same

Press, 1941) 308. Digger views came to the attention of historians in the 1930s, when Marxist historians sought anti-bourgeois antecedents. See Blair Worden. 'The Levellers in History and Memory c 1660–1960' in Michael Mendle (ed), *The Putney Debates of 1647, The Army, the Levellers and the English State* (Cambridge, Cambridge University Press, 2001) 256–82.

[74] Gerrard Winstanley, *The New Years Gift for Parliament and Army* (London, 1650) in Sabine (n 73) 358, 535.

[75] Winstanley, 'Fire in the Bush' in Sabine (n 73) 463, 464, 468.

[76] Winstanley, 'Law of Freedom' in Sabine (n 73) 590, 591–94, 595, 599.

grounds. Many, citing the Old Testament, insisted on a moral regime that would punish adultery, sodomy and blasphemy with death, and some supported the death penalty for perjury.

However, looking to Scripture was not entirely new. As early as 1573, Archbishop John Whitgift, who was anything but a radical, remarked that 'it is now disputed at every table, whether the magistrate be of necessity bound to the judicial of Moses, so that he may not punish otherwise than is there prescribed', a view that he considered absurd and seditious.[77] Sixteenth-century Anabaptists in Munster included blasphemy, adultery and disobedience to parents as capital offences. Many sectarians, unlike Anglicans, Presbyterians and Independents who insisted on an educated clergy, supported lay preaching and a few allowed women to preach. Parliament responded with a bill forbidding preaching by non-ordained ministers.

Although the Quakers, one of the few sects to remain in existence after the Restoration, were unusual in their refusal of 'hat worship' that reinforced social distinctions and in allowing a greater role for women, they shared much of the radical law reform programme. Priests perverted Scripture, as lawyers perverted the law. George Fox, a Quaker leader, opposed the use of Latin and law French in connection with the law. Lawyers and unjust laws should be abolished as abominations to the Lord. They opposed tithes, but did not support a religious code based on the Old Testament. Although Fox's many tracts ensured that their views were fairly well known, Quakers were frequently reviled. The Quakers were active during the 1650s and beyond.[78]

The Fifth Monarchy Men, millenarians looking forward to the end of the world, focused on law while waiting for that end. Sharing the anti-Normanism of many radicals, they condemned lawyers as 'compleat Knaves' or the 'antichrist's State-Army'[79] and rejected law French. People should plead their own causes. God's law should replace existing law. In 1654 Marchmont Needham's newsbook *The Observator* proclaimed that the Fifth Monarchists wished to bring in a 'catalogue of old dreaming Rabbies' and 'justle out Coke and Littleton'.[80] Like the Levellers, Fifth Monarchists favoured localised justice and deplored the system that allowed

[77] Quoted in BS Capp, *The Fifth Monarchy Men* (London, Faber, 1972) 169, from John Whitgift, *Works*, J Ayre (ed) (1851–53), vol I, 270, 272; vol III, 576.

[78] Michael Rogers, 'Quakerism and the Law in Revolutionary England' (1987) 22 *Canadian Journal of History* 149. See also George Fox, *An Instruction to Judges and Lawyers* (London, 1657) 20, 29. Ranters were a much-reviled group who were thought to have embraced antinomian beliefs that freed its members from the constraints of both Scriptural and secular law. See Christopher Hill, *The World Turned Upside Down: Radical Ideas during the English Revolution* (London, Temple Smith, 1972); Andrew Brastock, *Radical Religion in Cromwell's England* (London, IB Tauris, 2011) 85–88. JC Davis has suggested that the Ranters were a mythical group: *Fear, Myth and History: The Ranters and the Historian* (Cambridge, Cambridge University Press, 1986).

[79] John Rogers, *Ohel* (London, 1653) 222–23.

[80] Quoted in Capp (n 77) 162.

lawyers to enrich themselves by moving suits from one court to another. They were particularly concerned with laws relating to debt.[81] However, unlike most radicals, the Fifth Monarchists were not reluctant to use force, and during 1650s and 1660s attempted uprisings that were crushed.

Radical views began to impact the parliamentary army in 1647 and the New Model Army quickly became important in transmitting law reform ideas.[82] Although most army chaplains were not radicals or members of religious sects, the army provided the more radical among them with opportunities to preach radical messages.[83] An early indication of army interest in law reform can be found in *The Soldier's Catechism of 1644*, which called for the regulation of 'our courts' that in the past had been 'the Seats of iniquity and unrighteousness'. In August 1647 the *Heads of the Proposal*, a document combining both moderate and radical proposals, was drafted by the army 'grandees' and delivered to parliament. It recommended that 'the ruler and course of law, and the officers of it, may be so reduced and reformed as that all suits and questions of right be more clear and certain … and not so tedious and chargeable in the proceedings as now'. It proposed the two-witness rule in capital cases, no questioning that resulted in self-incrimination and changes to the law dealing with debtors.[84]

Divisions within the army became more visible during the Putney Debates of October 1647.[85] The debates opened with the presentation of the Leveller's *First Agreement*, a document recommending 'that in laws made or to be made every person may be bound alike, and that no tenure, estate, charter, degree, birth, or place to confer any exemption from the ordinary course of legal proceedings'.[86] *The Case of the Army*, another publication of 1647, advocated the reformation of legal proceedings and the abolition of imprisonment for debt, and called for a committee of 'conscientious persons … to reduce the number of laws to one volume'. It also propose hundreds courts and speedy trials.[87] Radical views, which tended to find support from the lower ranks, were contested by Cromwell, Ireton and the higher-ranking officers. However, Colonel Rainsborowe, a rare radical officer, urged the army in the direction of radicalism. England's good laws, he argued, had their origin in infringements on the power of kings and lords. Radical ideas and

[81] John Rogers, *Sagris* (London, 1653) 49–51.

[82] Mark Kishlansky suggests that radicalisation occurred in 1647. See Mark Kishlansky, *The Rise of The New Model Army* (Cambridge, Cambridge University Press, 1979).

[83] See Anne Laurence, *Parliamentary Army Chaplains, 1642–1651* (Woodbridge, Boydell Press, 1990); Leo Solt, *Saints in Arms* (Palo Alto, Stanford University Press, 1959).

[84] Robert Ram, *The Soldiers Catechism* (London, 1644) 9 (reprinted in 1645); ASP Woodhouse, *Puritanism and Liberty, Being the Army Debates* (London, JM Dent, 1938) 99. The two-witness rule was required in civil and canon law.

[85] See Michael Mendle (ed), *The Putney Debates of 1647: The Army, The Levellers, and the English State* (Cambridge, Cambridge University Press, 2001).

[86] Kenyon (n 8) 310.

[87] Woodhouse (n 84) 435n.

anti-monarchical sentiment grew in the army between 1646 and 1648.[88] But pressure from the army, whether radical or moderate, was not well received by parliament, and radical reform measures did not find a sympathetic parliamentary audience.

VIII. Print and Law Reform 1640–48

The decade of the 1640s brought with it an enormous change in the opportunities for publishing. It has been estimated that some 600–700 items had been printed during the 1630s, about 900 in 1640 alone, over 2,000 in 1641 and over 4,000 in 1642. The year 1642 witnessed a greater number than any year before the beginning of the eighteenth century.[89] This stream of publications offered enormous opportunities to present ideas to a wider public and to pressure parliament for reforms. The arena of law reform could no longer be limited to an elite composed of the government, lawyers, judges, members of parliament, aristocracy and gentry, but now included the reading public. The critiques emanating from the Levellers, new religious groups and the Fifth Monarchy Men came from a different class of people and appealed to a broader spectrum of English society.

The impact of printing on early modern culture and the concept of the political sphere have been much discussed by political and literary scholars. We have become more aware of both the importance and the limitations of the licensing system. While hostile to the licensing regime dominated by Archbishop Laud, parliament and successive revolutionary regimes supported licensing. The number of items published appears to have been greatest when control was at its weakest. Some items appeared with a licence, others without. Charges of seditious libel again became common.

Printed newsbooks that dealt with domestic as well as foreign affairs emerged during this period, allowing many to follow parliamentary business and the successes and failures of both royal and parliamentary armies. Some newsbooks were supporters of the king, while others were controlled by parliament, the Levellers or the army. Some had a fairly wide distribution, while others circulated primarily in London and the surrounding areas. Some had long runs, while others managed only a few issues.[90]

Petitions were not new in 1640, but now became common and were often printed. Hundreds of petitions, both printed and unprinted, were sent from local governments, grand juries and, later, the army and groups such as the Levellers.

[88] Ian Gentles, *The New Model Army in England, Ireland and Scotland, 1645–1653* (Oxford, Blackwell, 1992) 206–19.

[89] Cressy (n 36) 202, 293. Donald Veall suggests that George Thomason collected approximately 22,000 pamphlets; Donald Veall, *The Popular Movement for Law Reform 1640–1660* (Oxford, Oxford University Press, 1970) 74.

[90] Jason Peacey, *Politics and Pamphleteers: Propaganda during the English Civil Wars and Interregnum* (Aldershot, Ashgate, 2004) 129–45.

Addressed to parliament, they publicised grievances and/or proposed remedies. Petitions for law reform were addressed to parliament since it was assumed that law reform was in its hands.

Parliament's endorsement of the publication of Coke's *Second Part of the Institutes in* 1642 and the printing of the Third and Fourth Parts in 1644[91] suggests that parliament was largely supportive of Coke's view of the law. In 1642 William Lambarde's work was presented to and approved by the House of Commons. Its lengthy title, *The Courts of Justice Corrected and amended. Or The Corrupt Lawyer untrust, lasht, and quascht. Wherein the Partial Iudge, Counsellour, Great Mover, whispering informer, Favourite the Bar are full displayed, convicted and directed*, indicates its reformist content.[92]

An increasing number of law books were published in English. Among them were the *Reports* of Sir Henry Hobart and William Noy's *Treatise of the Principal Grounds and Maximes of the Lawes*.[93] There were new volumes to assist justices of the peace[94] as well as items such as Bacon's *Ordinances … for the better and more regular administration of Justice in the Chancery*. Books to aid legal professionals continued to grow in number and would, at least in part, compensate for the decay of the Inns of Court which had been the centre of English legal culture.

Though relatively few tracts focused on law reform between 1640 and 1648, those that did were most likely to come from Leveller, radical religious and army circles. The years between 1649 and 1659 would see many more publications on the subject of law reform. There were surprisingly few publications dealing with Star Chamber and High Commission, especially compared to the huge number dealing with the trials of Strafford and Laud or the issue of religious toleration.

Some reform topics received a good deal of attention, while others did not. At least 10 pamphlets demanded reform of imprisonment for debt. Many discussed the pros and cons of abolishing tithes. Anti-Norman themes were common. John Hare, the author of three anti-Norman tracts, demanded that 'all Laws and Usages introduced from Normandy … [be] abolished, and a Supply made from St. Edward's Laws, or the Civil, and that the Laws be divested of their French Rags (as King James of worthy Memory once royally motioned) and restored unto the English or Latin tongue'.[95] This kind of anti-Norman sentiment was typically accompanied by a vigorous denunciation of the legal profession.

[91] The Third and Fourth Parts of the *Institutes* were reprinted in 1648.

[92] Wilfred Prest, 'William Lambarde, Elizabethan Law Reform, and Early Stuart Politics' (1995) 34 *Journal of British Studies* 464.

[93] William Noy's *Treatise Principall Grounds and Maxims* (London, 1641) was reprinted in 1642 and 1651, and several times during the Restoration. His *The Compleat Lawyer: or A Treatise concerning Tenures and Estates* (London, 1656) was also reissued several times.

[94] *A Manual or Analecta* drawn from Lambarde, Crompton and Dalton appeared in 1641, 1642 and 1648. There were also handbooks for constables in 1641 and reprintings of Sheppard's volume in 1650, 1652 and 1654.

[95] See also John Hare, *England's Proper and only way, or the Normane Yoke once more encased* (London, 1648); John Hare, *Plaine English to our wilul bearers with Normanism* (London, 1647); John Hare, *St Edwards ghost, or Anti Normanism* (London, 1647).

Many law reform tracts favouring codification of the laws pointed to the example of Edward the Confessor's codification of the Saxon laws. Edward's example was often employed by those favouring a wholesale repudiation of the common law, but was also used by some moderates.

If many publications attacked the legal profession, others came to its defence or mixed criticism with support.[96] John Cooke, a lawyer who would later support the abolition of the monarchy,[97] both defended the legal profession and pointed to the problems of the legal system. Citing the dangers of precipitous reform, he referred favourably to James I's support 'for cutting off superfluous branches in Law Proceedings'. He defended the legal profession, blaming overly litigious clients for much of the legal profession's improper behaviour. But he also castigated lawyers who got 'more by the corruptions and delays of the Law, than by the Law itself', recommending limitations on their numbers and fees. He reprimanded lawyers who push 'themselves into parliamentary committee chairmanships'. Like many common lawyers, he thought Chancery ought to be limited to breaches of trust, fraud, deceit and accident, and opposed its practice of re-examining common law judgments. He opposed imprisonment for debt and benefit of clergy, and favoured land registration. Since the legal profession could not be counted on for law reform, he charged parliament to correct 'all abuses in Courts of Justice, and utterly breake the necke, and cut the very heart-strings of all fraud, deceit … and injustice whatsoever'. He ended his pamphlet on a hopeful note, saying 'methinks I see Justice which was heretofore fled into Heaven coming downe apace upon Earth amongst us'.[98] In a later pamphlet he declared 'I am for a Reform in Courts of Justice and not an extirpation' – it must not come to a 'Root and Branch' extirpation.[99]

Some reform publications featured a class-based analysis of the law and its problems. We have noted the anti-aristocratic and anti-hierarchical views of the Levellers and the appeal to the downtrodden voiced by Diggers and some religious radicals. Tracts opposing imprisonment for debt expressed greater sympathy for poor debtors than rich ones.[100] Other tracts pointed to the dangers of the vulgar and uneducated who were upsetting traditional social divisions and deferential practices. The fourteenth-century *Mirrour of Justice*, published in 1642 and again in 1646, vindicated the common law from 'aspersion' in 'these distracted times' and from the 'meaner sort of people' who believe that the laws were 'built upon a sandy foundation and traduce the common laws of England to bring the professors

[96] W L, *The Courts of Justice corrected and amended, or the Corrupt Lawyer* (London, 1642); Benjamin Nicholson, *The Lawyers Bane, or the Lawes reformation, and a new model* (London, 1647).

[97] John Cooke, *Monarchy, no creature of God's Making* (London, 1652).

[98] John Cooke, *The Vindication of the Professors & Profession of the Law* (London, 1646) Preface to the Reader, 2, 3, 5, 8, 22, 29; reprinted in 1652.

[99] *Unem Necessarium* (London, 1648) 65–69. See also *A Looking Glass for all proud, ambitious, covetous and corrupt Lawyers* (London, 1646); *The Malady and Remedy of Vexations and unjust Arrest and Actions* (London, 1646) 3, 5 expressed extreme hostility to attorneys and solicitors.

[100] *Imprisonment of mens bodyes for Debt* (London, 1641); Thomas Grantham, *A motion against Imprisonment for Debt* (London, 1642).

thereof unto contempt'. Nevertheless, the publication admitted that such negative views were 'nourished' because the law had been kept from public view and written in law French.[101]

The attack on capital punishment for theft now became a major feature of the reform program. The first organised demand was to be found in the Levellers' *Large Petition of March* 1647. Hugh Peters, a radical Independent clergymen, opposed the death penalty for theft and insisted on a two-witness requirement for felony. Peters stressed the importance of 'quick justice' and offered the example of Holland, where justice could be obtained 'as often and as naturally as their Cowes give milke'.[102]

If some law reform publications focused on particular reforms, such as imprisonment for debt or ending capital punishment for theft, a few offered more wide-ranging critiques of the legal system and/or proposals for its reform.[103] Benjamin's Nicholson's *The Lawyers Bane* claimed that the laws 'cry aloud for Reformation, a thing formerly often attempted without success' and proposed a new model of English law to be developed by an impartial commission chosen by the king and parliament. The law, a combination of common, civil and statute law, would be 'new', 'just', 'plain and easy and free from all dilemmas and ambiguities'. Written in plain and familiar English, it would eliminate the law's multiplicities and confusion. Local courts would provide justice at the people's 'own doors'. County courts would 'absolutely and sovereignly' handle all cases, except treason. Judges riding circuit who frightened people with their 'pomp' would no longer be necessary. Nor would attorneys and solicitors, since most parties would plead their own causes. Men of the long robe who darkened the sense and letter of the law would be eliminated from places of trust. Chancery, which had been erected to mitigate the strictness of the common law, had become 'a great burden and oppression: and should be eliminated'. The complexities of England property law would be replaced with one simple form of land tenure and the abolition of entails. Nicholson favoured reformation 'root and branch'. If only the branches were 'cut and lopped', they would 'spring and put out again, if the roote be still continued'.[104]

Others saw reform as restoration. There were those who sought to restore the lost Saxon legal system and others who looked back only a few decades. One of

[101] The quotation is from the English translation of 1646, Preface to the Reader. The 1642 edition was in French.

[102] Hugh Peters, *A Word for the Armie* (London, 1647) 12. Small cases would be decided in the parish. Peters favoured a land registry and opposed imprisonment for debt (at 11, 13). See also Robert Zaller, 'The Debate on Capital Punishment during the English Revolution' (1987) 31 *American Journal of Legal History* 126.

[103] *Questions propounded, or Quaeres, concerning remedies and taking away extreme and unnecessary charges, expenses, and troubles and long delays in just causes and suits in courts of Equity* (London, 1647). For an ironic anti-reform tract, see *Proposals of the Committee for regulating the laws* (London, 1647). It characterized Chancery as 'the Court of Iniquity' and ridiculed the idea of individuals pleading their own causes (at 5, 6).

[104] Benjamin Nicholson, *The Lawyers Bane or, the Lawes Reformation, and New Modell* (London, 1647) 1–4, 6, 8, 9–10.

the latter advised that the current parliament should follow 'The old Parliamentary Road, to the Path of the Predecessors … and make the Law run in their right Channels'. It should retrench excessive fees and find remedies for poor clients, who should not be made to suffer by 'monstrous Delays, that one may go from Tropick to another, and cross the Equinoctial twenty times, before his Suit be done'.[105] Those who looked to restoration might advocate either a total rejection of the then current political and legal system or a reformed common law regime.

An Experimental Essay Touching the Reformation of the Lawes of England was unusual in proposing that major reforms could be accomplished without parliament. Its author argued that although the common law had often been rectified by statutes causing a multiplication of laws, a better remedy would be reforms in land tenure that would both 'abolish and make void a great part of the Common Laws' and remove the 'grievance and burthensomeness of innumerable intricate laws'. The Court of Wards could then be eliminated and with it the need for an office to record land transactions. Tithes would be abolished, and wills, administered by 'conscientious men', could facilitate decisions in a 'short time'. Trespasses or wrongs of word or deed would be determined locally by 'conscientious men' with the power to make parties appear. Brief and plainly worded legal documents would be entered in all parishes and towns. There would be no need for common pleas, Chancery or duchy courts. As for the content of the laws, there would be no capital punishments except for treason, rebellion or murder. No lives should be lost for trivial matters, though felonies would require four fold restitution or work.[106]

England should replace its 'vast Body of the Law' with 'a few plain brief Lawes, like a new Magna Charta' printed 'in a Table or Little book'. The best way to reform the law without disturbance was to reduce it to 'first Principles, or Primitive Order'. Although the author recognised that his proposals would overturn most existing law and legal institutions, he nevertheless thought the 'roots and foundations of Law' were 'very good'. Prior to instituting reforms, 'a short draught' should be sent to foreign countries requesting comments on the 'Excellencies and Inconveniences' of their own laws. When the draft and comments were compared and amended, England would be in a position to have the best commonwealth 'than ever was in the world'. The author was optimistic that 'all this could be accomplished without any acts of parliament', and 'without any great trouble to any Body', by commissions at 'small charge' in a quarter of a year.[107]

There were obviously very different views on how much time and effort would be required to reform England's laws and whether reform should be limited to clearing away the unnecessary recent growths or should uproot the law 'root and branch'. If parliament had been inclined to implement the reforms advocated in printed media, it would have been faced with many contradictory proposals.

[105] *England's Teares* (1644), in *Harleian Miscellany*, 8 vols (London, 1744–46), vol VIII, 247.
[106] *An Experimental Essay Touching the Lawes of England* (London, 1648) 1, 2, 3, 5.
[107] ibid 6.

IX. English Law Reform and the New England Colonies

Little attention has been given to the similarities between English mid-century radical reformers and the emerging law of the New England colonies, aside from the insufficiently known study of GB Warden.[108] Brief law codes, demanded by Levellers and religious radicals, were a common feature of the New England colonies. New England codes, some of them introduced before the rise of English radical movements, tended to be short, easy to understand and written in the English language.

Merchants and Puritan clergymen appear to have played a significant role in the transmission of information about colonial legal developments. John Cotton's *An Abstract of the Lawes of New England* was published in England in 1641, as was his *The Powering out of the Seven Vials* (1642), which advocated the introduction of the Mosaic laws.[109] Hugh Peters, a vocal Independent minister who left England for New England in 1635, spent time in Sayebrooke, established by Puritan Lords Saye and Sele and Brooke. He was also active in Massachusetts, where he served on a committee to develop a law code and defended Massachusetts against the more radical Anne Hutchinson. Sometime after his return to England in 1641 as agent for the Bay Colony, Peters, who was characterised as the 'Vicar Generall and Metropolitane of the Independents both in New and Old England', would offer some of the laws and legal practices he encountered in New England when he became a member of the Hale Commission for law reform.[110] Henry Vane the Younger was another prominent transatlantic Puritan. He lived in New England between 1635 and 1637, becoming Governor of the Massachusetts Bay Colony. On returning to England, he became an active member of parliament supporting the

[108] GB Warden, 'Law Reform in England and New England, 1620–1660' (1978} 35 *William and Mary Quarterly* 668. Warden argues that the colonies implemented most of the law reforms sought by English law reformers. See also Edgar J McManus, *Law and Liberty in Early New England: Criminal Justice and Due Process, 1629–1692* (Amherst, University of Massachusetts Press, 1993); Richard Ross, 'The Career of Puritan Jurisprudence' (2008) 26 *Law and History Review* 227.

[109] Cotton's *Abstract* was reprinted in 1655 by the Fifth Monarchist William Aspinwall, who praised the code as 'surpassing all existing municipal laws and statutes'. He praised its capital penalties for blasphemy, idolatry, witchcraft, adultery, incest, sodomy and profaning the Sabbath, and the two-witness or confession standard for criminal convictions. Scripture provided the 'right rules of judgment in all causes both Civill and Criminal' (Preface to the Reader). See also John Cotton, *The Powring out of the Seven Vials* (London, 1642) 21 (reprinted in 1645). See also *The Capital Laws of New England, as they Stand Now in Force* (Boston, 1643); *The Book of General Laws and Liberties* (Cambridge, MA, 1648); *New Haven's Settling … and some Lawes for Government* (London, 1656) 12–13, 17 provided that the Mosaic laws relating to morals could not be altered. No capital punishments were permitted without two witnesses or its equivalent.

[110] See Carla Gordina Pestano, 'Hugh Peters' in *Oxford Dictionary of National Biography*. For Peters as a leading Independent in England and New England, see Thomas Edwards, *Second Part of Gangrena* (London, 1646) 61. *The Perfect Diurnal* in August 1645 wrote that Peters as an army chaplain rode 'rank to rank with a Bible in one hand and a pistol in another exhorting men to do their duty' (at 848). Peters became a supporter of Cromwell.

war party. He was a defender of religious toleration and supported Rhode Island's charter in 1641.

First developed in 1641, the Massachusetts *Body of Liberties* offered many of the provisions demanded by English radicals. There were provisions preventing vexatious suits and fraudulent conveyances. There was no imprisonment for debt, and litigants pleaded their causes without counsel. Its authors assumed the institutions of grand and petty juries, but allowed for a choice between jury and bench trials. Capital crimes, each supported by Scripture, included murder, adultery, blasphemy, witchcraft and bearing false witness if it resulted in death.[111]

However, the colonists did not make use of anti-Norman themes, there being little need or inclination to formally reject the complexities of England's feudal land law or the highly technical rules of the common law courts. Colonial law was simpler and the distribution of property was more egalitarian. Instead of primogeniture, most New England colonies adopted the Scriptural double portion for the eldest and equal distribution to both male and female heirs. Several colonies permitted both real and personal property to be liable for satisfying debts. Massachusetts, Plymouth and Connecticut had registries for deeds and conveyances. Probate administration was decentralised. Massachusetts had justices of the peace with roughly the same powers as in England. It adopted some writs, but was more sympathetic to litigants who had mistakenly chosen the wrong writ.[112] Massachusetts developed county courts that combined law and equity with appeals to the Court of Assistants or the General Court. The New England colonies did not follow the highly technical rules of pleading and several encouraged arbitration for settling disputes.[113]

Anti-lawyer sentiment was pervasive. Massachusetts forbade the taking of fees for legal advice for a decade and later forbade lawyers from sitting as deputies in the General Court. Colonists typically pleaded their own causes. Massachusetts judges were either elected or appointed by the legislature. With the exception of trials for felony, cases were usually decided by magistrates without legal training, employing a non-jury summary justice or by arbitration. Only felony trials required juries. Legal procedure was closer to that of England's courts leet

[111] *Massachusetts Body of Liberties* (1641).

[112] William Nelson, *The Common Law in Colonial America*, 3 vols (Oxford, Oxford University Press, 2008), vol I, 49, 71, 73–74.

[113] Rhode Island, West Jersey and North Carolina embraced juries. Massachusetts Bay colony and New Haven did not, preferring summary procedures by magistrates. New Haven magistrates wished to replace English laws with the 'judicial laws of God, as they were delivered by Moses' and the biblically sanctioned two-witness rule. New Englanders were more interested in confession and repentance than punishment. J Murrin, 'Magistrates, Sinners, and a Precarious Liberty: Trial by Jury in Seventeenth Century New England' in D Hall, J Murrin and T Tate (eds), *Saints and Revolutionaries: Essays in Early American History* (New York, Norton, 1984) 152–206, at 175, 188; Mark Cahn, 'Punishment, Discretion and the Codification of Prescribed Penalties in Colonial Massachusetts' (1989) 33 *America Journal of Legal History* 107.

and baron and borough courts than to those of the common law courts.[114] Many of the same or similar provisions would be included in the tracts of the radical English reformers.

New England colonists engaged in what Warden has called an 'orgy of code making'. Plymouth adopted a code in 1636, Massachusetts in 1641 and 1648, Rhode Island in 1650 and New Haven in 1655. The Old Testament exerted a powerful influence on these codes, most of which rejected capital punishment for theft and adopted the Scripturally prescribed capital punishments for adultery, sodomy and blasphemy.[115] There was no death penalty for poaching, fence breaking or thefts over a shilling in value. Most prescribed the two-witness requirement in criminal cases.[116] However, unlike English radicals, religious toleration was not on the colonial agenda; only the Rhode Island colony adopted religious toleration.

Warden suggests that the New England emigrants were probably familiar with and influenced by the outpouring of England's radical tracts. New England colonists, he argues, were more successful in adopting England's law reform proposals than were the English themselves. These proposals, he writes, were more likely to fall on fertile soil in New England than in England. However, one should point out that it was easier for the colonists to adopt some of these practices because their social and political institutions were not well entrenched and because distance prevented close supervision from England. Nor were New England laws treated as hostile to the common law. New England efforts to adopt Scriptural norms did not require the rejection of a pre-existing criminal law regime. Starting from scratch rather than altering a long-standing and much-cherished legal tradition made it easier to establish colonial law and institutions.

But we should not simply assume that New England colonists consciously shaped their law and legal institutions according to the specifications of English reformers as Warden suggests. Many colonial developments were already being put in place before the deluge of radical pamphlets. The commonalities between New England legal developments and the proposals of English radical reforms cannot be ignored, even if a causal relationship cannot be established. While it may not be possible to show either direct influence of English radicals on New England law-makers or New England colonial law and legal institutions on English radicals, it should be obvious that both developed from a common religious and cultural environment.

[114] GB Warden suggests that the Rhode Island Civil Code was heavily influenced by civil law as practised in Scotland and the Netherlands, as well as by Scripture. See GB Warden, 'The Rhode Island Civil Code of 1647' in Hall, Murrin and Tate (n 113) 138–51. Edward Billing, a brewer, drafted the first laws of West New Jersey; see Veall (n 89) 11.

[115] *New Haven's Settling in New England and some laws for government* (London, 1656) 17, 22–25. The Massachusetts *Body of Libertie* (1641) included the right to bail, the right against cruel and unusual punishment, and the right to a jury trial.

[116] Murrin (n 113) 152–206. For New Haven, see Gail S Marcus, 'Due Execution of the Rule of Righteousness; Criminal Procedure New Haven Town Colony 1638–1658' in Hall, Murrin and Tate (n 113) 99–137. The death penalty for adultery was adopted in Virginia in 1610 and in Massachusetts in 1631, 1641 and 1648. No Massachusetts jury ever convicted for adultery after 1644.

X. Conclusion

Major changes in the legal system had taken place between 1640 and 1642, the most dramatic being the end of the conciliar courts and the trials of leading Crown servants and judges. Between 1643 and 1648, in contrast, there were only a few minor law reform measures initiated in parliament, a body now largely devoted to governing, financing and supplying a war effort, religious reform, negotiation with the king, and concern with the rise of religious and political radicalism. These concerns were expressed in a deluge of pamphlets. Until the Crown's military defeat, Crown and parliament competed for control of the legal system, both claiming to have legitimate authority and both claiming to be the protector of liberty, property and the law. From the point of view of law reformers, little had been accomplished between 1643 and 1648. Radical law reform sentiment was largely expressed outside parliament. Few, if any, radical proposals were 'reforms' in the eyes of parliament. Nevertheless, we hear of an early 1648 grievance committee that included 'reforming courts of justice, and proceedings in law', and concern with legacies and administrations.[117]

The year 1648 would bring major changes to the structure of parliament and eventually to the nation. Pride's Purge, the forceful military expulsion of parliament's more conservative and often Presbyterian members, reduced that body to a relatively small remnant of the parliament that had assembled in 1640. The purge initiated a period in which the army would play a central role in the fate of parliaments, the fate of the king and the fate of successive governments.[118]

The purge of parliament was soon followed by the trial of Charles I, the first and only king to be put on trial for his life. The trial would require bypassing normal legal procedure and the creation of a new institution, the High Court of Justice, whose legality was contested by the king and many others. As an innovation without legal precedent, it led to an important rift in the parliamentary class as well as the broader public. The creation of the commission to try the king proved difficult and esteemed members of the legal profession, such as Bulstrode Whitelocke and Thomas Widdrington, who would play leading roles in several later governments, were horrified.[119] No sitting judge agreed to participate and many appointees either refused to serve or, once appointed, failed to attend. In the end, less than half the appointees participated in the trial. Charles refused to enter a plea, arguing that the trial was illegal and had no jurisdiction over a king, and that

[117] Whitelocke (n 42) vol II, 257, 268.

[118] See David Underdown, *Pride's Purge: Politics in the Puritan Revolution* (Oxford, Oxford University Press, 1971). A substantial number of the excluded Presbyterian members of parliament became Royalists.

[119] Whitelocke (n 42) vol II, 312, 478–87. Whitelocke favoured a settlement with the king and supported the Nineteen Propositions. See Ruth Spalding, *The Improbable Puritan: A Life of Bulstrode Whitelocke, 1605–1675* (London, Faber & Faber, 1975) 40, 82. Hugh Peters denounced the king as a 'murderer, tyrant and traytor'; quoted in Clive Holmes, 'The Trial and Execution of Charles I' (2000) 53 *Historical Journal* 308.

no one trained in the law could possibly consider it legal. The House of Commons, he claimed, was not, and never had been, a court of judicature. The questionable legality of the tribunal and the execution that followed created further rifts among the parliamentary elite and the wider public.

The trial and execution were widely publicised in England, Scotland and abroad, and resulted in deep political divisions, with Charles being depicted either as a Christ-like royal martyr or the monstrous 'man of blood' responsible for the war and all its ills. Would it be possible to create a new government based on military power that would be considered lawful or acceptable even if not lawful? Were the acts and ordinances that emanated from the new government lawful? Should Englishmen be willing to serve that government and, if so, under what conditions?

Although there was some overlap, two quite different law reform movements competed for public attention, beginning in the early years of the revolutionary era. As we shall see in the subsequent chapter, the two approaches to law reform would continue to compete with one another, especially in the print media. The radical movement would continue to flourish until 1660. The moderate movement, which had a lengthy history prior to 1640, would have a far longer future.

6

Commonwealth and Protectorate 1649–60

The fate of law reform, both moderate and radical, would be shaped by the tumultuous changes in government that occurred following the execution of the Charles I. The substance of moderate reform proposals remained much the same, but the opportunity to implement them fluctuated as one regime followed another. Each alteration of government created difficulties in gaining acceptance of and compliance with its legal proposals. It was a decade of political and legal instability and bitter conflict among a sometimes bewildering number of religious and political groups, some of which wished to initiate radical alteration in the legal system.

Parliament changed substantially between Pride's Purge in 1648 and the Restoration in 1660. The remaining members of parliament, derisively called the Rump, decided that the House of Lords was 'useless and dangerous and ought to be abolished'. The new government, the Commonwealth, now consisted of a single-house legislative body and a Council of State. When the Commonwealth government required the Engagement, a pledge of loyalty, there was controversy over whether individuals might honestly sign the oath if they had previously taken oaths of loyalty to the king. The controversy produced a variety of views on the nature and purpose of government and the grounds on which one might or might not accept or serve a regime based on conquest.[1] Could the Commonwealth's acts and ordinances be considered law? How could judges appointed by the Crown reconcile themselves to serving a government that had replaced and/or usurped the previous one? When offered the position of Commissioner of the Great Seal, Thomas Widdrington was reported to have 'some scruples in conscience' about accepting. Bulstrode Whitelocke also had reservations, as did many who had vigorously defended the common law against the Crown.

There was considerable interest in law reform in the Rump. As early as June 1649, a committee was established to develop proposals 'for regulating the proceedings burdensome to the people'. In October it decided to consider 'regulation of the proceedings of the law, and of all delays and charges in courts of justice' as well as 'all exorbitant fees, and other grievances'. A committee was appointed 'to present one or more bills', to consider the salaries and fees of judges and court officers, and

[1] See JM Wallace, 'The Engagement Controversy, 1649–52' (1964) 68 *Bulletin of the New York Public Library* 384.

to suggest those 'fit to be retrenched'. The lawyer-dominated committee that met for only two weeks accomplished little. On the advice of Bulstrode Whitelocke, it was decided to establish an extra-parliamentary committee to work on law reform.[2]

The Rump considered a substantial number of reform measures. The Council of State requested it to consider legislation for county probate courts,[3] aid to poor prisoners and regulation of proceedings at law and what laws 'are fit to be repealed'.[4] There was 'a great pique against the lawyers'. Some critics argued that it was 'not fit' for lawyers to practise while they were members of parliament. Others thought the proposal 'an odium upon the law and lawyers'.[5] Some bills originated in the Council of State, others in parliament and still others in response to petitions. Some petitions received a positive response leading to a bill, while others did not. A petition from Norfolk demanded that all courts be put down and that perjury become a capital crime. Another petitioned for the laws of England to be 'according to those God gave his people, and plain and short'.[6]

Chancery was again a subject of attention. Commissioners of the Great Seal, who replaced the Lord Chancellors and Lord Keepers, now turned to reform. Commissioners Whitelocke and Richard Keble, relying heavily on rules proposed by former Lord Chancellors Sir Francis Bacon and Thomas Coventry, drew up and published new orders for 'a further Reformation'. These called for the elimination of procedural abuses and rationalising the order in which cases were heard.[7] However, in November 1652, Whitelocke reported that 'the business of chancery was full of trouble this term, and no man's cause came to a determination, however just'.[8]

Jurisdictional issues, which had reduced in number since the abolition of the prerogative courts, continued in connection with the Admiralty and the Palatine Courts.[9] Matters of credit and debt and of imprisonment for debt remained a concern.

Whitelocke, often depicted as obstructing law reform, continued to press for reform. He attended the weekly meetings of parliament's committee for regulating

[2] Blair Worden suggests that law reform ceased to be an important feature of the Rump's agenda after late 1650; Blair Worden, *The Rump Parliament 1648–1653* (Cambridge, Cambridge University Press, 1972) 238. See also Derek Hirst, 'Making Contact: Petitions and the English Republic' (2006) 45 *Journal of British Studies* 26.

[3] Bulstrode Whitelocke, *Memorials of the English Affairs*, 4 vols (Oxford, 1853), vol III, 36. The first proposal which was rejected called for 24 local courts run by civilians. There were many delays and postponements; Worden (n 2) 205. See also Blair Worden, 'The Diary of Bulstrode Whitelocke' (1993) 100 *English Historical Review* 122.

[4] Whitelocke (n 3) vol III, 57, 59, 82, 83, 98, 118. Whitelocke suggested that the multiplicity of suits was caused by 'the greatness of our trade' not by lawyers; Whitelocke (n 3) vol III, 118, 123.

[5] William Leach, *A New Parliament* (London, 1651) 2.

[6] Whitelocke (n 3) vol II, 116, 553–54; vol III, 432. See also vol III, 88.

[7] *A Collection of such of the Orders heretofore used in Chancery, with additions of Commissioners to adorn and Profit for the Reforming of several Abuses in the said Court* (London, 1649). See also *A Collection of … Orders for … Chancery, … for better regulating Chancery procedure* (London, 1650).

[8] Whitelocke (n 3) vol III, 468.

[9] ibid 38, 140. Courts martial permitted both defence and prosecution witnesses to testify under oath.

the law and, between 1649 and 1651, participated in Council investigations of complaints about the law and the courts. In 1649 he was sent a proposal by the reform-minded lawyer Peter Ball that would 'English' and methodise the law and reform legal education. Ball argued that Whitlocke's 'high judicial power' as a Commissioner of the Great Seal made him the appropriate person to promote the scheme. While Ball had no objection to law French, he admitted that it kept clients and others from understanding their legal business. Ball also offered proposals for 'remagnifying ye Lawe, & rendering itt perfectedly intelligible to the professors [of law] & acceptable to ye people'. Like many other lawyer reformers, Ball wished to remedy the 'chaos' of the law and lawbooks. However, English law should continue 'in ye forme itt nowe is' because it provided certainty. Ball told Whitelocke that he wished to 'preserve itt from ruine in vigour & reputation'. Nothing was 'att present more disquieting ye people, than their feare & doubt of being deprived of their old laws, ye fence of all their Interests'.[10] Reform concern combined with caution was to be found among many lawyers. Whitelocke drafted the legislation requiring English to be the language of legal proceedings,[11] one of the very few reform measures that became law.

The creation of high courts of justice to try Royalist and other plotters hostile to the regime was considered a necessary reform by some and a travesty of justice by others. Critics questioned whether such courts had the authority to conduct trials. Several judges, including Henry Rolle and Whitelocke, were reluctant to participate, preferring traditional tribunals using traditional law and traditional procedures. Others opposed the new courts because cases were tried by commissioners who combined the functions of judge and jury.

Few bills became law. The year 1649 brought an end to the law requiring church attendance on Sundays, though an established church was retained. Adultery became a capital crime in 1650.[12] Although calls for harsher penalties had been common for decades, the demise of the ecclesiastical courts meant that legislative action was required if adulterers were to be punished. Efforts to establish English as the language of the law were realised in 1650 and 1651. Translation of the reports and other professional legal literature from law French to English was a significant part of the legislation.

[10] For Ball, see Wilfrid Prest, 'Law Reform and Legal Education in Interregnum England' (2002) 5 *Historical Research* 112.

[11] See Allan J Busch, 'Bulstrode Whitelocke and Early Interregnum Chancery Reform' (1979) 11 *Albion* 317. Busch rejects the negative views of Whitelocke found in the studies of Donald Veall, David Underdown and Blair Worden. Worden views Whitelocke as having a major responsibility for the Rump's law reform failures.

[12] Few were prosecuted and even fewer were convicted; Keith Thomas, 'The Puritans and Adultery: The Act of 1650 Reconsidered' in *Puritans and Revolutionaries: Essays in Seventeenth-Century History Presented to Christopher Hill* (Oxford, Clarendon Press, 1978) 257–82. In 1655 a proclamation called for the enforcement of the statute. See Derek Hirst, 'The Failure of Godly Rule in the English Revolution' (1991) 132 *Past and Present* 33. Conviction rates for buggery were about one per cent.

I. Law Reform Publications During the Commonwealth

The large number of publications dealing with law reform during the Commonwealth testified to the widespread public interest in this field.[13] Several were written by lawyers, while others were written by radicals of various persuasions. One of the more conservative lawyers, Henry Parker, a prolific polemicist best known for his theory of parliamentary sovereignty, has been insufficiently noticed as a contributor to law reform debates. Parker defended a learned judiciary, opposing Leveller advocacy of lay judges and 'illiterate mechanic jurors'. He was adamant about retaining a centralised legal system manned by trained lawyers and learned judges. He pointed out that the abolition of the ecclesiastical and other courts had resulted in a vast increase in the business of the remaining Westminster courts. Delays, often attributed to lawyers and court officials, were, he thought, the result of the increased business of the remaining courts. It was 'the great confluence of business that chokes up and obstructs Chancery proceedings'.[14] Another Parker pamphlet attacked proposals for decentralisation of courts adjudicating testamentary disputes. The ecclesiastical courts had disappeared, but the disputes they handled had not. Rejecting 'cantonisation', he favoured an expansion of the Prerogative Court of Canterbury to cover the entire country and an appeals procedure.[15]

Barrister John March's *Amicus republicae*, dedicated to the regicide John Bradshaw, President of the Council of State and the judge who presided in the trial of Charles I, was optimistic about 'these happy times of Reformation'. Like so many reforming lawyers, March characterised English law 'as just and as perfect' as any, though not completely perfect. Employing the standard language of the moderate reformer, he wrote: 'The tree grows the better for pruning, and cutting the exuberant and unnecessary branches.' His tract, which took the form of a series of queries, considered questions of debt, Chancery, land conveyance, trial by jury, benefit of clergy, pressing to death, and the death penalty for theft and manslaughter. Though many thought it a 'great grievance', March defended Chancery and believed that it had become excessively busy because it absorbed many cases previously adjudicated by the Court of Wards and Requests. He was one of several lawyers who commented on the problems that developed when a court was abolished. Opposing the 'total destruction' of Chancery, he wished to reduce its abuses, vexations and troublesome suits. He opposed the death penalty for theft,

[13] *Proposalls presented to (and most acceptably approved by the honorable Committee for regulation of the Courts of Justice* (London, 1650); *Several Proposalls, Tendered to the consideration of the Honorable Committee for Regulating of Courts of Justice, for a thorough Reformation thereof* (London, 1650). The reforms would save the commonwealth 'many hundred thousands pounds in few years' 1; *Certain assayes propounded to the consideration of the honourable Committee … Whereby it is made evident that most cases now in Chancery and other courts of equity may be reduced to tryal at law* (London, 1652).

[14] Henry Parker, *A Letter of Due Censure* (London, 1650) 7, 8, 21, 22, 24, 39.

[15] Henry Parker, *Reformation in Courts and Cases Testamentary* (London, 1650) 3–6, 8–10.

rejected benefit of clergy and argued that defendants in treason and felony trials, like those in misdemeanour trials, should be allowed counsel.[16]

The acrimonious pamphlet debate over tithes continued. Radical religious pamphlets favoured abolition, while those who supported an established church, however defined, advocated retention or other means of supporting the clergy.[17] The army supported abolition. The Rump, which was unfavourable to abolition, responded with an ordinance requiring payment. Issues of credit and debt were also discussed in a large number of tracts and pamphlets.[18]

Radical religious publications favoured either the replacement of the current law with the law of God or making secular law consistent with the law of God. Samuel Childrey proclaimed God the 'only lawmaker'. He opposed the death penalty for theft on biblical grounds and thought thieves might better be put in chains or sent to the galleys or mines.[19] Similar views were expressed by John More, who opposed pardons in cases of murder and manslaughter on Scriptural grounds.[20] Pardons should be abolished because they circumvented the death penalty for those who took a life.

Radical tracts continued to attack the common law and the legal profession. One suggested that there was no need for Littleton's tenures or Coke's reports. Lawyers promoted delay and with their 'old and counterfeit writs … ratchet clients from Court to Court'. The author bewailed the chaos of the laws and praised Denmark and Norway, where the 'letter of the law determined all'.[21] Leveller sympathiser John Jones wished that the law would return to its 'native, ancient

[16] John March, *Amicus republicae* (London, 1650) 55–66, 85–89, 108.

[17] Christophe Elderfield, *The Civil Right of Tithes* (London, 1649); Edward Bailey, *For the Stormy Storm and total routing of tythes* (London, 1651); *Lawless Tythes* (London, 1651); Peter Heylyn, *The Undeceiving of the People in the point of Tithes* (London, 1652); Samuel Duncan, *Severall Propositions of public Concernment* (London, 1652); R B, *The Country man's catechism or, the churches plea for tithes* (London, 1652); R B, *A Word of Information and advice touching Tithes* (London, 1652); Donald Lupta, *The Tithe-takers cart overthrown* (London, 1652); *The Two Main Questions … if Tithes be put down* (London, 1652); William Erbery, *The Grand oppressor or the Terror of Tithes* (London, 1652). Erbery, an army chaplain, was charged with blasphemy in 1652.

[18] William Leach, *Proposals for an Act for speedily settling at large all prisoners, both for damages and debt … as well for the benefit of creditors* (London, 1649); William Leach, *Proposals for an Act for prevention … of Debt* (London, 1650); William Leach, *Proposals for an Act for the more speedy satisfaction of creditors* (London, 1650). Leach favoured a registry for deeds and conveyances, but opposed county courts; William Leach, *Bills Proposed for acts, or proposals concerning the principal courts of England* (London, 1651) 5, 9, 24–25, 29. See also Joanna Cartwright, *The Petition of the Jews* (London, 1649) to 'release all prisoners for debt, according to the customs of other countries'; William Gery, *Abuses Discovered* (London, 1649); John Jones, *The crie of blood on behalf of the prisoners for debt* (London, 1651). There were also printed petitions addressed to parliament in 1649 and 1650. Completed legislation included an *Act for discharging poor prisoners unable to satisfie their creditors if not worth five pounds* (London, 1649) and *An additional Act for the further ease of relief of poor prisoners* (London, 1650).

[19] Samuel Childrey, *A Cry against a crying Sin* (London, 1652) 14, 15.

[20] John More, *More Sights for the Righteous* (London, 1654); John More, *A Trumpet Sounded* (London, 1654). See also John Brayne, *The New Earth* (London, 1653).

[21] Dalepater Mendemus, *Lex Exlex: or the Downfall of the Law, and the Gospell* (London, 1652) 21–24, 26–30, 32.

and proper habitation, language, … cheapness, briefness, [and] plainesse'.[22] James Frieze, who attacked 'corrupt Judges and mercenary Lawyers and cruel Gaolers', proposed that laymen serve as judges. He blamed corrupt lawyers and court officials for the ills of the legal system, and offered a plan that would save the litigants and the country £2,611,369 per year. The tract also proposed that witnesses be examined locally, saving the time and expense of travel to London. This author, despite his many criticisms, nevertheless wished to retain the law and leave the legal system largely unchanged. He looked to the past for methods of repair, arguing that repair was far better than a Leveller-inspired demolition.[23]

Hugh Peters, an Independent minister and New Model Army chaplain who would become a member of the Hale Commission, provided 'a short Model for the Law' in 1651. Peters, who was personally familiar with New England legal procedures, advocated replacing the existing system of courts with local arbitration and adjudication by laymen. Debt disputes would also be decided by laymen, and London would have several courts that would end suits within a week. Litigants could plead their own causes or use an unpaid advocate. Wills and testaments disputes would be decided by local justices of the peace without charge. Failure to pay one's debts would result in labour in the galleys, not imprisonment. All courts would be supervised by lay inspectors who would report injustices to the government. Hostile to both the common law and the lawyers, Peters recommended that 'all old legal records be destroyed'. A 'new body of laws', based on reason and Scripture, would replace the common law. Peters wished 'our Lawyers would urge … [Scripture] for Law' rather than 'obsolete precedents'.[24] His code, like the Massachusetts code, was essentially a list of criminal offences. His publications provoked replies and counter-replies.[25]

Certain Queries, or Considerations presented to the view of all that desire Reformation of Grievances, dedicated to Lord General Cromwell, demanded greater vigour in executing the laws against adultery, whoredom, swearing, blasphemy and drunkenness, and argued that capital punishments should be 'agreeable to

[22] John Jones, *The new Returna Brevium* (London, 1653), title page, 7. See also John Jones, *Everyman's Case or lawyer's routed* (London 1652); John Jones, *Jurors judges of law and fact* (London, 1650); John Jones, *Lawyers Unmask'd* (London, 1653).

[23] James Freize, *Why Not, Eight Queries made to the Parliament* (London, 1649) 1. See also *The Anti-Levellers antidote* (London, 1652) 5, 7, 21. The author also recommended ending the death penalties for petty felonies.

[24] Hugh Peters, *Good Work for a Good Magistrate* (London, 1651) 4–5, 29, 32–33, 41, 42, 47–48, 51–56.

[25] Rice Vaughan, *A Plea for the Common Lawes of England* (London, 1651) referred to Peters' 'slender knowledge' of its foundation and proposals that were either 'perplexed and obscure, impertinent, impossible, or but unseasonably proposed' (Dedication). Vaughan, a defender of the common law, favoured some reform. William Prynne labelled Peters 'the great New-modeller' (at 136). *A Just Vindication of Mr Peters* replied to Prynne. John Cooke defended the law and lawyers against Peters; *Unum Necessarium or the Poor Man's Case* (London, 1648) 68–69. See Carla Gordina Pestano, 'Hugh Peters', *Oxford Dictionary of National Biography*; Raymond Stearns, *The Strenuous Puritan: Hugh Peter, 1598–1660* (Urbana, University of Illinois Press, 1964) 308–10, 376–87. Veall places Peters among the moderates.

Scripture'. Theft would be punished by corporal punishments or commitment to a workhouse. If any Norman laws remained, it was 'high time to be the end of them'. The tract contained the usual tirade against the 'boundless fees' of the lawyers, and blamed both lawyers and litigants for the excessive number of vexatious suits. A summons should be used to initiate suits instead of writs. The practice of wealthier debtors purchasing land to evade creditors led the author to suggest that real property should be liable for the payment of debts. The author also favoured a register, modelled on those used in Holland, to record mortgages and other encumbrances. The tract also suggested that St Paul's Cathedral should be demolished or repaired and used to house the Westminster courts.

More secular than most radicals, Henry Robinson offered a plan featuring the complete replacement of the current courts with local non-jury tribunals to try lesser cases. Justices of the peace were to attempt arbitration before trial. There should be appeal from local to county courts that combined law and equity, staffed by salaried judges appointed by parliament. Although Robinson, like the Levellers, emphasised local courts, he had little use for juries. Leveller William Walwyn counter-attacked, defending the competent 'understandings' of jurors.[26]

Several pamphlets focused on juries. William Leach, a prolific pamphleteer, castigated their partiality, dishonesty and openness to bribery, and suggested that the secret ballot would reduce those evils. He was concerned with perjury and false witnessing, and pointed to the practice of bringing forward 'multitudes of witnesses' of unknown credit or those of 'ill life and dishonesty'.[27] John March favoured legislation providing for 'gentleman' jurors because most jurors were weak and ignorant.[28] Similar complaints about jurors characterised the entire early modern period, and most parliaments heard proposals for raising the educational and economic requirements for jury service.

The ill effects of the Norman Conquest were a common radical complaint. John Warr, a prolific radical pamphleteer, railed against the common law, characterising it as 'the badge of our oppression'. It was also 'full of uncertainty, nicety, ambiguity and delay'. Like most anti-Norman writers, he assaulted the legal profession. He rejected the notion of fundamental law, arguing that it merely confirmed past mistakes. He recommended local courts so that people might have justice 'right at their own doors'. Commenting favourably on James I's endorsement of the simpler, informal laws of Denmark, he proposed an 'An Abstract and Epitome of Laws'. Law reform was both necessary and possible.[29] As noted earlier, most lawyers and judges rejected the view that the Norman Conquest had had cataclysmic results for the law and were more likely to see continuity rather than a sharp break.

Although rarely, if ever, discussed in connection with Interregnum law reform, Thomas Hobbes' *Leviathan*, published in 1651, shared several radical law reform

[26] William Walwyn, *Juries Justified* (London, 1651) 3–4, 6.
[27] William Leach, *The Bribe-Takers of Jury Men* (London, 1652).
[28] March (n 16) 101, 105.
[29] John Warr, *Corruption and Deficiency of the Laws of England* (London, 1649) 7–16.

concerns. Hobbes attacked the clergy, the legal profession and the common law, and insisted that the body of law be 'short', and written 'in as proper and significant terms, as may be'. He castigated Sir Edward Coke and the judges who saw themselves as the proper interpreters of the law. Judges, for him, were simply subordinate officials who carried out sovereign authority.[30]

II. The Hale Commission

In January, 1652 the Rump's law reform committee, following the pattern recommended by Bacon and other Jacobean law reformers, decided that an extra-parliamentary commission would be better able to draft workable reform legislation than parliament and its committees. The commission's charge, cast in the language of moderate reform, was 'to take into consideration what inconveniences and irregularities in the proceedings in the law may be prevented, and the speediest way to reform the same'.[31] It was to eliminate abuses, not engage in radical restructuring, although there were pressures from the army and the sects to move the commission in a more radical direction.

The commission was initially chaired by Sir Matthew Hale, a well-respected lawyer of Royalist sentiment. Mary Cotterell, who analysed the commission's membership and minutes, found that it consisted of eight lawyers and 13 laymen. No members of parliament were selected by the Rump's law committee, then headed by Whitelocke. There were few radicals. Lawyers dominated the debates, but radical views were also heard. The commission met three times a week for six months, drafting and debating a series of reform bills in consultation with the parliamentary committee.[32] Expectations ran high, the *Faithful Scout* reporting that the members 'sit constantly to make speedy dispatch of that glorious work. The president, council and army are very unanimous in bringing it to a happy period'.[33]

Many of the commission's proposals are the familiar ones for reducing delays and costs of litigations. Common law courts would remain open all year for issuing

[30] Thomas Hobbes, *Leviathan*, DMG Oakeshott (ed) (Oxford, Blackwell, 1947) 256. See also Thomas Hobbes, *A Dialogue between a Philosopher and a Student of the Common Laws of England*, Joseph Cropsey (ed) (Chicago, University of Chicago Press, 1971).

[31] CJ, VII, 27 December 1651. For crimes and punishments, see Hobbes, *Leviathan* (n 30) chs 27 and 28.

[32] Mary Cotterell suggests that the commission was introduced to get around lawyers blocking the work of the parliamentary committee; Mary Cotterell, 'Interregnum Law Reform: The Hale Commission of 1652' (1968) 83 *English Historical Review* 689. For committee appointments, see Worden (n 2) 271–72. Worden suggests that army pressure was crucial to its formation. There were five army representatives; CJ, VII, 14. Hale chaired 11 meetings between 30 January and 23 February, and was replaced by William Steele, Recorder of London. Edmund Heward suggests that Hale's legal practice made it difficult for him to give much time to the commission; Edmund Heward, *Matthew Hale* (London, Robert Hale and Co, 1972) 37.

[33] *Faithful Scout*, 13–20 February 1652, 448.

writs and filing documents. Hale wished Common Pleas to undertake the first process in personal and mixed actions, and he, as well as other commission members, wished to reduce competition among the common law courts. Dissatisfaction with the writ of error, often used for delay, had been expressed for decades. The Commission recommended a system of appeals in all civil and criminal cases, except in capital cases. These would be reviewed by 20 members of parliament who were not lawyers, judges or court officials. A table of fees in common law proceedings was included, as was a bill for 'Fraudulent Contracts and Conveyances'.[34] Chancery reform, similar to those in Whitelocke's 1652 defeated Chancery bill, were included. Admiralty would remain and probate would come under the jurisdiction of the common law courts.[35]

The establishment of county courts proved to be the commission's most contentious issue and, in this instance, the proposed legislation appears to have originated outside the commission. Radicals wanted to replace the old local courts with county courts staffed by elected laymen.[36] At issue were Westminster control, jurisdiction and what opportunities for appeals, if any, might be offered.[37] Hale gave a lengthy speech against the proposed county courts and lay judges. Small claims courts, whose judges would be selected by justices of the peace, would be established to handle case of debt and damages under four pounds.[38] The commission rejected radical pleas for elected judges. Judges would not be penalised for wrong decisions. There would be no buying or selling of office, and no bribery of judges or officials. Fees for legal counsel, attorneys and court officials would be regulated.[39]

The commission also proposed civil marriage, one of the very few commission recommendations to become law. It is difficult to see how anything other than civil marriage could have been contemplated, since the ecclesiastical courts were now defunct. Wills and probate, also left hanging with the demise of the ecclesiastical courts, were to be placed under the jurisdiction of Common Pleas.

[34] Cotterell (n 32) 700–02; *Several Draughts of Acts* in Lord John Somers, *A Collection of Scarce and Valuable Tracts*, 2nd edn (London, 1811), vol V, 186, 240–43, 245; Donald Veall, *The Popular Movement for Law Reform* (Oxford, Oxford University Press, 1970) 179.

[35] See Busch (n 11) 321–22. Ludlow attributed the failure of the 1652 Chancery bill to the influence of lawyers in the Rump and to Whitelocke's committee. Parliament was dismissed before the third reading; Busch (n 11) 322–23. See also Stuart Prall, 'Chancery under the Puritan Revolution' (1972) 6 *American Journal of Legal History* 28. The commission recommended salaried masters appointed by parliament required to sit until a decision was reached. There were time limits for pleading, copies of pleas made available to the other side, a set order for chancery cases and established fees. Litigants would be fined for insufficient answers and frivolous exceptions; Somers (n 34) vol V, 202–11; Heward (n 32) 39–40; Veall (n 34) 180.

[36] Somers (n 34) vol V, 212–13. Cotterell suggests that Hale did not participate in writing the draft bill; Cotterell (n 32) 698.

[37] The court's jurisdiction was very broad and included capital crimes. Circuit judges would remain; Somers (n 34) vol V, 212–13.

[38] There were also proposals to abolish hundred courts, courts of liberties and the Palatine courts of Durham, Lancaster, Ely and Chester; Somers (n 34) vol V, 184–6, 231–34.

[39] Somers (n 34) vol V, 186–87, 188–89.

A probate registry was also included.[40] Credit and debt provisions were debated and drafted. Imprisonment for debt would be abolished, with debtors committed to workhouses until debts were repaid. Entails would be abolished. Radicals and moderates agreed that there should be a land registry, but disagreed over whether the registry should be limited to land transactions or should also include probate, wills, bills of exchange and assignment of debts.[41]

Several commission recommendations dealt with crime and criminal procedure. Benefit of clergy was to be abolished, as was pressing to death for a refusal to plead.[42] Offenders of the formerly capital crimes of horse stealing and pickpocketing would be required to wear an iron collar, with a failure to wear it to result in death.[43] There was no opposition to the death penalty itself. Manslaughter and acting as accessories before the fact would become capital offences. There was no suggestion that the Mosaic law should become the law of England, though the commission proposed the strict enforcement of the laws against drunkenness, profane cursing, swearing and Sabbath breaking.[44]

Radical influence was greatest on the creation of county courts and capital punishment for manslaughter. Criminal defendants would be allowed legal counsel if the prosecution had counsel. Defence witnesses, as well as prosecution witnesses, would testify under oath.[45] The commission did not recommend the two-witness rule for serious crime, nor did it propose codification of the common law or the statutes. Commission activities appear to have been reasonably well known, being followed in the newsbooks. Its proposals were printed for the members of the Barebones Parliament which assembled several months after the dismissal of the Rump.[46]

In the end, few of the commission's recommendations became law, though legislation ending fines for original writs and bills of review and civil marriage became law during the Barebones Parliament the following year. The Rump

[40] ibid 179–80, 186–87; Worden (n 2) 318–19, 320.

[41] See Seichiro Ito, 'Registration and Credit in Seventeenth Century England' (2013) 20 *Financial History Review* 137. There was also division as to where the registers should be kept. Registry proposals were introduced in 1650 and 1652–53.

[42] Hale wished to retain benefit of clergy. See Alan Cromartie, *Sir Matthew Hale, 1609–76: Law Religion and Natural Philosophy* (Cambridge, Cambridge University Press, 1995) 71.

[43] First-time offenders would be burned on the left hand, pilloried, the offence written on the forehead, sent to a house of correction and required to pay hefty damages. Perjury would be punished harshly, but not with the death penalty. Convicted perjurers would stand in the pillory, have their ears cut off, their nostrils slit, be burnt with a hot iron and be given six months in the house of correction; Somers (n 34) vol V, 190–91, 237.

[44] ibid 190–91, 234–39. Bigamy would become a capital crime. Women convicted of a felony would be hanged instead of burnt. A table of fees was to be hung in all courts trying criminal cases.

[45] ibid 181, 235. See John F Acevedo, 'The Ideological Origins of the Right to Counsel' (2016) 168 *South Carolina Law Review* 87. The issue was discussed in parliament in November 1649. Whitelocke viewed it as a beneficial reform; Whitelocke (n 3) vol III, 124.

[46] See also *A Second Supply to the draft of a great System concerning the Regulation of the Law* (London, 1653). See also *Supply to a Draught of an Act or system proposed (as is reported) by the committee for regulations concerning the law* (London, 1653).

debated the commission's report for two days. The bill for county registers for land transactions failed and, except for the probate bill of 1653, parliament did nothing more on law reform. Radical pressure may have moved the Rump in a conservative direction.[47]

Relations between parliament and the army deteriorated as fears of another military coup increased. As early as August 1652, when army officers petitioned parliament about what had been done about 'regulating of the law', it was reported that many thought it improper and arrogant for the army to petition 'their masters'. Cromwell was advised against petitioning 'with their swords in their hands'.[48] In April, troops forcefully ended the Rump's existence, making the army's power evident to all. The Rump's abrupt end also resulted in further ambiguity about the status of the judiciary. Cromwell ordered the existing judges to perform their duties, but did not issue them with new patents, since to do so would have involved exposing his lack of authority.[49]

III. The Barebones Parliament

It was during this ambiguous state of affairs that Cromwell called what has come to be called the Barebones or Nominated Parliament. Summoned in July 1653, it was far from a typical parliament, its members having been nominated by the Army Council and radical London churches rather than elected. Many considered it to be an illegitimate body lacking the necessary authority to make law. The absence of the Crown and an elected parliament left the law courts, juries, judges and the justices of the peace as the last links to England's traditional legal institutions.[50] The year of the Barebones Parliament was one of heightened fears, both within and outside of parliament, of social and cultural upheaval.

Although not quite as radical as is sometimes thought, the assembly included both radicals and moderates, the former having greater influence because the moderates were less faithful attenders. For the first and last time, radicals had a substantial voice in parliament. Moderates remained concerned with making the common law courts and Chancery less dilatory, but had no inclination to abolish the common law or the legal profession, or to substantially change the courts. They continued to insist that they wished to remove the dead branches or 'exuberances' of the law rather than pull it down 'root and branch'.

[47] Worden (n 2) 320–21.

[48] Whitelocke (n 3) vol III, 446.

[49] S Black, 'The Courts and Judges of Westminster Hall during the Great Rebellion 1640–60' (1986) 7 *Journal of Legal History* 36.

[50] See Austin Woolrych, 'The Calling of the Barebones Parliament' (1965) 80 *English Historical Review* 492; Whitelocke (n 3) vol IV, 32, 37; Austin Woolyrich, *Commonwealth to Protectorate* (Oxford, Clarendon Press, 1982); HA Glass, *The Barebones Parliament* (London, James Clark, 1899).

The central and most contentious issues before the Barebones Parliament were tithes, Chancery and a 'new model' of the law. There were also the usual concerns with the courts, the legal profession and fees. The committee on tithes supported abolition, but the larger body opposed it'.[51] There was a lively and acrimonious pamphlet debate defending[52] and attacking tithes,[53] as well as petitions to parliament on both sides.[54]

Chancery became a hotly contested issue between radical and moderate reformers. Whatever the differences between radical and moderate reform proposals, there was no doubt that Chancery 'was looked on as a great grievance, one of the Greatest in the Nation', and some members of the house affirmed 'horrible things' about it.[55] One member claimed that 23,000 cases were pending, some for 10, 20, 30 years or more.[56] Whitelocke, Commissioner of the Great Seal, an advocate in the Rump of Chancery reform who had worked with the Hale Commission, may be considered a representative of moderate Chancery reform. Moderates wished to reform Chancery along the lines suggested earlier; radicals wished to dismantle it. Shortly after the parliament opened, there was a resolution for abolition.

[51] *An Exact Relation of the Proceedings and Transactions of the Late Parliament* (London, 1654) 7; Margaret James, 'The Political Importance of Tithes in the English Revolution, 1640–60' (1941) 26 *History* 1, 14.

[52] Those defending tithes included John Gauden, *The Case of the Minister's Maintenance by Tithes* (London, 1653); William Prynne, *The Due Right of Tithes Examined* (London, 1653); Samuel Clarke, *A Caution against Sacrilege* (London, 1653); William Leach, *The Funeral of Symonie, Impropriations, and Tithes* (London, 1653); Counsellor Nortcliffe, *An Argument in defense of the Right of Patrons and Advowsons. And incidentally of the right of Tithes in Generall* (London, 1653) delivered to the committee on tithes September 1653; *The Right of Tithes Asserted: The Civil Right of Tythes* (London, 1653); *Some Modest and sober Considerations about Tythes* (London, 1653); Samuel Clarke, *A Caution against Sacrilege* (London, 1653); William Prynne, *A Gospel Plea* (London, 1653; *A Second Vindication of a Short Treatise on tythes lately written* (London, 1653); Bevill Turmiger, *A Brief Treatise … about Tithes* (London, 1653); Christen Elderfield, *Cuique suum, The Law of Tythes affirmed* (London, 1654); *The Case of Ministers Maintenance by Tithes* (London, 1653); William Prynne, *A Gospel Plea* (London, 1653; and *A Second Vindication of a Short Treatise on tythes lately written* (London, 1653). Hale supported tithes, suggesting that they were close to something close to real property.

[53] Opposed William Erbery, *The Grand Oppressor*; William Erbery, *Ministers for tythes* (London, 1653); Samuel Duncan, *Severall Propositions of publick concernment* (London, 1652); Donald Lupta, *The Tithe-takers cart overthrown, the down fall of tythes* (London, 1652); *Tithes: A Curse to all Nations* (London, 1654); *The Right of Tithes Asserted by our old Saxon Lawes* (London, 1653); *A Letter to a Christian Friend … Proposing the Groundlessness of the Plea for Tythes* (London, 1653); Isaac Graye, *Tithes a curse to all nations but Canaan* (London, 1654); *The Due Right of Tithes Examined* (London, 1654); John Spittlehouse, *An Explanation … of the Commission of Jesus Christ* (London, 1653); *A Letter to a Christian Friend … Proposing the Groundlessness of the Plea for Tythes* (London, 1653); *Mercurius Rusticus: The Downfall of tythes* (London, 1653); *No Age like unto this* (London, 1653); Ellis Bradshaw, *Downfall of Tythes no Sacrilege* (London, 1653); John Canne, *A Second Voyce from the Temple to the Higher Powers* (London, 1653); John Spittlehouse, *An Explanation … of the Commission of Jesus Christ* (London, 1653); H Culmer, *Lawless Tithe Robbers Discovered* (London, 1654); *Tithes totally routed by Magna Carta* (London, 1653).

[54] A petition of 1652 favouring a replacement for tithes led to a parliamentary debate; James (n 51) 11; *An Answer to the severall petitions … by the poor husbandmen, farmers and tenants for the taking away of tithes* (London, 1652). A petition of June 1653 for abolition was sent to Cromwell and Harrison; James (n 51) 13. Most religious sects were vigorous supporters of abolition.

[55] *An Exact Relation* (n 51) 12.

[56] ibid 12.

It would have ended the venue for trusts, fraud, mortgages, guardianship, business association and multi-party disputes. The committee for Chancery reform did not consult with the legal profession or Chancery officials. The bill was 'waved and layd aside' because it lacked any provision for pending and future cases, and a revised bill was introduced. One observer reported that Chancery supporters 'had little to say on the behalf of it'. Lawyers and clerks were said to be 'sad and sorrowfull' for 'feare of the losse of their great Diana'. After a single day's debate, the Chancery bill was voted down. Chancery therefore remained and its problems were left unresolved. When parliament was dissolved without a Chancery ordinance, the legal profession was said to have expressed 'great joy making 'Bonfires, and drinking Sacke'. A bill was prepared, for 'taking down the courts, and for the dispatch of the Causes depending and providing for the future in a summary way', so that cases of 20 or 40 shillings might be ended 'in a very short time, and much strife and going to Law' avoided. 'But the house being full of business … they let it alone till a fitter time and more leisure.'[57]

Like its predecessors, the Barebones Parliament concerned itself with matters of credit and debt. A petition by 1,000 prisoners 'for liberty, that Magna Charta may be in force, and no arrests for debt' resulted in 'serious debate', leading to an order for an act to redress prisoners' grievances. Somewhat stronger than earlier acts, commissioners were to investigate prisoner financial resources and recommend the release of those meeting certain conditions.[58]

Given the strong radical presence, it is not surprising that there were proposals for changing criminal law and procedure, for making punishments proportionate to offences, for eliminating the death penalty for theft and for making manslaughter a capital offence. These changes were meant to bring English law into line with the 'righteous law of God'.

A controversial bill establishing a High Court of Justice to handle cases of treason without common law procedures was read, debated and passed in a single day.[59] There were also bills to 'redress … delays and mischiefs arising by writs of error and writs of false judgment' and for curbing exorbitant legal fees. Legislation providing for probate of wills in all counties was approved.[60]

A vehement clash developed when a radical proposal to replace existing law with a new 'Body of the Law' was introduced. As anticipated, the lawyers were bitterly opposed, believing that its intention was 'to destroy the Law, and take away the Laws we had been fighting for all this while as our birth-right and inheritances'. There were several approaches to reforming the 'body of the law'.

[57] ibid 41.

[58] Whitelocke (n 3) vol IV, 32, 37, 44; CJ, VII, 316, 319, 322, 329–30; Charles Firth and R Rait, *Acts and Ordinances of the Interregnum 1642–1660*, 4 vols (London, Her Majesty's Stationery Office, 1911), vol II, 753–54, 860, 888; Stuart Prall, *Agitation for Law Reform and the Puritan Revolution* (Leiden, Martinus Nijhoff, 1966) 96–97; CJ, VII, 316, 319, 322, 329–30.

[59] CJ, VII, 297, 325, 334, 353–54; Firth and Rait (n 58) vol II, 352, 772–73; *An Exact Relation* (n 51) 8, 273. See Adele Hast, 'State Treason Trials during the Puritan Revolution, 1640–1660' (1972) 15 *Historical Journal* 37.

[60] *An Exact Relation* (n 51) 8; Firth and Rait (n 58) vol II, 352–57; CJ, VII, 342.

Some spoke generally without specifying what the new 'body' was to contain. Others complained that England's voluminous laws created uncertainty. Lawyers and judges, who often differed about the law, might be corrupt, partial or unaware of the circumstances of particular cases. Still others said that the statute books were so large that few could even afford to purchase the 'old musty statutes'.[61] Some thought that the laws should be 'easie, plain, and short' or 'reduced into the bignesse of a pocket book'. For some, this implied a summary of existing law. For others, it meant 'reducing' or consolidating good laws and eliminating 'useless' ones. Still others favoured a model in accordance with the 'word of God and right reason'. One member of parliament said that it was 'most falsely and wickedly reported' that proponents of new laws were engaged in 'endeavors tending to destroying the whole Laws, and pulling them up by the roots'. He thought that a new model of law would be 'a great work, and of high and great esteem with many, for the great fruit and benefit that would come by it'. Unfortunately, 'a thing of so great worth and benefit England is not yet worthy or, not likely in a short time to be so blessed as to enjoy'.[62] *An Exact Relation* characterised the House as 'modelized of Monsters, rather than men of reason and judgment'.[63]

The Barebones Parliament was dissolved by Cromwell in December 1653. While Cromwell would continue to support law reform, he was unsympathetic to proposals for abolishing the common law and dismantling Chancery, and had become impatient over debates over the words 'body' and 'model'. After the dissolution, he referred to those who had subverted the laws and liberties of the country and wished to replace them with 'the judicial law of Moses'.[64]

Dissolution came as a relief to the moderates who feared the abolition of the common law, and disappointed radicals. One moderate writer thought that the Barebones Parliament would have damaged 'the whole frame and body of the Laws and Justice', translated 'the Great Courts of Westminster into so many little courts and judicatures' and annexed equity to new courts.[65] Another noted that the parliament would have bid good bye to 'Coke and his reports', which would be of 'small account when there's no Courts'.[66] The radical Edmund Ludlow referred to the 'perfidious Cromwell' who had forgotten 'his most solemn professions and former vows'. Cromwell had 'ernestly solicited to reform the law and reduce the clergy to more evangelical constitutions' and then reacted negatively to the confusions brought by the ''immoderate zeal' of the Barebones Parliament. Ludlow thought

[61] *An Exact Relation* (n 51) 17.

[62] *An Exact Relation* (n 51) 16–18; Philostratus Philodemius, *Seasonable Observations on a Late Book intitled A System of the Law* (London, 1653).

[63] *An Exact Relation* (n 51) 15.

[64] Thomas Carlyle, *Oliver Cromwell, Letters and Speeches*, 2 vols (London, Methuen, 1904), vol II, 256–57.

[65] *Considerations touching the Dissolving or Taking Away the Court of Chancery … with a Vindication, or Defence of the Law from what is unjustly charged upon it* (London, 1653) 7.

[66] *The Downfall of Chancery* (London, 1653) 1.

that Cromwell had been 'readily embraced by the corrupt part of the lawyers and clergy', who under 'divers specious pretenses, put a period to parliament's sitting'.[67]

Radical pamphlets streamed from the presses in 1653 and 1654. We have noted the rancorous debate over tithes and the proposed abolition of Chancery. Another group of tracts addressed imprisonment for debt and the competing claims of debtors, creditors and prison officials. There were at least five printed petitions for relief addressed to parliament as well as legislation in 1652, 1653 and 1654 to relieve creditors and poor prisoners.[68] However, reformers on this topic were not as prolific as those writing for and against the abolition of tithes.

Fifth Monarchists were particularly vocal during the 1650s. The pamphlets of John Rogers and K Spittlehouse were laden with anti-Norman sentiment and condemnations of the clerical and legal professions, which Rogers characterised as 'the Two Plagues of this Nation', both of which 'must fall together'. Lawyers are characterised as 'Antichrists' State Army'. The Fifth Monarchists were adamant in wishing to establish the Law of God as the law of England. Rogers, confident that the Fifth Monarchy would eventually replace the law of England with the Law of God, charged parliament with not doing enough to change England's laws. During the remaining years of the Fourth Monarchy, parliament should 'see that all the Lawes of this Nation are agreeing to the Word of God'.[69]

The Barebones Parliament continued to have an impact after its demise. The Cromwellian *True State of the Commonwealth* characterised it as a combination of godly honest men and those wishing to promote 'a Subverting of the Fundamental Laws of the Land, the destruction of Propriety, and an utter extirpation of the Ministry of the Gospel. In truth, their principles led them to a pulling down all, and establishing nothing'. One 'party was for pruning away its exuberances and superfluities; the other for a hewing down of the main Body'. 'The more sober Judgments were for a regulation of the Law, by making it more succinct, intelligible, and certain, as also to remedy the abuses of it, and render it less tedious and chargeable to the People; yet nothing would serve the other, but a total eradication of the old, and introduction of a new.' They assumed 'to themselves only the name of Saints, from which title they excluded all others that were not of their judgment and opinion'. Fifth Monarchists had 'wrestled and fitted Scriptures for their turn' and demanded that 'all branches of the Fourth Monarchy' be 'rooted up and destroyed'. 'Nothing of moderation would content them.'[70] Radical pamphleteers

[67] Edmund Ludlow, *Memoirs*, CH Firth (ed), 2 vols (London, 1894), vol II, 365–66, 368–69.

[68] John Jones, *The Crie of Blood* (London, 1653); James Mullus, *Multo in parvo* (London, 1653); *The Prisoner's Remonstrance* (1654); *The Second Part of the Prisoners Remonstrance* (London, 1654).

[69] John Rogers, *Sagrir, or Doomes-day drawing nigh, with Thunder and Lightening to Lawyers of the Fourth Monarchy* (London, 1653) Dedication to Cromwell, To the Reader, 1, 10–11, 37, 39, 88, 110, 124, 125, 129. Rogers favoured the law in English, speedier trials held locally, punishments in keeping with crimes and sale of the Inns of Court (at 52, 54, 88, 137). See also SM Hoy, 'John Rogers: A Disillusioned Fifth Monarchy Man' (1975) 4 *Albion* 125.

[70] *A True State of the Commonwealth of England, Scotland and Ireland* (London, 1654) 9, 13, 14, 15, 18, 19.

such as Rogers were ridiculed by Marchemont Nedham for wishing to bring in the 'whole catalogue of old dreaming rabies, to jostle out Coke and Littleton'.[71] Nothing could be clearer than the opposition between moderate and radical reformers.

John Hall denounced those 'whom nothing could please, but the wildest and most extravagant devastations possible'. They were for 'setting up after the Kingdom of Jesus Christ', insisting only the godly could serve the government and claiming only they were fit to judge who and what was godly. Fifth Monarchists and other religious fanatics, being 'neither Politick' nor 'Rational', considered the law 'a noisesome building' incapable of 'repair or alteration … fit to be pulled down', wished to eliminate Chancery, throw out the statute book and shape a 'total alteration of the Law'.[72]

Albertus Warren too had been dismayed by the possibility that the common law would be destroyed and its courts dismantled. 'Those who most Carp at the law' were characterised as 'turbulent Spirits, pleased with no government, or else, Vulgar heads', many of whom were illiterate. The common law was the 'most incomparable reason in the world' and provided the best protection for property. Warren, however, was ready to support reform if done with 'great care', arguing: 'Where law is defective, or redundant, when the practice of it, is either prolix, chargeable or unnecessary … let all such excrescences be pared off.' Countering objection of the 'Law-Haters' that the common law was too obscure, too difficult to understand and too copious, Warren condemned the 'fierce Petitions against the Law' and those who wished England to 'fetch all our Species of Law from God's word literally'. Chancery was necessary and law could not exist without it.[73] Hall and Warren demonstrate the difference between radical and moderate law reform.

A few observers commented favourably on the radicalism of the Barebones Parliament. One member of parliament complained that the Speaker had wrongly accused the radical party of holding the 'principle of destroying and pulling down … though nothing was set up in its stead'. He denied that their 'destructive spirit' was manifested by its 'vote for removing Chancery'. Those members who refused to leave the building when the 'house adjourned had promoted the interest of Jesus Christ'.[74]

While it is difficult to determine public opinion from the large scattering of pamphlets and newsbooks that survive, Jason Peacey has shown that many

[71] Rogers (n 69) 39, 47, 49–55, 56–58, 59, 110, 125; *Observator*, October 1654.

[72] John Hall, *Confusion Confounded* (London, 1654) 2–3, 4–6, 18, 19.

[73] Albertus Warren, *Eight Reasons Categorical … that it is probable that the common law will stand* (London, 1653) 3, 4, 5; Albertus Warren, *A New Plea for the Old Law* (London, 1653) 2, 4, 14, 15, 21. In 1649 Warren thought that lawyers should assist in the reformation of the laws. It was easier to mend the practice than to make new laws regarding property; Albertus Warren, *The Royalist Reformed* (London, 1649) 5, 7, 8. Veall places Warren among those who opposed all law reform or against any further changes; Veall (n 34) 98–99.

[74] *A True Narrative of the Cause and Manner of the Dissolution of the late Parliament* (London, 1653) 3, 4, 5, 6. For a reply, see *An Answer to a paper entituled A True Narrative* (London, 1653) (actually January 1654).

outside London were informed of parliamentary activity.[75] *Several Proceedings in Parliament*, a licensed journal, reported on a number of law-related committees and bills. In July 1653, it noted that the committee on law was to consider the laws and ordinances hindering the progress of the Gospel, as well as the 'Order to a new Modelling of Laws and Law Proceedings, for a more speedy, cheap and equal distribution of justice'.[76] *The Moderate*, which was sympathetic to Leveller views, supported decentralising justice, ending imprisonment for debt and simplifying the law. Hostile to lawyers and to Law French, it proclaimed that the people were 'cheated by the Conquerers Lawes'.[77] The *Faithful Scout*, a newsbook favouring the abolition of tithes, devoted two pages to the dissolution of the Barebones Parliament.[78] Legislation dealing with incest, adultery, blasphemy and the relief of creditors was noted in several newsbooks.[79] The *Weekly Intelligencer* took note of committees on tithes and abuses. It reported that parliament was 'to begin in earnest to look after Justice and to tender the ease of the Oppressed' and noted that 'after large and serious Debate', Chancery should 'be quite taken away'. It later reported that its abolition had been rejected. Readers were also informed of the committee to consider 'A new Body of Law', a 'great undertaking' that would cause 'the greatest apprehensions'. Another issue referred to bills for 'reforming many abuses in the Courts of Common Law'. It reported at some length on changes in the marriage law and the marriage ceremony. It took note of bills for probate of wills and for poor imprisoned debtors and their creditors. The *Intelligencer* also reported on bills for apprehending highwaymen and erecting a High Court of Justice and the passage of legislation for the union of England and Scotland. The dissolution of the Barebones Parliament is noted with the vague comment that it had 'resigned their power' to the Protector.[80]

Several, albeit short-lived newsbooks favoured radical measures. One expressed approval of 'voting down' Chancery and the expected parliament either to 'new Mould it', or better regulate the court.[81] *Mercurius Rhadamanthu*, a publication that had only two issues, attacked all 'judges, justices, counsellors, attornies, sheriffs and clerks' and anticipated that the 'heroes at Westminster' would shortly 'destroy and take away' all of them and reform the law. It supported the abolition

[75] See Jason Peacey, *Politics and Pamphlets* (London, Routledge, 2004); Jason Peacey, 'The Print Culture of Parliament 1600–1800' (2007) 26 *Parliamentary History* 1–16. For an extensive treatment of parliamentary news, see Jason Peacey, *Print and Public Politics in the English Revolution* (Cambridge, Cambridge University Press, 2013). Peacey discusses the availability of parliamentary news.

[76] *Several Proceedings of Parliament*, 19–25 July, 3154, 3155, 3164.

[77] Laurent Curelly, *An Anatomy of an English Radical Newspaper*; *The Moderate* (Newcastle upon Tyne, Cambridge Scholars, 2017) 41, 52, 80; Joseph Frank, *The Beginnings of the English Newspaper 1620–1660* (Cambridge, MA, Harvard University Press, 1961) 179, 248.

[78] Frank (n 77) 179, 248.

[79] Jason Peacey 'Print Culture and Political Lobbying during the English Civil War' (2007) 26 *Parliamentary History*, 36, 38.

[80] *Weekly Intelligencer* 932, 933, 949, 959, 965, 967, 972–74, 997.

[81] *Mercurius Classicus*, 12 August, 4.

of the upper bench, but favoured the retention of Chancery and Common Pleas. Judges were denounced for not allowing defendants to speak for themselves, and for vilifying and threatening defendants with 'menacing words' and 'big looks' without hearing testimony, a practice that cost innocent lives. It supported the requirement for two witnesses because a single one might be perjured.[82]

Despite the radical proposals aired in the Barebones Parliament and the pamphlets of 1653 and 1654, the radicals had little prospect of success. There is little to support the view that the public at large favoured eliminating the common law, the common law courts and the legal profession or the replacement of professional with lay judges. There appears to have been considerable support for eliminating tithes, but how extensive that support was cannot to determined simply by counting pamphlets. Given the number of litigants using Chancery, its abolition without a replacement was unlikely to have had widespread appeal.

IV. The Protectorate

Shortly after the dissolution of the Barebones Parliament, Cromwell, backed by the army, established England's first government with a written constitution. It was composed of a Protector, Cromwell himself, a nominated Council of State, roughly analogous to the old Privy Council, and a single-house parliament. Together, the Protector and the Council of State were empowered to make ordinances binding until approved or disapproved by parliament. The disputed legal status of ordinances lacking parliament's consent made legislation during the First Protectorate Parliament impossible.[83]

Disturbed by the radicalism of 1653, Cromwell took a more moderate approach to law reform. According to John Thurloe, Cromwell's Secretary of State and spymaster, Cromwell spent much of his 'tyme in settling the Courts of Justice, which he intends to fill with the best and most learned men he can find in England'. Two months later, he reported that the Protector was 'very much resolved upon a solid and good reformation of the laws' and had entrusted the matter to distinguished lawyers in order to give 'the honour of reforming to their own profession'.[84] However, at about the time that arrangements were being made for parliamentary elections, Charles Fleetwood, a Cromwellian general, told Thurloe 'it is much wondered at that the regulation of the law goes so slowly'. 'The eyes of all men are upon my Lord Protector and if ever these considerations [law and tithes] are before the parliament, where there will be such a diversity of interests, I fear it may

[82] *Mercurius Rhadamantus*, 11–18 and 18–25 July 1653, 2, 7, 30, 34, 272–78.

[83] See David L Smith, 'Oliver Cromwell and the Protectorate Parliaments' in Patrick Little (ed), *The Cromwellian Protectorate* (Woodbridge, Boydell Press, 2007) 13–14.

[84] Letters Thurloe to Whitelocke, quoted in Ruth Spalding, *Contemporaries of Bulstrode Whitelocke* (Oxford, Oxford University Press, 1990) 372, 379.

prove as fatal as both have been in the last two parliaments.'[85] Fleetwood proved to be prescient.

The Protector and the Council, who governed before the parliament met, worked on a new Chancery ordinance, but had not consulted with Chancery officials or other legal experts.[86] Its provisions were largely in keeping with moderate reform, limiting the time for pleading, reducing staff, limiting the number of attorneys, requiring cases to be heard in the order published and allowing justices of the peace to take depositions. It would have no jurisdiction where common law remedies were available. An appeal process with both common law and Chancery judges was included.[87] Cromwell anticipated the easy passage of the ordinance, but instead faced strenuous opposition from parliament and the judiciary over its questionable legal status.[88]

The First Protectorate Parliament was quite different from its predecessor. Franchise requirements had been increased, as had the number of county seats. Some Royalists and Republicans, hostile to the very existence of the Protectorate, were returned. Although most members of parliament appear to have been moderates on questions of law reform, many were opposed to a government based on the backing of the army. There was therefore tension between parliament and the Protector from the beginning. The imposition of an oath of loyalty caused 100 members to withdraw.[89]

Cromwell's opening speech reinforced his rejection of radical reform. He repudiated the recent efforts to bring in the Mosaic law and attacked the Levellers and the Fifth Monarchy Men. Law reform must preserve social stability, retain a tithe supported ministry and include religious toleration. He reported having invited persons to make the laws 'plain, short and easie', which 'in due time' would be tendered'. 'Men of integrity would be introduced into the 'seats of justice', and Chancery reforms, as embodied in the Chancery ordinance, would satisfy 'all good men'.[90] Much to Cromwell's dismay, parliament, instead of following his

[85] Quoted in Ivan Roots, 'Cromwell's Chancery Ordinances: The Early Legislation of the Protectorate' in GE Alymer (ed), *The Interregnum: The Quest for Settlement 1646–1660* (Hamden, CT, Archon Books, 1972) 54. Fleetwood was married to Cromwell's daughter.

[86] Stuart Prall suggests that the Chancery Ordinance may have been the work of Bulstrode Whitelocke Commissioner of the Great Seal; Stuart Prall, *The Agitation for Law Reform during the Puritan Revolution, 1640–1660* (The Hague, Martinus Nijhoff, 1966) 106.

[87] Firth and Rait (n 58) vol II, 949–67. See Stuart Prall, 'Chancery Reform and the Puritan Revolution' (1962) 6 *American Journal of Legal History* 28; Prall (n 86) 105–13.

[88] See *The continuance of the High Court of Chancery vindicated … the abuses and corruptions being … proposed in Severall bills* (London, 1654); *A View of the Regulation of Chancery* (London, 1654); *Observations concerning the Chancery; with some proposals for the redress of the inconveniences in the practice thereof* (London, 1655); *A Letter of Advice Sent in a Letter* (London, 1655). See also *Some Considerations concerning the High Court of Chancery and the Ordinance made for the Regulation and limitations of that Court* (London, 1657); Edward Leigh, *Second Considerations concerning the High Court of Chancery* (London, 1658).

[89] Ivan Roots, 'Cromwell's Ordinances: The Early Legislation of the Protectorate' 154.

[90] *The Speech of His Highness the Lord Protector to the Parliament* (London, 1654) 5–7.

lead, focused on the legal status of ordinances. It repeatedly delayed consideration of the Chancery ordinance and suspended it twice before it was implemented without parliamentary approval. No legislation of any kind was completed before Cromwell dismissed the parliament in January 1655.[91] Although no legislation was completed, some 40 bills had been introduced. Those dealing with law reform included the seemingly perennial problems of creditors and poor imprisoned debtors, the elimination of the Court of Wards, probate reform, reinstating courts at York, clarifying the recent marriage legislation, and the courts in Ireland.[92]

When parliament ended, Cromwell expressed his disappointment, saying that he had hoped it 'might have proceeded to have made those good and wholesome laws which the people expected from you'.[93] He did not give up on law reform during the interval between his first and second parliament. He commissioned William Sheppard, a country lawyer, to draw up a law reform programme to be presented to parliament. Sheppard's *England's Balme*, the most important law reform publication of the Protectorate era, provided a comprehensive programme of reform. Printed under Cromwell's protection, it was submitted to parliament. At least one observer expected Sheppard's proposals to be implemented with minor changes. However, it also reported that the proposals had 'startled the lawyers and the city'.[94]

Under Sheppard's plan, the Westminster courts, which would remain largely unchanged, would add appellate judges to decide appeals in the court in which the case began. Prohibitions and injunctions would be severely limited and a court of requests for small suits would be established at Westminster. Lawyers, attorneys and court official were to be regulated and fees set. Probate would be handled by the common law courts by a cheap, short and clear process. Appearance in court would be by summons rather than arrest, but the summons would include the cause of action.[95] County courts with an expanded authority, manned by salaried, godly justices of the peace would provide quick and inexpensive justice close to

[91] See Hugh Trevor-Roper, *Oliver Cromwell and His Parliaments* (London, Macmillan, 1956); Peter Gaunt, 'Law Making in the First Protectorate Parliament' in C Jones, M Newitt and S Roberts (eds), *Politics and People in Revolutionary England* (Oxford, Blackwell, 1986) 161–86; Peter Gaunt, 'Oliver Cromwell and His Protectorate Parliaments: Conflict and Control' in Ivan Roots (ed) *Into Another Mould: Aspects of the Interregnum* (Exeter, University of Exeter Press, 1998); Patrick Little and David L Smith, *Parliaments and Politics during the Cromwellian Protectorate* (Cambridge, Cambridge University Press, 2007); Blair Worden, *God's Instruments: Political Conduct in the England of Oliver Cromwell* (Oxford, Oxford University Press, 2012) 230–59. Trevor Roper emphasised parliament's incompetent management; Gaunt provides a more positive view.

[92] CJ, VII, 350, 401, 415–16, 449; Firth and Rait (n 58) vol II, 1043; Little and Smith (n 91) 173; Gaunt (n 91) 163–86. There were ordinances dealing with the relief of creditors and poor imprisoned debtors, probate and granting administrations, and the creation of a High Court of Justice; Firth and Rait (n 58) vol II, 824, 869, 911–15.

[93] Quoted in Gaunt (n 91) 175.

[94] William Clarke, *Selections from the Papers of William Clarke* (London, 1891–1901), vol III, 61.

[95] William Sheppard, *England's Balme* (London, 1656) Dedicatory Epistle, 57–58, 66–69, 142. See Nancy L Matthews, *William Sheppard, Cromwell's Law Reformer* (Cambridge, Cambridge University Press, 1984).

home. Because juries were 'generally very corrupt', trial by jury would be replaced by summary justice in the county courts and courts baron. County land registers and parish registers to record satisfaction of debts and other agreements as well as land transactions would be established. Primogenitor would be replaced by a more equal division of property.[96]

Sheppard called for a reduction in the number of capital crimes, especially for small or trivial thefts. In keeping with the radical reformers, manslaughter and 'horrid blasphemies'. would now be punished by death. Penalties for perjury would increase. Counsel and sworn witnesses should be permitted in cases of serious crimes. A not guilty plea would eliminate pressing to death.[97]

Sheppard also called for 'one, plain, complete and Methodical Treatise or Abridgment of the whole Common and Statute-Law … to which all cases may be referred' in order 'to make … the obscure and incertain … cleer and certain'. The treatise would require both parliamentary confirmation and judicial affirmation that it was 'the settled Law'. Sheppard reassured his readers that his reforms would 'take away the Weeds', not the wheat. His 'rude Model' would remove 'offensive, oppressive and superfluous Laws', supply replacements for defective laws, clarify doubtful laws, and provide quick and easy justice.[98] Although he placed himself in the moderate camp, several provisions had more in common with the radical agenda.

V. Cromwell and the Judiciary

Although Cromwell intended 'to fill the Courts of Justice with the best and most learned men he can find', Thurlow reported that the Protector was finding it difficult to find 'fit persons'.[99] New patents were issued to several judges, but were denied to others appointed by the Rump. Some were reluctant to accept judicial office.[100] Despite his reservations, Matthew Hale agreed to become a judge of

[96] Sheppard (n 95) 42, 45–50, 113, 113–25. Defamation, once adjudicated in the ecclesiastical courts, would be transferred to the justices of the peace. See also William Sheppard, *A Survey of the County Judicatures* (London, 1656) Preface; William Sheppard, *A New Survey of the justice Pease* (London, 1657).

[97] Sheppard (n 95) 36, 37, 134, 159–160, 196–97, 210. He denounced the inadequacies of current laws dealing with 'lascivious gestures, wanton and filthy dalliance … whorish attire, [and] strange fashions' such as 'naked brests, bare shoulders, powdering'. Justices of the peace were to pay greater attention to laws against 'profane jesting … ballad fiddling, rhyming … tumbling, dancing upon the rope, singing … [and] bearbaiting' (at 162–64).

[98] Sheppard (n 95) To the Reader, Dedicatory Epistle, 56; Sheppard's *Epitome of all the Common and Statute law of the Nation now in Force*, published at Cromwell's special command, appeared the same year as *England's Balme*. See also Sheppard's *The Faithful Councellor; or the Marrow of the Law in England* (London, 1651).

[99] Thurloe to Whitelocke, quoted in Spalding (n 84) 373, 374.

[100] Stephen Black, 'Coram Protectore: The Judges of Westminster Hall during the Protectorate of Oliver Cromwell' (1976) 20 *American Journal of Legal History* 31.

Common Pleas. Whitlocke, again Commissioner of the Great Seal, was reluctant to accept the office because, unlike the common law judges who had 'certain Rules to guide them, a Keeper of the Seal had only his conscience to direct him'.[101]

Royalist rebellions during the period between Cromwell's first and second parliaments led to a series of controversial treason trials. High courts of justice and their trial procedure were established by ordinance without parliamentary approval. Assize judges resisted the ordinance and attempted to use traditional law and legal procedure. Several judges removed themselves from trying the causes, while others were quietly removed but not punished.[102] The questionable legality of non-parliamentary ordinances again cast doubt on the legitimacy of Cromwell's government.

The decision to implement the Chancery ordinance without parliamentary approval led judges to ignore the ordinance and proceed according to the traditional rules. Whitelocke, who favoured Chancery reform, opposed the Chancery ordinance, believing that the Council and Protector had no authority to make law: 'We cannot in judgment and conscience feel free to proceed on the Ordinance touching Chancery.' One judge objected on the grounds that Cromwell and Council 'had no power to make a law' and not being 'agreeable to any law … would be an occasion of injustice to many'. The ordinance was 'an illegal act … too much countenancing of illegal authority'. Critics also objected to the ordinance's lack of flexibility, protesting that the changes it introduced would lead to hardship and injustice. Whitelocke and Thomas Widdrington also complained that 'we had not the honor' of being 'advised with upon the making of this ordinance'.[103] After several meetings, the judges were 'gravely admonished … not to oppose his highness's intentions' and were dismissed from office. Whitelocke and Widdrington were replaced by judges without Chancery experience. Two additional judges were 'put out of their places' for not observing the Chancery ordinance. The ordinance was suspended.[104]

Whitelocke has not had a good press. As noted earlier, historians tend to see him as a conservative who sought to derail law reform. However, if one traces his career over time, a different picture emerges. Whitelocke was a reformer, albeit one who insisted on maintaining the common law and a centralised court system. When faced with the Cromwellian ordinances, even those he had helped to draft, he rejected them because they lacked parliamentary approval. Some judges and lawyers were uncertain about the legality of the Protectorate itself; others supported it on the grounds that law and its administration were necessary.

[101] Whitelocke (n 3) vol I, 373. Equity proceedings are '*secundum arbitrium boni viri*, and this arbitrium differeth as much in several men, as their Countenances differ'.

[102] Black (n 100) 41; Cromartie (n 42) 80–81, 84.

[103] Whitelocke (n 3) vol IV, 204–05. Master of the Rolls William Lenthall also spoke 'most resolutely against it'.

[104] ibid 191, 204–05; Black (n 100) 50, 53–55; Ruth Spalding, *The Improbable Puritan: A Life of Bulstrode Whitelocke, 1605–1675* (London, Faber & Faber, 1975) 203, 205; CJ, VII, 373, 376, 394, 414. Both Whitelocke and Widdrington were willing to become treasury commissioners.

Additional conflict with the judiciary developed over the validity of the new treason ordinance and the creation of high courts of justice. When a commission was created to try Royalist rebels in the north, two commissioners refused to recognise the validity of the treason ordinance because it lacked parliamentary approval. Although all common law and Chancery judges and the Master of the Rolls were named as commissioners, only one agreed to participate.[105] In 1658 two judges were questioned by the Council of State for their conduct on circuit. Doubts about the allegiance of the judges resulted in the cancellation of the next winter circuit. In November, 1658 Hale was said to have reservations about serving as a judge and was reported to have refused to sit until he had been 'satisfied in one part of the judges oath, and excused from sitting upon life and death' cases.[106] Whitlocke preferred using the regular courts and traditional procedure. Later Cromwell capitulated, agreeing to trying several conspirators at the upper bench (formerly King's Bench) using 'the course' of the common law.[107] Although the high courts of justice continued to function during the Protectorate, they never had the full support of the legal profession.

Another conflict with the judiciary occurred in the spring of 1655, when the merchant George Cony refused to pay customs duties and was imprisoned. Critics argued that the fines imposed by the Council violated the act abolishing Star Chamber and the other conciliar courts. Henry Rolle, Chief Justice of the Upper Bench, resigned over the illegality of the ordinance. The suit was eventually abandoned and a decision was avoided, but before it was over, several judges were removed and several lawyers were imprisoned. Trials based on ordinances lacking parliamentary approval eroded the legitimacy of the regime.[108]

VI. The Second Protectorate Parliament

The parliament which met from September 1656 to June 1657, and again in January and February 1658, was now augmented by a second chamber filled with Cromwell's trusted allies. About 100 elected members of parliament were refused their seats for not being 'of known integrity fearing God'. Another 50 withdrew in protest. Cromwell's opening speech in 1656 declared that if there was one general grievance, 'It is the Law'. He spoke of the 'great grievance in the execution and

[105] Cromartie (n 42) 81–82; James Hart, *The Rule of Law 1603–1660: Crown, Courts and Judges* (London, Longmans, 2003) 290–91. Acts erecting High Courts of Justice were passed in 1650, 1651 and 1653, and an ordinance in 1654.

[106] James Cockburn, *A History of the English Assizes 1558–1714* (Cambridge, Cambridge University Press, 1972) 245; Letter from Gilbert Mabbot to Henry Cromwell, in *The Correspondence of Henry Cromwell, 1655–1659*, Peter Gaunt (ed) (Cambridge, Cambridge University Press, 2007) 419

[107] Whitelocke (n 3) vol IV, 33.

[108] The legality of parliament's punishment of the Quaker John Naylor in 1656 raised the issue of whether the parliament might legitimately act as a court.

administration … of Law' as well as the 'wicked and abominable laws' that were within parliament's power to reform. He defended tithes and religious toleration, and referred to the injustice of hanging a man for a 'trifle' and the impropriety of pardons for murder.[109]

Though they were not implemented, Sheppard's reform proposals were prepared for parliament and printed. There were bills to eliminate the Court of Wards, to change feudal tenures to free and common socage, and to relieve poor prisoners and creditors. A bill proposing county land registries was debated and dropped.[110] General Lambert, who had governing responsibilities in the north, brought in a bill to settle courts of justice and equity at York and the northern counties that would have reinstated some of the functions of the abolished Council of the North.[111]

The Humble Petition and Advice (May 1657), which would have transformed the Lord Protector into a king, was thought to have been favoured by the legal profession, which on the whole preferred a more traditional constitution. The leading judges, Oliver St John, Widdrington, Whitelocke and William Lenthall, favoured a mixed monarchy. Whitelocke stated that 'the laws of England are so interwoven with the power and practice of monarchy, that to settle a government without something of monarchy would make so great an alteration in the proceedings of our law' as to make it impossible to 'forsee the inconveniences'. But the proposal making Cromwell king was opposed by the army, republicans and those who favoured the sovereignty of parliament.[112] After Cromwell refused the crown, excluded members were permitted to return to parliament. Legally binding ordinances issued when parliament was not in session were now explicitly forbidden and parliamentary approval would be required for the appointment of judges and others officers of state.[113] Parliament, not the executive, would control the judiciary. The changes led to republican protests in the House of Commons and in the army, as well as heightened fears of a Leveller revival and Royalist plots.

Despite the unsettled state of affairs, the legislation of 1657 granted religious toleration to those who acknowledged the Trinity and Scripture. Roman Catholics and those guilty of licentious practices were excluded. There were bills dealing with Admiralty and probate of wills. A much-debated bill for county registers of

[109] Wilbur Abbott (ed), *The Writings and Speeches of Oliver Cromwell*, 4 vols (Cambridge, MA, Harvard University Press, 1937–49), vol IV, 274; Ivan Roots, 'Lawmaking in the Second Protectorate Parliament' in H Header and HR Loyn (eds), *British Government and Administration* (Cardiff, University of Wales Press, 1974) 132–43.

[110] Firth and Rait (n 58) vol II, 1043; CJ, VII, 439.

[111] Clarke (n 94) vol III, 81; Whitelocke (n 3) vol IV, 161. The palatine jurisdictions of Chester and Lancaster were restored by a Proclamation in June 1658. For the role of the major generals in local administration and law, see Anthony Fletcher, 'Oliver Cromwell and the Localities: The Problem of Consent' in Jones, Newitt and Roberts (n 91) 187–294.

[112] Whitelocke (n 3) vol 372–73, 374. The document was printed. Lenthall, Speaker of the House of Commons (1640–53), again became Speaker in Cromwell's first parliament.

[113] Hart (n 105) 220, 221; Firth and Rait (n 58) vol II, 1048–56.

land was said to have gone nowhere due to opposition from the 'long robe'. There was also a hotly contested proposal for registering births, marriages and burials. A committee was appointed to prepare yet another bill for the relief of creditors and poor prisoners.[114] There were also bills dealing with bastardy, adultery and fornication, and for regulating the number and quality of attorneys and solicitors. Chancery remained contentious. The House voted not to receive a committee report dealing with Chancery, and no bill was introduced.[115] Although little legislation was completed, bills eliminating the Court of Wards and Liveries in England, Ireland and Scotland passed, as did others changing all tenures to freehold and abolishing purveyance. Both measures were retained in 1660–61.

VII. The Third Protectorate Parliament

With Cromwell's death in September, 1658, Oliver's son, Richard Cromwell, became Protector. Richard lacked the support of the army, the mainstay of the Protectorate, and inherited a divided Council. The government eroded and then collapsed under tension between the army, Protectorate supporters and those opposed to the monarchical character of the Protectorate. Royalist sentiment increased, as did the belief that the Protectorate lacked legitimacy. It had never been very popular and continued to be tainted by its military basis.

Richard called on Parliament for the 'work of reformation, both in manners and in administration of justice'.[116] Using the language of moderate reform before parliament, Nathaniel Fiennes, Keeper of the Great Seal, reminded his auditors that 'Judgment and Justice' should 'run down in a clear and swift stream'. If 'Rubbish, Mud, or Weedes … got into the Channels, it may be cleared' by 'scouring the Channel' not digging 'down the Banks' and allowing 'an Inundation of Arbitrary Power and Jurisdiction' to be let loose upon the nation. It was essential to avoid the 'those dreadful Confusions' of the recent past.[117]

The legislative and executive consensus essential for successful law reform became even less possible during the Ricardian Protectorate. There was disagreement about the powers of the Protectorate and the legality of its legal proceedings, as well as disputes over the judicial and legislative functions of the Other House.[118]

[114] CJ, VI, 427, 439, 441, 524. Civil marriage was no longer the only form of marriage.

[115] CJ, VI, 528; *The Diary of Thomas Burton* (London, H Colburn, 1828), vol II, 80. The extent to which the Chancery ordinance was implemented is not clear. Busch suggests that Whitelocke's successors, Nathaniel Fiennes and Lord Lisle, enforced the ordinance until their dismissal in April 1659; Busch (n 11) 329. Donald Veall suggests that resistance to Chancery reform was primarily the work of the Chancery bar and court officials; Veall (n 34) 252.

[116] Richard Cromwell, *The Speech … made to both Houses of Parliament* (London, 1659) 4, 5, 9.

[117] *The Speech of Nathaniel Lord Fiennes … Made before his Highnesse, and both Houses of Parliament* (London, 1659) 13, 14–15, 16, 18–19, 22.

[118] Lord Keeper Fiennes and William Prynne defended the judicial powers of the upper house; *A Plea for the House of Lords* (London, 1657), Preface. See Little and Smith (n 91) 191–95; Derek Hirst,

There were clashes between pro- and anti-Protectorate supporters and between civil and military supporters. The result was the forced resignation of the Protector and the dissolution of the parliament.

VIII. Law Reform and the Press During the Protectorate

Pamphlets on the subject of law reform dropped off precipitously in 1655, rose again briefly in 1656 and did not increase again until the tumultuous year of 1659. The reduction in 1655 stemmed from orders dealing with unlicensed and scandalous books, and perhaps from reduced interest from the high point of 1653–54. Newsbooks, except those allowed by Cromwell and the Council of State, were suppressed. Law reform publications were various. Some again offered a defence of the common law and legal profession, while others proposed a legal system in accordance with Scripture. Cromwell was portrayed as a providential saviour or an unlawful tyrant. There was no consensus on law reform either in parliament or in the printed media.

Among the defenders of the common law, there were those who were hostile to all change, as well as those who defended the common law and the legal profession, but favoured moderate reform. *The Exact Law Giver*, for example, defended the 'Antiquity, Excellency and Perfection' of the common law and its use of Latin, French and English. Its author also supported the legal profession and condemned the 'conceited Novelists and malevilous spirits' with their 'rash and overmalepert censures of our Common Law'. He pointed to the 'certainty and sure principles' of the common law. No other law could be 'so well exprest, nor any Case in Law so succinctly sensibly and fully reported and demonstrated'. Excessive delays were not caused, as so many thought, by lawyers, but rather by the 'artfulness and perverseness of clyants', with their 'contentious depositions' and propensity to seek 'judgement after Judgment and Decree after Decree'. Lawyers are defended from 'unjust calumnies', as were the assizes that brought justice to the entire country.[119]

William Prynne attacked the Cromwellian regime and its programme of law reform. He admitted that there might be a few grievances and abuses in the law, but these were 'not in the Theory, but Practice of our Laws'. Remediation should in the hands of judges, not military 'Reformadoes of the Law' who 'under pretext of reforming some petty Abuses' created abuses 'of a far more grievous, general, and transcendent nature, subverting the very Fundamental Law, Liberties of the whole Nation'. Army reformers had acted against the law of God and the land without 'any colour of lawfull Authority' and had 'disseised' and 'disinherited' many 'without any other Law or Title' than that of the 'longest sword'. Prynne repudiated

'Concord and Discord in Richard Cromwell's House of Commons' (1988) 103 *English Historical Review* 339.

[119] *The Exact Law-Giver* (London, 1658) 2, 3 7, 8.

efforts 'to engross all Law and Justice for the future into their own hands alone and suppress all Courts of Justice, Judges, as dull and useless tools, as some of late have stiled them'. He reviled 'their New Voluminous Whitehall folio Edicts, Ordinances … altering our former Laws and Statutes' and the practice of soldiers riding with assize judges in order 'to overawe and control them'.[120]

In an assize charge of 1658, Oliver St John, Chief Justice of Common Pleas, refuted radical proposals for autonomous local courts. 'New judicatories will disunite & make severall laws in ye nation', creating 'as many petty states as there are laws'. 'One law, one state.' Like many common lawyers, St John also rejected the radical notion of a sharp break at the time of the Norman Conquest. The courts should not be tampered with, though their jurisdictions should be clarified to prevent 'delay and mistakes in judgment'. St John rejected the addition of courts to assist the poor who were unable to travel to Westminster, arguing that existing local courts provided access to law and that the assizes provided legal services 'in your owne counties'. By 1658, St John thought it better to tolerate lesser inconveniences 'to avoid ye greter'.[121] Like so many revolutionary-era lawyers and judges, he had little sympathy with the radical law reform agenda. The radical reformers pushed many moderate reformers into becoming more defensive.

Another example is provided by William Style. Style hoped that his *Registrum Practical*, which provided a 'brief but concise' alphabetical treatment of the 'rules, orders and observations' of the common law, would 'satisfie those great Antagonists of the law who need to have things made a very plain' and 'vilify the Law'. He defended common law and the lawyers, and denounced the 'clamour of some infatuated Spirits of this distempered Age, who … labor to bring all things into confusion' and rail 'against the Common Laws of this Nation, and the practice thereof'. 'The vulgar and ignorant were 'ever thirsting after change and alteration'. Many 'things disliked and inveighed against' were wrongly characterised as 'fit … to be abolished or reformed'. The common law was 'never so excellent and desirable' and neither the law nor its practice contained the 'considerable inconveniences' of 'such dangerous consequences as some pretend'. 'Reform was difficult and dangerous.' 'Only "Grave and Learned Judges and Sages of this Nation" might order and regulate law and legal practice … without impairing the excellences of the Laws.'[122]

Writing about the same time, another barrister praised common law as 'nothing less than the Perfection of Reason and consonant to the Law of God, grounded

[120] William Prynne, *A Summary Collection of the Principal Fundamental Rights, Liberties, Properties of all English Freeman* (London, 1656), 20, 22, 26, 29, 31. Prynne supported the Restoration.

[121] Cornelia D Smith, 'A Seventeenth Century Judge Views the Law: Oliver St John's Introduction to His Charge at the Thetford Assizes in 1658' (1986) 130 *Proceedings of the American Philosophical Society* 55, 59, 69, 70, 82.

[122] William Style, *Regestrum Practical; Or, the Practical* (London, 1657). 'Reports were taken in unsettled times, wherein the Law was almost at a Stand.' Earlier 'the Laws flow'd' in 'more open, and uninterrupted Channels' and 'were in a more splended and flourishing condition'; Epistle Dedicatory, Preface to the Reader.

upon long experience and so brought to Perfection'. Its enemies are characterised as few in number and worth, imbued with the 'spirit of levelling' and novelty, and dissatisfied with all forms of government. However, the writer, like a substantial number of moderate lawyer-reformers, admitted that England's 'excellent laws' contained 'exhuberancies' that should be ''lopped off'. He denounced the 'false and groundless' and 'frivolous and trivial' lawsuits that had 'crept in'. He favoured reforming irregularities in the Court of Common Pleas, the summons to initiate cases and reduction in the number of attorneys, solicitors and clerks. The 1654 ordinance, the author suggested, was insufficient to restrain the 'swarms of suits' for slander, occasioned by 'contentious spirits'. Several recent acts and ordinances 'gave too much to Equity', leaving too much to judgments and interpretation according to every man's conscience'. Praising Sheppard's proposals, the author hoped for reform during 'this blessed flourishing spring' of the Protector's 'Justice'. Unlike most reformers, the author thought reform possible 'without the help of the Legislative Powers, or new Law made'.[123]

Printed and published according to Order and dedicated to the Protector, his council and common lawyers, *The Humble Inquiry, Partly Approving and Partly Disapproving the Practice of the Law* praised lawyers for their knowledge, dignity and glory, but also pointed to abuses. It castigated lawyers for giving 'unsound and unfaithfull advice', 'managing … ill causes at Trials or Hearings' and an inclination to 'palliate or extenuate wrong[s]' and to 'misguide' witnesses, juries and judges. Attorneys and solicitors were also criticised. The author then offered a series of queries, among them whether it was best to abolish lawyers, whether common pleading, terms and circuits should be ended because shire business was too often managed by persons of the weakest parts and the least experience, whether common pleading led to a multiplicity of suits and encouraged 'men of contentious spirits' to pursue 'causelesse vexatious and frivolous actions', and whether arbitrators might be preferable to lawyers. Additional queries included whether some things were now so corrupt that it was too difficult to separate abuse from use and therefore it would be better to remove them altogether. It also asked whether the legal system would be improved if three judges were required to hear and determine causes, whether there should be 'sharp fines' for lawyers who supported unjust causes, and whether lawyers should be salaried or equal fees should be charged to defendants and plaintiffs. Although unanswered, his queries left no doubt that this defender of the common law and common lawyers was open to considerable reform. This tract looked to the Cromwellian government to implement the necessary reforms.[124]

[123] D W, *A Perspicuous Compendium of Several Irregularities and Abuses in the Present Practice of the Common Law of England* (London, 1656) Dedicatory Letter, 1–2, 7–8, 12–13. 16–18.

[124] *The Humble Inquiry, Partly Approving and Partly Disapproving the Practice of the Law* (London, 1656) 2, 4, 15–16, 17, 21. See also *A New Case Put to an Old Lawyer, or, Lawyers look about You* (London, 1656) 2, 4, 8, 11–13.

Chancery and the Cromwellian Chancery ordinance attracted a number of writers. In 1655 there was *Observations concerning the Chancery with some proposals for the redress of the inconveniences in the practice thereof.* In 1657 another publication discussed the limitations of the Chancery ordinance.[125] On the other hand, Edward Leigh, a defender of the ordinance, thought that England had never seen 'a better or more accurate and excellent [ordinance]'.[126]

If Leigh lauded Cromwell's reform efforts, the author of *The Second Narration* viewed the Protector as a tyrant. The pamphlet condemned the Protector's 'High Court of so called Justice', his judges and commissioners of the Great Seal, and 'that abominable Corruption … in the Law and Administration of Justice, which the Protector himself said was not to be endured'.[127]

Best known as a work of historical analysis and political theory, James Harrington's *The Commonwealth of Oceana*, which was dedicated to the Lord Protector, commented briefly and somewhat obliquely on the issue of law reform. Using the language of the moderates, Harrington argued that 'There was danger in the plausible pretence of reforming the law' unless the government be 'first good, in which case it … bringeth not evil fruit'. If evil, 'you can never reform the fruit, or, if a root that is naught bring forth fruit of this kind that seemeth to be good, take the more heed, for it is the ranker Poison'. Harrington's idealised version of England retained judges who rode circuits assisted by local magistrates, juries 'according unto the more ancient laws and customs of this nation' as well as quarter sessions 'according unto the ancient custom'. *Oceana* assumed that there would be professional lawyers educated at the Inns of Court and Chancery, as well as judges 'as they have heretofore been'.[128]

The most extended reform publication of the Protectorate era was *England's Balme* of 1656, the work of William Sheppard, discussed earlier. Printed under Cromwell's protection, Sheppard's comprehensive proposals were submitted to parliament, which ordered a committee to evaluate them.[129]

Religious radicals offered a very different kind of law reform. The militant Fifth Monarchists, who were at their height during the Barebones Parliament, were hostile to the Protectorate. Fifth Monarchists William Aspinwall and John Spittlehouse insisted on rigorous adherence to the law of God. Aspinwall urged that the Kingdom of Christ be established in England. Scripture made it clear that capital punishment must not be applied in cases of theft, but required it

[125] *Some Considerations concerning the High Court of Chancery* (London, 1657).

[126] Edward Leigh, *Second Considerations concerning the High Court of Chancery* (London, 1658) 1–12. Leigh advised the removal of anything in the ordinance that might be harmful. Parliament passed the ordinance in 1657, but only for the life of that Parliament. It lapsed in February 1658.

[127] *A Second Narration* (1658) in *Harleian Miscellany or, a Collection of Rare, Curious and Entertaining Pamphlets and Tracts*, 8 vols (London, 1744), vol III, 452, 458, 467.

[128] James Harrington, *The Commonwealth of Oceana and a System of Politics*, JGA Pocock (ed) (Cambridge, Cambridge University Press, 1992) 41, 94, 100, 167, 191, 203, 204.

[129] Sheppard (n 95) Dedicatory Epistle.

for blasphemy, cursing God, profaning the Sabbath, cursing parents and giving false witness against a man's life. Aspinwall, who had spent time in New England, published John Cotton's *Abstract of law* in 1655, a code he viewed as 'far surpassing all the Municipal Laws and Statutes' of any other nation.[130] Spittlehouse agreed that the law of God must be the law of England and provided Scriptural proofs for his assertions.[131] William Medley declared Protectorate laws 'inconsistent with Gospel Spirit' and advocated county judicatures, appeals and the ability to plead one's own cause.[132] A Fifth Monarchist pamphleteer called the Protector the betrayer of the Saints and 'no friend of God'. It condemned the Protectorate's 'monarchical foundation', its rule by 'power of the sword', its 'tyrannical wicked power' and its support for tithes. For this writer, Cromwell had betrayed the Barebones Parliament and wrongfully imprisoned Fifth Monarchists.[133] Risks of Fifth Monarchist plots were tracked by the government's spy system. Government fears were not imaginary: Venner's Rebellion of 1657 justified government apprehension.

Quakers also believed that the 'unchangeable and perfect' law of God must be the 'rule of Law-makers and the ground of all just Laws'. However, unlike the Fifth Monarchists, they did not insist on all the Old Testament penalties. Richard Farnsworth wrote that all unjust laws and lawyers should be abolished as 'an Abomination to the Lorde' and George Fox criticised a legal system that required litigants to travel hundreds of miles.[134] Fox also insisted that English replace law French as the language of the law 'so that every countryman may plead his causes'. 'All the law books in the nation' should be 'thrown away' and replaced with law 'in short and plain words'.[135] In 1654 and 1655, Quaker John Camm expressed disappointment in Cromwell's failure to end legal oppression. A Quaker tract sent to Cromwell and his counsellors emphasised the distinction between 'the righteous law of God' and the law of man, and complained that law-makers were opposing the former.[136]

Examining English laws by the standards of antiquity, reason and Scripture, a lengthy radical anti-Cromwellian publication found many to be 'repugnant'

[130] William Aspinwall, *The Legislative Power is Christs Peculiar Prerogative* (London, 1655) To the Reader, 26, 30–31, 43. See also Bernard Capp, *Fifth Monarchy Men: A Study in Seventeenth Century English Millenarianism* (London, Faber & Faber, 1972); LF Solt, 'The Fifth Monarchy Men: Politics and the Millennium' (1961) 30 *Church History* 314; Andrew Bradstock, *Radical Religion in Cromwell's England* (London, IB Tauris, 2011) 120–35.

[131] John Spittlehouse, *Royal Advocate* (London, 1655) The Epistle, 2, 8, 11.

[132] William Medley, *A Standard Set Up* (London, 1657) 16, 17, 10.

[133] *The Protector (so called) in Part Unvailed* (London, 1655) 1, 37, 43, 55, 77.

[134] Farnsworth, quoted in R Michael Rogers, 'Quakerism and the Law in Revolutionary England' (1987) 22 *Canadian Journal of History* 156, 159; George Fox, *The Law of God, the Rule for Lawmakers, the Ground of all Just laws, and the corruption of English Laws and Lawyers Discovered* (London, 1658) 5–8, 20, 21–22, 28.

[135] Rogers (n 134) 159, quoted in Christopher Hill, *Liberty against Law: Some Seventeenth Century Controversies* (London, Allen, 1996) 260. Quakers, who numbered about 5,000 in 1654, grew to 20,000 by 1657 and 60,000 by the end of the decade; Bradstock (n 130) 95.

[136] John Camm, *Some Particulars concerning the Law, sent to Oliver Cromwell* (London, 1654). There was another printing in 1655.

to the laws of God and burdensome to the people. The Law of God must be the 'foundation' of all laws. Proof of these laws were to be found in Scripture, not in 'Books or Rolls', Magna Carta and the many other old statutes that 'savor[ed] of the Anti-Christ'. The author supported radical demands for new county courts, pleading one's cause, the abolition of imprisonment for debt and the development of a new 'body of law' that was 'short, easie, and few'. Currently both courts of law and equity were 'oppressive' and against the law of God. Cases previously adjudicated in more than one court led to an overcrowded Chancery, which in turn led to oppression. Lawyers, attorneys, solicitors, clerks, sergeants, sheriffs and jailors are compared to 'Egyptian Locusts'. Most land tenures were inconsistent with 'Gospel Spirit', while entails were against God-given law. Primogeniture must be ended because Scripture prescribed only a double share for the eldest male. Juries too were 'no Scripture way'.[137]

Like many religious radicals, Booth insisted that many punishments were contrary to Scripture. Capital punishment for theft must end, but should be introduced for manslaughter. The ruler's pardoning power in the case of murder was impious. Currently there was no 'considerable law' against adultery or fornication because the law prescribing the death penalty had been 'so penned, that few, or none will ever be convicted upon it'. He also took the position that conviction on the basis of single witness was against the law of God.[138] James Freise, author of several pamphlets on imprisonment for debt, looked to 'the Lords Instrument of Englands Honor', Cromwell, to restore the ancient law of England in its purity 'grounded on the Judicial Law of God'.[139]

Although the newsbooks of this period have been well studied, little attention has been given to their role in informing the public about law reform measures introduced and/or debated in Parliament. *Several Proceedings of Parliament* in 1654 and 1655 made frequent mention of the contentious debates on the legislative power and the Protector's speeches to parliament. The *Proceedings* noted bills that were offered for elimination of the Court of Wards, relief of creditors and poor prisoners, the regulation of Chancery and abuses of habeas corpus. Petitions from the West Riding of York favouring a court of justice in York and five surrounding counties were noted. Parliamentary debates on Chancery were reported between October 1654 and January 1655, as was Cromwell's speech denouncing parliament's failure to produce good laws. Most items were reported without comment.

[137] A Booth, *Examen Legum Angliae, or, The Laws of England examined by Scripture, Antiquity and Reason* (London, 1656) To the Reader, 4, 9, 15, 17, 25, 29–30, 45, 58–59, 62, 65, 77, 84, 85, 93, 95–96, 100, 105, 110, 112, 114, 124, unpaginated appendix.

[138] Laws were also lacking against 'wanton and filthy dalliance', 'whorish attire', 'naked breasts' and 'powdering', and curling women's hair and insufficient for gaming, bear and bull baiting, stage players, and ballad singers; Booth (n 137) 54, 55, 56, 115, 121–22, 127–28, 130–31. Similar language also appears in Sheppard's *England's Balme*.

[139] James Freize, *A Moderate Inspection into the Corruption of the Politique part of the Common Law of England* (np, 1656) 3–4, 5, 8. See also L P, *The Prisoners Enlargement* (London, 1656).

Law reform, discussed extensively in *A Perfect Diurnal* between April and November 1654, provided weekly discussion on the legislative power, security of property against fraud, the high cost of witness travel, removal of cases to Westminster, creditors and imprisoned debtors, bankruptcy reform, clandestine marriage and the Chancery ordinance. In 1655 all newsbooks, except those allowed by Cromwell and the Council of State, were suppressed. Additional efforts to tighten control were taken in 1658.[140]

There continued to be the significant publication of legal literature mostly in English. We have already taken notice of Styles' *Practical Register*. Lawyer Edmund Wingate's *The Body of the Common Law of England* provided an abstract based on Sir Henry Finch's earlier work as well as a collection of statutes that had altered the common law.[141] In 1654 the reprint of Finch's *A Summary of the Common Law* included the statement that although English law was 'accounted so abstruse and intricate, that it has always seemed an Impossibility to reduce it to method', Finch had 'clothed it with a logical method' and produced an excellent one.[142]

Lawyer Michael Hawkes' *The Grounds of the Lawes of Englan*d provided 200 'grounds', a term he equated with principles, maxims or erudition. A supporter of moderate law reform. Hawkes reminded readers that King James I had advised Coke to 'reduce the common law into a more commodious method'. While Coke had doubted the 'fruit' of that labour and Bacon had avoided the task, Finch had succeeded 'in reducing rationally, the body of our Lawes into a compendious method'. Hawkes promised to simplify the vast bulk of material that 'confounded memory' and seconded Sir John Doddridge's wish to purge the laws of their 'great confusion of tedious and superfluous reiterations'. Only parliament could alter the law and no changes should be made 'unless for necessity and impulsive causes … that arise' from 'public mischiefs and inconveniences which happens to all commonwealths'.[143]

These were years in which many law reports or abridgements were translated into English. Coke's were not translated, but abridgements of Coke's, Dyer's and Plowden's reports were 'Englished'. The number of translations during the Protectorate suggests a serious effort to make the law more accessible.

Edward Bulstrode, whose publications were dedicated to Bulstrode Whitelocke, his powerful relative, condemned the radical reformers and defended the common law and the Protector. The radicals had 'held up their swords to cut down (pretended) superfluous branches of our Law, have cut down the law itself, both root and Branch'. Fortunately, these 'oppressors of our Law' had been stopped

[140] Peacey, *Politics and Pamphlets* (n 75) 160–61.

[141] E W, *The Body of the Common Law*, 2nd edn (London, 1655). Later editions appeared in 1662, 1670 and 1678.

[142] Sir Henry Finch, *A Summary of the Common Law digested into certain Tablets* (London, 1654) Advertisement to the Reader.

[143] Michael Hawkes, *The Grounds of the Lawes of England* (London, 1657) Preface. The 'table' of the 'grounds' or 'maxims' were borrowed from Finch and Noy.

'by the wisdom and fore-sight of the Supreme Magistrate'. Patriots like Whitelocke had been 'vigilant and industrious, for the Preservation of our laws'. English law is praised for its antiquity, certainty, equality and quick execution, and its judges for their learning and wisdom. Their interpretations were 'grounded upon the Evidence of Reason and upon the prudent advisements and mature men who were *Ieges loquents*'. While Bulstrode admitted that the law had expanded too much, leading to obscurity and bulk, its foundation was 'good' and its 'known Maxims' could not be changed. Although abrogating ancient laws would be disastrous, some of 'rust' currently attached to the laws might be removed.[144]

There were few reform publications in 1657 and 1658.

IX. Scotland and Ireland

Cromwellian-era law reform efforts had a considerable impact on Scotland and Ireland. Commissioners were sent to Scotland with instructions to impose English law 'as near as the constitution and use of the people there and the present affairs will permit'. They were authorised to set up new courts and appoint law officers, to decentralise justice and to simplify the law. However, serious implementation had to wait until the army had conquered Scotland.[145]

Oliver St John, a prominent Cromwellian judge and commissioner in Scotland in 1652, believed that there could be no unity between the two countries without a single legal system, pointing out that Wales had not become united with England until English laws had been introduced there. In 1654 an Ordinance of Union abolished feudal lordships, heritable jurisdictions, military service and wardship. A mixed Scottish-English commission was to administer justice. Legal fees were regulated, Latin was abolished in legal documents and legal language and procedure were simplified. The laws governing debt were made more attractive to debtors and the burning of witches was forbidden. English judges were sent on circuit and justices of the peace were re-established. However, these reforms proved short-lived, disappearing with General Monck's departure from Scotland in 1660.[146] As James Harrington observed: 'If England have no Army in Scotland, Scotland will receive no Law from England; and if England have a Army there, her hold consisteth not in the Union but in the force.'[147]

[144] *The Third Part of the reports of Edward Bulstrude*, 2nd edn (London, 1688) Dedicatory Epistle dated 1 November 1658. Reports are characterised as 'anchors of Law'. See the comment on 'rust' from *The Reports of Edward Bulstrode* (London, 1657) Dedicatory letter.

[145] See J Irvine Smith, 'The Transition to Modern Law, 1532–1660' in *An Introduction to Scottish Legal History* (Edinburgh, Stair Society, 1958) 25–43.

[146] Quoted in Smith (n 121) 44; see also 41. See also Whitelocke (n 3) vol 390; Brian Levack, *The Formation of the British State: England, Scotland and the Union 1603–1707* (Oxford, Oxford University Press, 1987).

[147] James Harrington, *Political Aphorisms* (London, 1659) 6. In 1659 it was said that Scotland was 'without all law' and that there were 'no judicatures in Scotland to exercise of justice or by any courts,

Although the English had attempted to impose English law and English legal institutions on Ireland for centuries, they had a fragile hold there. Courts equivalent to King's Bench, Common Pleas, Exchequer and Chancery were established along with two presidency courts. Chancery, which offered cheaper and quicker justice than the other courts, was the most popular of the English-imposed courts. In 1614 a parliamentary committee attempted to standardise and display fees, and, during the reign of Charles I, Lord Strafford instituted reforms to expedite and reduce the cost of litigation. During the revolutionary decade, there were efforts to reduce and regulate fees, to keep litigants from bringing small cases to Dublin, to improve debt procedures and to prevent the manipulation of juries. Law reform in Ireland was thus consistent with Stuart efforts to improve English administration and control.[148]

Reform efforts were revived and extended by Cromwell, Henry Ireton and Fleetwood after 1649, and even more by Cromwell during the Protectorate. In 1649 Cromwell was said to have 'settled courts of judicature at Dublin' that proceeded 'by way of the chancery'. The Rump passed a bill for courts of justice in Ireland, and in 1651 parliamentary commissioners were instructed to recommend permanent legal arrangements for Ireland.[149]

Commissioners recommended reform measures again in 1653, noting the absence of a Chancery court and the inadequate arrangements for registering land conveyances. Fleetwood, a powerful English government representative in Ireland, requested the re-establishment of Chancery as well as combining the four major courts into two. Reforms were to reduce delays. The new system operated between 1650 and 1655, when Fleetwood was replaced by Henry Cromwell. Ludlow, a strong supporter of law reform in England, hoped the English would take 'Ireland for a precedent, and when they see how easy and cheap a rate property is there preserved, they will never permit themselves to be so cheated and abused as now they are'.[150]

In 1655 Irish judges became salaried, and English became the language of the law. Chancery was re-established the following year. In 1659 there were orders aimed at simplifying and speeding cases. The English found it easier to impose reforms in Ireland than to legislate them in England. However, these English-sponsored reforms were imposed in the context of efforts to subjugate Ireland and involved massive land confiscation and colonisation. For the English, Scotland and Ireland were ripe for reform; the Scots and the Irish no doubt viewed the reform efforts in another light.

superior or inferior'. Quoted in FD Dow, *Cromwellian Scotland 1651–1660* (Edinburgh, John Donald, 1979) 242.

[148] John Adamson, 'Strafford Ghost: The British Context of Viscount Lisle's lieutenancy of Ireland' in Jane H. Ohlmeyer (ed) *Ireland from Independence to Occupation 1641–1660* (Cambridge, Cambridge University Press, 1995), 137.

[149] TC. Barnard, *Cromwellian Ireland: English Government and Reform in Ireland 1649–1660* (Oxford, Oxford University Press, 1975) 251–53, 259, 278–79.

[150] Ludlow (n 67) vol III, 123.

Little on the pamphlet front dealt with Irish law reform, with the exception of the publications of John Cooke, who became Chief Justice in Munster in 1649 and judge in the Court of the Upper Bench in 1655. Cooke, who had worked with Strafford on revising the Irish statutes, produced a number of reform pamphlets between 1646 and 1659 defending the legal profession and the common law. But he also proposed that debts be paid in instalments, noting that 'although the Irish people were very poor, yet debts were much better paid in Ireland than in England'.[151] In Munster, fees were reduced, and law and equity were fused in the same court. Litigants were able to handle many legal matters close to home. TC Barnard concluded that English law became more influential in Ireland during this period and that these reform 'achievements were of the same modest order as in England'.[152]

X. 1659

I treat the year 1659 separately in order to show that the number of publications favouring law reform is, in itself, a poor gauge of widespread public interest in law reform and an even poorer one for the possibility of its success. The year 1659 is one of the most tumultuous in English political history. It saw the collapse of the Protectorate, the revival of the Commonwealth and the Rump, army generals competing for influence and power, calls for the restoration of monarchy, and deep anxieties about the viability of the political and legal system. This political instability was accompanied by an outburst of publications aided by the inability of the revived Commonwealth government to control the press. It was the collapse of government control rather than a sudden increase in reform enthusiasm that led to the increase in publications.

The Protectorate ended when the army dissolved parliament and reinstated the Rump. Though the revived Rump owed its existence to the army, parliament and army were often at odds during the few months of its troubled existence. Nor was the restored Rump, which had been opened with army officers lining the room, a unified body. It contained a relatively conservative group wishing for little more than an effective stable government and a republican, fiercely anti-monarchist faction opposed to both the Stuart and Protectorate forms of monarchy. The Rump was immediately confronted by an effort to reinstate members excluded from parliament in 1648. Outside the parliament, there was both monarchist sentiment and radicals hoping for a regime that adhered to Scripture. Support for the revived republic was narrow and the army remained a looming presence with the ability to topple the government at any moment.

[151] Quoted in Veall (n 34) 148.

[152] John Cooke, *Monarchy no creature of God's making* (London, 1652) Introduction; Edward MacLysaght, *Irish Life in the Seventeenth Century* (Dublin, Irish Academy Press, 1978) 422, 424, 437; Barnard (n 149) 279, 292.

Unsettled conditions were aggravated by differing views of the legitimacy of the government. Judicial compliance was again a problem. Two Protectorate judges refused to serve and were dismissed. Assizes were disrupted and short-staffed. The legal profession became increasingly wary of what many of them believed to be an illegitimate, military-based government. Neither law reform nor other kinds of legislation proved feasible. There was insufficient time for bills to make their way through the necessary readings, committees and debate. Longer-lasting and more cohesive parliaments had great difficulty in completing legislation, and the revived Rump laboured under more disadvantages than most.

A few, mostly familiar, reforming measures were introduced. There were again bills to reform abuses and fees of clerks, attorneys and solicitors, and to reform and regulate Chancery.[153] The republican Ludlow thought that the Rump 'retained the design of regulating the practice of the law, and relieving the people in that particular', but was again hampered by the hostility of lawyers and clergymen. He believed that Whitelocke and St John now opposed law reform, and that parliament was 'falling in' with the corrupt interests of the lawyers and clergy.[154] Although some have treated 1659 as another lost opportunity for law reform, reform legislation was virtually impossible in the face of the political and parliamentary reality.

XI. Law Reform and the Press in 1659

Pamphlet output, spurred by the government's inability to control the press, grew to formidable proportions and contrasted sharply with the relatively meagre output of law reform publications in 1657 and 1658. In 1659, radical publications, many inspired by religion or Fifth Monarchy adherents, were most vocal. A mélange of proposals was offered as the republic crumbled, but none became law.

Supporters of the revived republic themselves had differing views, some wishing to retain the common law with a few moderate reforms[155] and others favouring a major transformation. Some tracts were characterised by a virulent anti-lawyer sentiment; some favouring abolition, some reform. Fifth Monarchy Men, favouring full implementation of the Mosaic law and the acceptability of armed rebellion, raised fears of a radicalism that might topple the existing political, social and legal world.[156] Decentralisation of the legal system was proposed again, some tracts advocating complete localisation, others merely enhancing local courts without imperilling the Westminster courts. In 1659 radical voices were the loudest.

[153] Veal (n 34) 96.

[154] Ludlow (n 67) vol II, 133. See also vol II, 210.

[155] eg, *England's Safety in the Laws Supremacy Hostile to Protector and all Monarchy* (London, 1659) 7, 10.

[156] A tract of 1659 indicated that Christ was the only king, and God's laws, the laws of the Old and New Testaments, would be the laws of the country; PG Rogers, *The Fifth Monarchy Men* (Oxford, Oxford University Press, 1966) 101.

A few examples demonstrate the lack of consensus over law reform. Harringtonian ideas circulated widely and Harrington's *System of Politics* sounded the familiar complaint that England's laws were 'perplexed, intricate, tedious or voluminous' and rained 'snares upon the People'. The 'fewest, plainest and brief' laws were best and permitted the least arbitrary power to the judiciary. Harrington's 1659 *Aphorisms Political* stated that people will always desire the government by laws and 'abhor that of Arms'.[157]

Despite its conservative title, *The Vindication of the Law as it is now Established* offered a Baconian programme of moderate reform.[158] Rejecting both those who would have the law 'totally eclipsed' or cast 'into a New Mold' and those who refused all change, the author favoured reforms that were 'more a matter of order and explanation than alteration' and did not involve 'dangerous innovation'. His proposals would give '"light" to the laws', not create a 'new Nature'. Using Baconian language and ideas, the reform plan had three parts. The first dealt with the common law, the second with the statutes and the third with the creation of auxiliary volumes for the study of the laws.

As for the first, the common law itself was not faulty; what was faulty was the manner of its 'Registry, Expression and Tradition'. Currently, the laws were 'subject to great uncertainties and variety of opinion Delays and Evasions' that armed the contentious and wearied honest subjects. Chancery overflowed with business because the law was 'often obscure and doubtful'. Judges were 'absolute' in doubtful causes and current legal practices meant that 'men's assurance of their Land, and Estates by Patents, Fines, Recoveries, Deeds, Devises, Wills' was often in doubt.[159]

Using the familiar agricultural metaphor, the author indicated that his reforms 'tendeth to pruning and grafting the Law; and not to plow up, and planting it again'. The 'entire body and substances of Law' would remain, 'only discharged of the idle and unprofitable or hurtful matter, and illustrated by Order'. He would 'reduce' or 'perfect the 'Course or Body of the Common laws' contained in the yearbooks and reports. Obsolete cases would be removed and those that consisted of 'solemn and long debates' where there was no current legal issue would be entered 'as Judgments only and Resolutions' without arguments. Cases merely of 'iteration and repetition' would be purged and 'idle queries, and prolix cases' shortened with their 'tautologies and Impertinancies … cut off'. Only the best-reported and best-argued cases would be retained.[160] The author may well have had Bacon's *De Augmentus* before him as he wrote, some of his phrases being identical to those of Bacon.

[157] James Harrington, 'A System of Politics' in JGA Pocock (ed), *The Commonwealth of Oceana and a System of Politics* (Cambridge, Cambridge University Press, 1992), 288, 289; James Harrington, *Aphorisms Political* (London, 1659) A2.

[158] Veall suggests that no part of the interregnum reform movement was influenced by Bacon and that the defeat of the prerogative meant the defeat of Bacon's conception of the law; Veall (n 34) 98–99.

[159] *Vindication of the Laws of England as they are now established* (London, 1659) 5, 6, 7.

[160] ibid 9, 10.

Given the number of 'ensnaring penal laws', work on the statutes was even more necessary. Some might be retained, but with lesser penalties. 'Dormant and useless statutes' would be removed and concurrent statutes now 'heaped one upon the another' would be reduced 'to one clear and universal Law'. Following Bacon, modification of the statutes 'must of necessity come to this Honourable House of Parliament, and the House will best like that which itself guides, and the Persons that themselves employ'. Commissioners named by the house should 'prepare and propound to the Parliament'.[161]

The third part of the *Vindication* recommended the creation of auxiliary texts for the 'Study and Science of the Law'. Following Bacon, these included 'institutions', 'a treatise de Regulii Juris' and an improved book of legal terms. Institutions would provide both 'a perspicuous and clear Order or Method', 'an universal Latitude or Comprehension' and a 'little pre-notion' of evrything, like 'a model toward a great Building'. The *Regulii Juris* were most important, but no existing rules were satisfactory, either in English or in other languages. The author of the *Vindication* did not mention Bacon's *Maxims of the Law*. And, as for the 'terms of the law', the author found none of the available collections satisfactory.[162] Like Bacon before him, ordering and reworking the sources of the law was central to reforming the law.

The author of the *Vindication* found precedents for law reform in Greece and Rome, and in the efforts of French kings who made 'perfect and uniform Law' by reducing provincial customs 'into a very brief method'. He also cited Henry VIII's commissions for purging the common law and rationalising ecclesiastical law, and Edward VI's law reform efforts. James I's proposals to 'reduce' the laws and the well-advanced 'good pains taken' by Bacon and a group of lawyers, 'though now lost', were also mentioned favourably.[163]

Many pamphlets of 1659 focused on the shortcomings of the legal profession. The title of William Cole's *A Rod for the Lawyers, Who are Hereby Declared to be the Grand Robbers and Deceivers of the Nation* alone indicates the hatred found in some quarters.[164] *The Honest Design: or the True Commonwealth's-man*, a pamphlet addressed to the army, claimed that every family in England was cursed by both laws and lawyers. The author offered a multi-faceted programme that included land registration and legal decision-making by local 'lay elders' with appeal of their decisions being limited to Parliament. William Sprigge again attributed the excessive power of common law lawyers and judges to the Norman Conquest. If a few, brief and plain laws were introduced, there would be no need for many books and

[161] ibid 13, 14.
[162] ibid 12, 13.
[163] ibid 5, 6, 7, 8, 9.
[164] William Cole, *A Rod for the Lawyers* (London, 1659) 13. Lawyers were 'Insatiate Cannibals' who gorged themselves on the poor and innocent. If lawyers refused to pursue 'honester callings', they would perish. George Gregory recommended that lawyers, attorneys and solicitors be speedily suppressed; George Gregory, *A Bakers Dozen* (London, 1659) 4, 8.

volumes of reports, cases, precedents and commentaries. Addressing parliament, he advised that 'we are now Rasa Tabula, and your Honours may write as you please upon us'. Don't 'build on old Foundations'. The entire fabric of the law must be demolished.[165]

The legal profession also had its defenders. For the author of *The Exact Law Giver*, there was no just cause to cast aspersions on lawyers who were being wrongly blamed for lengthy delays in law. It was the disputatiousness and 'stomachfulness and perverseness of Clyents' that were to blame. Clients, not lawyers, attempted to reverse judgment after judgment and decree after decree.[166]

Publications again supported a more local administration of justice, some favouring local trials handled by laymen, while others favoured handling by legal professionals. One wished lay elders to decide all cases. Another, who wanted 'God's Lawes to be enthroned', favoured judges in every city.[167] Yet another wanted all ordinary civil cases to be determined locally with no appeal except to Parliament.[168] The Republican William Cole wanted local trials while the suits were 'fresh [and] green … when the Witnesses are alive, and in the Places wherein their Lives and Conversations are known'. Individuals speaking in their own case or using a friend would ensure speedy justice and equity without sophistry or quibbles. Cole also complained of assizes where cases were 'passed over in Hugger-mugger for want of Time'.[169] John Milton suggested that each county should be 'a little commonwealth' and make 'their own judicial laws, and execute them by their own elected judicatures, without appeal, in all things of civil government between man and man'.[170] Another pamphlet proposed peace-makers in all counties to hear and determine cases so that there would be 'no going to Law one with another'.[171]

Land tenure issues were also explored in 1659. Several publications favoured a single type of land tenure or an end to primogeniture. Proposals for a land registry were again voiced, some advocating county registration, others parish registration.[172] Some favoured registration only of land transactions, others

[165] William Sprigge, *A Modest Plea* (London, 1659) 25, 118. Peter Chamberlen, who thought God's laws should rule, was also critical of corrupt lawyers. He thought it possible to retain 1,000 lawyers as well as judges provided with sufficient clerks and registers; Peter Chamberlen, *A Scourge for a Denn of Thieves* (London, 1659) 4; *The Declaration and Proclamation of the Army of God* (London, 1659) 4, 6; *Twelve Queries humbly proposed to the Consideration of the Parliament and Army* (London, 1659) 1–2, 4–5, 7.

[166] *The Exact Lawgiver* (London, 1659).

[167] Peter Chamberlen, *The Declaration and Proclamation of the Army of God* (London, 1659); Chamberlen's *A Scourge for a Denn of Thieves* (London, 1659) noted that 'Jesus Christ is the only one Lawgiver' (at 4).

[168] *Long Parliament Work* (London, 1659) 11. *The Honest Design: or the True Commonwealth's Man* (London, 1659) favoured trials judged by honest God fearing elders (at 4–5).

[169] William Cole, *A Rod for Lawyers* in *Harleian Miscellany*, vol V, 307–10, 311.

[170] Quoted in Alison Chapman, 'Milton and Legal Reform' (2016) 69 *Renaissance Quarterly* 529, 553–55, 557–58.

[171] *Several Proposals … to the Serious Considerations of the Keepers of the Liberties of the People of England* (London, 1659) 2.

[172] *The Honest Design* (n 168) 1; Sprigge (n 165).

registries that included a wide range of transactions.[173] The administration of wills was again debated, some favouring local administration and local registries, and others a central registry in London.[174]

Neither the common law courts nor Chancery received much attention in 1659. At least two publications supported special courts for merchants. One argued that summary procedure without counsel were 'more speedy, cheaper' and would advance navigation and trade. Both argued that common lawyers possessed insufficient knowledge of 'bargains in trade and commerce' to deal with merchant disputes.[175]

The pamphlets of 1659 debated capital punishment. The death penalty for theft was opposed by arguments from Scripture because it was irrational or because it was inhumane. One Rump supporter, wishing the penalty to be agreeable to 'Scripture and humanity', opposed it for small offences, noting that offenders often escaped capital punishment only because of mercy on the part of jurors or judges. Restitution, imprisonment or hard labour were typically offered as replacements.[176] Several who most opposed capital punishment for theft favoured the penalty for manslaughter and/or perjury.[177] One favoured capital punishment for forgers and falsifiers of deeds, as well as death 'without mercy' for embezzlers and perjurers.[178] Imprisonment for debt was also revisited.[179] The abolition of tithes was vigorously aired in parliament, in petition and in print. The number of pamphlets on this topic again exceeded those on any other law reform issue – I located 20.

XII. Conclusion

The year 1659 was one where radical religious ideas circulated widely. Several tracts insisted that God's law was the fundamental law of England. One proclaimed

[173] Cole (n 169) vol V, 308; *Long Parliament Work* (n 168) 11; Edward Billing, *A Might of Affection, Manifested in 31 proposals* (London, 1659) 3–4. Some also favoured a registry for wills.

[174] Cole (n 169) vol V, 308; *Several Proposals* (n 171) 2.

[175] Cole (n 169) vol V, 308; *Twelve Queries* (n 165) 7. See also *A Bill for the Establishment of a Court-Merchant*; Sprigge (n 165) 73. See also *The Honest Design* (n 168) 3; *The Looking Glass of England's Liberty* (London, 1659), 3; Billings (n 173) 2, 3–4.

[176] *Long Parliament Work* (n 168) 5–6. For punishments proportioned to the offence. See *England's Safety in the Laws Supremacy* (n 155) 14; *An Exact Description of the Government of the Commonwealth of Geneva* (London, 1659). Several Quaker publications favoured ending the death penalty for theft; Billing (n 173) 3, 7. Billing drafted the first laws of West New Jersey. Veall treats him as a moderate; Veall (n 34) 98. See also Thomas Lawson, *Appeal to the Parliament Concerning the Poor* (London, 1660); George Fox, *59 Proposals* (London, 1659). Fox wished to retain the death penalty for murder. See Rogers (n 134) 156, 160.

[177] Cole (n 164) vol V, 306. If hanging for theft was retained, 'great men' should be hanged first because they 'robbed the power of a law than highway men' (at 306).

[178] William Ball, *Law and State Proposals Humbly Presented to the Supreme Authority, the Parliament of England* (London, 1659).

[179] *England's Safety in the Laws Supremacy* (n 155) 4; William Gery, *Proposals for Reformation of Abuses* (London, 1659) 1–2, 9; Billing (n 173) 7; *To Parliament of the Commonwealth* (London, 1660). The

that the laws as practised in England were simply 'the Remains and Relics of Antichristian Superstition and Tyranny'. 'Gods Statutes and Judgments' should be the basis of English law. What was needed was 'the Legislative Power of Jesus Christ and the Law of God'.[180]

The pamphlets of 1659 were many, but the proposals offered little that was new. Nor was there anything remotely close to a consensus on what kind of reforms were desirable. Given the variety of reforms offered and the power struggles within and without parliament, there was little chance of law reform of any kind. Reformist publications, especially those inspired by Scripture, flourished most during periods of the most political disruption. These were the very periods that were least likely to achieve legislative success.

It was not long before General Monck brought his troops from Scotland and dissolved the faction-ridden parliament. Bells would soon ring in London to welcome Charles II and a governmental structure and legal system that recalled, if it did not precisely replicate, those of his father. The laws and the constitution would be considered again, both in Parliament and in the press by a different parliament, a different monarch, a different religious scene and in a different publishing environment.

process for initiating cases of debt was again discussed, some favouring arrest and some the summons: *England's Safety in the Laws Supremacy* (n 155) 14; *Several Proposals* (n 171) 2; *Reasons for the Continuance of the process of Arrest* (London, 1659). See also *Good Old Cause Dress'd: the Cause of God and of these Three Nations* (London, 1659).

[180] *Legislative Power* in *Problemes published for the Information* (London, 1659) 5–8.

7

The Restoration Era 1660–88

We now turn to the Restoration era, a period typically viewed both as a conservative one, disinterested in law reform, and as the beginning of the 'long eighteenth century' rather than an integral part of the seventeenth century. To better understand the place of the Restoration era in the history of English law reform, we examine what was and was not restored, note the reform measures considered by Restoration-era parliaments, review contemporary comment on law reform issues and highlight continuity with many earlier reform initiatives.

Important measures were decided by the Convention before the Cavalier Parliament met. The king and a two-house parliament were restored, the latter bringing lay lords and bishops back into the law-making process and the House of Lords to its judicative role.[1] The Act of Indemnity and Oblivion (12 Car II, c 11) provided official forgiveness to all those who had participated in civil and military actions against Charles I, except the 19 regicides. Although hostility and suspicion remained, there would be no bloodbath, and England returned to a civil, if not harmonious, society. Legislation enacted after the death of Charles I was invalidated. English therefore ceased to be the language of the courts and legal proceedings, and adultery was no longer a capital offence.[2] Prior decisions of the courts were to be treated as legitimate, but the acts of Interregnum parliaments were not. Marriages performed between 1642 and 1660 were confirmed. Judges loyal to Charles I returned, though their ranks had been depleted by death. Some interregnum judges were retained.[3]

With the exception of the prerogative courts, most courts and legal institutions remained intact. The ecclesiastical courts were restored, but High Commission and the *ex officio* oath were not. The Court of the Marshalsea was restored.[4] The Court of Wards and Liveries, abolished in 1646, was abolished again in 1660 along with tenure by knights service and tenure *in capite*. The landed class, regardless of religious or political affiliation, unanimously supported the abolition of feudal

[1] Arthur Turberville, 'The House of Lords under Charles II' (1929) 44 *English Historical Review* 400.

[2] 12 Car II c 12 (1660). But see *A Letter to a member of Parliament favoring a law to punish adultery with death* (London, 1675).

[3] JS Cockburn, *A History of the English Assizes 1558–1714* (Cambridge, Cambridge University Press, 1977) 246.

[4] Although reinstated in 1660 and criticised in parliament in 1689–90, the court had become an anachronism by the eighteenth century; Douglas Greene, 'The Court of the Marshalsea in Late Tudor and Stuart England' (1976) 20 *American Journal of Legal History* 281.

tenures and the obligations that accompanied them. Basically unchanged were the common law, the common law courts, the assizes, the justices of the peace,[5] trial by jury and the structure of the legal profession. Completing parliamentary legislation remained difficult and time-consuming, and few bills of any kind became statutes.

Since legislative efforts dealing with law reform were shaped by the religious, political and parliamentary environments as well as by dissatisfactions with the law and legal system, we divide the era into three fairly distinct political, religious and parliamentary environments, 1661–78, 1679–81 and 1682–88, looking first at parliamentary activities and then at commentary on law reform issues.

I. Parliament and Law Reform 1661–78

By the time the 1661 elections brought the Cavalier Parliament into being, which has typically been portrayed as loyalist and focused on the preservation of the law, stability and the Anglican church, many things had already been settled. Its members portrayed themselves as returning England to the rule of law and traditional English institutions, and frequently contrasted themselves to the unlawfulness of interregnum regimes.[6]

Completing legislation remained difficult, requiring three readings in each house, committees meetings in both houses and, if amendments were offered, agreement on those as well as royal assent. Julian Hoppit has shown that only 28.2 per cent of bills of any kind became law during the reigns of Charles II and James II, and that 11 of the 20 parliamentary sessions lasted less than 50 days. Those during the reign of Charles averaged 6–10 weeks.[7] About one-third of all bills originated in the upper house between 1660 and 1681.[8]

The House of Commons, though emphasising its loyalty to the Crown, soon found itself opposed to the king's religious policy. Charles II's Declaration from Breda had offered possibilities for toleration and/or comprehension, but the staunchly Anglican House of Commons responded by passing a series of repressive acts. These measures were considered to be reforms by those who supported and implemented them. Others saw toleration or comprehension

[5] The political composition of the justices of the peace changed in 1660 and again during the Popish Plot, in 1680 and again in 1685; Anthony Fletcher, *Reform in the Provinces: The Government of Stuart England* (New Haven, Yale University Press, 1986) 20–25. See also Norma Landau, 'The Changing Persona of the Justices and Their Quarter Sessions, The Justices at Quarter Sessions' in Lorna Hutson (ed), *Oxford Handbook of English Law and Literature* (Oxford, Oxford University Press, 2017) 239–55.

[6] See Tim Harris, 'Tories and the Rule of Law in the Reign of Charles II' (1993) 8 *The Seventeenth Century* 9.

[7] Julian Hoppit, 'Patterns of Parliamentary Legislation' 31 *Historical Journal* 109, 113–29. See also Julian Hoppit, and Joanna Innes, *Failed Legislation* (London, Hambledon Press, 1997) 8

[8] Andrew Swatland, *The House of Lords in the Reign of Charles II* (Cambridge, Cambridge University Press, 1996) 68.

as reform. Legislating the religious establishment and establishing penalties for non-conformity would remain contentious throughout the Restoration era. The staunchly Anglican Cavalier Parliament passed the Corporation Act of 1661, the Act of Uniformity in 1662, the Conventicle Act of 1664 and the Five Mile Act of 1665, as well as the Second Conventicle Act of 1670, all prescribing severe penalties and restrictions on Protestant dissenters. The king's 1672 Declaration of Indulgence, designed to dispense with the penalties of these laws, as well as to aid Roman Catholics, initiated a legal crisis. Viewing royal indulgence as a threat to law itself, parliament responded with the Test Act barring Roman Catholics from public office.

Comprehension legislation to broaden the church was typically accompanied by bills granting toleration for Protestant dissenters. Efforts began early when Sir Matthew Hale introduced a bill transforming the king's Declaration of Breda into law. Companion bills for comprehension and toleration were introduced again in 1667–68, 1673 and 1680, the latter providing the basis for the toleration legislation of 1689.[9] Legislative efforts aimed at repression, comprehension and toleration were accompanied by numerous publications supporting and attacking each alternative.

II. The Courts

The courts, central and local, common law and equity, ecclesiastical and temporal, received a good deal of reform attention, much of it similar to earlier efforts. In 1660 and 1661 there were bills to regulate fees in courts of justice. In 1662 a bill was introduced in the House of Commons aimed at eliminating 'Corruption, Grievances, Abuses, Delays, Vexations, Exactions and unnecessary expenses in the Law and Correction of Public Justice'.[10] In the following year, there was a bill to prevent 'unnecessary suits, delays, expenses, extortions and other abuses in the Courts of Justice and Proceedings at Law'.[11] A 1663–64 bill to prevent unnecessary 'Delays, Expenses, Vexations and Grievances in Courts of Law and Equity, and supply some Defects in Law, and Legal Proceedings and Executions' was read and a 'Grand Committee for Courts of Justice' was ordered to meet and

[9] *The Parliamentary Diary of Sir Edward Dering 1670–73*, B Henning (ed) (New Haven, Yale University Press, 1940) 112, 114–18, 120, 131; John Spurr, 'The Church of England, Comprehension and the Toleration Act of 1689' (1989) 104 *English Historical Review* 927; Roger Thomas, 'Comprehension and Indulgence' in GJ Nuttall and Owen Chadwick (eds), *From Uniformity to Unity* (London, SPCK, 1962); Walter Simon, 'Comprehension in the Age of Charles II' (1962) 31 *Church History* 189; Henry Horwitz, *Revolution Politics: The Career of Daniel Finch, Second Earl of Nottingham, 1647–1730* (Cambridge, Cambridge University Press, 2008) 87–91, 94–96; Henry Horwitz, 'Protestant Reconciliation in the Exclusion Crisis' (1964) 15 *Journal of Ecclesiastical History* 201.

[10] CJ, VIII, 316, 331, 336, 339, 340.

[11] CJ, VIII, 535, 546.

develop a bill.[12] Three separate bills emerged.[13] In May 1663 a 'bill for regulating abuses in the Law and Courts of Justice' was read and a committee was appointed to prepare a bill to prevent fraudulent conveyances.[14] A few months later, there was a request for bills regulating 'abuses and delays in the Execution of Justice' and for limiting 'the Exhorbitancy of Fees'.[15] A list of the fees of all court officials was to be hung in every court. Several reform measures were sent to the House of Lords with a request for 'quick Dispatch'.[16] Although the House of Commons agreed to the changes desired by the upper house, parliament was prorogued before any proposed legislation on law and court could be completed.[17] The problem of excessive fees was often discussed together with the sale of court and other offices. The Act of 1551 that provided punitive measures for selling offices had not been enforced, though there had been many subsequent legislative efforts to prevent their purchase and sale. Another failed effort occurred in 1660.

The long-sought but difficult to achieve rationalisation of the statutes was reintroduced in 1665 and 1666. In 1665 the Speaker of the House of Commons announced that parliament was sending 'Several Bills for the Regulation of the Law' to the king which would 'prune some exuberant Branches, and to pull away the ivy that robbed this tree of her just Nourishment'. He explained 'the best laws in time may grow obsolete' and that 'fraud and Tricks' began to prevail when such laws were left unchanged.[18] Lord Chancellor Clarendon encouraged a lower house committee to confer with the upper house about rationalisation efforts. In 1666 a House of Commons committee conferred with the House of Lords and the judges 'who have already taken pains and made progress in perusing the statute law, and consider of repealing such former statute Laws' as needed repeal and, 'if expedient, of reducing all laws of one Nature under such a Method as may conduce for a more ready Understanding and better Execution of such laws'. In discussing the matter with Samuel Pepys, William Prynne, a member of the house committee, referred to the 'many faults' of the laws, especially 'their obscurity through multitude of long statutes'. He told Pepys that he was 'about to abstract out of all a sort; and as he and the Parliaments come, get them put into laws, and the other statutes repealed, and then will be a short work to know the laws'.[19] This project, which was similar to earlier efforts, was no more successful than the efforts of pre-revolutionary and revolutionary parliaments.

[12] CJ, VIII 535, 546; Hoppit and Innes (n 7) 74.

[13] CJ, VIII, 486, 535, 546.

[14] CJ, VIII, 486, 487.

[15] CJ, VIII, 573, 574, 576, 579; *The Diary of John Milward*, Caroline Robbins (ed) (Cambridge, Cambridge University Press, 1938) 98, 104. The bill failed after a second reading.

[16] CJ, VIII, 596, 610.

[17] CJ, VIII, 610, 613, 614.

[18] LJ, XI, 675.

[19] Samuel Pepys, *The Diary of Samuel Pepys: Diary*, 11 vols, R Latham and W Matthews (eds) (London, Bell, 1970–83), vol VII, 109–10.

There was a bill to prevent vexatious suits in 1670 and another the following year to prevent delays in courts of justice. Legislation reforming abuses and delays in legal proceedings was introduced yet again in 1673.[20] Lord Chancellors and Lord Keepers continued to promote law reform. In 1675, after the Lord Keeper spoke on the need to reform delays and abuses in the administration of justice, a bill was ordered.[21] Further legislation aimed at avoiding unnecessary suits and delays was introduced in 1677, this time passing the lower house and having two readings in the House of Lords.[22] Although the legislation was lost when the session ended a few days later, it was passed in the next session. The Cavalier Parliament, like its predecessors, wished to reform overly long, costly and vexatious lawsuits.

Parliament also wished to remedy the long-term problem of the lack of finality of judgments. This was largely, but not entirely, a matter of conflict between the common law courts and Chancery, which took cases after judgment in the common law courts. The appeals jurisdiction of the House of Lords also proved contentious. When revived in 1660, the upper house again heard Chancery appeals and writs of error. In 1663 and 1664 the upper house was attacked for delaying the execution of court judgments.[23] The upper house had also taken over some of the jurisdiction of the abolished Star Chamber, one lawyer in 1663 indicating that: 'The jurisdiction of the Star Chamber is now transformed into the House of Lords, but somewhat in a Nobler way.'[24] Lawsuits in 1673 and 1675 challenged the jurisdiction of the House of Lords. Although the decisions in *Skinner v East India Company* and *Shirley v Fagg* narrowed the jurisdiction of the upper house, the House of Lords continued to hear Chancery appeals.[25]

There was some discussion of reviving abolished courts. Reinstating a court similar to Star Chamber was proposed in 1662 by Lord Chancellor Bridgman, albeit modified to restrict its jurisdiction to causes mentioned in the earlier Star Chamber Act. The following year, a similar proposal resulted in a draft bill, but it too came to nothing.[26] Matthew Hale was reported to have stated that 'since the

[20] CJ, IX, 289, 296; LJ, XII, 486, 488, 490.

[21] CJ, IX, 317, 322, 324, 332, 342, 374; LJ, 486, 499, 502, 503, 508; Edward Cooke, *Memorabilia* (London, 1681), 7. It passed the lower house and had a second reading in the House of Lords; Hoppit and Innes (n 7) 128, 129.

[22] Hoppit and Innes (n 7) 142–43.

[23] CJ, VIII, 543. The Statute of Amendments and Jeofails provided that writs of error could not be maintained except for material error (16 and 17 Car II c 8).

[24] Quoted in William Holdsworth, *A History of English Law*, 17 vols (London, John Murray, 1903–72), vol IV, 367.

[25] James S Hart discusses the role of the House of Lords in remedying effects of irregularities in judicial procedure. The upper house could set aside but not reverse Chancery decrees; James S Hart, *Justice upon Petition: The House of Lords and the Reformation of Justice 1621–1675* (London, Routledge, 2000) 250, 257; James S Hart, 'The House of Lords and the Appellate Jurisdiction in Equity 1640–43' (1983) 2 *Parliamentary History* 49; Swatland (n 8) 73, 75, 76. The House of Lords retained its role in impeachment trials and the trial of peers. Sir Matthew Hale felt that peers had insufficient knowledge to judge appeals. See also John Selden, *Of Judicature in Parliament* (London, 1681); Sir Robert Atkyns, *A Treatise of the True and Ancient Jurisdiction of the House of Peers* (London, 1699).

[26] LJ, XII, 382, 474, 499.

putting down of that court, that there has been in a few years more perjuries and frauds unpunished than there had been in a hundred years before'.[27] The demise of Star Chamber helps to explain the large number of legislative efforts to curb frauds and perjuries and the increased Chancery business. The abolition of a busy if unpopular court had solved some problems, but generated others.

Petitions in 1661, 1663 and 1664 resulted in bills to resurrect the Council of the North in order to alleviate problems caused by the distance and costs of travel to London. Critics of the 1663 bill warned of putting arbitrary power in the hands of commissioners, the absence of jury trials, the danger of giving judicial power to shopkeepers and the potential damage to existing inferior courts. Although it was expected to pass, the bill was dropped. In 1665 there were rumours that the king would establish a court in the north by prerogative.[28] Similar objections to the absence of juries arose in 1667 when a special court to adjudicate disputes arising out of the Great Fire of London was proposed.[29] Common lawyers remained alert to efforts that might erode the jury trial.

Earlier interest in creating a new system of local courts did not revive, though there were continued efforts to limit withdrawal of suits from inferior to Westminster courts. Legislation regulating the inferior courts was considered in 1675, and bills allowing commissioners to take affidavits in the country for use in the central courts were introduced.[30]

Although there were fewer jurisdictional conflicts between the ecclesiastical and temporal courts during the Restoration era, reform and regulation of the ecclesiastical courts was discussed in 1668, 1670 and 1675 and again in 1679–80.[31] Probate and the administration of wills were the subject of reform from 1665 to 1673, but the proposed legislation made it clear that the spiritual courts would retain that jurisdiction.[32] Legislation relieving the problems of those who died intestate was introduced in 1667–8, 1670 and 1671. The 1671 bill, which became law, modified the conduct of administrators and the pattern of distribution of

[27] Philip Warwick, *Memoirs of the Reign of Charles II* (Edinburgh, London, Longmans, 1813) 191–92 In about 1660, the Duke of Newcastle defended the Star Chamber as a valuable institution, though he admitted its abuses. He defended the Council of Wales on the ground that it saved litigants from travelling to London; T Slaughter, *Ideology and Politics on the Eve of the Restoration: Newcastle's Advice to Charles II* (Philadelphia, American Philosophical Society, 1984) 65–66.

[28] LJ, XII, 310, 366–67; Andrew Marvell, *The Poems and Letters of Andrew Marvell*, MM Margoliouth (ed). 2 vols (Oxford, Clarendon Press, 1971), vol II, 36; Rachel R Reid, *The King's Council in the North* (Wakefield, Longmans, 1921) 457. Reid suggested that the bill was defeated by northern common lawyers (at 548).

[29] 18 & 19 Car II c 7; LJ, XII, 110. A Fire Court was established by Parliament because of the need to rebuild London quickly. It was not a common law court. Cases were decided by three judges. See Jay Tidmarsh, 'The English Fire Court and the American Right to Civil Jury Trial' (2016) 83 *University of Chicago Law Review* 1894.

[30] CJ, XI, 102, 119, 317, 381, 387, 392, 404, 413.

[31] A Grey, *Debates of the House of Commons from the year 1667 to the Year 1694* (London, 1763), vol I, 110–11; CJ, IX, 199, 680; RB Outhwaite, *The Rise and Fall of the English Ecclesiastical Courts, 1500–1800* (Cambridge, Cambridge University Press, 2006) 80, 81, 83.

[32] CJ, XI, 596.

personal property, substantially reducing the business of the ecclesiastical courts.[33] In 1672–73 the House of Lords considered defects in the Henrician Statute of Wills, offering a bill remedying current grievances and inconveniences shortly before parliament was adjourned.[34]

Tithes remained contentious, though revolutionary-era proposals to abolish them were not considered. The prevention of clandestine marriage, legal marriages performed secretly by a clergyman, was a growing, if not novel, concern. Legislation was introduced on this in 1661, 1666, 1667, 1670, 1677, 1685, 1687 and 1690.[35]

In 1665 a bill to regulate proceedings in courts of equity had two readings, but was not committed.[36] An ordinance issued by Lord Chancellor Clarendon was directed at correcting the 'manifold disorders and undue practices' that had 'gotton into the office of the six clerks'.[37] In 1676–77 the House of Commons resolved that Chancery should not have jurisdiction over cases determinable at common law.[38] On the whole, there was less hostility expressed towards Chancery than earlier as, over time, it developed more rules and principles that became more predictable.[39] Collections of frequently printed Chancery orders declared that they were 'reforming several abuses in the said court, preventing multiplicity of suits' and providing 'more expeditious and certain Course for relief'.[40]

Chancery remained the subject of some criticism, with reform efforts both from within the court and by parliament. Internal reform had been promoted by

[33] Grey (n 31) vol I, 121, 122; CJ, VIII, 408; IX, 63, 65, 70; LJ, XI, 469; LJ, XII, 218, 226, 249, 348, 565; An Act for the Better Settling of Intestate Estates 17 Car II c 6; 22 and 23 Car II c 10 (1670); 29 Car II c 3 (1677).

[34] LJ, XII, 348, 565. The statutes of the 1670s, though modified in 1837, governed testamentary requirements until the post-Second World War period; Lloyd Bonfield, *Communities and Courts in Britain, 1150–1900* (London, Hambledon, 1997) 138, 139. Bonfield considers the reforms of the 1670s to be far more important than the Interregnum shift to the secular courts. See also Edward Whitaker, *The Bishops Courts dissolved, or the law of England touching Ecclesiastical Jurisdiction stated* (London, 1681).

[35] CJ, VIII, 626, 628, 728, 749; LJ, XII, 358. See RB Outhwaite, *Clandestine Marriage in England 1500–1850* (London, Hambledon Press, 1993) 13. There had been bills to prevent the elopement of women in 1610 and 1614. Bills continued to be introduced until Hardwicke's act was passed in 1753.

[36] Another bill of 1668 to regulate the Six Clerks in Chancery also failed; Hoppit and Innes (n 7) 89, 100.

[37] *An Ordinance made eighteenth day of July … 1666* (London, 1666) 1. There were several efforts to reform the Six Clerks during the next few decades.

[38] David W Raack, 'A History of Injunctions in England before 1700' (1986) 61 *Indiana Law Journal* 585.

[39] See George Carew, *Reports or Causes in Chancery* (London, 1665); *The Transactions of the High Court of Chancery* (London, 1671); Michael Boyle, *Rules and Orders to be observed in the High Court of Chancery in Ireland* (London, 1685); Anthony Colquitt, *Modern Reports* (London, 1682); *1700 Cases in Chancery, Kings Bench and Common Pleas* (London, 1685); Walter Williams, *Some Reasons Humbly offered … for passing the bill entitled an act for the better reviewing of causes in Chancery and other courts of equity* (London, 1690); Walter Williams, *Orders and Rules to be humbly proposed* (London, 1700); Henry Horwitz, 'Continuity or Change in the Court of Chancery in the Seventeenth and Eighteenth Centuries' (1996) 35 *Journal of British Studies* 24.

[40] *A Collection of such of the orders before used in Chancery* (London, 1660) reprinted in 1661, 1669, 1676 and 1688. Several reprints included alterations and additions by Lord Chancellor Clarendon.

earlier Lord Chancellors and Lord Keepers, but, given the frequent repetition of their orders, they appear to have had few long-lasting, let alone permanent, results. Lord Chancellor Clarendon and Sir Harbottle Grimstone, Master of the Rolls, attempted internal reform. Grimstone's orders 'for Reforming of several Abuses … preventing multiplicity of Suits, motions, and unnecessary Charges to the Suiters' were largely based on Whitelocke's interregnum reforms,[41] which in turn were based on those of earlier Lord Chancellors. Bills regulating proceedings in courts of equity and Chancery fees were also introduced.[42] Lord Shaftsbury, Lord Chancellor in 1672–73, drafted reforms that were submitted to several law officers for comment, but these were dropped when he lost office.[43]

Shaftsbury's successor, Heneage Finch, Lord Nottingham (Lord Keeper 1673–75 and Lord Chancellor 1675–82), accomplished somewhat more, and made serious efforts to rationalise the rules of equity.[44] Often called the 'father of equity', Nottingham sought to regularise and make the concept of 'conscience' more predictable, and made considerable progress in rendering Chancery rules more 'certain and known'.[45] He made important additions to the law of mortgages and trusts, and developed regulations for using injunctions. Drawing on Bacon's Chancery orders of 1619, those of the 1649 Commissioners of the Great Seal and Clarendon's 1661 compilations, Nottingham developed procedures to prevent delays, to treat the parties fairly and to keep Chancery injunctions from interfering with suits at law.[46] His tenure at Chancery helped to mitigate, if not end, the long-standing conflicts with the common law courts.

Sir Francis North, who succeeded Nottingham as Lord Keeper, was similarly committed to 'amend the course of the proceedings in the Chancery'. He provided 'new rules and orders for regulation of abuses, and melioration of dispatch' and worked 'to prevent the trouble, and charge of motions and rehearings'. Since Chancery had 'more business and greater value' than other courts' and was 'coming to possess almost all the justice in the nation', its 'abuses' were more keenly felt. Some 'mischiefs' were caused by plaintiffs, while others were caused by defendants who brought in 'false pleas' and writs after long delays. North favoured the creation of lesser courts of equity as well as reforms relating to hearing delays,

[41] John Lord Campbell, *The Lives of the Lord Chancellors and Lord Keepers of the Seal of England*, 8 vols (London, J Murray, 1846), vol III, 190; *A Collection of … Orders in Chancery* (London, 1651) 6–7, 19, 23, 28–29, 36. There were also editions in 1666 and 1688

[42] CJ, VIII, 586; John Milward, *The Diary of John Milward*, GE Aylmer and Carolyn Robbins (eds) (Cambridge, Cambridge University Press, 1938) 252.

[43] K Haley, *The First Earl of Shaftesbury* (Oxford, Clarendon Press, 1968) 310, 312; Campbell (n 41) 316n.

[44] Roger North thought that Lord Bridgman and Lord North gave too much 'liberty to counsel and officers' so that 'no very commendable tirades of the court run high'; Mary Chan (ed), *The Life of the Lord Keeper North* (Lampeter, Edwin Mellen Press, 1995) 312–23, 325–30, 331–34, 336–37, 350–52; GE Alymer, *The Crown's Servants* (Oxford, Oxford University Press, 2002) 330, 352.

[45] Dennis Klinck, 'Lord Nottingham and the Conscience of Equity' (2006) 67 *Journal of the History of Ideas* 123.

[46] *Lord Nottingham's Chancery Cases*, ed and intro by DEC Yale, 2 vols (London, Bernard Quaritch, 1957–61), vol I, 5.

injunctions, interlocutory orders, rehearings, the regulation of attorneys and the private examination of witnesses. He designed a new book of orders to regulate the court. He also referred to the 'inequitable torment inflicted upon suiters by vexatious and false adversaries assisted by knavish confederating officers and other chicaccaneries'. He agreed with the common complaint that it was sometimes preferable to give up one's debt than go to law. His commonplace book commented on the relationship between equity and the common law, querying 'where the Chancery is regular in its remedy, why is not that Law?' and providing a list of equitable rules to be incorporated into the common law.[47] However, he feared he would 'never live to see such amendments as may be for the profit of the Kingdome'.[48] Throughout the Restoration era, Lord Chancellors, Lord Keepers and Masters of the Rolls made efforts to reform Chancery from within, but despite these efforts, complaints about Chancery continued.

The boundary between the law and equity was never clear, but became somewhat more stabilised as a result of successive Lord Chancellor and Lord Keeper efforts. However, conflict was not eliminated. In 1661 Judge Jenkins complained of the 'the excess in Chancery … in examining judgments at common law and examining suits pending at common law'. The chancellor 'ought to do nothing else but compel the executor of trusts and moderate the rigour of forfeitures: the common law ought to try frauds'.[49] In 1665 a bill to regulate equity passed in the lower house, but not the upper house.[50] In 1677 the Commons resolved that 'the extraordinary Power and Jurisdiction and other courts of Equity in matters determinable at the Common Law, is grievous to the Subject and that a bill should be drawn'.[51] Nothing was done. Less hostility was expressed towards Chancery than in earlier years as it was gradually becoming more rule-oriented and appeared less capricious.

Admiralty jurisdiction, which had long been a matter of contention, was discussed in 1662 and 1663. Though the 1663 bill, which involved shifting foreign contracts relating to navigation from the common law courts to admiralty, was rejected, another bill was ordered to improve merchant law and erect merchant courts in major ports.[52] During the 1663 debates, Heneage Finch, defending the interests of the common lawyers, claimed that if the civilians got jurisdiction over foreign contracts, they would have 'at one blow gotten the Barbadoes, Jamaica, the American Islands, Virginia and New England and … have planted the civil

[47] Quoted in M MacNair, 'Common Law and Statutory Imitations of Equitable Relief' in Christopher Brooks and Michael Lobban (eds), *Communities and Courts 1150–1900* (London, Hambledon, 1997) 119. MacNair suggests that if North's proposals had been implemented, there would be little left of Chancery jurisdiction (at 119). For North on Chancery reform, see Chan (n 44) 324–34.

[48] Chan (n 44) 312–23, 325–30, 331–34, 336–37; GE Aylmer, *The Crown's Servants: Government and the Civil Service under Charles II, 1660–1685* (Oxford, Oxford University Press, 2002) 57.

[49] *Eight Centuries of Reports*, 4th edn (London, 1885) xxi.

[50] CJ, VIII, 606, 608; LJ, XI, 664, 665.

[51] CJ, IX, 388.

[52] LJ, XI, 377, 378, 416; Marvell (n 28) vol II, 34–35.

law there'.[53] A 1670 bill to broaden admiralty jurisdiction was defeated.[54] The common law courts continued to issue prohibitions shifting cases to themselves, and the competition for jurisdiction in many areas of commercial law continued.

Interest in urban courts of conscience to handle small claims revived. Several bills were introduced to establish courts in Southwark and Westminster.[55] There were long debates in 1661 and 1662 on establishing a court in York, though this was probably intended to be a court of wider jurisdiction.

Habeas corpus legislation was introduced in 1668, 1670, 1673, 1674, 1675, 1677 and 1679. Its lengthy legislative history illustrates the difficulties in completing legislation. The 1668 bill had only two readings before parliament was adjourned,[56] and in 1673 parliament was dismissed shortly after the introduction of a habeas corpus bill. Some speakers argued that the bill was not strong enough, while others claimed that no legislation was necessary. In 1674–75 legislation was introduced to prevent prisoners from being sent beyond the sea to avoid habeas proceedings. In 1677 yet another bill passed in the House of Commons, but had not passed in the upper house before parliament ended. In 1679 legislation was finally enacted preventing illegal imprisonment of the subject.[57]

III. Reform and the Legal Profession

The legal profession, which had been the subject of constant criticism during both the pre-revolutionary and revolutionary periods, continued to be the subject of reform. Some measures involved the tenure of judges, others the regulation of lawyers and attorneys. A draft bill of 1662 dealing with judicial tenure aroused little interest because the king had for several years employed the good behaviour standard that Charles I had agreed to. After 1672, when judges in the central courts again became dismissible at the pleasure of the king, there were politically motivated transfers and dismissals that brought renewed attention to judicial tenure. In 1674 a House of Commons bill attempted to regulate judicial salaries and make dismissal by the Crown more difficult. Those who felt that complete security of tenure would make judges too independent, below the king, but above

[53] Quoted in George F Steckley, 'Merchants and the Admiralty Court during the English Revolution' (1978) 22 *American Journal of Legal History* 167, 175. Steckley rejects Stuart Prall's view that Admiralty jurisdiction had been settled during the Interregnum and emphasises the continuing struggle between the common law courts and Admiralty throughout the Interregnum and Restoration eras.

[54] LJ, XII, 308; Steckley (n 53) 178. In 1673 the appointment of lesser Admiralty judges was moved from the Lord High Admiral to the Crown.

[55] Hoppit and Innes (n 7) 120, 122, 124, 126, 132.

[56] Milward (n 42) 253, 279, 299; Paul Halliday, '11,000 Prisoners: Habeas Corpus 1500–1800' in P Brand and J Getzler (eds), *Judges and Judging in the History of the Common Law and Civil Law* (Cambridge, Cambridge University Press, 2012) 259–76.

[57] Paul Halliday, *Habeas Corpus from England to Empire* (Cambridge, MA, Harvard University Press, 2010); Helen Nutting, '"The Most Wholesome Act": The Habeas Corpus Act of 1679' (1960) 65 *American Historical Review* 527.

the people, opposed the proposal.[58] Impartiality rather than independence was their goal.

There were also issues involving the relationship between judges and juries. In 1667 a measure against 'menacing and fining and imprisoning juries' for their verdicts was debated, but the impeachment of the most offending judge was unsuccessful.[59] However, Bushel's case in 1670 determined that judges were forbidden from interfering with jury assessments of matters of fact. Many pamphlets treated the decision in Bushel's case as a major reform. On the one hand, juries often did as they pleased in capital cases or cases involving the Conventicle Act; on the other hand, some judges had the reputation for menacing and threatening juries that refused to convict. From time to time, judges were removed without explanation and new ones were appointed. Judicial purges increased during the reign of James II.[60]

As in the past, juries were criticised for being improperly influenced and lacking in education and integrity. A bill for 'returning able and sufficient Jurors' passed both houses, but failed due to the prorogation of parliament. Another, dealing with abuses in returning juries, was introduced in 1678.[61]

The impeachment of Lord Chancellor Clarendon for high treason in 1667 again raised the issue of whether impeachment should be considered a desirable tool for keeping judges and ministers of the Crown responsible or was merely a device to bring down political opponents. Though Clarendon's accusers were unable to prove their accusation of high treason, the Lord Chancellor was forced to flee the country.[62]

The high fees of the legal profession, lawyers, attorneys, solicitors and court officials continued to be denounced, and in 1663–64 their 'exorbitant' fees were considered by the lower house's committee for regulating the law.[63] Similar bills were introduced in 1667 and 1668. Legislation to prevent the sale of offices failed after two readings in the lower house in 1667.[64]

IV. Credit and Debt

The seemingly intractable problems of imprisonment for debt and bankruptcy continued. Poor debtors unable to pay their debts were imprisoned, making them

[58] John Kenyon, *The Stuart Constitution* (Cambridge, Cambridge University Press, 1986) 420.

[59] Milward (n 42) 88, 159–60, 163, 167, 170, 174, 187, 191. See also AF Havighurst, 'The Judiciary and Politics in the Reign of Charles II' (1953) 66 *Law Quarterly Review* 72–78, 229–52. CJ Keyling was accused of 'usurping a lordly dictatorial power' for illegally fining and imprisoning grand and petty juries.

[60] Kenyon (n 58) 421–26; AF Havighurst, 'James II and the Twelve Men in Scarlet' (1951) 69 *Law Quarterly Review* 222. James removed 12 judges in three years.

[61] CJ, VIII, 610, 613; Hoppit and Innes (n 7) 104, 146, 147.

[62] See Clayton Roberts, 'The Impeachment of the Earl of Clarendon' (1957) 13 *Cambridge Historical Journal* 1. Impeachment proceedings were considered for Lord Danby and Sir William Scroggs, Lord Chief Justice of the Court of King's Bench.

[63] CJ, VIII, 579. A bill to regulate attorneys in 1677 failed.

[64] Hoppit and Innes (n 7) 98, 106, 110.

even less able to pay, while rich ones might live easily in prison to avoid their debts. Measures that emptied prisons from time to time did little to alleviate the underlying problems. Debtor-creditor issues would be taken up again and again. Bills for the relief of poor prisoners were read in 1662–63 and 1664–65.[65] In 1666 Milward mentioned legislation under which small debtors would be set free, although indicating that the bill was 'much spoken against'.[66] A bill was introduced again in 1674.[67] A few bills such as the acts in 1671 passed; others failed. Those that became law were short-lived because legislation was typically limited in time. These were sticking plasters that did not really address the basic problems.

Officials managing the prisons were repeatedly condemned for rapacity and inefficiency. In 1664–65 the House of Commons ordered a bill 'for regulating of Prisons and to prevent Abuses and Miscarriages in Keepers of Prisons, in giving liberty to Prisoners, whereby their Creditors are defeated of their Debts'.[68] In 1665 there was a bill to relieve creditors from frauds committed by the Warden of the Fleet and the Marshal of the King's Bench, and in 1668 another to regulate the King's Bench and Fleet prisons. Given the widespread use of credit by nearly all elements of society, it is not surprising that the problems of individual debtors and creditors would attract repeated parliamentary concern.[69]

V. Crime Control

Crime control remained a persistent problem. As had been the case earlier, reform typically took the form of increasing punishment for highway robbery, house-breaking, robbery and the theft of horses and cattle.[70] Measures against house and corn burning at night reached the statute book.[71] Moor burning was discussed repeatedly.[72] Legislation against child stealing was introduced in 1661 and again in 1673.[73] In 1669 there was a move to make the punishment for extortion harsher, and in 1663, 1666, 1668 and 1675 efforts were made to provide harsher punishments for duelling.[74] The available punishments for perjury were thought to provide an insufficient deterrent, and bills were offered in 1660, 1670, 1674 and 1675.

[65] CJ, VIII, 399, 403, 405, 408, 586, 587, 591, 593, 608.

[66] Milward (n 42) 97.

[67] Hoppit and Innes (n 7) 124n.

[68] 81 CJ, VIII, 593.

[69] CJ, VIII, 580; Hoppit and Innes (n 7) 146. Bankruptcy, which had often been viewed as a means of evading legitimate debts, was the subject of a bill in 1661–62. See Craig Muldrew, *The Economy of Obligation: The Culture of Credit and Social Relation in Early Modern England* (New York, St Martin's Press, 1998).

[70] Milward (n 42) 115–17, 139, 141, 211–13, 258; CJ, XII, 269, 328, 681; XV, 374, 376; XVI, 252.

[71] 22 and 23 Car II c 1.

[72] Hoppit and Innes (n 7) 120, 128.

[73] ibid 120.

[74] 22 and 23 Car II c 25.

Efforts to mitigate capital punishment for theft, which had been a goal of many revolutionary-era reformers, continued to sound in a few pamphlets, but were not a concern of the Cavalier Parliament.[75] A comprehensive game law in 1671 was, no doubt, considered to be a reform by its gentry and aristocratic beneficiaries.[76]

Transportation continued to be employed as an alternative to capital punishment. Quarter session records suggest that after 1660, it was being used both as an independent sentence and as an alternative to capital punishment.[77] An act to transport those convicted of felony 'within clergy' or for petty larceny was discussed in Parliament in 1663, 1664 and again in 1670.[78] Although Member of Parliament John Milward thought transportation 'would be of more force than the present law of hanging',[79] it was not considered an ideal solution because of the problem of returnees, and because the ability and desires of the colonies to absorb this type of labour fluctuated. In 1677, a year of low demand, convicts due for transportation were said to have been pardoned because 'they know not what to do with them'.[80]

Frauds, particularly those associated with land transactions, were a continuing concern. Legislation to prevent fraudulent conveyances was often accompanied by proposals for land registration. In 1663 a House of Commons committee was ordered to 'expedite and bring in' a bill to prevent fraudulent conveyances and assurances. Two months later, the committee was instructed to bring in bills for preventing frauds by merchants and others who cheated creditors. In the spring of 1664 the committee on fraudulent conveyances was revived and a bill was proposed 'for the registering of Conveyances of Sales and Mortgages, and for regulating the offices for Recording and keeping of Judgments, Statutes and Recognizances'.[81]

The problem of fraud and deception in land transactions remained a major one throughout the early modern period. Tudor legislation of 1536 made some inroads into the problem, but reform proposals continued to be offered throughout the late sixteenth and seventeenth centuries. The Great Fire of London in 1666, which had destroyed many houses and a myriad of deeds and other documents, again stimulated interest in fraud and registrations and proposals for a Fire Court. Legislative activity relating to land was particularly great in the 1670s. Legislation, probably drafted by Lord Chancellor Nottingham, was introduced

[75] A 1665 bill dealing with the trial and conviction of petty treason, murder and other felonies, and another for the felonious stealing of cloths from the rack at night both received two readings in the lower house; CJ, 88, 110.

[76] The 1677 and 1678 bills to prevent unlawful deer stealing failed; Hoppit and Innes (n 7) 140, 146, 147.

[77] See AH Hamilton, *Quarter Sessions from Queen Elizabeth to Queen Anne* (London, 1878).

[78] LJ, XI, 529, 531, 546, 548, 550, 561, 587, 591; Grey (n 31) vol I, 236–37.

[79] Milward (n 42) 89.

[80] WG, *Proposals* (np, 1695) 467. Those guilty of horse theft and highway robbery were among the most frequently transported. In 1670 Maryland and Virginia prohibited the transportation of convicted felons.

[81] CJ, VIII, 549, 544, 548.

in 1674, but the bill was dropped and parliament prorogued. Nottingham, Sir Matthew Hale and other judges played key roles when a similar bill was introduced the following year. It passed the lower house, but failed due to prorogation. Despite the backing of the judges and the support of both houses, it required many sessions before becoming a statute. In 1677 the landmark statute 'for the Prevention of Frauds and Perjuries' finally became law. The statute had a great impact, making land transactions and several other kinds of contracts more certain and secure. Transactions now required written evidence. Most oral contracts would no longer be considered sufficient, thus substantially reducing opportunities for perjury and fraud. Some contemporaries believed that it resulted in reduced interest rates, increased land values and gave the government increased information for levying land taxes.[82]

Registration of land, often introduced in connection with bills to prevent fraudulent conveyances, was again a concern of Restoration-era parliaments. Two bills emerged in the 1662–63 session, one to prevent frauds in conveyances and the other for a registry of deeds and conveyances.[83] Registration efforts, like so many reform measures, were stymied as much by parliamentary prorogations as by opposition. There was, as there had been in the past, opposition from those who argued that registration would increase rather than prevent fraud by increasing the number and variety of fraudulent documents and endangering long-time possessors lacking sufficient documentation. In 1669 a committee of the House of Lords proposed a registry suggesting that uncertain titles were causing a decline in the value of land and rents. Debate followed, and the judges requested to prepare a bill.[84] The following year, the House of Lords ordered a bill 'that henceforth no estates shall be transferred' or conveyed without enrolment.[85] In 1671 the lower house debated a bill to establish a register 'for Deeds, Securities, and Perpetuities'. Some favoured a registry at Westminster, though it made searches expensive and difficult, while others preferred that registration take place 'where the lands do Lie'.[86] Opponents emphasised the dangers of innovation, general disturbances and the threat to those with long possession but uncertain titles. The bill failed and little was heard about a registry for several years.[87]

[82] 29 Car II c 3. Six categories of agreement and contracts now had written requirements. Over time, perjury became punishable at common law and punished primarily by monetary penalties. See KM Teevan, 'Seventeenth Century Evidentiary Concerns and the Statute of Frauds' (1983) 9 *Adelaide Law Review* 252; Philip Hamburger, 'The Conveyance Purpose of the Statute of Frauds' (1983) 27 *American Journal of Legal History* 354.

[83] CJ, VII, 480, 482, 487; CJ, VIII, 545. A 1664 registration bill failed.

[84] LJ, XII, 284; John Spurr, *England in the 1670s: The Masquerading Age* (Oxford, Blackwell, 2001) 129–30.

[85] LJ, XII, 381.

[86] Grey (n 31) vol I, 372. According to one Member of Parliament, the sense of the House favoured an office of enrolments in every county; *The Parliamentary Diary of Sir Edward Dering 1670–73*, B Henning (ed) (New Haven, Yale University Press, 1940) 71–72.

[87] Marvell (n 28) vol II, 208; Grey (n 31) vol VI, 144–48; CJ, XI, 736, 455, 468.

As had been the case in the past, there was legislation to contain atheism, heresy, profaneness and blasphemy. A bill was introduced in 1666, perhaps with Thomas Hobbes' *Leviathan* in mind, but was dropped when parliament was prorogued.[88] In 1680 there was another such bill.[89] In 1674 the punishment for heresy was discussed. When the judges were queried as to whether there was any statute or common law remedy available other than the ecclesiastical law that might be used against heretics, they replied in the negative, but said that the ecclesiastical and common law might act together. An obstinate offender might face the writ of *de haeretico comburendo*, burning the heretic, or, if it was a first offence, the writ *de excommuicatio capiendo*, imprisonment, might apply. When parliament was prorogued, the bill was dropped. In 1675 the House of Lords considered the abolition of the long-obsolete writ *de haeretico comburendo*, and in 1677 a law ending the legal burning of heretics was enacted.[90]

The 1677 legislation ending the burning of heretics again raises the question of dating reforms. The statute authorising the writ had been repealed as early as 1559. The last burning of a heretic occurred in 1610 and the last case was in 1631, a case in which the king intervened to prevent the burning. Should we date the reform at 1559, 1610, 1631 or 1677? The same kind of dating issue arises when any obsolete or nearly obsolete offence is officially ended considerably after having fallen into disuse.

Law reform may not have been a dominant concern of the Cavalier Parliament, but it received considerable attention. As we have seen, there were bills offering reform of the courts and bills to alleviate vexation, high costs, delays and excessive fees. Institutional factors such as the length of time parliament was actually in session and the time necessary to complete legislation (even legislation with little opposition) help to explain why so many reform measures did not become law. Compared to the reform efforts of the pre-1640 period, there were somewhat fewer reform measures dealing with jurisdictional conflicts. Chancery continued to be the subject of reform measures, although the ferocity that led to interregnum efforts to abolish Chancery was no longer expressed.[91] The ecclesiastical courts continued to be the subject of reform, but their control over tithes, moral offences, marriage, wills and administrations remained largely intact. As had been the case in the past, parliament legislated on the legal consequences of Protestant and Roman Catholic nonconformity. There was less effort to reform the legal profession, but judicial tenure remained a concern, as did the regulation and reform of attorneys and legal fees. Parliamentary interest in codification of the common law and the reduction and simplification of statutes diminished, but did not entirely

[88] See Jon Parkin, 'Beating the Bear: The Anglican Attack on Hobbes in the Later 1660s' (2013) 34 *History of Political Thought* 432, 452. Another atheism bill failed in 1667. Hobbes considered heresy in his *Dialogue between a Philosopher and a Student, of the Common laws of England.*

[89] Hoppit and Innes (n 7) 156.

[90] LJ, XIII, 717; CJ, I, 591, 674, 713.

[91] But see Henry Neville, *Plato Redivivus* (London, 1681) 50–51 (in the 1745 edn).

disappear.[92] The common law was rarely challenged. Reform measures in the area of debt or creditor relations and the criminal law continued to be introduced. It would be difficult to argue that the Cavalier Parliament had little or no interest in law reform.

VI. Pamphlets and Debate 1660–78

Although this period witnessed far fewer publications than the two preceding decades, law reform was discussed both in and out of parliament. Here we look at evidence relating to Restoration attitudes towards law reform, as well as several of the more interesting law reform proposals, some of which focused on pending legislation.

No one was in a better position to comment on law reform than Sir Matthew Hale, a much-admired judge who had been a key participant in and observer of the revolutionary-era law reform efforts as well as a highly respected judge. Reflecting on the recent past, his 1668 preface to CJ Rolle's *Abridgement* indicated that efforts to impose a new model of laws had been defective and dangerous, being either too 'strait or too loose: too narrow, or too wide'. Things that looked well initially either 'disjoyn or disorder the Fabrick' or required continual amendments and alterations. However good a new model might be, it would take a long time to be sufficiently known or understood. 'Even a more imperfect body of Laws well known … is more of use and convenience to the good of society, than a more perfect and complete Body of Laws newly settled.' Admitting that the common law was 'more particular than other Laws', making legal rules 'more numerous, less methodical' and longer to learn than others, it had the benefit of preventing 'arbitrariness in the Judge, and makes the Law more certain'. 'General Laws' might be 'comprehensive, soon learned, and easily digested into method', but, when applied, left 'great latitude to partiality, interest, and variety of apprehensions to misapply them'. It was the wisdom of English law 'not to rest in Generals, but to prevent arbitrariness and uncertainty by particular Laws, fittest almost to all particular occasions'. Hale recognised that parliaments had 'taken off, or abridged' parts of the law, that 'usage and disuse hath antiquated others', and changes in commerce had rendered some proceedings less useful. Thus, when Justinian found that the Roman law had become 'contradictory, obsolete … or too voluminous', he reformed and codified it. Edward I, 'England's Justinian, similarly had reduced

[92] A December 1670 letter from Henry Oldenburg Secretary of the Royal Society to Wilhelm Leibniz indicates that Leibniz was 'laboring at to make Law more brief and clear, by substituting for its infinite cases a single complex of few and almost simple rules'. Oldenburg admitted the difficulty of the task, but wished him success and expressed the view that he hoped the project would find patrons and champions for the 'Important work'. He indicated that he would bring Liebniz's efforts to the attention of England's civil lawyers; *The Correspondence of Henry Oldenburg*, A Rupert Hall and MB Hall (eds and trans) (Madison, University of Wisconsin Press, 1970), vol VII, 1670–71, 311.

English law into 'a better compendium which make up now the body of the Civil laws' and had contracted 'the Laws into a narrower compass and method, at least for ordinary study'. Though English law could not be 'demonstrated or deduced by Syllogisms', it might be reduced to 'general heads' and formed into a digest at least for study. Reform was 'a work of time', requiring 'many industrious and judicious Hands and Heads to assist it'.[93]

Hale's expanded treatment of law reform, the *Amendment and Alteration of the Law*, viewed law reform as 'a choice and tender business, neither wholly to be omitted when the necessity requires, and yet very cautiously and warily to be undertaken'. It was necessary to avoid 'the over-busy and hasty and violent attempt in mutation of laws under pretense of reformation', as well as a 'wilfull and over strict adhering in every particular to the continuance of the laws in the state we find them'. Although little reform had been possible during the recent 'tumultuous' and 'unseasonable times', there were abuses that now required reform. Reform must be gradual and consistent with the 'frame and basis' of the government. If possible, it should be undertaken by 'court and judges without troubling a Parliament', but he warned that if the legal profession refused responsibility, 'it shall be done by other hands'. Because Hale, like Coke, thought that parliaments were likely to enact statutes that created unanticipated negative consequences, 'judges and other sages of the law' should prepare legislation and be present during parliamentary debates. None without the 'most authentic injunction by the king and his supreme council' should meddle with reform. Parliament, however, could only be effective during periods of 'tranquility at home and little engagement abroad'. Much of what 'wise and honest men do now desire' with respect to reform was what they once had 'industriously decline[d]' out of fear that change would get out of hand. Lawyers who had initially favoured reform became less and less sympathetic during the turmoil of the previous two decades. It had been inappropriate to attempt reform when government had been 'fixed upon a tottering and unwarrantable basis'. England had been able to withstand the turmoil of the Civil War and its tumultuous aftermath because the common law had been incorporated into the country's 'very temperament, complexion and constitution'.[94]

Looking to the past for exemplars, Hale emphasised that Edward I, 'the English Justinian', had brought English law to 'a very Great Perfection'. 'Silently and without Noise', he had abrogated 'many ill and inconvenient Usages, both in the Courts of Justice, and in the Country', leaving the law 'very little differing from that which we

[93] Henry Rolle, *Les Abridgment des plusiers Cases et Resolutions del Common Ley*, 2 vols (London, 1668), vol I, Preface by Sir Matthew Hale.

[94] Matthew Hale, *Amendment and Alteration of the Law* in Francis Hargrave, *A Collection of Tracts Relating to the Laws of England* (London, 1787) 253, 254, 255, 257–62, 264, 266, 268, 269–74. In a discussion of parliament, Hale indicated that 'parliament had sovereign and sacred authority … in making, confirming, repealing and expounding Laws'; Matthew Hale, *The Origins and Institution, Power and Jurisdiction of Parliaments* (London, 1707) 49.

now hold and practice'.[95] Since that time, 'Additions and Alterations' to the law had been 'in the subject Matter' of the law, not its 'Rules, Methods, or way of Administration'. Hale remained an advocate of cautious, moderate reform.

Hale's catalogue of necessary reforms included the 'length and Nicety of Pleadings', and control of clerks who enlarged their pleadings to gain larger fees. Courts were 'overforward to Countenance … frivolous Exceptions' that contributed 'nothing to the true Merits of the Cause'. Inferior courts were so 'ill served, and Justice there so ill administered' that litigants, despite greater expense, sought justice at Westminster. He favoured a reduction in the multitudes of attorneys, but rejected the widely held view that the greed of the legal profession was the cause of the multiplicity of suits; instead, it should be attributed to England's increased population and the 'great Increase of Trade and Trading Persons'.[96] Whatever criticisms Hale had, he firmly believed in 'the Excellency of the Laws of England above those of other nations' and that trial by jury was 'the best Trial in the World'.[97]

When friends questioned Hale on the question of rationalising the law, they voiced the commonly held view that the common law could not be 'formed into a rational science, by reason of the indigestedness of it, and the multiplicity of cases in it, which rendered it very hard to be understood, or reduced into a Method'. Hale was said to have replied that he was 'not of their mind' and immediately produced 'a scheme of the whole order and parts of it, in a large sheet of paper, to the great satisfaction' of his friends. However, when pressed to 'compile a body of the English law', he was reluctant to put forward his sketch, saying that this should be the work of a committee of leading lawyers, at the direction of the king.[98]

Hale's *Pleas of the Crown: or, A Methodical Summary of the Principal Matters relating to that Subject* and his *The Analysis of the Law: being a Scheme or Abstract of the several Titles and Partitions of the Law of England Digested into Method* should be seen as related to that project.[99] William Blackstone viewed Hale's *Analysis of the Law* as 'the most natural and scientifical of any, as well as the most comprehensive' of 'all the schemes hitherto made public for digesting the Laws

[95] Matthew Hale, *History of the Common Law of England*, Charles Gray (ed) (Chicago, University of Chicago Press, 1971) 101–02.

[96] ibid 111, 112, 113. He also complained of the 'multitude of new laws, both Penal and others', which led to 'new Questions, and new Suits of Law', 'as well as the multiplication of Actions upon the case' (at 113). *A Treatise showing how useful the enrolling and registering of all Conveyances of land may be* (London, 1694), often attributed to Hale, proposed voluntary registers that would record future but not past titles.

[97] Hale (n 95) 160; for the jury, see 160–66.

[98] Gilbert Burnet, *The Life and Death of Sir Matthew Hale* (London, 1682) 73. However, on another occasion, he expressed the wish for a 'complete *corpus juris communis*' compiled out of 'the many books of our English laws'; Hale (n 95) 105.

[99] There were editions of *Pleas of the Crown* in 1678, 1682, 1685 and 1694. A seventh edition appeared in 1773. Hale desired something more 'methodical' than Rolle's alphabetically arranged *Abridgment*. The preface to the 1682 posthumous corrected edition suggests that the work was now 'well accepted and esteemed' and that Hale carried the text with him on his circuits.

of England'.[100] Hale believed that equity should be reduced to 'certain Rules and Principles' so that it might be studied as a 'science', but did not make such an attempt himself.[101] His monumental *History of the Pleas of the Crown*, published after his death, was used by many generations of lawyers and judges. Shortly after Hale's death in 1682, the House of Commons asked his executors to print the manuscript and appointed a committee to monitor the matter.[102]

Although of a very different political persuasion from Hale, Francis North, Lord Guilford, the Chief Justice of Common Pleas, was, like Hale, concerned with 'regulating what was amiss in the law'. As Lord Keeper between 1682 and 1685, North recognised: 'In process of time as well from the nature of things changing as corruption of agents, abuses will grow up; for which reason the law must be kept as a garden with frequent digging, weeding, turning, & That which in one age was convenient and, perhaps, necessary, in another becomes an intolerable nuisance.' He recorded his reflections first in in a commonplace book and later on 'a second view … digested his thought and brought what he had digested into the form of a tract, and thereon designed to prepare acts of parliament as he had encouragement and opportunity'.[103]

After his death, North's brother found drafts of several bills that he had 'prepared to put forward as opportunity offered'. North had strategically prepared his innovations in such a way as not to 'crowd' them into a single bill, 'but to pass them in separate bills for readier dispatch in the two houses'. He hoped to prevent 'long debate' on a single item from 'retarding all the rest upon which no question was made'. North, like Hale, believed that legal experts should lead the law reform effort:

> If the gentlemen of England in parliament would find in their hearts to trust fit persons, as the chiefs of the law for instance … taking whome they would to their assistance and act, debate, and hear in public; to draw up a law out of particulars, as the ancient way was, and then unless gross mistakes are showed to pass it upon their authority, there would be some hopes of an effectual regulation in a multitude of particulars all agree need it.

Like Bacon and his fellow reformers of the Jacobean era, North recommended that the judges together with other 'great men' meet together during 'vacation of parliament' and follow a procedure that would ensure that reform bills might be framed in an 'orderly, concise, and proper' way. North's biographer also reported that the judge 'had a great hand in the statute of frauds and perjuries'. His papers

[100] John Austin considered William Blackstone's *An Analysis of the Laws of England* 'a slavish and blundering copy of Sir Matthew Hale's'; David Lockmiller, *Sir William Blackstone* (Chapel Hill, University of North Carolina Press, 1938) 76.

[101] Gilbert Burnet, *The Life and Death of Sir Matthew Hale* (London, 1681), 76.

[102] It was printed only in 1736.

[103] Roger North, *The Life of the Right Hon Francis North, Baron Guilford*, 3 vols (London, 1826), vol III, 140–41, 142–43.

contained 'hints, concerning the defects, absurdities, abuses, and irregularities' in the common law and 'the practice of it and included material for a parliamentary bill as there might be opportunity and encouragement'.[104]

While Lord Chief Justice of Common Pleas and later as Lord Chancellor, North attempted court reform. On becoming Chief Justice of Common Pleas, he 'saw the desolate state of the court', which was 'a sort of derision in Westminster Hall', and 'meditated seriously to rescue the true and ancient seat of the common law, from the Present dereliction to a better imployment'. 'He worked to restore the court 'to a capacity of holding pleas in parr with the King's Bench', which had 'by subtile countrivances' deprived 'the court instituted for common pleas, of almost all resort of those causes'. He instituted a number of reforms in the proceedings of the court and issued a new set of rules and orders.[105] Although a leading figure in the Tory reaction, North, like Bacon and Hale, was a judge who favoured moderate law reforms formulated by the legal profession and enacted by parliament. Hale and North, two of the most prominent Restoration-era judges, supported law reform.

Hale was not the only critic of the law. The 1660 fictional *New Atlantis begun by Lord Verulum*, an alleged continuation of Bacon's *New Atlantis* dedicated to the newly restored Charles II, argued that earlier law reform had been prevented by the country's domestic and foreign problems and by the artifice of lawyers. Expressing extreme hostility to the 'inter-regnum of tyranny and oppression' when 'all laws, both divine and humane, have lain dead', or 'at least fast asleep', the author looked to the king to be 'our Solomon, our second Justinian'. The Crown was the preferred agent of reform because parliaments were 'factious or dilatory'. This Bacon inspired publication favoured repealing old laws, milder punishment for petty larcenies, changes in the laws of inheritance and debt, the abolition of primogeniture and dower, and the registration of sales and conveyances of land and judgments. Just as Bacon's *New Atlantis* proposed sending agents abroad to collect scientific information, the author recommended that students of the law be dispatched to foreign countries to collect useful information.[106]

Jus Gentium or England's Birthright (1660) similarly argued that despite the fact that law reform had been attempted by a 'lawless, illegitimate, and bastard power', it should now be attempted by 'lawful Authority'. Invoking King James I, the author emphasised the need for greater certainty and clarity in the common law and statutes, and that both should be in the English language. He also provided a scathing attack on legal proceedings which led to 'delay, overburdening, and deluding litigants'.[107]

[104] ibid vol III, 140–43.

[105] Chan (n 44) 50–51, 106, 302, 320–24. North favoured the elimination of trial by battle, changes in the law relating to executing and administration of wills, voiding marriages without the consent of parents and guardians, altering liberties that delayed justice and occasioned 'cavils', oppression by attorneys and reforming jail conditions (at 279, 282, 288–89, 290, 291, 292, 293).

[106] RH, *The New Atlantis* (London, 1660), Dedication to Charles II, 49.

[107] *Jus Gentium or England's Birthright* (London, 1660.

There was some, albeit slight, interest in making the law more comprehensible. William Phillipps, for example, responded to the old complaint that the English law lacked method. Agreeing that it was 'not capable of Exquisite Method', he nevertheless offered his 'Principles of the Law', in the form of alphabetically arranged maxims 'worthy of publique view'.[108] When it was updated in 1670 and again in 1671, William Style's 1657 *Practical Register* retained its condemnation of the ignorant who vilified the law. In 1674 there was an advertisement for an elaboration of William Sheppard's alphabetically arranged 1656 *Epitome of all the common and Statute Law. A Grand Abridgment of the Common and Statute Law* appeared the same year. This 1656 work, which was well received by the 'learned in the law', urged 'a more Comprehensive work of the same nature' in order to provide 'a Sure Guide' to 'what is either Common or Statute Law of England'.[109]

Fabian Philipps, a prolific Royalist lawyer, condemned reformers who failed to distinguish between the 'right' and 'abuse of Law'. Their 'pretended Reformation' of the laws had been 'driven on by a Mechanic Party that did not understand them' and endeavoured 'all they could to subvert and take away those very laws'. He noted that some writers had even wanted the moral and judicial laws of Moses or the laws of Holland and Sweden to replace English law.[110]

Thomas Hobbes resumed his attack on the common law and its judges and lawyers. His *Dialogue Between a Philosopher and a Student of the Common Laws of England* (1681) attacked the Cokean concept of the artificial reason of the law and the traditional distinction between statute law and common law, indicating there was just 'law'. He rejected the use of precedent, arguing that 'if Judges were to follow one another's Judgments in Precedent Cases, all the Justice in the World would at length depend upon the Sentence of a few Learned, or unlearned ignorant Men, and have nothing at all to do with the Study of Reason'. It was not 'Wisdom but Authority that makes a law'. The law itself was not difficult and might be learned in a couple of months, and the meaning and sense of statutes could be 'easily found out by the Preamble, the time when it was made, and the Incommodities for which it was made'. The statute book, not cases determined by the judges, was the authoritative statement of the laws.[111]

[108] William Phillipps, *The Principles of Law Reduced to Practice* (London, 1660), Preface to the Reader.

[109] William Sheppard, *Proposals for the Printing A Grand Abridgement of all the Common and Statute Law to this Present year 1674* (London, 1675). See also, William Sheppard, *The office of a Justice of the peace* (London, 1662). The 1662 enlarged edition expunged the acts and ordinances of the Interregnum. William Sheppard, *The Court Keeper's Guide for the keeping of courts leet and courts baron* (London, 1662 and 1685). See also William Sheppard, *Actions on the Case for Slander or a Methodical Collections under certain Heads, of Thousands of Cases … With a Table annexed for the ready finding out anything therein* (London, 1662; 2nd edn, 1774); William Sheppard, *Grand Abridgement of the Common and Statute Law of England. Alphabetically Digested* (London, 1675). The abridgement, designed for both legal professionals and non-professionals, was an updated and enlarged version of his earlier *Epitome* minus the acts and ordinances of 1649–60.

[110] Fabian Philipps, *The Antiquity, Legality, Right and Use … in Chancery* (London, 1663). In the Preface, he also wrote of judges being threatened and 'pulled out' of their courts.

[111] Thomas Hobbes, *Dialogue Between a Philosopher and a Student of the Common Laws of England*, Joseph Cropsey (ed) (Chicago, University of Chicago Press, 1971) 31, 35, 56–57, 71–72, 113

Like many, Hobbes emphasised the covetousness of lawyers who made the law unnecessarily difficult and accused them of 'magnifying' the learning of lawyers and making it law. He also emphasised accessibility, arguing that the laws should be as available as the Bible. He weighed in on the relationship between equity and the common law, and recommended that the reversal of errors in all courts should be handled by Chancery. Surprisingly, given his anti-clericalism, he thought that clergymen were the best Lord Chancellors. His critique included commonly held views on the relationship between law and equity, felony and misdemeanour, and felony and trespass. He ridiculed a concept of larceny which excluded the taking of corn and the legal rules on what objects can and cannot be stolen.[112]

Hobbes criticised the law of treason and characterised benefit of clergy as a 'relick of the old usurped Papal privileges, which is by now by many Statutes so pared off', and described it as a 'legal kind of Conveying Mercy'. He also favoured registries for conveyances of land, expressing a preference for one that would register locally, 'where the Lands ly'.[113]

Colonial ventures offered considerable opportunity to shape the law and legal institutions. The *Fundamental Constitutions of Carolina*, drawn up in 1669 by a group of aristocratic proprietors that included the future Lord Shaftsbury, envisioned a feudal society combined with elements taken from the law reform agenda. The colony would be peopled by a hereditary landed aristocracy, lesser landholders, serfs and slaves. It was to adopt grand and petty juries, but the latter's verdicts would be decided by majority rule. There were leet courts for civil and criminal cases for landholder dependents as well as local courts to handle all civil and criminal causes except treason, murder or other death penalty crimes. At the apex, a court of proprietors would have the authority to mitigate all laws or suspend death sentences of inferior courts. Carolina would have local registries of 'all deeds, leases, judgments, mortgages and conveyances'. No lawyers were to be permitted in the colony, it being 'a base and vile thing to plead for money or reward'.[114] Reformist measures were to be combined with repressive control in the hands of a proprietary oligarchy.

The *Enchiridion Legum* of 1673 by Thomas Sheridan was one of several publications that combined a defence of the law with a programme of reform. The author defended the law from critics who attacked the 'barbarous' languages of the law, charged that English law had no 'method or order' and claimed English law lacked

(probably written sometime between 1662 and 1675; published in 1681). See also Alan Cromartie, *A Dialogue between a Philosopher and a student, of the Common Laws of England* (Cambridge University Press, Cambridge, 2005), Introduction, xiv–lxxi.

[112] Hobbes (n 111) 62, 69, 70–72, 84, 86–87, 88.

[113] ibid 78, 79.

[114] *The Fundamental Constitutions of Carolina* (London, 1670). John Locke, Shaftsbury's secretary, was involved in the project. In 1691 judicial offices were appointed 'during pleasure'; Scott Gerber, *A Distinct Judicial Power: The Origins of an Independent Judiciary, 1606–1787* (Oxford, Oxford University Press, 2011) 179, 180. In 1683 Pennsylvania judges were appointed for good behaviour (at 271).

maxims or 'fundamental grounds whereon they consist'. Sheridan refuted the charge that judicial opinion could make or alter the laws. The private opinion of a single judge could not alter the law. Such change required the concurring opinion of several judges who must provide 'reasons' for their judgment. He explained why English law consisted of three languages and pointed out the inconveniences of methodising and its peril for students.[115]

Nevertheless, there were things 'worthy' of reform. These included proceedings that tend 'to the delay, overburdening, and deluding of the subjects in their suits, or to the defrauding of the law itself in the withdrawing or declining of it from its native sure and upright course'. Sheridan pointed to defects in trials and legal proceedings stemming from the inadequacies of juries, judges, lawyers, attorneys and court officials. Jurors, men of 'simple mean capacities' and 'small substances', lacked 'understanding and indifferency' and, all too often, failed to appear. Though generally 'upright and learned', judges were occasionally led by 'affection or, or by some other private respects'. Sheridan's remedy was an additional oath administered publicly to the judges at every assize. Masters of Chancery should be required to swear that they had taken no gift or reward for their favour. Counsellors – that is, barristers – often had 'diverted' and 'sometimes overthrown' proper legal proceedings 'by their multitudes, insufficiency, advice of dilatory, or defensive Pleas'. Too many were admitted to the bar with insufficient experience and inadequate legal education. Attorneys were far too numerous. Therefore, the statutes regulating them should be enforced. Abuses by court officers and their clerks required reform, particularly their excessive fees and wasteful forms of document preparation. The courts themselves must reform the 'incertainty and intricate ambiguity of Pleadings' that brought 'damage and danger' to England's subjects.[116]

Sheridan claimed that the much-desired 'Reformation of the laws' had often been 'thwarted'. The reigns of Edward VI, Mary I and Elizabeth I had been too troubled for successful reform. James I and Sir Francis Bacon had 'pitched upon to form a new scheme of new Law' or 'a remodel of the old', but 'that glorious Enterprise' had been prevented by religious discontent and the 'artifice of the Lawyers'. Parliament too had resolved upon a 'new Method of Laws' before being turned out by their 'own idol', Oliver Cromwell. Sheridan, like most moderate reformers, recommended changes only in the law's 'superstructure' that had grown 'cumbersome', not fundamental change in the substance. He complained of the 'almost numberless' intricate laws, many of which were unknown to those regulated by them. He provided an extensive but familiar critique of the central courts, the legal profession and overly long lawsuits. He proposed limiting the number of legal professionals in each court, replacing fees with salaries and limiting the length of suits. Cases undecided after six months should be decided by parliament.

[115] *Enchiridian Legum* (London, 1673) 57, 67–68, 74–75, 79, 80.
[116] ibid, 112–16, 117, 118, 119–20, 122–24, 125–27, 128–31, 135–38, 139.

All courts would be supervised by a new body reporting to parliament and empowered to suspend, degrade, punish and collect information of improper conduct by judges while on circuit.[117]

Debate on the advantages and disadvantages of land and other types of registration continued unabated both in and out of parliament, with advocates to be found along the whole spectrum of political persuasions. The Royalist Duke of Newcastle recommended county registers for all deeds and land conveyances, but expected the lawyers to oppose it.[118] Fabian Philipps opposed county registers, believing that they would lead to greater uncertainties. The newly expanded version of *The Reforming Registry* characterised registration as a 'Pandora's Box' and in over 400 pages denounced the 'many Mischiefs and Inconveniences which will unavoidably happen'. Deeds could easily be forged and counterfeited, and dates changed. Registries would also encourage informers.[119] In 1662 William Petty thought that both the introduction of public loan banks and land registration would reduce the number of lawsuits.[120] *Some Reasonable Proposals* (1669) advocated a register of estates to reduce the number of lawsuits relating to titles of land. In 1670–71 there were more tracts for and against this.[121] Sheridan advocated a Domesday-like survey of all the lands, manors, and customs which, when registered, would allow land disputes to be 'speedily and cheaply decided'.[122] The author of *The Grand Concern of England* estimated that county land registers would save the public £50,000.[123]

VII. Parliament 1679–81

The Cavalier Parliament that ended in 1678 was followed by three short-lived 'exclusion' parliaments primarily concerned with the law of succession and efforts to exclude the Catholic Duke of York from the throne. Largely following the laws relating to the descent of landed property, the law of succession was deeply embedded in English law. Its alteration was viewed by many as a threat to

[117] Thomas Sheridan, *A Discourse of the Rise & Power of Parliaments, of Laws, of Courts of Judicature* (London, 1677) 39, 41–44, 61, 64–68, 71.

[118] Thomas Slaughter, *Ideology and Politics on the Eve of the Restoration: Newcastle's Advice to Charles II* (Philadelphia, American Philosophical Society, 1984) 32.

[119] *A Reforming Registry* (London, 1671) 3, 4, 8, 14–15, 19, 29, 47.

[120] William Petty, *The Economic Writings of Sir William Petty*, Charles Hull (ed) (Cambridge, Cambridge University Press, 1963), 26. See also Josiah Child, *Brief Observations Concerning Trade* (London, 1668) 6.

[121] Seiichiro Ito, 'Registration and Credit in Seventeenth Century England' (2013) 20 *Financial History Review* 137, 150–51.

[122] Sheridan (n 117) 68–94, 222.

[123] *The Grand Concern of England* (1673) in *Harleian Miscellany*, VIII, 527; RH (n 106) 21; Richard Preston, *The Moral State of England* (London, 1670) 63. Pamphlets also appeared in 1667 and 1668. See Seiichiro Ito, 'The Making of Institutional Credit in England, 1600–1688' (2011) 18 *European Journal of Economic Thought* 487.

tradition and the security of property. For others, a change in the law of succession was necessary to save England from Catholicism. Proposals for changing the law of succession were not entirely novel. The succession had been altered during the reign of Henry VIII and discussed again during Elizabeth I's reign when the possible succession of the Roman Catholic Mary Queen of Scots was a matter of concern. It was aired again when the Elector Palatine was briefly considered as a possible replacement for Charles I. Whigs or proto-Whigs viewed exclusionary legislation to prevent James II's succession as a major legal reform, Tories and proto Tories as a major legal disaster.[124]

None of the three 'exclusion' parliaments lasted long enough for legislation to be enacted. The first was prorogued after two months. When it met briefly again, no legislative business was transacted, with the exception of the Habeas Corpus Act. The exclusion bill of the second Exclusion Parliament was rejected by the upper house, as were other methods of limiting a Popish successor. Parliament attempted to impeach several judges and was prorogued by an angry king and dissolved a week later. The last Exclusion Parliament, which met only for a week, again raised the issues of succession, corrupt judges and the exclusion of bishops from voting in capital cases.

This brief period was characterised by renewed concern with judicial independence and tenure. Charles II had been making judicial appointments at the royal pleasure since 1672 and in 1680 dismissed a justice of common pleas. A House of Commons committee appointed to examine judicial proceedings reported that judges were 'Arbitrarily, Illegally and Partially Favoring Papists', 'excessively oppressing His Majesty's Protestant Subjects' and 'subverting the fundamental laws of this kingdom'. Judicial refusal to bail in bailable cases was labelled a 'high Breach of the Liberties of the Subject'. Resolutions for the impeachments of several judges and for a bill to 'hold their Places and salaries *quamdiu se bene gesserint*' soon followed[125] Charles II called no parliaments after the dissolution of the third Exclusion Parliament, ending the possibility of any legislation, reform or otherwise.

VIII. Publications 1679–81

Publications relating to the law during this period focused on the succession issue. The abeyance of the Licensing Act in 1679 helps to explain the nearly 200 publications which dealt with the law of succession.[126] The Popish Plot trials and

[124] See Mark Knights, *Politics and Opinion in Crisis 1678–81* (Cambridge, Cambridge University Press, 1994) 80–81, 104; JR Jones, *The First Whigs: The Politics and the Exclusion Crisis, 1678–1683* (Oxford, Oxford University Press, 1961).

[125] Knights (n 124) 111–12.

[126] See Howard Nenner, *The Right to Be King: The Succession to the Crown of England 1608–1714* (Chapel Hill, University of North Carolina Press, 1995); OW Furley, 'The Whig Exclusionist Pamphlet Literature in the Exclusion Campaign, 1679–81' (1957) 13 *Cambridge Historical Journal* 19.

Crown efforts to prosecute leading Whigs for treason resulted in another burst of printed commentary, as did the issues of judicial behaviour and the appropriate relationship between judges and grand juries. Controversy that emerged from the prosecutions of the prominent Whigs, Stephen College and Lord Shaftesbury, for treason in part turned on the procedures and legal standards for indicting accused traitors. The Whigs argued that grand juries must actively examine the credibility of the evidence, several insisting that grand jurors could not reach the level of belief necessary for indictment if they only heard witnesses for the prosecution. Grand juries should be able to reject the testimony of Crown witnesses considered unworthy of credit. The opposite view held that grand juries properly could hear only prosecution witnesses because they were only to determine whether there was sufficient evidence to proceed to a jury trial. Therefore, all that was needed was a 'probability' that the accused might be guilty. To do otherwise would require the defendant to undergo two trials. Pamphlet literature on the issue largely disappeared after the Whig defeat.[127] The issue of whether bishops should continue to sit in capital cases in the House of Lords was explored in print as well as in parliament.[128]

IX. Parliaments and Pamphlets 1685–88

James II called a parliament shortly after his succession in 1685. Although initially supportive of the new king, its mood changed as the country experienced rebellion in Scotland and the Monmouth Rebellion in England, the latter aimed at replacing James with Charles II's illegitimate Protestant son. The defeat of the Monmouth Rebellion resulted in the trial and execution of a substantial number of its participants. The trial brought further attention to the high-handed behaviour of the presiding judge.

There was also concern over what were thought to be illegal actions on the part of the king. Attention focused on the illegal intrusion of Roman Catholics into civil and military offices in violation of the Test Act, the king's Declaration of Indulgence providing toleration to Roman Catholics and Protestant dissenters, the harsh punishments for supporters of the Monmouth Rebellion and the illegality of the revived ecclesiastical commission. The birth of a Roman Catholic heir to the throne kept succession issues alive, and the widely publicised trial of seven

[127] See Barbara J Shapiro, *Beyond Reasonable Doubt and Probable Causes: Historical Perspectives on the Anglo-American Law of Evidence* (Berkeley, University of California Press, 1991) 54–93; Sir John Hawles, *The Grand Juryman's Oath and Office Explained* (London, 1680); Sir John Somers, *The Security of English men's Lives* (London, 1681); *Ignoramus Vindicated* (London, 1681); *The Letter of the Grand Jury of Oxford to the Grand Jury of London* (London, 1681); *A Modest Vindication of the Proceedings of the late Jury* (London, 1681); *Guide to English Juries* (London, 1682); *Billa Vera: or the Arraignment of Ignorance* (London, 1682); Henry Care, *English Liberties* (London, nd).

[128] Thomas Hunt, *The Examination of the Right of Bishops to Judge in Capital Causes in Parliament* (London, 1680); Henry Briggs, *Considerations* (London, 1682); *England's Wants or Several Proposals* (London, 1685) 10–11, 14, 15.

bishops for refusing to read the Declaration of Indulgence in church was viewed as an illegal attack on the established church. All of these matters would be subject of reform measures after James fled the country and was succeeded by William III and Mary II, Protestants in the Stuart line.

If relatively few publications focused on law reform topics between 1660 and 1688, a substantial number took up reform of imprisonment for debt, many written in the context of proposed legislation. There were printed petitions to parliament and the Crown on the subject in 1671, 1680, 1687, and 1690. Several favoured continuing the current use of arrest to initiate cases of debt, while others preferred the summons. While the majority emphasised the miserable conditions of the imprisoned, there was also emphasis on the need for speedier payment of creditors.[129] Sir William Petty's belief that labour was the source of a nation's wealth led him to suggest that insolvent debtors might be made slaves, and insolvent thieves and cheats forced to make multiple restitutions rather than punished with death, the pillory or whipping. Financial punishments were preferable to those that deprived the state of labour.[130]

Whigs writers were largely silenced between 1682 and 1688. However, the Whig Declaration of the Duke of Monmouth attacked the judiciary for being 'suborned and forsworn', 'corrupt and mercenary' and for 'wrestl[ing] and misapply[ing] the Laws'. It supported parliamentary involvement in judicial appointments and terms of good behaviour.[131] Harsh treatment of the Monmouth rebels by 'the hanging judge' Jeffreys, and the role of the judiciary in the trials of the Rye House Plotters, reinforced antagonism towards what was thought to be a politicised judiciary.[132] The judiciary again became a reform issue during the last years of Charles II's reign and the short period of James II's reign. From the time of his restoration in 1660 to his death, Charles dismissed 11 judges; James dismissed 12 during his three-year reign.[133] Deploring the sorry state of the judiciary, Andrew Marvell commented: 'Alas! The wisdom and probity of the law went off for the most part with good Sir Matthew Hales, and justice is made a meer property.' The 'parliamentary machinations of wicked men' were 'more compendiously acted by twelve judges in scarlet'.[134]

[129] *Some Reasons humbly offered to Parliament for the continuance of the writ of capias, and process of arrest, in actions of debt* (London, 1671); *The English man's question whether imprisonment of the body for debt and damages, be more advantageous* (London, 1673); William Cole, *Legal and other reasons … why the subjects of England, should be imprisoned for debt or damages* (London, 1680); *Reasons for passing a bill in Parliament to erect Courts of Conscience … to relieve poor debtors and creditors* (London, 1680); *To the Kings Most Excellent Majesty the humble address of poor distressed prisoners for debt* (London, 1687).

[130] Sir William Petty, *A Discourse of Taxes* (London, 1689). Petty also favoured decreasing the number of lawsuits and the reduction of legal fees.

[131] *The Declaration of James, Duke of Monmouth* (London, 1685) 5, 6.

[132] *A New Martyrology, or, The Bloody Assizes* (London, 1689).

[133] Havighurst (n 59) 62–78, 229–52.

[134] Andrew Marvell, 'An Account of the Growth of Popery and Arbitrary Government in England' in *Complete Prose Works of Andrew Marvell*, Andrew Grosart (ed) (New York, AMS Press, 1966) IV, 315; *England's Wants* (London, 1685).

One of the few reform publications during the reign of James II, *England's Wants, or Several Proposals*, supported digests of civil and ecclesiastical laws in the English language to be read in the nation's churches, the regulation of lawyers and attorneys, and the reform of some pleadings. It recommended that overly harsh laws be mitigated because they led juries to foreswear themselves when they lowered the value of stolen goods. It favoured capital punishment for some perjurers and transportation and the pillory for others, as well as monetary rewards for bringing in highway robbers. Although the pamphlet recommended hard labour, a form of punishment that was becoming an attractive alternative to capital punishment, the author believed that some crimes should remain 'absolute felon'.[135]

X. Legal Publication and the Legal Profession

Legal publications continued to issue from the press, so that the legal profession was increasingly well provided with printed as well as manuscript case reports. Readily available to the affluent were the statutes at large, usually published in large multiple volumes as well as the more accessible abridgments. Most law reports were again published in law French after 1660, although some of the more recent reports and abridgements were in English. Regardless of the language of publication, lawyers of this and later eras had access to an increasing number of case reports. The professional life of a Restoration era common lawyer was very different from those of the sixteenth and early seventeenth centuries. The growing availability of legal literature was accompanied by the continuing decline of the Inns of Court. The oral emphasis and community of the Inns of Court and Chancery ceased to be the centre of legal education. Printed books increasingly provided the basis of legal learning. Publications commenting on the legal profession continued to be negative. Satirical poetry of the Restoration era attacked Judges Scroggs and Jeffreys, the former for his involvement with the Popish Plot trials and the latter for the excesses of the 'Bloody Assizes'.

XI. Conclusion

The Cavalier Parliament which met between 1660 and 1678 actively sought to implement many of the law reforms that had been sought by moderate reformers for a century and a half. It therefore belongs in the company of its Elizabethan and Jacobean predecessors and the moderate reformers of the revolutionary decades. Although efforts to implement those reforms largely lapsed between 1679 and 1688, attention being limited primarily to the succession and to judicial abuse,

[135] *England's Wants, or Several Proposals* (London, 1685), 14, 15, 17, 19, 20.

reform efforts would revive again in the years following the Revolution of 1688. Law reform publications became particularly sparse between 1682 and 1688.

Although the period 1660–78 had witnessed the introduction in Parliament of many law reform measures, few became statutes. The same pallid results had occurred in the parliaments of Elizabeth I, James I and the parliaments of the Interregnum. Failure, most often attributed to the opposition of lawyers, was often the result of frequent prorogations, unexpected dissolutions and factional differences about the desirability of legislative proposals. Julian Hoppit, who has studied parliament under the later Stuarts, found that legislative output before the Glorious Revolution was 'infrequent, unpredictable and numerically inconsiderable'.[136] Given these institutional problems, it is not surprising that so few law reform bills became law. Parliaments between 1679 and 1688 were too few and too occupied with the impending Roman Catholic succession issue. In evaluating the successes and failures of the Restoration era, it is necessary to bear in mind that revolutionary-era parliaments were no more successful in passing law reform legislation than their predecessors. The reform efforts of the Cavalier Parliament were not negligible, but it, like earlier parliaments, experienced a similar lack of success.

Both contemporaries and historians have been quick to blame the lawyers for the failure of parliamentary reform. Yet many judges and lawyers participated in drafting reform statutes, and Lord Chancellors and Lord Keepers often introduced or supported law reform measures. Lawyer authored pamphlets offered modest reforms accompanied by defence of the common law. Most parliaments appointed a committee for courts of justice early in the session, typically with a substantial number of lawyers. The House of Lords made constant use of the judges in drafting legislation. Whatever the legal professions' responsibility may have been, far too little has been attributed to the difficulties of the law-making process.

[136] Hoppit (n 7) 110, 123, 124, 128–29.

8

Revolution and Beyond 1688–1740

Although law reform has not typically been associated with the Revolution of 1688 and its aftermath, there was considerable reform activity during the immediate post-revolutionary period and the early decades of the eighteenth century. Reform began with the Convention Parliament, which gave the Bill of Rights the force of a statute. However, as it evolved from a series of drafts from the Declaration of Rights, the statute became an increasingly less sweeping reform document. Dropped provisions included judicial appointments on terms of good behaviour, allowing counsel for defendants in cases of treason and felony, providing a copy of the indictment for the accused and requiring two witnesses to the same fact in treason trials. These omissions became part of the post-1688 law reform agenda. Most other items on the post-1688 parliamentary law reform agenda resembled the proposals of earlier parliaments.

I. Parliament

Parliaments now met more frequently with longer sessions and thus had greater opportunities to complete legislation. The passage rate of bills increased, but remained low. Law-making continued to be a ponderous affair, with relatively few bills reaching the statute book.[1] Many foundered in committee or after introduction into the House of Lords. Failed bills were frequently reintroduced the following session, often failing again, while still others simply dropped out of sight. Bills that did reach the statute book were often poorly enforced, so that new ones replicating them were introduced. Still others were enacted for a brief period only and required re-enactment.[2] Many of the abuses discussed in parliament were the same or similar to those that had troubled earlier parliaments or were new measures designed to correct or slightly modify older ones. During this period, the House of Lords, aided by the judges, became the more important source of

[1] The failure rate was 60 per cent between 1689 and 1697, and 48 per cent between 1697 and 1705. Of the bills in Hoppit's 'law and order' category, only 16.6 per cent received a second reading; Julian Hoppit and Joanna Innes, *Failed Legislation; Extracted from the House of Commons and Lords Journals* (London, Hambledon, 1997) 4–5.

[2] See Wilfrid Prest, 'Law Reform in Eighteenth Century England' in Peter Birks (ed), *Life of the Law* (London, (Hambledon Press, 1993) 113–24.

parliamentary reform initiatives.[3] Law reform measures tended to cluster during periods of Whig dominance.[4]

This chapter begins with several fairly broad initiatives seeking to reform expensive and cumbersome court practices and procedures. It then looks at measures directed at individual courts. Roughly following the pattern of earlier chapters, it moves on to measures directed at regulating the legal profession, and then considers problems associated with local justice and justices of the peace. As in earlier chapters, it looks at the seemingly intractable problems of debtors, creditors and bankruptcy, proposals to provide greater security to landholders, and the criminal law. What stands out is the number of times the same or similar bills are introduced.

Although reform proposals remained much the same, the legal environment did not. Earlier reform efforts occurred during a period of enormous litigation, extremely busy, overcrowded courts and record high levels of participation. Despite demographic growth, the post-1688 period saw a precipitous drop in the quantity of litigation.[5] The business of Chancery and the common law courts fell 'at a truly spectacular rate' and there were declines in the ecclesiastical, leet and borough courts as well.[6] By 1750, borough courts had only 5–20 per cent of their sixteenth- and seventeenth-century business. Outside of London, prosecutions for serious criminal offences also fell.[7] For smaller landholders and others, the courts were either no longer accessible because of the increased cost of litigation or were no longer thought to be an appropriate venue for their disputes. In general, there

[3] Henry Horwitz, 'Changes in the Law and Reform of the Legal Order 1685–1760' (2002) 21 *Parliamentary History* 301.

[4] See Prest (n 2) 113–24.

[5] David Lemmings, *Law and Government in England in the Long Eighteenth Century* (London, Palgrave Macmillan, 2002) 56–80; Craig Muldrew, *The Economy of Obligation: The Culture of Credit and Social Relations in Early Modern England* (Basingstoke, Macmillan, 1998) 203–04.

[6] Christopher Brooks, 'Interpersonal Conflict and Social Tension: Civil Litigation in England 1640–1830' in AL Beier, D Cannadine and JL Rosenheim (eds), *The First Modern Society* (Cambridge, Cambridge University Press, 1989) 362.

[7] For the decline, see Christopher Brooks, 'Litigation, Participation and Agency in Seventeenth and Eighteenth Century England' in D Lemmings (ed), *The British and Their Laws in the Eighteenth Century* (Woodbridge, Boydell, 2005) 155–81; Henry Horwitz, 'Continuity and Change in the Court of Chancery in the Seventeenth and Eighteenth Century' (1996) 35 *Journal of British Studies* 24; Wilfrid Prest, 'The Experience of Litigation in Eighteenth Century England' in D Lemmings (ed), *The British and Their Laws in the Eighteenth Century* (Woodbridge, Boydell, 2005) 133–54. WA Champion attributes the decline to the increasing costs of litigation, increased legal fees, preparation of legal papers and the stamp duty for legal papers that began in 1694; WA Champion, 'Recourse to the Law and the Meaning of the Great Litigation Decline, 1650–1750: Some Clues from the Shrewsbury Local Courts' in Christopher Brooks and Michael Lobban (eds) *Communities and Courts in Britain 1150–1900* (London, Hambledon, 1997) 179–98. Shrewsbury experienced a sevenfold decline between 1660 and 1725. Historians have also noted the increased negotiability of informal written debts, promissory notes and bills of exchange; Brooks, 'Litigation, Participation and Agency in Seventeenth and Eighteenth Century England' (at 161). Debt and credit had been the chief type of litigation in the local courts, common law courts and Chancery during the period of greatest litigation; Peter King, *Crime, Justice and Discretion in England 1740–1820* (Oxford, Oxford University Press, 2000) 134–35. Litigation began to increase in the late eighteenth century, but the increase was greatest in the local courts.

appeared to be less need for the courts, yet newspapers in the 1720s and 1730s reported complaints of declining access to the courts.[8] The central courts were largely becoming the territory for the wealthier classes. The decline in civil litigation and the gradual increase in non-jury trials in civil cases meant that the proportion of the population serving on juries must also have declined.

II. The Courts

In November 1689 parliament launched a major 'Inquiry into irregularities of the Courts of Law', creating committees to investigate the courts of Westminster Hall, the Court of Chancery, the courts of the Grand Session in Wales and the ecclesiastical courts. Parliament was informed of earlier commissions to regulate the courts. The drafters recognised that 'Whereas many good laws made in former reigns' had been designed 'to suppress the corruptions and undue practices' of officers and attorneys, 'enriching themselves by non-execution or mis-execution of the laws', these practices 'of late years had escaped unpunished, to the great scandal of the Government'. New legislation was therefore needed.[9] A new bill ordered judges to provide lists of officers and offices as well as tables of their ancient fees. Oaths should require judges to observe the statutes aimed at the buying and selling of offices and the partiality of judges. There would be a table of fees hung in all courts and offices. This bill, which was reminiscent of many similar earlier ones, became law.[10]

In April 1690, 'An Act for the Benefit of the Subject in relation to the Practice and Execution of the Law' was introduced in the House of Lords, but did not have a smooth passage. After receiving a petition from officers of several courts, the upper house consulted the judges about 'object[ions] against the passing of that Bill'. As had happened so often in the past, parliament was adjourned before the legislation was completed.[11] In 1692 and 1693 the House of Commons again requested a table of fees.[12] In February 1693 the upper house again considered a bill dealing with the buying and selling of offices.[13] A bill regulating proceedings in the Crown Offices of the King's Bench became law.[14]

[8] Lemmings (n 5) 75.

[9] Arthur Cross, 'The English Law Courts at the Close of the Revolution of 1688' (1917) 15 *Michigan Law Review* 539.

[10] *An Exact Table of fees, of all the Courts at Westminster, as they were delivered in Parliament* (London, 1694); *An Exact Table of Fees ... delivered to Parliament* (London, 1697). Chancery and Exchequer bills must exclude 'impertinent matter to increase the charge of defendants'. Bill read January 1689/90; LJ, XIII, 435; XIV, 153, 157, 159, 165; XIV, 352, 554, 403, Hist Mss Commission Report, XIII, pt v, 17–25.

[11] LJ, XIV, 448, 450, 459, 479, 480.

[12] CJ, X, 708, 714.

[13] LJ, XV, 235. Officers petitioned against it. Though amended, it did not pass.

[14] A Bill for better discovery of judgments in the Courts of the King's Bench, Common Pleas and Exchequer received the royal assent; *The Parliamentary Diary of Narcissus Luttrell 1691–1693*, Henry Horwitz (ed) (Oxford, Oxford University Press, 1972) 416, 477, 480.

Early in 1694, the House of Commons sent 'An Act for preventing frivolous and vexatious Suits' to the upper house. After consultation with the judges and the attorney general, the bill was amended and returned to the lower house.[15] Two years later, a House of Lords committee was instructed to report on 'the proper Methods to restrain the great Expense and Length of Suits in the Courts of Law and Equity'. Legislation 'for the better preventing frivolous and vexatious Suits' became law in early 1697 and, about a year later, material on 'methods to restrain the great Expense and Length of Suits in the Courts of Law and Equity' was sent to a select committee.[16]

Among the many reform proposals initiated by the House of Lords were those dealing with the number of counsel to be heard in a case, limits on the number and qualifications of attorneys, and restraints on unnecessary rehearings. However, the judges reported rehearings to be rare in Exchequer and non-existent in Common Pleas. The upper house also considered legislation disallowing 'frivolous pleadings' in the King's Bench and regulating 'frivolous writs of error'. Judges were ordered to discuss regulating counsel fees. After a good deal of discussion, the bill passed, but was rejected by the House of Commons.[17] Irregularities in the courts in Wales as well as its officials and fees were examined in 1688–89.[18] Legislation to prevent frivolous and vexatious suits in Wales and the Counties Palatine became law in 1696–97 and again in 1699–1700.[19] There were also numerous proposals for establishing urban courts of conscience.[20]

Another period of reform activity began in 1705. The House of Lords inquired into defects in the 'Laws relating to the Administration of Justice and to consider of proper Methods to Prevent Expensive Suits'. Lord Chancellor John Somers, the most active law reformer of the decade, headed a committee that introduced a bill drafted by the judges. It gained rapid approval, but was watered down by the House of Commons after underofficers, clerks and attorneys objected to threats to their incomes.[21] The Act of 1705–06 for 'the Amendment of the Law and

[15] LJ, XVI, 364, 400, 416, 38.

[16] 11 Wm c 9 (1698–99 frivolous suits). Another act dealing with frivolous suits was offered in 1698–99.

[17] LDS MSS, III, 69–70, 71; HJ, XVI, 193, 214, 225, 252, 260; CJ, XII, 72.

[18] LJ, XIV, 223, 231, 259, 294; 1691–92; LJ, XV, 86, 89.

[19] LJ, XVI, 578; 196, 236, 240, 248. See also 8–9 Wm and Mary c 16 (1696–97). A bill to end frivolous and vexatious suits in Wales and the Counties Palatine was introduced in 1709. It provided that in all personal actions in which jury found damages to be under 40 shillings, plaintiffs should not recover or gain more than the amount of damages. The rule already existed in the Westminster courts by legislation enacted during the reigns of Elizabeth I and Charles II, but had not been applied to inferior courts. LDS MSS IV, xvn.

[20] LJ, XIV, 257, 265, 269, 297, 377, 395, 416; *The Parliamentary Diary of Narcissus Luttrell* (n 14) 9, 371; Hoppit and Innes (n 1) 160, 178. Between 1689 and 1702, there were bills for courts of conscience to handle small suits in Westminster, York, Exeter, Southwark, Tower Hamlets, Bristol, Gloucester, Newcastle on Tyne, Norwich, Greenwich, Holborn, Finsbury and several places in Kent. There were complaints about removing cases from urban courts to the common law courts.

[21] The bill was amended to avoid a quarrel over the trial of peers; 4, 5 Anne c 16; Arthur Turberville, *House of Lords in the Eighteenth Century* (Oxford, Clarendon Press, 1927) 77; William Sachse,

the Better Advancement of Justice', favoured by Queen Anne, provided considerable improvement in both common law and in Chancery pleading and procedure.[22]

Little was heard about replacing law French and Latin as languages of the law and legal proceedings until 1707, when legislation was introduced requiring acts of parliament and the proceedings of courts of justice to be in English. The legislation, introduced at the time of the Union with Scotland, also required the use of regular rather than the arcane court hand and the end to confusing abbreviations. It provided that misspellings and clerical errors would no longer be considered errors.[23] The provision requiring English as the language of the courts did not become law until 1731.[24]

III. Chancery

Chancery, which had long been the subject of complaint, continued to receive attention. Regulation of Chancery proceedings was considered as part of the House of Lords' 1689 concern with abuses in the courts of justice.[25] In the autumn of 1690, the judges were instructed to draw a bill 'with all convenient Speed to limit the Power of the Court of Chancery', to 'retrench' its 'Expenses and Delays' and to block its encroachment on the jurisdiction of the common law courts.[26] In December 1690 the committee reviewing Chancery and other equity courts requested the Commissioners of the Great Seal to 'prepare and bring the Bill'. After judicial comment, additional debate and further discussion with the judges, an amended bill was passed and sent to the House of Commons.[27] A bill to prevent unnecessary delays in Chancery, regulate its fees and expenses, and stop it from giving relief after judgment in non-equity cases was discussed by the House of Lords, though no bill was produced. By late November 1691, another Chancery reform measure was approved by the House of Lords, only to be rejected by the lower

Lord Somers: A Political Portrait (Manchester, Manchester University Press, 1975). Somers became Lord Keeper in 1693 and Lord Chancellor four years later.

[22] LJ, XVIII, 52, 68, 70, 77–78, 87; Lds MSS, VI, 36, 355–7; 3 and 4 Anne c 7; William Cobbett, *The Parliamentary History of England*, 36 vols (London, R Bagshaw, 1806–20), vol VI, 518.

[23] Peter M Tiersma, *Legal Language* (Chicago, University of Chicago Press, 1999) 36.

[24] Lords MSS, VII, xxiii; Turberville (n 21) 177; Ruth Morris, 'Great Mischiefs: An Historical Looked at Language Legislation in Great Britain' in D Kibbee (eds) *Language, Legislation and Linguistic Rights* (Amsterdam, J Benjamin, 1998) 32–54.

[25] It voted down a clause forbidding the sale of offices by Masters of Chancery and ordered a more far-reaching bill regulating and preventing the selling places in Chancery or elsewhere; LJ, XIV, 161; Sachse (n 21) 73–74.

[26] LJ, XIV, 519, 522–23, 531, 535, 556, 561, 564, 565, 567. See David W Raack, 'A History of Injunctions in England before 1700' (1986) 61 *Indiana Law Journal* 539. Another House of Lords committee was ordered to draw yet another bill to prevent unnecessary delays in Chancery and to regulate fees and expenses; Lords Mss, 1689, No 160, 313–32; Lords Mss 244, 17–25; 1690; LJ, XIV, 161.

[27] LJ, XIV, 588, 566, 590, 670, 679, 683, 684, 685, 690.

house.[28] Shortly afterwards, 'An Act for the better reviewing of Causes in Chancery and other Courts of Equity' received a second reading in the upper house before disappearing.[29] Chancery reform was pursued vigorously in the House of Lords between 1689 and 1692, but made little progress. Further attempts were made in 1695 and 1696,[30] but Chancery reform failed in parliament after parliament.

Chancery was scrutinised again in the early years of the new century. A reform tract of 1701 condemned its 'dilatory and expensive proceedings' and offered several remedies in connection with a bill 'now depending in the House of Commons'.[31] The House of Lords investigated Chancery in 1704 along with other courts and again in 1705. Although somewhat watered down, the legislation of 1705–06 provided considerable improvement in both common law and Chancery pleading and procedure. Parliamentary interest in Chancery reform dwindled, along with the business of Chancery during the course of the eighteenth century.[32]

IV. Ecclesiastical Courts

The ecclesiastical courts and High Commission were scrutinised. High Commission, which had been revived by James II, was dissolved by William III in 1688, ending Crown prosecution for ecclesiastical offences. A House of Lords committee of I689–90 investigated 'irregularity and what is fit to be redressed in the Ecclesiastical Courts'.[33] Gilbert Burnet, the Whig bishop who had tried to reform the Salisbury court in 1689, described them as 'the most corrupt courts of the nation, in which they think of nothing but squeezing and oppressing people by all the dilatory and fraudulent ways that are possible'.[34] A 1696 bill passed in the upper house, but was defeated in the lower house.[35] Two years later, the House of Commons

[28] Lords, MSS 1690–91, October No 304, 128–41; Lords MSS, 1690–91, No 304, 138; Hoppit and Innes (n 1) 188–89.

[29] LJ, XV, 117.

[30] Hoppit and Innes (n 1) 206, 214.

[31] *Observations on the Dilatory and Expensive Proceedings in the Court of Chancery* (London, 1701).

[32] Horwitz (n 7). See also Samuel Burroughs, *The History of Chancery* (London, 1726); Roger Acherley, *The Chancery as a Court of Equity Researched* (London, 1733); Hoppit and Innes (n 1) 160, 176, 208; LJ, XVIII, 52, 68,70, 77–78, 87; Lords MSS, VI, 36, 355–57.

[33] LJ, XIV, 345; CJ, IX, 199, 680. The bill would have eliminated excommunication for litigants in party cases and as well as *ex officio* proceedings when rights or profits were contested in church courts; LJ, XVI, 704; CJ, 11, 526, 527, 553; MSS HL, II, 226–27. In 1693 legislation allowing those in the province of York to dispose of their personal estates by bills 'notwithstanding the Custom of that Province' became law; LJ, XV, 736; RB Outhwaite, *The Rise and Fall of the Ecclesiastical Courts 1500–1850* (Cambridge, Cambridge University Press, 2005) 90–91. See LJ, XVII, 456; Sir Robert Atkyns, *A Discourse concerning the Ecclesiastical Jurisdiction* (London, 1689). In 1729 and 1738 the judges were requested to prepare legislation dealing with wills and exemplification; Hoppit and Innes (n 1) 310, 332. For 1740, see 336.

[34] HC Foxcroft (ed) *A Supplement to Burnet's History of My Own Time* (Oxford, Clarendon Press, 1902) 105, 131, 503.

[35] LJ, XVI, 704; CJ, 11, 526, 527, 553; MSS HL, II, 226–27.

initiated legislation regulating the ecclesiastical courts.[36] In 1696 legislation shifted many tithe cases to the justices of the peace. In 1713 legislation preventing excessive excommunication passed both houses, but failed because the session ended on the same day that the lower house passed the bill.[37] In 1732 a House of Commons committee was 'to consider of the abuses and exactions of the ecclesiastical courts' in England and Wales. The bill, which passed the lower house, did not emerge from the House of Lords, probably blocked by the bishops.[38] There were bills again in 1733 and 1734.[39]

Although the ecclesiastical courts were revived at the Restoration, they continued to decline. The passage of the Toleration Act meant that their role in the prosecution of Protestant dissent was largely eliminated. Defendants frequently failed to appear. Defamation and matrimonial cases declined, as the latter were shifting to Doctor's Commons in London. A substantial amount of their business was shifted to the Exchequer Court of Equity, which shared equity business with Chancery.[40] As their jurisdiction diminished the ecclesiastical courts were no longer seen as a substantial threat to the common law courts.

A bill to prevent clandestine marriage was considered in 1689. Although it passed both houses, protesters objected that marriage was so sacred, so 'religiously contracted and consummated, it cannot be nulled'.[41] Legislative efforts to prevent clandestine marriages, especially those of heiresses and minors, continued throughout the early eighteenth century.

Concern with the reform of morals and manners, which had long been a function of the church courts, was revived in the 1690s. The Society for the Reformation of Manners was at the height of its activity between 1690 and 1710. As enforcement declined in the ecclesiastical courts, it increasingly became the duty of justices of the peace. In 1689 William III complained about the lack of statute law for the punishment of adultery and fornication. Legislation against blasphemy and profaneness received the royal assent in 1698. A similar bill of 1721 was rejected on the grounds that existing laws covering immorality were sufficient.[42]

[36] CJ, 12, 199.

[37] LJ, XIX, 530, 580, 613.

[38] Prest (n 2) 16. Opponents argued that the ecclesiastical courts were superior and less expensive and employed a better method of handling facts; *The State of The Ecclesiastical Courts* (London, 1733), 17, 22–23.

[39] Outhwaite (n 33) 107, 116, 117; Stephen Taylor, 'Whigs, Tories and Anti-clericalism; Ecclesiastical Courts Legislation in 1733' (2000) 9 *Parliamentary History* 329.

[40] Donald Spaeth, *The Church in an Age of Danger* (Cambridge, Cambridge University Press, 2000) 77, 78. A court decision of 1703 (*Matthew v Burdett*) ruled that church courts could not discipline the laity under the canons (at 63).

[41] LJ, XIV, 287, 329, 343, 346, 415. Another bill passed in 1692; 4 Wm and Mary c 18. See Humphrey Prideaux, *Clandestine Marriage* (London, 1691); RB Outhwaite, 'Clandestine Marriage in England 1500–1850' (1995) *Economic History Review* 1144.

[42] Martin Ingram, 'Reformation of Manners in Early Modern England' in *The Experience of Authority in Early Modern England* (Basingstoke, Macmillan, 1995) 73, 81; Outhwaite (n 33) 100, 101; Keith Thomas, 'The Puritans and Adultery: the Act of 1650, in DH Pennington and Keith Thomas. *Puritans and Revolutionaries* (Oxford, Oxford University Press, 1978) 282.

V. The Legal Profession

The legal profession remained a topic of reform in the years after 1688. Concerns centred on the salarying of judges and on making judicial tenure secure from interference by the Crown. Although change in the terms of judicial tenure had been included in an early draft of the Declaration of Rights, it had not been included in the Bill of Rights. Richard Temple's speech of 1688 recalled that the Westminster Hall judges had been an 'Instrument of Slavery, and Popery, ordinary Justice destroyed, and extraordinary ways promoted'.[43] The following year, several judges of the previous reign were attacked and some were replaced. Although a bill 'ascertaining the Commission and Salaries of the Judges' passed both houses, it failed due to the king's refusal to assent to legislation that would have effectively ended royal control over the judiciary. However, royal vetoes had become rare and, in this instance, there was said to be 'a general resentment of the denial of the judges bill'.[44]

When the long-sought proposal for a salaried judiciary and removal only for cause upon the address of both houses of Parliament finally became law in 1710, the *Guardian* characterised it as the best ever passed.[45] The measure limited the Crown's ability to ensure a compliant judiciary and ended the fees and gifts that had supported the bench. Although there had been many calls for salaried court officials, the prospect of a government-funded court bureaucracy was not seriously considered, and the cost of court services continued to be borne by litigants. Since there were only 12 judges, judicial salaries were unlikely to become a costly drain on Crown finance. Despite the growth of the population, reformers did not propose increasing the number of judges as a means of reducing delays. The size of the judiciary remained roughly the same as in the medieval era. By contrast, France had hundreds of judges to handle the country's legal business.

However, complaints continued. Criticism focused somewhat less on judicial corruption than on uncertainty arising from the clash between current judicial opinions and those of their predecessors. Although eighteenth-century judges were less likely to be accused of being overly deferent to the Crown, they were often allied with one or another of the political parties. Judges were increasingly recruited from those who had held the position of solicitor or attorney general rather than from sergeants or other highly respected lawyers. Almost all judges had previous Crown service and many had been members of parliament.

[43] Anchitell Grey, *Debates of the House of Commons from the Year 1667 to the Year 1694*, 10 vols (London, 1763), vol IX, 7; Lois Schwoerer, *The Declaration of Rights* (Baltimore, Johns Hopkins University Press, 1689).

[44] The comment was made by Gilbert Burnet; Horwitz (n 3) 84 quoting HMC Finch IV, 442. The sale of offices, both judicial and non-judicial, was frequently attacked, though the financial interests of office-holders continued to make abolition unlikely. Legislation was introduced in 1690 and 1693 and again in 1700, 1702 and 1725.

[45] Joseph Addison, *The Works of*, 4 vols (London, 1721), vol IV, 144, 328–29, 4 July 1713.

Judges were deeply embedded in patronage networks, and Lord Chancellors were typically leading politicians, appointed and removed as Whigs or Tories dominated the government. When Whigs dominated between the Act of Settlement and 1760, patronage was in the hands of a single party. Some Lord Chancellors were 'virtually government ministers'.[46] Sir John Somers, a major political figure as well as a judge, was impeached when the ministry changed. Robert Walpole ruthlessly excluded his political opponents. Philip Yorke, Lord Hardwicke, who served as LC King's Bench and Lord Chancellor, was a leading politician, as was William Cowper, Lord Keeper and Lord Chancellor. Lord Mansfield, who became Chief Justice of the King's Bench in 1756, served simultaneously as a judge and a powerful member of the cabinets of Duke of Newcastle and William Pitt.[47] English judges became more independent from the Crown in the post-1688 decades, but most were deeply enmeshed in the fierce party politics of the day.

Parliamentary efforts continued to focus on attorneys and solicitors rather than counsellors (barristers), though its efforts to regulate their numbers, activities and fees met with relatively little success. Reform proposals had not changed and continued to be directed at reducing the number of attorneys and their clerks, limiting their fees and improving their education. Legislation limiting fees when successful did not solve the problem because it was not well enforced. Legislation was introduced in 1690–91 and again in 1693, 1698, 1700, 1701, 1709 and 1729.[48] Attorney members of parliament, looking out for their financial interests, were typically blamed when bills failed.[49] However, there was some fee regulation by the courts.[50]

VI. Justices of the Peace and Juries

Justices of the peace became less supervised, but, like the judges, were appointed and dismissed with political changes at the centre.[51] Summary justice by justices

[46] Wilfrid Prest, 'Judicial Corruption in Early Modern Europe' (1991) 133 *Past and Present* 67, 87–88. Lord Chancellor Thomas Parker was impeached for corruption in 1725.

[47] David Lieberman, *The Province of Legislation Determined: Legal Theory in Eighteenth Century Britain* (Cambridge, Cambridge University Press, 1989) 132, 138, 140–45.

[48] Lords, MSS 1690–91 No 1200, 29 -88; Lords MSS 1699–1702, 62–64.

[49] Robert Robson, *The Attorney in Eighteenth Century England* (Cambridge, Cambridge University Press, 1959) 7–13, 32, 139.

[50] CJ, XII, 72; LJ XVI, 214, 225; 491, 493, 506, 508; *Lords Manuscripts*, IV, xv, 62–63; 2 George II c 26; Hoppit and Innes (n 1) (1701). For legislation regulating solicitors in Exchequer, see 2 Geo 2 (1729) c 23. See also Norma Landau, *Justices of the Peace 1679–1760* (Berkeley, University of California Press, 1984); Lemmings (n 5) 19–55; John Beattie, 'London Juries in the 1690s' in JS Cockburn and Thomas A Green (eds), *Twelve Good Men and True: The Criminal Trial Jury in England, 1200–1800* (Princeton, Princeton University Press, 1988) 214–53. Beattie found London jurors tended to be experienced and came from London's substantial and prosperous citizens (at 250).

[51] A total of 656 out of 3,700 were removed between 1700 and 1704. Judges expanded the use of the writ of *certiorari* to quash judgments of the justices of the peace; Landau (n 50) 7–8, 345–46, 347;

of the peace expanded as ecclesiastical, manorial and other local courts decayed.[52] Dissatisfaction with local magistrates continued to be expressed. 'An Act to prevent the Delay of Proceedings at quarter sessions' became law in 1692–93 and was made 'perpetual and more effectual' in 1697.[53] There were bills in 1698–99, 1700, 1701, 1702, 1704, 1704–05, 1706 and 1710–11 to increase the property qualifications for the justices of the peace.[54] What counted as reform depended on whether or not one viewed greater power and authority for the landed gentry as a good, bad or indifferent development. Whatever the criticism of the justices, they provided the most common legal experience of English subjects during the eighteenth century and were the face of justice for the many who never came into contact with the central courts.

Parliament continued to hear complaints of juror lack of social and economic standing, ignorance and susceptibility to pressure.[55] They also heard the long-standing complaint that jurors violated their oaths by their 'pious perjuries', that is, refusals to convict accused felons to avoid the death penalty.[56] There were efforts to regulate juries in 1696, 1698 and 1730.[57] In 1726 a newspaper indicated that 'whoever considers the Nature of Juries, the Persons of whom they usually consist, the unhappy Prejudices by which they are too often misled and their notorious Conduct in some late Instances' understands that it was 'dangerous to trust to them the Determination of Things, on whose issue the Safety of the Constitution manifestly Depends'.[58] Party politics influenced jury selection as well as the selection of grand jurors, judges and justices of the peace.

Some changes in the role of juries occurred without legislative action. Until the end of the seventeenth century, juries heard about 90 per cent of all civil cases. This figure was halved between 1710 and 1715, and by 1745, judges were deciding

Julian Hoppit, *A Land of Liberty? England 1689–1724* (Oxford, Oxford University Press, 2000) 466. See also Lemmings (n 5) 19–55.

[52] Norma Landau, 'Conviction and the Development of the Penal Law' (2005) 23 *Law and History Review* 173; D Gray, 'Justices at the Roots: the Current State of Research on Summary Proceedings and Petty Sessions', presentation to the British Crime Historians Symposium, Milton Keynes, The Open University, 6–7 September 2012).

[53] LJ, XV, 223, 234, 253, 402; JHL, XVI, 138, 162; *The Parliamentary Diary of Narcissus Luttrell* (n 14) 416, 453.

[54] Landau (n 50) 150–54; Hoppit and Innes (n 1) 238–39, 276, 278, 282. Legislation passed in 1732. Non-felonious crimes such as assault and riot were handled in quarter sessions. Since some of these cases ended with monetary payments or a settlement between prosecutor and defendant, they were often difficult to distinguish from civil suits; Norma Landau, 'Indictment for Fun and Profit: A Prosecutor's Reward at Eighteenth Century Quarter Session' (1999) 17 *Law and History Review* 507.

[55] However, in 1701 the House of Lords blocked an effort to fix minimum property qualifications for juries.

[56] See Barbara J Shapiro, 'Oaths, Credibility and the Legal Process' (2012) 6 *Law and Humanities* 145; (2013) 7 *Law and Humanities* 19.

[57] A tract of 1733 opposed the current system of appointing juries on the grounds that control by Crown-appointed officers might lead to packed juries; *Reasons for Explaining* (London, 1733) 15, 16, 20.

[58] Quoted in Lemmings (n 5) 176 from the *Whitehall Journal*, April 1723, 275.

about 80 per cent of civil cases.[59] If the change was viewed positively because of juror inability to understand complex cases, the development for others was an undesirable erosion of the jury. Demands for summary justice by justices of the peace, or for the creation of merchant courts, were often opposed on the grounds of reducing the role of juries.[60]

VII. Religion and the Law

Parliament also considered reform in several specific areas of law. Enacted shortly after the Revolution of 1688, the Toleration Act changed the laws that had disrupted the country and its politics for generations. Protestant dissenters could now practise their religion without legal penalties, thus diminishing the business of ecclesiastical courts and justices of the peace. However, Protestant dissenters remained legally excluded from university education and public office, and intra-Protestant differences remained a feature of English religious and political life.[61]

Legislative proposals for religious toleration were often accompanied by measures for comprehension designed to bring Presbyterians back to the church. Comprehension bills foundered in 1689 and again in 1697.[62] The practice of occasional conformity, in which some Protestant and Roman Catholics attended Anglican services from time to time in order to be eligible for public office, was debated in parliament in 1702, 1703 and 1707. Legislation forbidding the practice became law in 1711. Although the statute was repealed in 1719, the law defining the relationship between religious affiliation and civil status remained a significant aspect of the English legal system and would continue to have a profound impact on post-1688 political life and legal experience.

Whether legislation dealing with toleration, comprehension and occasional conformity was considered to be reform or the opposite depended on the views of the actors who espoused or rejected it. The law preventing occasional conformity was a reform measure for Tories, but not for Whigs. Historians have frequently praised the Toleration Act as a desirable reform measure, but typically have not viewed comprehension and occasional conformity in the context of 'reform'. Last but not least was the 1714 Act of Succession barring Roman Catholics from succession to the Crown.

[59] Lemmings (n 5) 71, 75, 100, 121.

[60] One tract complained that neither judges nor juries were capable of understanding the 'variety of circumstances', or the 'new and unusual Contingencies' in merchant cases; *Essays upon Several Projects* (London, 1702) 307, 312.

[61] Toleration was not extended to Roman Catholics or to those who rejected the Trinity.

[62] See John Spurr, 'The Church of England, Comprehension and the Toleration Act of 1689' (1989) 104 *English Historical Review* 927.

VIII. Debt and Credit

Issues of debt and imprisonment for debt remained a significant area of parliamentary action, especially in 1690. There were bills dealing with the plight of poor imprisoned debtors, especially their harsh treatment by jailors and bailiffs, as well as the related issues of how to ensure that creditors were not defrauded. No easy answers were to be found.[63] As before, there was considerable sympathy for those unable to repay their creditors and with no means of earning money to do so, but it was countered by the equally strong feeling that those debtors able to pay should not be allowed to shirk payment or live well in prison by paying jailors for their keep. There were again a number of efforts to make more kinds of assets liable for debt. Reform measures also focused on prison conditions, and jailors who exploited their positions and escapes. Parliament frequently acted to alleviate the plight of the poor imprisoned debtors who were periodically released.[64] Since each piece of legislation covered only the currently imprisoned, there were bills to relieve poor indebted prisoners almost every year between 1690 and the end of the century, and at least eight more between 1700 and 1730.

Reform publications probably exaggerated the numbers of imprisoned debtors. Craig Muldrew's investigations indicate that relatively few were actually imprisoned and that most debts were settled or forgiven.[65] Despite dissatisfaction with imprisonment for debt and the numerous acts passed allowing poor prisoners to petition for release, imprisonment for debt was not abolished.

Measures reforming bankruptcy law were introduced, some focusing on bankrupts who defrauded creditors by concealing assets and others on relieving bankrupts. There were bills in 1693 and in 1705, when a major reform of the bankruptcy laws was undertaken offering more equal treatment of creditors and debtors. Honest bankrupts gained legal protection and bankrupts would no longer to be treated as criminals.[66]

IX. Land Registration

After 1688, parliament actively pursued a number of bills to ensure the security of land titles. Bills to prevent clandestine mortgages passed the lower house

[63] A House of Lords bill of 1696 would have relieved creditors by making compositions with debtors possible if two-thirds of the creditors agreed.

[64] The sessions of 1690–91, 1691–92, 1695–96 and 1696–97 saw bills to prevent escapes from prison. Legislation releasing prisoners was introduced in 1689, 1690–91, 1694, 1695–96, 1697–98, 1702, 1703, 1710, 1711, 1712, 1714 1717–18, 1724, 1725, 1728–29 and 1729–30.

[65] Craig Muldrew found contemporary estimates of those imprisoned and released to be excessive. In 1691, 105 were released in the five main London and environs. In about 1719, he found 201. In 1728, 623 were released from the Fleet. Most were insolvent tradesmen; Muldrew (n 5) 696. However, the Act of 1722 was said to have resulted in the release of 6,000 prisoners.

[66] Once the bankrupt disclosed all his assets and complied with the required procedures he was discharged of his debts. L Leventhal, 'The Early History of Bankruptcy Law' (1918) 66 *University of*

in both 1691–92 and 1692–93, one becoming law in 1692.[67] A bill of 1693 was designed to eliminate 'bad titles, double mortgages and other encumbrances in deceit of purchasers'.[68] Provisions for a registry of conveyances, deeds and wills were introduced in both the 1693–94 and 1695 sessions.[69] In 1696 John Evelyn queried: 'Will ever those swarms of locusts, lawyers and attornies, who fill so many seats vote for a public Register, by which men may be secured of their titles and possession, and an infinity of suits and frauds prevented?'[70] In 1709 the *Tattler* referred to forgery, falsehood in titles of land and 'records which had been hidden or buried by time, chance, or design'.[71] In 1697 a bill to more easily acknowledge deeds was rejected, but legislation providing registries in Yorkshire and Middlesex passed without opposition.[72] Bills establishing registries in Berkshire, Huntingdonshire, Surrey and Wiltshire were also introduced, but a national registry was resisted. Though some 24 bills were introduced between 1689 and 1750, there was never a consensus as to whether registration would result in greater security or greater fraud. England never adopted national land registration.

X. Scotland and Ireland

Constitutional and legal relations with Scotland and Ireland were revisited after 1688. There were proposals for union with Scotland in 1689 and again in 1702–03. When Union was completed in 1707, Scotland retained its law and law courts. Nevertheless, the House of Lords instructed judges to report on the laws of both countries relating to habeas corpus and to prepare legislation providing a uniform law for high treason. Methods of prosecution and trial of accused traitors were to be the same in England and Scotland, and torture was to be declared illegal. Transportation was to be extended to Scotland.[73]

Ireland in the 1690s was the scene of considerable legal reform, most of which involved the incorporation of recent English reforms.[74] It was no doubt easier to

Pennsylvania Law Review 223; Muldrew (n 5) 383; 4 Anne c 17 (1705); 10 Anne c 15 (1711). Additional bankruptcy legislation was introduced in 1706, 1707, 1710, 1719, 1725, 1731, 1732 and 1734; CJ, XV, 388; LJ, XIII, 285; House of Lords Mss, VII, 78–82, 4; Hoppit and Innes (n 1) 254–55, 256, 260–61, 314, 315, 320, 321.

[67] 4 Wm and Mary c 16.

[68] LJ, XVI, 455, 468.

[69] CJ XII, 11, 35, 41, 42, 130, 142, 172, 179, 181, 184, 188, 192, 195, 196. Some bills provided for registration of wills, while others did not. There were also bills in 1696, 1698 and 1699; Hoppit and Innes (n 1) 212, 218, 226, 228, 234, 235, 332, 336, 337.

[70] John Evelyn, *Diary and Correspondence*, W Bray (ed), 4 vols (1850–52), vol III, 357.

[71] Addison (n 45) vol IV, 62.

[72] 2 and 3 Anne c 4; 6 Anne c 20 c 62. The bill for Yorkshire emphasised the needs of the clothing manufacturers to borrow more easily on their estates. Legislation established registries in Middlesex (1709), West Riding of Yorkshire (1704), East Riding (1709) and North Riding (1731).

[73] LJ, xviii, 651, 658; J Irvine Smith, 'The Rise of Modern Scots Law, 1660–1707' in *An Introduction to Scottish Legal History* (Edinburgh, 1958) 25–43. There was a single Lord Chancellor for both countries.

[74] There were acts to allow the use of affidavits taken in the country (1692), to eliminate the writ *de heretico comburendo* (burning of heretics) (1695), settling intestate estates (1695), preventing delays

legislate reform for the subjected Ireland than for England. In 1719 legislation declared that the British parliament had the right to pass laws for Ireland and that the British, not the Irish, House of Lords would handle Irish appeals.

XI. Crime

Far more is known about crime and punishment in the eighteenth century than in earlier centuries.[75] Perhaps the most important finding of recent scholars for our purposes is a pattern that combined an increasing number of capital statutes with a decline in the number of those convicted and executed for serious crimes. Law on the books and legal practice were growing further and further apart. There was a growing interest in exploring intermediate forms of punishment somewhere between no punishment, which resulted from acquittals and pardons on the one hand, and capital punishment, on the other hand. However, complaints about the unfairness and unreasonableness of capital punishment were more likely to be voiced outside parliament than in it. There was a continuing shift to summary justice for lesser crimes, a change lauded as reform because of fewer delays, and condemned for the absence of juries.

The responsibility for the prosecution of crime remained largely in private hands. Given the reluctance or inability of the victim to incur the costs both of time and money, there was a growing inclination to provide rewards and immunity from prosecution to informers. While some viewed the addition of informers to be a necessary reform, others felt that paid informers were responsible for increased false prosecutions and perjured evidence. The threat of prosecution alone often proved sufficient to elicit compensation. Many cases were settled out of court.

From time to time, there were spurts of heightened, and sometimes hysterical, reactions to crime that appear to have been concentrated in London and its environs, probably because London victims were less likely to know the accused

in judgments to prevent arrest of judgments and superseding execution (1695), to prevent vexations and oppressions by arrests and suits of law (1695), to prevent frauds by clandestine mortgages (1697), for the easy and speedy recovery of small debts (1697), to relieve poor prisoners for debt and damages (1698), to regulate fees and redress abuses in the Marshall's Court (1698) and to settle disputes by arbitration (1698). Reform of the appeals procedure in the Irish Court of Chancery was considered in 1698.

[75] For a discussion of differences between sixteenth-, seventeenth- and eighteenth-century studies of crime, see GR Elton, 'Crime and the Historian' in *Studies in Tudor and Stuart Politics and Government*, 4 vols (Cambridge, Cambridge University Press, 1983), vol III, 289–304; John Beattie, *Policing and Punishment in London, 1660–1750* (Oxford, Oxford University Press, 2001); Richard Ward, *Print Culture, Crime and Justice in Eighteenth Century London* (London, Bloomsbury, 2014). A large percentage of news dealt with crime. 206, 209. For the later eighteenth century, see James Oldham, 'Law Reporting in the English Newspaper 1756–1786' (1987) 31 *American Journal of Legal History* 177. See also Peter Thomas, 'The Beginning of Parliamentary Reporting in Newspapers, 1768–1774' (1951) 74 *English Historical Review* 623, 634–36; Andrea McKenzie, '"Useful and Entertaining to the Generality of Readers": Selecting the Select Trials, 1718–1764' in David Lemmings (ed), *Crime, Courtrooms and the Public Sphere in Britain 1700–1850* (Farnham, Ashgate, 2012).

than those in small towns or rural areas. There was also growing concern with shoplifting, pickpocketing and embezzlement, crimes more typical of urban than rural settings.[76] London magistrates and grand juries were particularly concerned with enforcing laws, recommending new legislation and pushing for non-capital punishment for some felonies. The search for secondary punishments for some felonies was gaining support.[77]

For the most part, parliament followed the path of making punishments harsher and removing benefit of clergy. However, benefit of clergy was now extended to women.[78] The reading test was abolished in 1706 so that benefit of clergy became available to all those accused of lesser felonies for the first time.[79] The disconnect between the increasingly harsh criminal law and the declining number of executions of felons did not seem to have bothered parliament. Harsh punishments and wide discretion in the hands of justices of the peace, judges, grand juries and trial juries continued to prevail.[80] The decline in the number of those executed was also influenced by the practice of using transportation as a penalty rather than as a condition of pardon and the frequency of pardons.

The most applauded legislation was the treason legislation of 1696. Efforts to reform procedure had been included in the early drafts of the Declaration of Rights, but were not included in the Bill of Rights. Legislation was repeatedly introduced, but passage encountered difficulties resulting from prorogation, delays, differences between the two houses and changes in the various drafts. A treason bill of 1690–91 failed, and one of 1692 was stalemated over a provision dealing with the trial of peers.[81] In 1693–94 legislation became bogged down

[76] Shoplifting became a crime again in 1689 and a capital crime in 1696, though only a few of the convicted were executed. It became a non-capital offence in 1813; John Beattie, *Crime and the Courts in England 1660–1800* (Princeton, Princeton University Press, 1986) 78–79.

[77] John Beattie, 'London Crime and the Making of the "Bloody Code" 1689–1718' in L Davison (ed), *Stilling the Grumbling Hive: The Response to Social and Economic Problems in England 1689–1750* (New York, St Martin's Press, 1992) 49–76.

[78] 3 Wm and Mary c 9.

[79] 6 Anne c 23.

[80] Douglas Hay views discretion as a ruling class device to manipulate the poor and to emphasise the sacredness of property; Douglas Hay, 'Property, Authority and the Criminal Law' in *Albion's Fatal Tree* (London, Allen Lane, 1975) 17–63. John Beattie also emphasises discretion and shows how it might be employed by prosecutors, grand jurors, juries and judges. The liberal use of the pardoning power also meant that the increase in death penalty statutes was mitigated in practice. Pardons for felony property offences in London between 1660 and 1800 reached 61.7 per cent. Beattie found the 'scale of undervaluation' of stolen goods to be 'frequently staggering'; Beattie (n 76) 203, 424, 403, 625–26. Beattie (n 77) 49–76. Peter King's investigations show that mitigation was not capricious and was related to the character, youth, poverty and respectability of the accused. Pardons recommended by the judges on circuit were usually accepted; Peter King, *Crime, Justice and Discretion in England 1740–1820* (Oxford, Oxford University Press, 2000) 113. However, Leon Radzinowicz suggests that parliament intended enforcement and attributes the discrepancies between legislation and the high rate of pardon to the differences between legislators and judges; Leon Radzinowicz, *The History of the Criminal Law and its Administration from 1750* (London, Stephens & Sons, 1948). See also John Langbein, 'Albion's Fatal Flaws' (1983) 99 *Past and Present* 96.

[81] *The Parliamentary Diary of Narcissus Luttrell* (n 14). The bill of November 1692 allowed defendants a copy of the indictment, party witnesses on oath and required two lawful witnesses to the same

in the House of Commons.[82] When the much-revised bill finally became law in 1696, it provided safeguards for persons accused of treason. These included corroboration by two witnesses and the right to see the indictment and a copy of the juror panel. This allowed defendants to have counsel and to call witnesses who testified under oath.[83] Earlier versions of the bill had been more generous, offering procedural protections to accused felons as well as those accused of treason. In 1701 legislation provided that defence witnesses in cases of felony could testify under oath. The same or similar issues had occasionally been raised in the past in connection with the trials of John Lilburne, the Popish Plot trials and the Rye House Plot, but had not originally been an essential part of the moderate reform agenda.

Although benefit of clergy had been repeatedly eliminated for most serious felonies, post-1688 parliaments continued to re-enact its removal, typically for the same crimes. A statute of 1692 removed clergy from those convicted of stealing cloth from the rack or stealing or embezzling government ammunition and stores. However, those claiming clergy were no longer required to prove that they could actually read.[84]

Legislation provided rewards for informers when felony prosecutions were successful. A bill of 1692 offered rewards in cases of burglary and other felonies. In 1693 there was a similar bill for highwaymen.[85] A bill dealing with highway robbery had failed in 1690.[86] In 1698 there was a bill to improve the apprehension, prosecution and punishment of felons who committed burglary, housebreaking, robbery or horse theft.[87] Yet, on the whole, the failure rate of such felony bills was quite high.

During the 1706–07 wave of reform activity, legislation was offered to check a perceived increase in burglary and housebreaking. A House of Lords bill included the repeal of a clause in the 1698 legislation that allowed those using benefit of

treason, and process to bring in witnesses and counsel assigned by judges. Many of those opposed believed that legislation should be delayed until the war with France had ended. Others argued that new legislation was unnecessary or would make treason too difficult to punish (at 194–95, 206, 236–38, 264, 265).

[82] Henry Horwitz, *Parliament, Policy and Politics in the Reign of William III* (Manchester, Manchester University Press, 1977) 64, 74, 124; Alexander H Shapiro, 'Political Theory and the Growth of Defensive Safeguards in Criminal Procedure: The Origins of The Treason Trials Act of 1696' (1993) 11 *Law and History Review* 215; Samuel Reznick, 'The Statute of 1696: A Pioneer Measure in the Reform of Judicial Procedures in England' (1930) 2 *Journal of Modern History* 5; James R Phifer, 'Law, Politics and Violence: The Treason Trials Act of 1696' (1980) 12 *Albion* 235.

[83] Prior to 1696, felony defendants had been allowed to consult lawyers, but counsel could not speak in court.

[84] Lords MSS, VI, 8–9; LJ, II, 313. 323; 3 Wm and Mary c 9; 8–9 Wm and Mary c 41. Benefit of clergy was abolished in the US federal courts in 1790. It was abolished in the UK and Ireland in 1823.

[85] LJ, XIV, 288; *The Parliamentary Diary of Narcissus Luttrell* (n 14) 479. The provision was extended to burglary in 1706.

[86] Hoppit and Innes (n 1) 180, 218.

[87] LJ, XIX, 715, 743, 750. See David Friedman, 'Making Sense of English Law Enforcement in the 18th Century', *University of Chicago Roundtable* (nd, np); Hoppit and Innes (n 1) 182, 283, 284, 286. Bills on stealing and killing cattle in 1714, 1715 and 1717 failed; Hoppit and Innes (n 1) 224, 230, 311, 312.

clergy to be burnt on the cheek instead of the hand, it being argued that visible cheek burns made it impossible to find employment, making such persons more dangerous. The pre-1698 punishment was reinstated and the judges were empowered to commit offenders to a workhouse or house of correction for a period not exceeding two years. New legislation 'encouraging the discovery and apprehending of housebreakers' was passed in 1707,[88] as did legislation to prevent robberies in houses in 1713.[89]

Dissatisfaction with inadequate punishment for perjury continued, though with less reference to Scripture. The House of Lords introduced legislation in 1691, 1694, 1701 and 1702 making perjury and subornation of perjury a felony in certain types of cases.[90] In 1729 a bill dealing with perjury, subornation of perjury and forgery became law[91]

Transportation, which had been used in the past as an alternative to the death penalty, became the primary punishment for felony in 1717. The Black Act of 1723 aimed at destroying disguised gangs of poachers. Fifty new felonies were added, including maiming cattle, destroying young trees, extortion, blackmail and setting fire to corn, hay, houses and barns. Some offences imposed the death penalty, while others imposed fines for first offences and transportation for the second. The legislation was viewed as a reform by some and as punitive oppression by others.[92] Statutes sometimes developed out of judicial decisions. New statutes followed in the wake of the judicially developed doctrine that the taking of items attached to the land was not larceny. Several capital statutes were passed, each concerned with one or two sometimes newly introduced crops.[93]

There were also statutes dealing with forgery, a crime once handled by Star Chamber as a misdemeanour. Forgery had been viewed by some as an increasingly serious problem as new financial documents such as Bank of England notes and seals, South Sea company bonds, army debentures and lottery tickets came into common use. Separate statutes for different documents quickly increased the number of capital crimes. Some 29 acts relating to forgery became law during the reign of William III and Queen Anne alone, and the number increased during

[88] House of Lords, MSS New series VII, viii; 89–90; LJ, XVIII, 236, 320. A bill preventing robberies became law in 1713.

[89] LJ, XIX, 599. In 1720 there was another bill to prevent robbery, burglary and other felonies; 6 Geo 1 c 22.

[90] LJ, XV, 443, 445, 466, 449, 450, 456, 461, 463, 465, 466. For a similar bill of 1702, see LJ XVII, 30, 33, 39; Lords MSS, IV, xxxiii, 425–426; *The Parliamentary Diary of Narcissus Luttrell* (n 14) 293, 321. However, a 1701–2 bill was rejected. The Lord Chief Justice argued it would make the assizes so 'long and tedious, that the country cannot bear it'. It was also suggested that its provisions would discourage prosecution. Although passed in the upper house, it was rejected by the House of Commons.

[91] 2 Geo II c 25. Although forgery became a capital offence, there were few trials; Randall McGowen, 'Making the "Bloody Code": Forgery Legislation in Eighteenth Century England' in Norma Landau (ed) *Law, Crime and English Society* (Cambridge, Cambridge University Press, 2002) 117–38; House of Lords MSS, IV, 425, 426.

[92] 9 George I c 22, extended in 1725, made permanent in 1758 and repealed in 1825.

[93] Jerome Hall, *Theft, Law and Society* (Indianapolis, Bobbs Merrill, 1952) 39, 41, 46, 47.

later reigns. While historians have most often attributed the rapid multiplication of statutes to the growth in commerce or to public panic about forgery, Randall McGowen argues that there was no panic and points out that the legislation did not cover the private instruments that formed the bulk of England's commercial transactions.[94]

The 1736 repeal of the 1604 witchcraft statute provides something of a puzzle, since prosecutions and convictions for witchcraft had virtually ceased many decades earlier. If abolition is to be considered a reform, should that reform have an early eighteenth-century date or should it be dated from the time when the law had become largely obsolete?[95] When a practice dies out, should it be considered reform only if it is legislatively abolished?

The atmosphere in which post-1688 reform efforts occurred was quite different from that of 1640–60. Measures were introduced without the background of civil war, rapid regime change and inflammatory pamphleteering, some of which had insisted on the demolition of the entire legal system. Yet, as in the past, many bills never reached the statute book.[96] As earlier, the vagaries of the legislative process made law reform difficult. War and political conflict of the post-1688 era also diverted parliament from reform. While lawyer opposition or delaying tactics sometimes may have been at play, law professionals continued to play a major role in drafting and amending legislation, and served on parliamentary committees for law reform. Some changes in the law were the product of judicial decision-making, some as a result of legislation and some through disuse and obsolescence. Major changes in contract and tort law in the eighteenth century were the work of judges, not the legislature.

There were about 50 capital statutes in 1688. The numbers began to expand, though the rise was particularly rapid in the late rather than the early eighteenth century. Legislation increasingly offered monetary rewards to ensure that criminals would be prosecuted in spite of fears that such payments encouraged false accusations and false testimony. The practice of putting short expiry dates on legislation meant periodic re-enactments were necessary. Other statutes were enacted to fill loopholes in previous enactments. Still others can be attributed to changes in agricultural and commercial practices. There was a tendency for statutes to deal with a particular crime such as sheep or horse theft rather than using more sweeping general statutes, a practice that multiplied their numbers. Statutes were also being extended to include various kinds of commercial and later industrial property.

[94] McGowen shows that many forgeries were punished as misdemeanours and that few were prosecuted and convicted under the new statutes; McGowen (n 91) 117–38.

[95] 9 Geo II c 5. The last witchcraft trial in England was in 1716. The accused was convicted but pardoned. Most judges were sceptical by the Restoration era; Matthew Hale was an exception. LC John Holt was the judge in 12 cases; no defendants were found guilty.

[96] Thirty-six per cent of bills relating to law and order became law during the reigns of William III and Anne. Other bills passed at the rate of 53 per cent; Hoppit (n 51) 477.

Private prosecution remained the norm. Summary procedure was sometimes utilised, avoiding a jury trial. When crime appeared to be particularly rampant, paid informers were sometimes employed to increase convictions. The wide discretion of prosecutors, jurors and judges made it possible for many accused criminals to avoid prosecution, indictment and conviction or to gain pardon.[97] There was growing interest in finding a replacement for the death penalty, but the English were willing to live with a disconnect between harsh law on the books and its evasions in practice.

XII. Law Reform Publications 1688–1740

Publications dealing with law reform in this period rose and fell with the meetings of parliament. Many were directed at pending legislation. Reform publications peaked in 1694–98 and 1705–10. Another small wave occurred between 1726 and 1730.[98] Publications tended to fall into two types: brief pamphlets that were for or against measures currently before parliament or longer works dealing with several types of reform. The lengthier publications were frequently reprinted, ensuring that the ideas presented in them had a longer life and a wider audience than the ephemeral tracts and broadsides of the mid-seventeenth century. Since many of the publications are relatively unknown, I will discuss them at some length.

Tory lawyer Sir Bartholomew Shower's *Reasons for a New Bill of Rights*, written before passage of the 1696 treason law, focused on judicial reform. Shower complained of judicial overly 'complaisance to prerogative', excessive judicial discretion and circuit court judgments that differed from one another. The practice of granting new trials when a verdict displeased the judges should be ended. He also sought changes in the Habeas Corpus Act, which led too many persons to be improperly imprisoned due to vagueness in the causes of their commitment. Too much was 'still reserved to judges' to commit 'upon pretense of contempt to them'. Shower also recommended that treason law should be reformed to allow the accused a copy of the indictment and legal counsel. 'What rule of justice is there to warrant its denial', he queried, 'when, in a civil case of a half penny value, the party may plead either by himself or advocate?' Such criticism, typically raised by Whigs, had become relevant as Jacobites now worried about accusations of treason. Given the current 'plague of lawsuits' and 'vexation … now was the season' to regulate the courts. Shower, like so many before him, singled out the 'exorbitances' of Chancery, complaining of its 'dilatoriness and expenses', its

[97] The pardoning rate for those convicted of capital crimes was about 60 per cent in 1700; Beattie (n 75) 433–35.

[98] For legal publishing more generally, see Michael Lobben, 'The English Legal Treatise and English Law in the Eighteenth Century' in D Duchy, J Monballys and W Wijffels (eds), *Auctoritates xenia R Van Caenegan oblata* (Brussels, Koninklijke cademie, 1987) 69–88.

'too arbitrary' power and its uncertain rules that were the 'single and sudden thoughts of a lord keeper'.[99]

Robert Molesworth, a prominent Whig, addressed law reform issues in his often-reprinted *An Account of Denmark.* Formerly ambassador to Denmark, Molesworth noted that Danish judges were salaried, took no fees and held their posts *durante bene placito.* Danish laws 'exceed[ed] all … for Justice, Brevity, and Perspicuity'. Not only were they 'Grounded upon Equity, and all contained in one Quarto Volume written in the Language of the Country', but were 'written with so much plainness' that any literate person 'could understand his own Case, and plead it too if he pleases, without the Assistance of Counsel or Attorney'. Denmark's 'plain and clear' laws preventing vexatious suits made it possible to go through three court levels for less than £12. No important suit was said to last much longer than a year. 'None of that Chicane' that 'destroys and raises so many great Estates in England' existed because there were only a few Danish lawyers. 'Biased and partial' inferior courts were rare as there was a system of appeals. When no positive directive could 'be found in the law', litigants sought out its Chancery-like equity court. Molesworth characterised Denmark as having little crime because clippers, coiners, highway robbers and housebreakers were treated with 'great severity'. Despite its despotic government, a government that Molesworth abhorred, Denmark possessed an admirable legal system and offered a 'practicable' model for England. The *Account*'s many editions ensured that Molesworth's ideas circulated for at least half a century.[100]

Reform was also to be found in the fictional *Free State of Noland*, which, like Thomas More's *Utopia*, portrays an imaginary state having the same religion, language and law as England. Once a monarchy, Noland was now a free state or republic with a parliament-like body and a hierarchy of courts with a system of appeals. There were parish courts of conscience for small debts, hundred courts for civil matters, and county courts to hear cases in law and equity of greater value. There were no circuit courts and, unlike the English assizes, its county courts sat until all their business was completed. Provincial-level courts determined errors and appeals in equity and adjudicated first instance cases of £200 or more. All cases were tried by the common law and juries. While the author admitted that increasing the number of courts would result in a great increase in law business, the increase would cause little oppression because charges would be less than the cost of an arbitration dinner. The number of lawyers too would increase, but their cost would be dramatically reduced.[101] The fictional Noland, like Molesworth's Denmark, was to serve as a model for England.

[99] Bartholomew Shower, 'Reason for a New Bill of Rights; Humbly submitted to the ensuing Session of Parliament' (1692) in *A Collection of Scarce and Valuable Tracts*, Sir Walter Scott (ed) (London, 1812), vol X, 569.

[100] Robert Molesworth, *An Account of Denmark, as it was in the year 1692* (London, 1694) 139, 214, 219, 227. There was a fifth edition in 1745.

[101] *The Free State of Noland* (London, 1692) 2nd edition 1701. Sometimes attributed to Daniel Defoe or Lord Somers. Jonathan Swift's *Gulliver's Travels* also used fictitious lands to criticize English legal practices.

The 'want of a due, and impartial administration of Justice' and the exorbitant fees of counsellors, attorneys, clerks, gaolers and other corrupt officers were the principal themes of James Whiston's angry 1696 *England's Calamities Discovered*. His remedy was 'just Impeachments, and reasonable accusations … against those, who … either contrary to Law, or by illusion and corrupt practices of the Law, seek to invade and destroy' the people's liberties and properties. He looked to parliament for the necessary 'reformation'.[102]

In 1699 attorney Richard Collins, who also directed his complaints to parliament in 1698, blamed the evils of the legal system principally on the 'gross corruption' of its judges. Despite England's superior laws, foreigners had cheaper and quicker legal process.[103] Two years later, a 'well-wisher to his country' complained that despite England's many commissions for 'revising of the law', none had been 'effectual'. Given that England was currently experiencing a 'full and tranquil Peace', now was 'the season' for reform.[104]

Reforming the law to meet changing conditions was a major theme of William Pudsey's *The Constitution and Laws of England Considered* (1701). Pudsey complained of the widespread belief that the laws must not be touched, despite the obvious 'alterations in the fundamentals of the common law' over time. Not only had the law been altered by 'judicial resolutions', but every new Act of Parliament changed it. Parliament should improve the law along several fronts. Enforcement was far too 'loose and accidental'. The assizes, held too infrequently, were decaying, as were the old courts leet and baron and county courts. Too many cases were removed from the county courts to Westminster. Pudsey recommended revival of local courts with an enlarged jurisdiction. Justices of the peace should be divided into honorific and well-trained categories, with only the latter deciding criminal and property cases. To the objection that expansion of the justice of the peace's summary jurisdiction would diminish juries, he responded that juries might be retained. Juries, however, also required reform, now being 'mean and ordinary, even contemptible'. Attorneys, 'a nuisance in all ages', should be regulated to reduce their numbers, fees and delaying tactics. He also supported pleading in English and the enrolment of land transactions.[105]

The years 1706 and 1707, in which several law reform bills were introduced in parliament, saw the publication of *Proposals humbly offered … For Remedying the Great Charge and Delay of Suits at Law and in Equity*. Its frequent reprinting

[102] James Whiston, *England's Calamitie Discovered* (London, 1696) 4, 5, 6, 12, 13, 19, 26, 38; James Whiston, *Farther arguments for passing the bill against the sale of offices* (London, 1689?).

[103] Richard Collins, *The Cause of England's Misery: or A Brief account of the Corrupt Practices of the Law* (London, 1698) 4, 10–14, 16, 113.

[104] *Overtures for Correcting and Amending the Laws* (np, 1700) Dedication.

[105] William Pudsey, *The Constitution and Laws of England Considered* (London, 1701) 7, 12, 13, 14–15, 16, 25, 85, 101, 113, 131–32, 169–70, 188–89, 196–97, 199–200, 211, 219–21, 253, 260, 271–75, 285–86, 290, 294, 305. William Nelson also favoured both honorary and paid justices; *The Office and Authority of the Justice of the Peace* (London, 1707) 365.

ensured that its proposals circulated for several decades.[106] Like many moderate reformers, its author thought that although England's law was 'already the best in the World', many grievances remained for parliament to address. The 'primum mobile of the Mischiefs and Inconveniences' was the 'smallness' of judicial salaries, which led judges to take fees and sell offices. Suppressing the sale of offices would raise judicial esteem and make trials more 'indifferent, impartial and quick of Dispatch'. The author complained of the assize system, suggesting that the judges sitting together in Westminster functioned better than when on circuit, being 'kept steady' by their fellow judges.[107]

It was also necessary to reform the 'dilatory and senseless Customs, Rules and Forms of the several Courts'. The high costs and long delays in Chancery were denounced. The author looked to Chancery's leaders to suppress many offices and reduce the fees of the rest. Replying to the objection that cheaper justice encouraged litigation, the author denied that the English were particularly litigious. While the institution of the jury was defended, jury trials currently provided insufficient security. Men of worth simply would not attend trials for 12 pence or less. Furthermore, 'mean' and ignorant jurors relied excessively on judicial direction, so that cases were in effect tried by judges.[108] Ambivalence about the jury was a staple of reform for several centuries.

Law reformers of the eighteenth century, like earlier ones, made use of the language of pruning and purifying the law or eliminating its weeds. The satirical *The Law Corrupted* employed a variation: 'For Iron rust, the Workman takes the File.' It recommended codification, ending condemnation of defendants who remained mute, reducing delays and eliminating multiplication of the same suit, but expected the lawyers, the 'people's foe', to oppose the recommendations. This tract, unlike most reform publications, recommended that reforms be initiated by the queen and her ministers. Like several other reformers, the author thought that 'Now that the war was over, now was the time' to implement reform.[109] These proposals circulated for several decades.

Another pamphlet of 1707 also suggested that the times were fully 'ripe for a regulation' and that parliament would 'meet with all imaginable encouragements' in the endeavour. The usual complaints are outlined and the usual remedies offered. Exorbitant expenses, especially in courts of equity, were justly 'ranged among our first-rate grievance'. Actions at law for 'slender debt' cost litigants twice as much as the debt itself. There were unnecessary expenses in filing affidavits and unnecessary interrogatories and their copies in Chancery. Attorneys and solicitors

[106] First published in 1706 and reprinted in 1707. It appeared again in 1724 with additions, and again in 1725, 1727, and 1730.

[107] *Proposals humbly offered ... for Remedying the Great Charge and Delay of Suits of Law and Equity ... to the House of Commons* (London, 1706) 3, 5, 6.

[108] *Proposals humbly offered* (n 107) 9, 11, 12, 13, 14, 15.

[109] *The Law Corrupted* (London, 1706) 1–2, 3, 8–9, 12, 13, 18, 19, 22. It was reprinted in 1707. It appeared again in 1724 with additions, and again in 1725, 1727 and 1730. For a critique of lawyers, see Bernard Mandeville, *The Grumbling Hive* (London, 1705) 4, 5, 17.

should be regulated and their numbers reduced. Legislation could 'influence the Courts themselves to regulate several more of the Abuses, or give Foundation, to a further Regulation by the Legislature'. But 'till the Parliament has begun, till some good Law is made to redress the present extravagant charges', the author had little hope of reform as long as offices were 'the property of the officers'.[110] Despite the constant pleas to end the sale of offices, the practice remained an integral part of the structure of early modern law and governance.

About a decade would pass before another full-scale attack appeared. Thomas Baston's tract, published first in 1716 and again in 1728 and 1732, focused on the 'universal complaints of the tediousness and chargeablness of the Law' and the 'multitude of our Laws' that led to 'endless disputes' that might 'last a lifetime'. A reformation in the laws was as necessary as had been the earlier reformation in the church. Again we hear the familiar complaint about the sale of law offices. The common law courts rather than the ecclesiastical courts should handle cases of adultery, fornication and blasphemy. Baston opposed the division between courts of law and courts of equity that required litigants to go from one court to another. He looked to the Lord Chancellor, the judges and reform-minded lawyers to remedy abuses of the courts. Echoing the long-standing criticism of the legal profession, he attacked the 'knavish lawyers' who encouraged litigation. There were 10 times more lawyers than necessary in England, more 'than in all Europe'. He favoured abolishing imprisonment for debt and capital punishment for theft, but bewailed the lack of 'due and severe' punishments for 'Perjury, Frauds, Cheats, clandestine mortgages, [and] selling Estates over and over'.[111]

Law reform interest revived in 1724, bringing with it a new wave of parliamentary reform measures and reform tracts. The anonymous author of *Proposals humbly offered to the Parliament for remedying the great charge and delay of suits at law and in equity*, published twice in 1707, noted that it was time for a third edition.[112] When it was first published in 1707, it seemed as if Parliament had been in a 'good disposition to have done something in this affair'. A new edition had therefore been prepared for parliament's upcoming session. According to the author, 'grievance[s] of the last seventeen years' had much increased and were 'still growing'. The 'prodigious Charge and Delay' in lawsuits was a 'grievance universally complain'd of'. The 'vox populi' was now lifted up against the grievances in the law that had 'well nigh swallowed up the common justice of the Kingdome'. Parliament should put a 'speedy stop' to these grievances. Readers were reminded that in the past, when 'public grievance' had become great, parliament had 'pluct' evils up 'by the very Roots'. Invoking its abolition of Star Chamber and the Court

[110] *Reasons humbly offered to both Houses of Parliament, for Passing a Bill for Preventing Delays and Expenses, in Suits of Law and Equity* (London, 1707) in *Harleian Miscellany*, VIII, 400, 401, 406, 407. It was printed twice in 1707 and again in 1726.

[111] Thomas Baston, *Thoughts on Trade and a public spirit* (London, 1716) Preface, 71–74, 87, 79, 82, 83, 84, 87, 88, 114–30, 134–35, 137–38.

[112] There were seven editions before the last edition in 1730.

of Wards as examples of legislatively enacted reform, the author urged the 'present parliament' to 'imitate them'.[113]

Law Quibbles, published in 1724 together with *An Essay on amending and reducing the laws of England*, advocated changes in the laws relating to small debts, a reduction of legal offices and fees, and a registry for deeds and conveyances. Such measures would cause funds to be 'freely advanced' on mortgages, lower the interest rate and allow trade to be 'more effectually carry'd on'. County registries transmitting information to Chancery would prevent many suits and unjust prosecutions. Legislation to prevent fraudulent conveyances and a compilation of the penal laws was also recommended. Like many earlier reformers, the author proposed that the laws on a single subject be listed under one heading and put into 'one concise and accurate Statute'.[114]

An Essay on the Amendment of the laws of England, published in 1724 and again in 1726 and 1736, offered criticisms and remedies. Although English law itself was not difficult, it had been made so by the legal profession and by the multiplication of laws. The author's remedy was the familiar one, that England's 'long and accumulated Acts' should be reduced 'under every individual Head, by one concise and Accurate Statute'. Reduction to about a quarter of their current number would not injure the legal profession. 'Though not easie to be performed', the task of reform was 'practicable'. If undertaken, those 'eminent in the law' would be deserving of an 'immortal Reputation'.[115]

Specific proposals included reducing delays in common law and equity cases, posting fee schedules and eliminating unnecessary paperwork. New legislation was necessary because current law was not effective. 'Either evidence is not ready or some excuse or another is eternally in the way.' Except for cases of great consequence, counsellors and attorneys should be punished for dilatory pleas. Attorneys must be regulated and their fees reduced. Also recommended was a national registry for deeds and conveyances, the argument being that Yorkshire and Middlesex had registries which 'hath been experienced to be very beneficial and advantageous to the Subject'.[116]

Like so many reformers, the author insisted that better-educated jurors would make better judgments. In criminal cases, jurors must not be 'too forward in giving their Verdicts, or be any Ways biass'd by others, where the life of a man, who perhaps does not deserve death, may be taken away'. Offenders were often 'scandalously brought off, by laying the indictment for an attempt only', thereby incurring only fines and imprisonment. Many crimes were insufficiently prosecuted or

[113] *Proposals humbly offered to Parliament for Remedyng the Great Charge and Delay of Suits of Law and Equity* (London, 1724) Preface, i–iv. A tract with the same title dealing with Ireland appeared in 1725 and 1726, A seventh edition appeared in 1730.

[114] *Law Quibbles* (London, 1724) 11–12, 19, 20, 30–31, 61–63.

[115] *Essay on the Amendment of the Laws of England*, 4–5, 31–32, 33, 70 (using the 1726 edn).

[116] ibid 21–22, 61, 62–67, 76.

needed harsher penalties. Sacrilege, rape and sodomy were insufficiently punished. Blasphemy should be a capital crime. Bribery, which was thought to be on the increase, should also be made a capital offence. Perjury, which currently incurred a fine, imprisonment or the pillory, should be more heavily punished. Informers should be respected rather than reproached because so many statutes were 'wholly unexecuted'. The *Essay* called for a new office to 'detect and inform against criminals … from the highest to the lowest' so that every crime should 'impartially meet with the punishment that is due to it, and our Laws in general be no longer useless'.[117]

Christopher Tancred's 1727 *Essay for a General Regulation of the Law and the more Speedy of Justice*, dedicated to the Lord Chancellor, offered a combination of novel and familiar reforms. Tancred looked to parliament for 'a much quicker Dispatch in the Administration of Justice' because only the legislative power had the capacity to provide remedies. There were too many vexatious suits for trespass, slander and battery, and far too many unnecessary delaying procedures. He recommended a general plea to replace the ancient intricate method of pleadings and the abolition of unnecessary offices in courts of law and equity. He called attention to the 'growing and exorbitant Power of the Courts of Equity', especially condemning the use of injunctions to stay suits begun in other courts. Conveyancing must be simplified and a general register created for all securities affecting lands, hereditaments and encumbrances to eliminate fraudulent lawsuits and defective titles.[118] Tancred praised quarter sessions and recommended the enlargement of their 'power and jurisdiction'. Legal fees should be reduced, attorneys regulated and juror qualifications modified to ensure jurors of birth and education. Poorly educated jurors were overawed by judges, who as a result 'became sole arbiters of fact as well as law'. Like Molesworth, Tancred looked to Denmark as an exemplar. Its courts operated with far fewer delays and lower costs than the English courts and had an effective appeals system that was lacking in England.[119]

Another gap in reform publications ended in 1736. *Law Visions, or Pills for Posterity*, a lengthy, fictional satirical treatment of corrupt lawyers and legal procedure, reiterated the familiar complaints and reform proposals. It referred to a

[117] ibid 10–11, 14, 15, 16, 17, 20, 21, 30, 75. If perjury resulted in the loss of life, it should be a capital offence. If the perjury resulted in loss of lands or possessions, it should be punished as a felony and the perjurer's estate confiscated. Subornation of perjury in a court of record in cases of life, lands or goods should become a felony without benefit of clergy.

[118] Christopher Tancred, *Essay for a General Regulation of the Law* (London, 1727) 4, 7, 8, 17–18, 24–26, 27, 83, 85, 104–05. See also Christopher Tancred, *A Draught of a Bill, for the more easy and speedy recovery of small debts* (London, 1730).

[119] Tancred, *Essay* (n 118) 7–8, 27, 28, 55, 56, 94, 96, 97, 102, 138. Tancred recommended that perjury and barratry by legal professionals should be capital crimes. See also Tancred, *A Draught of a Bill* (n 118). For a more severe treatment of perjury, see Guy Miege, *The New State of England* (London, 1701) 6; *The Present State of England* (London, 1707), vol I, 290; and *Britannia fortior, or the New Present State of Great Britain* (London, 1709) 32–35. Miege's work, which appeared in several editions, contains chapters describing English courts.

recent parliamentary proposal fixing fees of court officers, noting that the 'sudden end of that session put an End to all at that time'.[120]

An attack on judges for introducing new precedents, a critique of the legal profession and a call to reduce the law 'to a form of decency and utility' dominated JA Purves' 1737 *Law and Lawyers Laid Open*. Though critical of lawyers who opposed regulation of legal fees, Purves insisted that most barristers favoured a 'reduction, if prudently, and by proper Instruments, it be entered upon'. Like many, his ire was directed primarily at the 'swarms' of solicitors and attorneys. He was disturbed by judges who overturned precedents, creating great uncertainty in the law, and queried whether the cavalier rejection of earlier precedents meant establishing 'a pope in every court of justice'.[121] The way in which judges were to make decisions at this time and the role of precedent in making these decisions remained problematic for Purves and for many others.

Repeating the complaints of the previous two centuries that the laws were 'too bulky to be useful' and contained too many contradictory and obsolete statutes, Purves invoked both Justinian and Bacon's law reform scheme. Like Bacon and James I, he wished to 'perfect', not enervate the law. He blamed lawyers for thwarting Bacon's reforms. Interestingly, Bacon's discussion of compiling and amending of our laws and his 'offer of a digest of our Laws' was reprinted in 1737 and again in 1741, suggesting a continuing interest in Baconian reform. Recognising that reform of the statutes was 'difficult and laborious' as well as 'expensive and chargeable', Purves nevertheless thought it 'feasible', 'glorious to the King and advantageous to the Public'. The king should communicate his desire for reduction of the law to the House of Commons, which he thought 'ready to give their utmost Assistance'. Reform should be undertaken now because England was at peace.[122]

Despite its neutral title, *The Present State of the Practice and Practisers of the Law* offered a broad range of reforms. Doubtful and obsolete laws should be expunged, good ones abridged and the 'thousands of volumes' of glosses, commentaries and expositions 'turned into Wastebaskets'. The author complained of the 'prolixity of pleadings' and the huge number of documents to be copied, querying whether arrest or summons should be preferred to ensure the appearance of defendants. Proceedings should be shortened in order to make the law less precarious, tedious, uncertain and costly. He condemned jurors who improperly focused on points of law, overbearing counsel who intimidated witnesses, and judges who were all too often divided among themselves. Also deplored were the reversals of

[120] The fictional author reports that 'I myself have heard many of your Order [lawyers] lament the great Uncertainty of the Law' and 'complain of its unwieldy Corpus', too 'bulky for a thorough knowledge, even to a person of Extraordinary Capacity'. Bacon is invoked for reducing the body of laws; *Law Visions, or Pills for Posterity* (London, 1736) 2, 12, 15, 17, 18, 21.

[121] Purves, *Law and Lawyers Laid Open* (London, 1737) xv–xvii, xix, xx, xl, 242, 253, 257.

[122] ibid xviii, 3. Purves supported the establishment of courts leet and courts of conscience for Westminster, Southwark and London (at xxx). He also discussed judicial alteration of precedents and the excessive number of attorneys. He was familiar with Hale's manuscript on law reform and cited Lord Chief Justice Holt as a supporter of reform.

judgments by the King's Bench, the Exchequer and the House of Lords. Courts of conscience for small debts in all cities and market towns would remedy the excessive number of cases in the superior courts.[123]

Two topics in particular attracted the attention of late seventeenth- and early eighteenth-century law reformers. The first was debtor–creditor relations and the associated issues of imprisonment for debt and bankruptcy; the second was the pros and cons of a registry for land and other transactions. While hardly new topics, the number and intensity of such publications marked the years following the Revolution of 1688.

Both before and after 1688, there were numerous bills and pamphlets dealing with the problems of poor imprisoned debtors, their improper treatment by jailors and bailiffs, as well as the related issues of how to ensure that creditors were not defrauded by those able to pay their debts. No easy answer was to be found, and parliament from time to time continued its earlier practice of periodically freeing impoverished debtors and enabling creditors to more easily obtain what was due to them. Most printed proposals were directed at persuading parliament to support bills already introduced or to improve on existing legislation. Publications dealing with the reform of creditor–debtor matters were particular numerous in 1690 and 1691.[124]

Although not all shared the same view, publications sought rather than opposed change. Moses Pitt, himself in difficulties over debt, thanked parliament for its recent gracious 'Act for Relief of poor Prisoners for Debt or Damages', which released thousands from starving conditions, but urged further reform.[125] *Labour in Vain*, another tract of 1700, argued that imprisonment left imprisoned debtors with no opportunity to repay their debts. English practice was compared to the 'good law in the Seigniory of Biscay' and to the practice in Holland that forbade creditors from keeping insolvent debtors in prison unless the creditor maintained them there.[126] Several publications indicated that England lagged behind other countries in their handling of debtor–creditor relations. Such publications typically appeared at the time parliament met or was about to meet. There were at least eight during the 1690s and at least six more during the first decade of the new century.[127]

[123] *The Present State of the Practice and Practisers of the Law, Wherein a is shewn the Obscurity, Uncertainty and Expensiveness* (London, 1740?) vi, vii, 3. 4, 6, 7 10–11, 13, 18–19, 24, 36–42, 54, 61.

[124] *Petition of thousands of poor and perishing prisoners for debt* (London, 1690); *Reasons humbly offered for passing the bill for the better recovery of bankrupts estates* (London, 1694); *Considerations upon the bill for the relief of poor prisoners* (London, 1696); *Some Considerations humbly offered, in relation to the bill now depending in Parliament for the further relief of creditors in cases of escapes* (London, 1698). For Guy Miege on the excessive severity to insolvent debtors, see *The New State of England* (London, 1701) 6.

[125] Moses Pitt, *The Cry of the Oppressed* (London, 1691).

[126] *Labour in Vain* in *Harleian Miscellany* VI, 346, 354. See also *The most indigent poor prisoner's letter to a worthy member of parliament* (London, 1700); *The petition a case of the poor prisoners for debt* (London, 1700).

[127] *Petition to House of Commons of thousands of poor and perishing prisoners for debt* (London, 1690); *Observations and reasons humbly offered to the present parliament on the behalf of the creditors* (London, 1690); *Reasons humbly offered for passing the bill for the better recovery of bankrupts estates* (London, 1693);

Another cluster of publications appeared in 1714. One complained that the earlier legislation had failed to discharge even half the prisoners. *The Case of Insolvent Debtors considered: with Proposals for the Relief both of them, and their Creditors* referred to 'thousands locked up in Gaols, and sacrificed to the insatiable voracious Appetite of the Law' that ruined both debtors and creditors. The author again suggested the example of France and other countries in eliminating imprisonment for debt. Referring to the relief measure being considered in parliament, the author insisted that 'most everyone wishes Success to see [its] good Design, or is ashamed to oppose it'.[128] A broadside, *Reasons … for Debt* also encouraged the passage of the bill before Parliament, indicating it would discharge at least 60,000 insolvent prisoners and praising those who 'endeavor to promote so just and pious an Act'.[129]

The piercing cryes of the poor and miserable prisoners for debt, another work of 1714, addressed to the Queen and both houses of parliament, commended the superior arrangements of France, Scotland, Holland, Italy, Spain and the civil law. Rather than creating new summary courts as some suggested, the tract favoured the expansion of county courts and courts baron. It also recommended standing committees of parliament to inspect jails, regulate the legal profession, reform the laws and listen to complaints.[130] Yet another publication favouring ending imprisonment for debt also noted that the French had long since eliminated the practice. The author of *The Committees Memorial* insisted that honest creditors wanted only their debts, not the ruin and misery of debtors. Gaolers, the 'vilest Miscreants in the World', took fees sufficient to 'maintain a good Fleet of Ships'.[131] The 1720s saw even more publications on the subject.[132] There were at least five pamphlets on the topic in 1729.[133]

Reasons humbly offered … to the House of Lords against repealing the relief of creditors by making composition with their debtors (London, 1694); *Considerations upon the bill for the relief of poor prisoners* (London, 1696) 2nd printing; *Reasons against the read bill, for relief of creditors, and preventing escapes* (London, 1698); *Some considerations humbly offered, in relation to the bill now depending for the further relief of creditors* (London, 1698). The year 1707 saw the publication of *Observations upon the Bill for the ease of insolvent debtors Reasons humbly offered to the Parliament assembled for the relief of poor prisoners.*

[128] *The Case of Insolvent Debtors considered, with Proposals* (London, 1724) 10–11.

[129] *See also Reasons … for Debt* (London, 1714) unpaginated. See also *Reasons humbly offered for a more extensive act for the discharge of prisoners* (London, 1714); *The case of the poor Insolvent prisoners for debt, in the several goals [sic] of this Kingdom* (London, 1716?).

[130] *The Piercing Cries of the poor and miserable prisoners for debt* (London, 1714) 7, 9, 10–11, 14, 16, 17, 27, 29. See also *Reasons humbly offer'd for a more extensive act for the discharge of prisoners* (London, 1714); Thomas Baston, *Thoughts on Trade and a Public Spirit* (London, 2016).

[131] *The Committees Memorial* (nd), unpaginated; *Reasons for an Act* again appealed to parliament to reform imprisonment of poor prisoners (London, 1719) 1–2; *The cries of the poor prisoners, humbly offered to the serious consideration of the King and Parliament* (London, 1716); *Reasons humbly offered for a general and unlimited act, for discharging of poor prisoners for debt* (London, 1715).

[132] In 1724 there was *The case of insolvent debtors considered.* See also *The case for prisoners for debt considered* (Dublin, 1725); *Reasons against confining persons in prison for debt* (London, 1726); *The Case of Prisoner for Debt Considered* (Dublin, 1727); *Reasons offered For the Bill* (London, 1726) indicated that legislation had already remedied the problem in Scotland.

[133] *The Arbitrary Punishments and Cruel Tortures Inflicted on Prisoners for Debt* (London, 1729); *The unreasonableness and Ill Consequence of Imprisoning the Body for Debt* (London, 1729); *A Speech*

Bankruptcy reform was also frequently discussed. Thomas Goodinge's *The Law against Bankrupts* (1695) reported that while bankruptcy earlier had concerned only the capital or 'famous marts', it now extended to country towns and villages and thus had become a 'Matter of Public Consideration'. Current laws dealing with fraudulent bankruptcy were insufficiently severe. Goodinge expressed regret that bankrupts by accident were subject to the same penalties as fraudulent bankrupts.[134] *Gravamina mercatoris* recommended a bankruptcy court to service London and the suburbs that would prevent 'the excesses and enormities' caused by current bankruptcy laws.[135]

Discussions of bankruptcy law reform, like discussions of debt and credit, typically appeared when parliament was about to meet. There was still ambivalence about relief because it was widely believed that bankruptcy was used to avoid legitimate debts. A tract of 1705, written by a member of parliament in support of a recently introduced bill, noted abuses by insolvents who retreated to bankruptcy in order to 'injure and abuse their creditors'. The author reported that a parliamentary session had ended before legislation could be completed, but that the bill, now enlarged, was before the present parliament.[136] However, portions of the proposed legislation were unjust, in that they allowed creditors to 'pounce' on bankrupts after they had already 'given up all'. Many bankruptcies, the author believed, were caused by recent trade disruptions, not by efforts to avoid payments.[137] Similar discussion of the bankruptcy law reform was to found in pamphlets of the 1730s.

XIII. Land Registration

Although legislation had repeatedly been introduced to register land and other kinds of transactions, debate became particularly intense in the 1690s, when reformers argued that registration would not only reduce fraud and defective titles, but would also reduce fees and eliminate unnecessary court officials. When the 1694 tract attributed to Matthew Hale outlining the benefits and deficits of land registration was reprinted in 1710, Lord Keeper North responded. North favoured

without doors, in behalf of an insolvent debtor in Fleet Prison (London, 1729); *Some Objections Humbly offered to the Consideration of the Hon. House of Commons Relating to the presented intended Relief of Prisoners* (London, 1729); *A Letter to my Lord S****** Concerning the Prisons for Debts* (London, 1729); *Heads of a bill for relief of insolvent debtors* (London, 1733) (concerning Ireland); *Some considerations Humbly Offered to the High Court of Parliament for the Benefit of Creditors, and Relief of Honest Insolvents* (np, nd).

[134] Thomas Gooding, *The Law against Bankrupts* (London, 1695) Preface to the Reader.

[135] *Gravamin mercatores* (London, 1695); *Remarks, on the bankruptcy bill* (London, 1705), 2–4, 6, 7–8.

[136] *Remarks on the bankruptcy bill* (n 135) 2–4, 6, 7–8. Bankrupts' assets should be divided among all their creditors, so that some would not suffer greater losses than others.

[137] See also *Some Considerations Humbly offered to the High Court of Parliament for the benefit of Creditors, and the Relief of Honest Insolvents* (np, nd, probably 1719) 3; *The Case of the Poor confined Debtors within the several Prisons of this Kingdom* (np, nd)

registries covering land conveyances and grants of land as well as rent charges, wills and revocations, statutes and recognisances and decrees.[138] Edmund Bohun, a prolific writer on legal topics, thought that without a register, 'the uncertainty of Titles and Pedigrees would become an intolerable Grievance'. Although parliaments had 'ever been hammering at a Reform by Way of Registrar, and sometimes fancied they had it', their efforts had been defeated by 'the more modern trick of Lease and Release'. It was 'ridiculous and senseless' for 'a Nation pretending to Literature and Law, That a Man should be capable to Sell his Estate over and over again in the same Morning'. Bohun also noted that 'few Law Suits for Land' now turned on 'nice Questions of Conveyancing' and instead involved 'Mortgages, Descents, Dormant Intails' as well as 'Trusts, and Equities in Chancery'. Though he anticipated opposition to registration from the legal profession, he insisted that his conversations with prominent legal practitioners indicated that some lawyers 'were much for it'.[139]

Debate over registries continued in lawyer John Asgill's 1698 *Essay on a Register*, which favoured a register. It provoked a reply that argued that there were already laws against clandestine settlements and that parliament could prevent existing loopholes without a registry. Registration would not make land transactions 'easier, safer, and cheaper', and a new office to administer it would provide greater extortion and oppression. Such schemes were 'like Pandora's Box'.[140] Asgill then stated that registration would save half the money it currently cost to enrol transactions and that a public registry of 'all Deeds, Conveyances, Wills, and other Encumbrances' would provide 'better satisfaction and more certain Security to purchasers'.[141]

A few post-1688 publications focused on the reform and regulation of the courts and the legal profession. Lord Chief Baron Sir Robert Atkyns thought that Chancery's jurisdiction, once 'modest and moderate', had 'grown and enlarged' 'wonderfully', despite remedies often 'endeavor'd' by parliament. He opposed the court's practice of offering relief after judgments in the common law courts and urged a legislative remedy.[142] After the failed Chancery legislation of 1691–92, Walter Williams, a prolific writer on Chancery reform, thought that it was 'one of the chief cares of Parliament' to keep Chancery within its due bounds and jurisdiction.[143]

[138] *Life of Lord Keeper North* (ed) Mary Chan (Lampeter, Edwin Mellen Press, 1995) 296–97.

[139] Edward Bohun, *Arguments and Materials for A Register of Estates* (London, 1698) 1, 2, 3, 5, 6, 7, 8, 9, 14, 21 285. Bohun recommended registering 'all conveyances, assurances, last wills, instruments and agreements concerning lands, except Leases at Rack' because it would 'be a clearer Evidence than any is yet'. He claimed that the 'most publick spirited' now supported a registry.

[140] *Some Reflections on Mr Asgill's Essay on A Registry* (London, 1698) 16, 18, 36, 37, 38, 45, 53, reprinted in 1699. The author rejected the claim that registration was 'easier, safer, cheaper' and suggested that Asgill lacked understanding of the law of conveyances (at 37).

[141] John Asgill, *A Reply* (London, 1699). See also *A Proposal for the erecting County Registers for Freehold lands* (London, 1696).

[142] Robert Atkyns, *An Enquiry into the Jurisdiction of the Chancery* (London, 1695) Title page, 16, 46.

[143] Williams suggests that nothing was being done because of the royal practice of relieving subjects on petition. Parliament should decide whether or not such petitioning should continue; *Some Reasons*

An unusual 1707 publication seeking parliamentary redress for the 'public calamity' caused by lawyers referred positively to the 'good progress' of the 1653 Barebones Parliament, remarking that it was a 'real pity' that 'so Pious a Design did not succeed, but hath slept ever since'. Claiming respect for 'our Judicious and Pious Judges and Honest Lawyers', the author complained that many lawyers 'ruined many and stopped justice'. He condemned the 'evil Practitioners in the Law' who practised 'by Fraud, Craft and open violence' and hoped that the 'good Lord' would deliver us from 'Sollicitours, Clerks, Registers, [and] Attorneys'.[144]

Lawyers and attorneys continued to be vilified in a variety of venues. In *Gulliver's Travels* (1726), Jonathan Swift wrote: 'It is a maxim among lawyers, that whatever has been done before may legally be done again, and therefore they take special care to record all the decisions formerly made against common justice and the general reason of mankind. These, under the name of precedents, they produced as authorities to justify the most iniquitous opinions.' Lawyers were bred 'in the art of proving by words … that white is black and black is white, according as they are paid'. They padded fees, bribed judges and encouraged 'fraud, perjury, and oppression' in a 'peculiar cant and jargon of their own that no mortal can understand'. Brobdingnagian laws were written in brief sentences, expressed in the most plain and simple interpretation.[145]

Complaints about jurors for the most part continued to be lack of education and financial status that rendered them unable to withstand the pressures of local figures of importance or judges who took advantage of their ignorance to control their decisions. There was also the familiar condemnation of 'pious perjuries' that freed criminal defendants from capital punishment. Since the abolition of Star Chamber and the 1670 Vaughan decision that forbade judges from punishing juries, there was no institutional remedy for dealing with juries refusing to convict despite overwhelming evidence.

Crime continued to attract a good deal of attention. Reform-oriented commentary centred on increasing penalties, eliminating benefit of clergy and condemning 'pious perjuries'. There was also some interest in reducing the death penalty for theft. For the author of the anonymous *Solon Secundus, or Some Defects in the*

Humbly offered for passing the bill entitled An Act for the reviewing of Causes in Chancery and other courts of Equity (London, 1690?) 1–2. See also Walter Williams, *Some Few Reasons* (London, 1691); Walter Williams, *A manifestation of the king's part and power to relieve his subjects against erroneous and unjust decrees in Chancery* (London, 1683); Walter Williams, *The Substance of the enacting clauses … for regulating proceedings in Chancery* (London, 1696); Walter Williams, *Orders and Rules proposed to his Majesty* (London, 1700); Walter Williams, *Observations on the Dilatory and Expensive Proceedings in the Court of Chancery* (London, 1701); Walter Williams, *Proposals humbly offered … to the regulation of proceedings in Courts of Equity* (London, 1701); *The Locusts: or, Chancery Painted to the Life* (London, 1704). See also Roger Acherley, *The Jurisdiction of Chancery Researched* (London, 1733), who attempts to distinguish the jurisdictions of the common law and equity courts.

[144] *A True Relation of … Practitioners* (London, 1703) Preface to the Reader, 5, 17, 19.

[145] Jonathan Swift, *Gulliver's Travels*, 2 vols (London, 1726), vol II, 77–78; see also vol I, 262. Swift also satirised informers, punishment for fraud, corrupt judges, legal precedent and trials that might take 30 years; vol I, 75–78, 95–96, 129, 262; vol II, 75–77.

English Laws, not 'one in five thousand ever reads a capital statute' and for that reason 'gentle and simple' alike fell 'within the lash' and 'teeth' of the law, hazarding the 'loss of their lives and estate'. Hanging failed to clear the roads of highwaymen, and transportation, though preferable to hanging, did not 'do the business'. The author recommended that highwaymen be imprisoned and required to perform bodily labour, and that convicted thieves be sent to workhouses and required to repay what they had stolen. Punishments such as whipping and being paraded through the streets at the 'cart's tail' were not only 'barbarous and beastlike' but also 'unjust and ineffective at preventing crime'. Commenting on juries that refused to convict the obviously guilty, he noted an instance in which a grand jury made 26 of 28 proposed indictments, but the jurors convicted only one of the indicted.[146]

A tract of 1690 recommended the elimination of capital punishment, arguing that it was preferable to cure rather than destroy. It proposed restitution plus penal labour such as work in the mines.[147] In 1701 it was suggested that, given the increase in highway robbery and house burning, those convicted of such crimes, as well as murderers and housebreakers, should suffer more painful executions. The addition of 'torments' would reduce the number of executions. The writer also criticised the lengthy time before trial, housing accused felons together with debtors in county jails, and composition between thieves and their victims. Receivers of stolen goods should be punished in the same way as thieves. Selling convicts as slaves or sending them to work in the mines was rejected, the former because they might be ransomed and the latter because of the possibility of escape. Despite the harshness of the author's proposals, he was insistent that the evidence of crime must be very certain, 'as clear as the midday sun'. There should be no conviction if the 'least partere' of evidence was lacking.[148] *An Essay Concerning the Original of Society* in 1727 referred to press comments on parliament's consideration of punishment for felony and 'introducing afflictive Services instead of the capital Animadversion'. The author thought that the 'notion of Felony hath been stretch'd by our Lawyers (especially in our Acts of Parliament) too far … making many things which were once trespasses into felonies'. If addressed with 'modesty', reforms to 'supersede and excuse the Rigor of many Penal Sanctions now in Force' would be received favourably.[149]

[146] *Solon Secondus, or Some Defects in the English Laws* (London, 1694) 5–6, 10–11. The author praised the law ending the hanging of women for slight matters, noting that, though women had once been excluded from benefit of clergy, they 'have it now'.

[147] *Taxes No Charge*, in *Harleian Miscellany*, VIII, 505.

[148] *Hanging not Punishment Enough* (London, 1701) 3, 4, 5, 7, 9, 11, 14, 16, 17, 21. George Ollyffe, who believed neither executions nor transportation were preventing crime, argued that crime reduction was possible by adding torture to execution, by marking convicted felons with non-removable burns or scars and by hard labour. Felons who refused work should not be fed; *An Essay humbly offer'd for an Act of Parliament* (London, 1710?). See also Randall McGowan, '"Making Example" and the Crisis of Punishment in Mid-eighteenth Century England' in Lemming (n 7)185–205.

[149] *An Essay Concerning the Original of Society* (London, 1727) 60, 66, 67. See also Allen Fifield, *Reasonableness and Necessity of Human Laws and Penalties* (London, 1739).

Although there was little activity relating to the systematisation of either the common law or the statutes in the decades following 1688, there were a number of efforts to make law easier to understand. Thomas Wood's *An Institute of the Laws of England* sought to refute the widespread belief that there was no way to know the laws 'but by a Tedious Wandring about' or by 'long study at the courts of justice'. He called for putting the 'Heap of Good Learning' into some order and 'bring[ing] the Laws of England into a Method'. Sounding very much like Jacobean and later reformers, he wrote that 'Monstrously over grown' statutes should be put 'under their Proper Heads' and then 'thrown into one short and plain Act'. Optimistic about the possibility of reform, he remarked that it was 'a Comfort that our legislators' now 'seem Resolved to Break this Heartstring of the Law, and to Banish from our Courts the Arts of Petty-Fogging, Sophistry and Cavil; which Have Flourished too long Amongst us'.[150] Ten printings of Wood's *Institutes* before 1772 kept his reform proposals in circulation.

Giles Jacob, whose life was devoted to legal publishing, emphasised making the law more understandable. His *A Treatise of Laws: or a General introduction to the Common, Civil and Canon Law* (1721) insisted that 'Collection without method' was 'a fruitless Labour'. Abridging and methodising could bring the law into a much 'Narrower Compass than is commonly supposed'.[151] His later *The Student's Companion; or the Reason of the Laws of England* (1725) provided 'a Body or View of the Law in its most Useful and Essential Parts' and was therefore superior to earlier publications of 'overgrown Prolixity' that lacked 'a due method', which he likened to a 'wilderness' without a guide.[152] Simplification and accessibility also provided the rationale for his *The Common Law Common-Plac'd* (1726), a work that brought the substance and the most prominent law cases currently 'dispersed in the Body of the Law … unto a small Compass'.[153] His *Every Man his own Lawyer*, published in 1736, 1737, 1740 and again in 1750, would provide 'some light' on the law for ordinary readers. He characterised the publication as 'an Instructive Treatise, writ in the easiest Method and adopted to every Capacity, whereby the unskillful, and those who are Ignorant in the practice of the law may in some Measure be their own Advisers, and readily avoid the Common Errors too often happening in the

[150] Thomas Wood, *An Institute of the Laws of England: Or, the Laws of England in their Natural Order*, 2 vols (The Savoy, 1720) Preface, i, ii, iv, v. Wood divided the law into 'Persons, Estates, Crimes and Misdemeanors; or Pleas of the Crown, Courts of Justice or Jurisdiction of the Courts'; I used the 1724 edn. See also Thomas Wood, *Some Thoughts concerning the study of the law of England in the two Universities* (London, 1708), which praised Finch's *Law, or, a Discourse thereof* as still 'the most methodical book extant' (at 19). See Robert Robinson, 'The Two Institutes of Thomas Wood: A Study in Eighteenth Century Legal Scholarship' (1991) 35 *American Journal of Legal History* 432.

[151] Giles Jacob, *Treatise of the Laws* (The Savoy, 1721) Preface.

[152] Giles Jacob, *The Students Companion: or the Reason of the Laws of England* (The Savoy, 1725) Preface.

[153] Giles Jacob, *Every Man his Own Lawyer, or a Summary of the Laws of England in a New and Instructive Method* (The Savoy, 1736) Preface, v–vi. Jacob's *The Statute Laws Common-placed* was to reduce 'the several branches of the Law to a proper Bounds, freeing them from a Confusion of Method, and perfecting what I find little more than begun by my industrious Predecessors' (Preface). See Julia

Prosecution of Suits'. It would provide sufficient knowledge of 'our laws and statutes, concerning civil and Criminal affairs' in order to enable laymen 'to defend Themselves and their Estates and Fortunes'.[154]

Sollom Emlyn, whose publications are not usually considered part of the reformist repertoire, treated a number of law reform issues in the second and subsequent editions of the popular *Collection of State Trials*. He combined fulsome praise of the laws of England with a reform agenda. Despite its many 'Excellencies and Advantages', the law had 'defects and Blemishes' and no 'experienced Lawyer' could deny that 'some things need to be mended'. The largest obstruction to reform for Emlyn was the 'blind Veneration' and 'supposed Perfection' of the law. He drew attention to the 'tediousness and delay' of civil suits that 'necessarily' arose 'from our Methods and Forms of Law' and the nicety of 'special Pleadings'. He objected to terms such as *vi et armis* in indictments when there was 'no pretence or colour of truth in them'. Echoing the Whig pamphleteers of 1680–82, he queried how a juror could give a verdict under oath unless he believed the entire charge in the indictment to be true. Legal proceedings should be conducted in English and special forms of writing eliminated.[155] This long-sought reform, which was briefly in force during the Interregnum, was enacted a year after his publication appeared. Emlyn also criticised the practice of confining juries without food or drink until they reached a verdict, arguing that restraint could 'never be a means of informing their Judgment' or 'convincing their Understanding'. He was unusual in rejecting the unanimous decision requirement because 'many minds' could not be expected to see 'things in the same Light'.[156]

Several features of the criminal law also required reform. Though rarely used, the plea of *peine forte et dure* should be replaced by a not guilty plea. The law did not distinguish appropriately between 'heinous felons' and those of a less degree. Capital punishment for 'lighter Crimes' such as 'Pilfering and Thieving' was unreasonable when the 'enormous crime' of adultery could not be prosecuted criminally. Non-capital punishments were 'intended to reform the Criminal, and deter him from offending again'. Prisons bred 'rogues' who grew to be 'harden'd Villains'. Jailors were denounced for 'Oppressions and Extortions'. Emlyn approved of judicial discretion to punish 'smaller crimes and misdemeanors' with fines, imprisonment,

Rudolph, '"That Blunderbuss of Law": Giles Jacob, Abridgment and Print Culture' (2008) 37 *Studies in Eighteenth Century Culture* 197.

[154] Sollom Emlyn, *A Complete Collection of State Trials*, 2nd edn (London, 1730). Henry Rolle's *Un Abridgment des Plusiers Cases* continued to be published, prolonging the availability of Hale's 1668 discussion of law reform.

[155] Emlyn (n 154) Preface. There were editions in 1739 and 1742 (3rd edn). Emlyn contrasted public prosecution, the separation of judgments about fact and law, the absence of torture to gain confession and the use of the jury with the less desirable practices of other countries. He praised the king's inability to detain even 'the meanest subject at his mere will and pleasure', the need for lawful warrants and the protection of habeas corpus. He celebrated recent changes in the procedures for prosecuting treason that had recently been extended to felonies.

[156] ibid Preface. If 12 votes were necessary, a jury of 23 might decide by a majority or two-thirds vote.

the pillory and whipping. He thought that magistrates should be restricted from 'arbitrary punishments' and warned that discretionary power to exact extravagant fines or perpetual punishment might be used for 'private Revenge, or the Rage of party'.[157]

We again encounter the complaint of and remedy for the 'Multiplicity and Voluminous of our Laws'. Emlyn thought that law would become 'more plain and easy' if obsolete laws were removed and the remainder collected 'under several Heads into so many distinct Acts'. He found it 'strange' that none of the numerous authors of reports and institutes had 'hitherto thought fit to make any considerable collection of this kind or thoroughly to methodize or digest this sort of learning'.[158] He hoped that publication of the state trials that were included in the collection would provide instructive examples for judges and lawyers. He reminded readers that judicial opinions 'in direct contradiction to the known Fundamental Laws' had resulted in the 'downfall' of judges who had 'made no scruples to murder the Innocent'. The published trials could also instruct lawyers with examples of those 'who with rude and boisterous Language abuse and revile the unfortunate Prisoner' and 'browbeat his Witnesses'.[159] He hoped that readers would 'use their utmost Endeavors to promote this Amendment of whatever appears to need it'. His plea for reform remained in circulation for the remainder of the century and beyond in subsequent editions of the *Collection of State Trials* It was one of the most widely circulated law reform publications of the eighteenth century.

Published after his death in 1726, the treatises of Sir Geoffrey Gilbert were designed to provide a more analytical treatment of a wide variety of legal topics. His account of the Court of Exchequer, for example, was characterised as 'a concise and Methodical Account'. His treatment of the law of devises and revocations proclaimed that it was arranged according to 'the most exact Logical and Analytical Plan'. The preface to his treatise on civil actions, while admitting that the Court of Common Pleas had often tended to 'oppression' and 'indulgence to Delay and Vexation', noted that judges had been led to 'regulate and amend' its practice. His treatise was to 'lay down the fundamental rules by which the judges directed their opinions' and his 'method' would 'in a Great Measure advocate the True Understanding of the Practices of the Law'.[160] Gilbert's treatise on the law of evidence was

[157] ibid. Emlyn also complained of 'petty, but chargeable suits' and excommunication 'for the minutest contempts' in the ecclesiastical courts. See Randall McGowen, 'The Problem of Punishment in Eighteenth Century England' in Simon Devereaux and Paul Griffiths (eds), *Penal Practice and Culture 1500–1900; Punishing the English* (Basingstoke, Palgrave Macmillan, 2004) 210–31. There was a dramatic decline in public whippings in London during the first half of the eighteenth century: Jason Peacey, *Policy and Punishment in London, 1660–1750* (Oxford, Oxford University Press, 2001) 446–47.

[158] Emlyn (n 156) Preface. Emlyn was responsible for publishing Sir Matthew Hale's *The History of the Pleas of the Crown* in 1736.

[159] Emlyn (n 156) Preface.

[160] Geoffrey Gilbert, *An Historical View of the Court of the Exchequer* (The Savoy, 1738) Preface; Geoffrey Gilbert, *An Historical Account of the Original and Nature, as well as the Law of Devises and Revocations* (London, 1730), Preface; Geoffrey Gilbert, *The History and Practice of Civil Actions*

preceded by a precis of John Locke's *Essay on the Humane Understanding* to give its material more rational support. It has been suggested that Gilbert's treatises may have been envisioned as a larger work, perhaps a general abridgement or encyclopaedia of the law.[161]

Interest in 'method', which was so widespread in the years before the Civil War, had not disappeared. William Hawkin's *Treatise of the Pleas of the Crown* is not typically treated as a reform publication. Following the method of Hale, Hawkins claimed not only 'to Vindicate the Justice and Reasonableness of the Laws concerning Criminal Matter', but also 'to reduce them into as clear a Method, and explain them in as familiar Manner, as the Nature of the Thing would bear'.[162]

William Blackstone's famous *Commentaries on the Laws of England* also responded to the long-sought but elusive goal of putting the law into a rational order. Blackstone saw himself as marking out 'a Plan of the Laws of England so comprehensive as that every Title might be reduced under some or other of its general Heads: and at the same time so contracted that the Gentleman might with tolerable application contemplate and understand the whole'. Like earlier critics and reformers, he complained of the law's antiquated forms and obsolete practices, referring to the edifice of the laws as a long-neglected 'old Gothic castle' in need of repair. Although opposed to 'crude and abortive schemes for amending laws', he pointed to 'the most promising sensible' reforms that had taken place. He favoured punishments more proportionate to the crime and reserving capital punishments for the most serious. He thought that counsel might be permitted to those accused of felony. 'Certainty' not 'severity' was most effective at preventing crime.[163] Though ambivalent about legal change by legislation because it might disrupt the common law, Blackstone's *Commentaries* belongs to the long tradition of moderate legal reform.

Although there was a great deal of crime reporting to be found in the newsbooks and periodicals of the eighteenth century, we know relatively little of the extent to which criticism of the legal system and law reform proposals had become a feature of the many popular periodicals of the period. However, a few examples are suggestive. In 1704 *The New Athenian Oracle* discussed benefit of clergy, whether those accused of treason, felony or slanderous words should have counsel, 'weak and ignorant juries', fraudulent contracts and the appropriate punishment

(London, 1737) Preface; Geoffrey Gilbert, *History and Practice of the Court of Common Pleas* (London, 1737). Gilbert's works were published posthumously.

[161] Michael MacNair, 'Sir Jeffrey Gilbert and His Treatises' (1994) 15 *Journal of Legal History* 258.

[162] William Hawkins, *Treatise of the Pleas of the Crown* (London, 1716–21) Preface, 21, 23.

[163] William Blackstone, *Commentaries on the Law of England* (1765–69, 11th edn, 1788), vol I, 35; vol III, 267–68; vol IV, 16, 18. Blackstone viewed his *Analysis of the laws of England* as belonging to the tradition of Hale's *Analysis of the Law*, a work he characterised as 'the most natural and scientifical of all the Schemes hitherto made public for digesting the Laws of England' (Oxford, 1756) v–viii. See David Lieberman, 'Mapping Criminal Law: Blackstone and the Categories of English Jurisprudence' in Landau (n 91) 139–61; JW Cairns, 'Blackstone; An English Institutist: Legal Literature and the Rise of the Modern State' (1984) 4 *Oxford Journal of Legal Studies* 318.

for highway robbery. It considered whether punishments, with the exception of treason and murder, should be changed from capital punishment to permanent or temporary slavery.[164] *The Athenian Oracle* indicated that debtors should be obligated to pay their debts, should not be severely treated by creditors and should be allowed sufficient funds to support themselves.[165] Daniel Defoe's *Review* was used as a vehicle for criticism of the law in 1704 when he addressed the problem of the 'multitude of Statutes' that had been 'superseded by Custom' and were now 'Dormant'. Defoe, himself burdened with debt problems, also proposed reforms in debtor-creditor law.[166] The *Tatler* in November 1709 addressed the problem of forgery and falsehood in land titles that had been 'hidden or buried by time, change, or design'.[167] A satirical description of law students, legal education and the fraudulent practices of lawyers appeared in *The Spectator*. It is likely that these examples are only the tip of the iceberg and that the periodical press will yield more information about the early eighteenth-century interest in improving the law and the courts.[168]

XIV. Conclusion

This chapter has covered a period of some 50 years. Parliamentary and public concerns as expressed in print media fluctuated, with high points in 1689–94 and 1705–06, and flurries in 1727 and 1737. Interest flagged about 1710, diminishing as the century proceeded. Highlights of the first period were the revised treason statute and the Toleration Act, the latter perhaps being more important because it altered the legal status of so many. Only gradually were protections for felony defendants such as counsel for the defence and oaths for defence witnesses implemented. There was a diminished concern with the courts, though Chancery received a good deal of attention until about 1710. Judges were given security of tenure and adequate salaries, but continued to be criticised for overawing juries. There was uncertainty and considerable difference of opinion about the role that

[164] *The New Athenian Oracle* (London, 1704), vol I, 8–9, 107–08, 180–81, 184, 185–86.

[165] *The Athenian Oracle* (London, 1728), vol II, 555; vol III, 82, 199, 241.

[166] Defoe's' *Review*, May 1704, quoted in J Hoppit, 'Patterns of Parliamentary Legislation, 1660–1800' (1996) 39 *Historical Journal* 109, 130–31. See also Daniel Defoe, *Remarks on the Bill to prevent frauds committed by bankrupts* (London, 1706); Daniel Defoe, *Vox Dei and Nature showing the Unreasonableness and folly of Imprisoning the Body for Debt* (London, 1711); Daniel Defoe, *An Essay on Projects* (New York, AMS Press, 1999) 77; G Lord et al (eds), *Poems on Affairs of State: Augustan Satirical Verse, 1660–1718* (New Haven, Yale University Press, 1968–75), vol 6, 88. See also Michael Quilter, 'Daniel Defoe: Bankrupt and Bankruptcy Reformer' (2004) 23 *Journal of Legal History* 53.

[167] Addison (n 45) vol IV, 62; Beattie (n 75); Ward (n 75). A large percentage of news dealt with crime. For the later eighteenth century, see Oldham (n 75).

[168] David Lemmings, 'Negotiating Justice in the New Public Sphere: Crime, the Courts and the Press in Early Eighteenth Century Britain' in David Lemmings (ed), *Crime, the Courts and the Press in Early Eighteenth Century Britain 1700–1830* (Farnham, Ashgate, 2012) 119–46.

precedent should play in judicial decision-making. Although monarchs became less active in making judicial appointments, the emergence of political parties gave judicial appointments a partisan flavour. Judges had become increasingly independent of the Crown, but many were deeply involved in politics. Although judges were responsible for many changes in the law, reformers looked to parliament, not judges, for remedies.

Over the half-century, there were numerous parliamentary efforts to regulate attorneys, solicitors and court clerks, none of them very successful. Justices of the peace were given greater authority. Ambivalence about juries continued. On the one hand, juries, along with the common law, were seen as essential components of the English legal system, while on the other hand, jurors were viewed as poorly educated, possessing insufficient property to be independent, and prone to the influence of judges and local power-holders. They were often characterised as law-breakers or oath violators as a result of the practice of 'pious perjury'. However, the utilisation of juries declined with the growth of summary procedure by justices of the peace and the gradual withdrawal of juries from civil cases. The common law was left substantially unchanged by parliamentary legislation, though legislation and media frequently addressed issues relating to debt, imprisonment for debt and bankruptcy. Most measures dealing with the criminal law were directed at reducing crime. These included proposals for both more and less harsh punishments.

The next and final chapter attempts to assess the continuities and changes in law reform efforts from the beginning of the reign of Henry VIII to circa 1740 and reassesses the revolutionary-era reform in the context of both pre-1640 and post-1660 reform efforts.

9

Conclusion

This final chapter has two parts. The first summarises the study's key findings and places the more studied and better-known reform efforts of the Civil War and Interregnum reform era into a longer timeframe. The second addresses questions that emerge from my account of law reform, but are unanswerable or only partially answerable. It therefore indulges in speculation and suggestions, some of which stem immediately from my account of early modern law reform and some, of a more general nature, that might be of use to scholars interested in law and legal systems more generally.

The law and legal institutions of England consisted of a mélange of several kinds of law and courts that had developed over a long period of time and interacted with one another against a background of changing political, demographic and economic environments. Though England's legal institutions did not form a neatly arranged system, one can nevertheless chart the introduction of new courts and the modifications of older ones, competition among different parts of the system and the efforts of those who wished to alter all or parts of it. It also provides an opportunity to assess some of its problems and weaknesses.

My treatment of early modern law reform has given a larger role to religion than is usual and has emphasised the impact of religious legislation on the legal lives of English subjects. The changing nature of the legally established religious regime which began with the Henrician Reformation, as well as issues of religious toleration, comprehension and occasional conformity, are discussed in terms of their legal consequences. The punitive measures and legal disabilities that governed the lives of Protestant dissenters and Roman Catholics made those who failed to conform less than equal subjects. Religious quarrels had legal consequences and legislative intervention in religious matters probably aroused more public interest than any other type of legislation.

Some law reform measures stemmed from those who wished English law to conform to Scripture. The most prominent was the movement to end capital punishment for theft and to impose it for adultery. Quarrels over altering the law of succession also revolved around religion. Concern with the law of succession arose in connection with the marriage of Mary I, the marriage and succession of Elizabeth I, rumours of making the Elector Palatine king, the exclusion of Roman Catholics from the Crown, the Jacobite opposition to the replacement of James II and the Protestant succession that formally made Protestantism part of the constitution.

I have treated the growth of professional publications as part of the law reform movement. Legal professionals wanted and needed greater order and clarity of what was generally agreed to be a chaotic mass of undigested legal material. The development of printed professional materials played an important role in shifting oral transmission of the law towards the written and printed, thus modifying the nature of legal learning and the legal profession itself. Lawyers increasingly relied on books.

The study has taken account of the striking changes in the number of Englishmen and women who sought out courts as a means of solving their differences. The dramatic increase from circa 1580 correlates roughly with the Elizabethan and Jacobean interest in law reform. The substantial decline in litigation that began in about 1680 was accompanied by a comparable decline in the number of lawyers. The supply of lawyers appears to have roughly tracked demand for their services. Although the hostility expressed towards lawyers, and especially attorneys, was a commonplace throughout the early modern period, it is unclear just how many lawyers were necessary or desirable. However, the question of how many lawyers and other legal professionals are desirable is one that faced many polities over a long period of time and remains an open question to this day in many places. How many is too many? How many are enough? The same question can be asked in connection with judges and courts. Would English justice have become less lengthy and less costly if there were more courts? Why did the English settle for only 12 judges when both the population and the rate of litigation increased?

This study has posited two quite different law reform movements. One is a moderate movement that existed throughout the entire period. Its reform agenda was primarily directed at improving existing law and legal institutions. This moderate movement was intersected by a short-lived radical movement seeking major transformations in the law and legal institutions during a period of particular political instability.

I trace what I have labelled the 'moderate' movement for law reform roughly from 1509 to the mid-eighteenth century. During the Tudor and early Stuart period, it was voiced primarily by the Crown, Crown officials and parliament, and focused on a variety of legislative measures to improve existing law, legal institutions and the legal profession. Henry VIII's reign saw the expansion of Chancery, the development of the conciliar courts and new courts created in the wake of the Reformation. Despite the turbulence of the reigns of Edward VI and Mary I, reform efforts continued with the young king, who exhibited a great deal of interest in reform. The movement became stronger during Elizabeth I's reign, encouraged by her Lord Chancellors, Nicholas and Francis Bacon, and had the support of several prominent lawyers who sat in parliament. Moderate reform supported by Crown and parliament peaked during the reign of James I. Given the belief that new law and modification of existing law was properly the work of parliament, law reform was not possible between 1629 and 1640, when no parliament met. Law reform before 1640 was largely promoted by the Crown and the parliamentary elite. Until 1640, printed publications played virtually no role.

The period from 1640 to 1660 was quite different because it was accompanied by a deluge of printed pamphlets, petitions and broadsides that brought two quite distinct law reform agendas to the attention of the public at large. However, the first phase of revolutionary-era reform remained in parliamentary hands. It focused on the impeachment trials of Lord Strafford, Archbishop Laud and the judges who had supported the Crown position on the legality of ship money. The king's chief ministers were charged with treason. Parliament abolished the formerly popular conciliar courts, which had become associated with the now distrusted king and his closest advisors, as well as High Commission. The connection between the Crown and parliament on law reform was severed, and the country was to experience a civil war between the armies of the Crown and the forces of parliament. Both sought to control the legal system, which was in a state of disarray.

The short-lived radical reform movement was promoted by two somewhat overlapping groups. The first was the more politically inspired Levellers and their allies who advocated the democratisation of the entire political and legal system. It featured intense hostility to the legal profession, the common law and its courts centralised in Westminster, and advocated autonomous local courts in which trials took place without professional judges and lawyers. The movement was democratic in its values and was hostile to the social hierarchy that privileged the aristocracy and the gentry.

Inspired by an anti-Norman vision of English history, the Levellers and their allies wished to eliminate the common law, the legal profession with its confusing law French and the tyrannical monarchy introduced by force in 1066. They envisioned an entirely different legal system that harked back to the simpler and less aristocratic Saxon period. They favoured the replacement of the complexities of English law with a simple, brief law written in an English language that could be easily understood. They favoured religious toleration, opposed the tithes that supported the clerical establishment and favoured reforms of local justice that would make local courts independent from the centralised courts in Westminster.

Levellers, more than any other mid-seventeenth-century reform group, promoted the expansion of privileges for criminal defendants, arguing on behalf of counsel for the accused, oaths for defence as well as prosecution witnesses and the requirement of two witnesses for conviction. These demands had not been a significant part of the pre-1640 moderate parliamentary movement.

Some of these demands were also promoted by religiously inspired radicals who wished to make English law conform to the law of God. They rejected the death penalty for theft on Scriptural grounds, but favoured it for adultery and sodomy for the same reason. On biblical grounds, they insisted that two or sometimes three witnesses be required for a conviction. Most advocated religious toleration and the end to a learned clergy supported by tithes. Some rejected the centralisation of English justice and favoured local courts manned by godly laymen with little or no interference from Westminster. They favoured tight control or abolition of the legal profession. Together, the two movements presented an alternative vision of the law and England's legal institutions.

This study has also pointed to the very considerable overlap between the English religious, radical, reform programme and the laws and law codes being developed in colonial New England, though the latter did not approve of religious toleration or the end to a learned clergy. Although the radical law reform movement had a great impact during the revolutionary years, it ceased to be a significant element in law reform thinking after 1660, except for its role in making contemporaries cautious and fearful of major changes in the law and legal system.

In 1640 printed materials began to play a large role among both radical and moderate reformers. Debates for and against reform poured from the presses and were now available to a larger audience. Publications streamed from the presses as restrictions on printing could no longer be enforced. Radical publications ended with the Restoration, although occasionally radical proposals might be included in the writings of later moderates.

While the large quantity of law reform pamphlets and broadsides has drawn historians to this cache of material, it remains unclear whether and to what degree radical law reform proposals had public support. The printed newsbooks, well explored for their political and literary impact, remain to be systematically examined for their role in transmitting law reform proposals to the public. Restoration and post-Restoration law reform publications were fewer in number, but tended to be longer, with the exception of single-page efforts devoted to imprisonment for debt and other matters of credit and debt. Restoration and early eighteenth-century pamphlets that appeared in more than one edition suggest that these publications had an eager audience for a long period of time.

Radical reformers of the revolutionary decades were responsible for many law reform publications. Although these publications have traditionally been at the centre of historical work on revolutionary-era law reform, more attention has been given here to the less-known moderate efforts of parliament. Fear of social and religious upheaval dampened but did not end parliament's promotion of moderate reform. I suggest that the number of publications is an inadequate indication of public support. The largest numbers of law reform publications appeared in 1653–54 at about the time of the Barebones Parliament and in 1659, which were particularly turbulent years. The expansion of publications did expose a larger portion of the population to issues relating to the legal system.

Although interest in radical change diminished rapidly at the Restoration, parliament continued to pursue a moderate law reform agenda with little fanfare or publicity. As a result, its legislative activity in the area of law reform has been neglected for too long. This post-Restoration agenda was very similar to that of pre-1640 moderates, and reform bills continued to be introduced during and after the Restoration. The familiar moderate agenda continued to be pursued by early eighteenth-century parliaments. After 1714, fewer proposals were offered.

The reforms desired by moderate reformers changed little. Parliament after parliament, and an account of them, though necessary, makes for tedious reading. Jacobean reform proposals were much like those of the Restoration and beyond. The most striking features of moderate reform are the continuity of its critique and the continuity of its proposals. The moderate reform proposals of the post-Restoration era has been largely ignored because that period has been considered to be conservative and punitive. However, a conservative political stance proved compatible with the moderate's agenda. There was no reason why post-Restoration parliaments should be hostile to reforms directed at reducing costs and delays or reducing the jurisdictional conflicts among the courts. With the exception of repressive religion legislation, most of the proposed reforms were not matters of high politics. Restoration and early eighteenth-century law reform efforts have been ignored largely because historians and others did not anticipate their existence and because modern pre- and post-Restoration historians do not share a research agenda.

What follows is a brief account of those groups or institutions responsible for promoting reform, and a summary of complaints about courts, criticism of the legal profession, the justices of the peace, and juries and of reform efforts in particular areas of law.

Prior to 1640, the Crown and its servants were key members of the reform community. When parliament and the Crown were at loggerheads, reform was promoted first by parliament, and then by parliament, part of the Cromwellian army, the Levellers and their allies, and radical religious groups. The period from 1643 to 1660 marked the point of greatest tension between the two types of law reform. After 1660, radical reform supporters disappeared, and the Crown showed little interest in law reform.

Parliament was always the key to law reform. Much of this book has therefore concentrated on parliament. One of the most striking features of early modern parliaments is their inability to complete legislation. On some occasions, parliament was dismissed or prorogued before legislation was complete, while on other occasions, time-consuming procedures limited successful legislation. On still other occasions, efforts at law reform legislation were diverted by more pressing issues or the lack of parliamentary preparation. Law reform proposals were introduced in most parliaments, but were rarely high on the agenda. Many of the legislative measures that were successful were renewals or slight modifications of older ones. Statutes that were 'continued' received little publicity after their initial passage.

Parliamentary interest continued to focus on the faults of the courts and legal profession rather than the law itself. The common lawyers were largely successful in convincing parliaments that they should not meddle with the common law. Because some areas formerly under the jurisdiction of Star Chamber were not part of the common law, fraud and forgery became the subject of some reform bills.

I. The Courts

During the sixteenth century, the most significant changes in the legal system were initiated by the Crown, the most noteworthy being the rapid expansion of

Chancery, the creation and expansion of the conciliar courts, the new status of the monarch and parliament in shaping the established church and the new courts resulting from the Reformation. Thereafter, momentum was to be found in parliament, whose attention to law reform was centred on reforming various aspects of the courts and the statutes. Corruption by court officials was a continuing concern and there were many efforts to control their fees. However, the most pervasive and disruptive problems were the conflicts over jurisdiction. Parliament gave a great deal of attention to what was perhaps the major weakness of the legal system. To one degree or another, the common law courts were in competition with the ecclesiastical courts, Chancery, Star Chamber, the Court of Requests, the Council of the North and Admiralty. There was also competition for business between the King's Bench and Common Pleas. In many instances litigants who failed in one court went on to another, thus increasing the costs and delays that so often attracted reform attention in parliament. Sir Edward Coke was the most vocal of those defending the common law courts and arguing for jurisdictional reforms that would give priority to those courts.

The most striking development in the system of courts was the rise and then the fall of the conciliar courts. Their addition to the complement of existing courts altered the legal system significantly, as did their abolition. One of the most puzzling features relating to the conciliar courts was Star Chamber, which for many years had been a much sought-after venue for solving legal conflict. It had garnered praise from leading legal figures such as Coke and Bacon, but would be abolished as an agent of tyranny only a few decades later. Its loss was not mourned and was little spoken of. After the dissolution of the conciliar courts, jurisdictional tensions continued between others, but, with the exception of the attacks on Chancery, were not as angry or bitter.

A second major weakness in the legal system was the absence of a clear system of appeals, without which it was difficult to know when a legal case was finally decided. There was some appeal within the common law courts from Common Pleas to the King's Bench. The common law courts were often in conflict with Chancery over the latter's attempts to serve as an appeals court for wrong decisions made by the common law courts. Over time, the House of Lords took over some appeals, but which appeals were to go where was never spelled out.

II. The Legal Profession

There was a good deal of reform interest in the judiciary expressed in parliament, though criticism was more likely to be focused on the failings of individual judges than the judiciary as a whole. There were attacks on Lord Chancellor Bacon, Lionel Cranfield, judges in the ship money case, Restoration judges who fined jurors for their verdicts, judges in the Popish Plot trials, judges in the Rye House Plot and the judge in the Monmouth Rebellion prosecutions.

Parliament, which had been concerned with the relationship between the Crown and the judiciary for many years, attempted to change the security of the judges' position by supporting measures giving judges tenure on good behaviour rather than by the grace of the Crown. It became supportive of providing the judges with salaries that would reduce 'corruption' by eliminating the then normal practice of accepting gifts and/or bribes.

During much of the time discussed, judges and their courts were burdened with more cases than they could handle, thus contributing to the much complained-of long delays. Prior to 1640, judges were more identified with the Crown than would be the case later on, often having prominent positions as Crown advisors. Judges combined legal and administrative duties. Before 1640, judges were involved in supervising justices of the peace and were expected to report to the king about conditions in the counties they visited while on assize. However, the repudiation of the ship money judges for siding with the king reduced the bond between the Crown and the judiciary. During the revolutionary period, some judges resigned, were replaced or had difficulty accepting governments that they thought to be illegal. Although their administrative roles were reduced in the post-Restoration era, there were occasions when they continued to be agents of the Crown. Charles II and James II were not reluctant to dismiss non-compliant judges. Legislation making judicial tenure more secure was much applauded for reducing incentives for corruption, but many eighteenth-century judges, especially those holding the offices of Lord Chancellor or Lord Keeper, were deeply involved in partisan politics.

The judiciary was involved in the legislative process throughout the early modern period. Judges advised the Crown on legal issues and frequently provided legal advice to both Houses of Parliament. Lord Chancellors had a major role in supporting law reform. Given the constant complaints about 'slow process', it is surprising that there was little interest in increasing the size of the judiciary. Twelve common law judges served the entire country for centuries.

III. Lawyers

Lawyers were criticised throughout the period, attorneys and solicitors receiving the most criticism and becoming the subject of a good many reform measures. During the revolutionary decades, many radical reformers called for eliminating all lawyers, echoing the absence of lawyers in the early New England colonies. Throughout the entire period, the House of Commons had a fairly large contingent of lawyers who were actively engaged in parliamentary debate and statute drafting.

Expressions of hostility should not be surprising. Lawyers have never been popular and most people who came into contact with lawyers came to them when they had troublesome problems. Lawyers were thought to be greedy, their fees outrageous, and fond of fomenting and prolonging lawsuits. Radicals argued that they were unnecessary, and every man should be able to defend his own case or be advised by a friend. The radical attack on lawyers was part of their general attack on the learned professions, physicians and clergymen, as well as lawyers. Moderates reformers offered reform measures, particularly for attorneys, but insisted that they were a necessary and valued part of the legal system. Lawyers, like judges, were active in government and parliamentary circles and were deeply involved in drafting statutes and parliamentary debate. A substantial number of law reform publications were written by lawyers. If there was any theme that predominated, it was praise of the common law and its continued capability to serve the nation's legal needs, combined with a willingness to reform the courts and the high costs and long delays in the legal process. Although some explored the addition of new local courts, they were insistent on retaining the central courts at Westminster. Many lawyers who contributed to growth of professional literature of law characterised their efforts as a means of clarifying the law and making it more accessible and understandable.

IV. Court Officials and Clerks

Court officials who handled many of the routine aspects of litigation came under a great deal of criticism, especially for drawing out legal documents and for charging excessive fees. Time and time again, reformers promoted fixed and publicly displayed fees. Although such bills were sometimes successful, their repetition suggests that statutes requiring posted fee schedules were frequently ignored. However, judges in their respective courts often attempted to regulate the attorneys and officials who served them.

V. Justices of the Peace

Though not part of the legal profession, justices of the peace were an essential part of the legal system throughout the early modern era. It is difficult to imagine English government or the English legal system without them. Already by the late sixteenth century the justices were said to be laden with 'stacks of statutes'. Like many legal officials, justices of the peace had administrative as well as legal duties. Over time, there were substantial changes in their duties. They lost jurisdiction over felonies quite early on, a task they had shared with the assize judges. As time passed, their responsibilities in quarter sessions were reduced and their role in handling cases by summary procedure increased. Though they were an essential part of English government and justice system, justices of the peace were not legally trained. And most of the information necessary to perform their duties was provided in the popular printed manuals of Lambarde, Crompton and Dalton and later Burns.

Justices of the peace were rarely praised. When under the scrutiny of parliament, they were criticised for corruption, partiality and failure to perform their duties. Bills calling for better-educated, harder-working and higher-status justices were frequently offered. The quality and impartiality of local justice varied a great deal from one locale to another. It also varied with the temperament of particular justices of the peace and the amount of time each was prepared to devote to their many legal and administrative duties. However, pamphlets of the revolutionary decades largely ignored the justice of the peace when proposing alternative forms of local justice and local government.

VI. Juries

Although the jury trial has been the hallmark of English justice, the English, or at least their parliaments, were ambivalent about juries throughout the early modern period. Trial by jury was repeatedly praised as being far superior to any other kind of trial, but the jury was frequently the subject of reform proposals. The most common complaint was 'corruption' caused by jury partiality and the likelihood of their being subject to pressure. Jurors, who were recruited from a social class less esteemed and less wealthy than members of parliament, were criticised for their low social and economic status and lack of education. They were often called 'ignorant', unable to understand the cases they heard or likely to be pressured by judges. These complaints were to be heard throughout the early modern period.

There were frequent complaints of their 'pious perjuries' that mitigated capital punishments contrary to law. Jury 'nullification' of law was often perceived as a problem in the area of crime and its punishment. Jurors were also criticised by merchants who found jurors insufficiently knowledgeable about business affairs and international commerce to make appropriate decisions in merchant disputes. And when, after the Great Fire of London, a non-common law fire court was created to settle legal issues stemming from destroyed houses and other structures, the absence of juries led to opposition. The institution of the jury was often praised, but that praise was frequently countered by complaints of its incompetence, lack of independence and ignorance.

Until its abolition, Star Chamber had jurisdiction over corrupt jurors who gave verdicts against the evidence. After its abolition, some control was exercised by the judiciary, but that too was reduced during the Restoration when Vaughan's judgment in Bushel's case determined that judges could not punish juries. The increase in summary procedure reduced reliance on juries. Jury participation in civil trials would decline rapidly during the eighteenth century.

When parliament concerned itself with juries, it almost always emphasised their defects. Juries were typically characterised as illiterate, vulgar, lacking in education and sufficient property. However, recent historical research on the early modern jury reveals a quite different institution. A recent survey of jury research presents a picture of jurors as responsible members of their local communities, that is, yeoman, farmers, artisans and tradesmen. Many served on juries frequently and became quite experienced. London juries of the late seventeenth century, while not belonging to the top echelon of urban society, were nevertheless substantial propertied members of the urban elite.[1]

Grand juries were rarely the subject of criticism or reform, perhaps because they were largely drawn from the same social milieu as members of parliament. An exception occurred during the Restoration period when the issue of the threshold for indictment generated a substantial partisan literature. Grand juries also performed a political function. On some occasions, and particularly during the revolutionary years, they petitioned parliament either to support or oppose parliamentary measures. In such cases they may be viewed as pressure groups that portrayed themselves as giving voice to the views of the county.

VII. Areas of Law

Parliament was more concerned with some areas of law than others. If legislation dealing with religion was the most contentious, matters associated with creditor–debtor relations and with crime and crime control received a good deal of attention.

The problems associated with credit and debt and the institution of imprisonment for debt were continually discussed in parliament. They were the subject of many publications, which were particularly numerous during the revolutionary and post-Restoration periods. Most repeated the theme that imprisonment was unreasonable because it allowed wealthy debtors to live well, while poor debtors not only lived in misery but were also deprived of the opportunity to work and thus to pay their debts. Jailors were constantly condemned. Though imprisonment for debt was much criticised, parliament did not find an alternative. Its practice was to periodically empty the prisons of poor debtors. Since this kind of legislation was limited in time, it required frequent renewal. The competing interests of creditors, debtors and bankrupts were often discussed in parliament and were the subject of many publications.

VIII. Crime and Crime Control

Crime control is doubtless a problem for most, if not all, societies. Most early modern countries had a catalogue of crimes, both serious and less serious. Crimes in

[1] For a survey of historical research on the jury, see Thomas A Green, 'A Retrospective on the Criminal Trial Jury, 1200–1800' in JS Cockburn and Thomas A Green, *Twelve Good Men and True: The Criminal Trial Jury in England, 1200–1800* (Princeton, Princeton University Press, 1988) 358–400. Green discusses the differing views on the passivity of juries.

England were classified either as felonies, which required the death penalty, or less serious crimes that did not. Some crimes had a lengthy history, but new offences in either category required new statutes. Non capital offences of various kinds were handled by the ecclesiastical courts, Star Chamber, quarter and petty sessions and by summary procedure, which became more prominent in the latter part of the era. Counting the number of bills and statutes does not prove to be a good indicator of parliamentary concerns about crime, since many statutes did little more than renew earlier ones or make minor modifications.

Crime control was often discussed in parliament. The most frequently proposed measures removed benefit of clergy for first-time felony offenders. There was frequent concern with highway robbery and horse theft, crimes associated with outsiders to the local community. There was also a good deal of attention given to fraud and forgery, which were not crimes under the common law. New crimes required legislative action. Perjury was a matter of concern throughout the early modern era. Legislation, however, did not always result in changed behaviour, since many laws were not well enforced. Adultery and sodomy were felonies, but prosecutions were few and convictions even fewer. A major change in punishment developed as transportation of convicted felons became a common substitute for capital punishment and later became a separate punishment. Despite the increase in death penalty statutes, fewer executions actually took place.

Harsh criminal punishments were combined with a good deal of discretion in their implementation. Looking at legislation alone does not tell the story. Discretion occurred at every level. Private prosecution prevailed throughout the period and many injured parties refused to prosecute. Arbitration and agreements between victims and perpetrators often evaded jury trials in which capital punishment was required. Grand juries might refuse to indict and trial juries often practised 'pious perjuries' by reducing the value of theft amounts to small amounts, regardless of the actual value of the items stolen, in order to evade capital punishment. Evidence about the character of the accused might allow respected members of the community to be treated differently. Trial outcomes were often related to the good or bad reputation of the accused. And after sentence, judges often sought pardons, a great many of which were granted. Law on the books was considerably modified by a variety of legal actors. The combination of harsh punishment and the wide use of discretion was a feature of the early modern legal system.

IX. Criminal Procedure

Some aspects of the legal system that are of particular interest to modern citizens were largely absent during much of the early modern period. The question of oaths for criminal defendants was aired briefly in connection with the Jacobean interest in reconciling the laws of Scotland and England, but then disappeared until it became a central issue for the Levellers. They stressed the need for defence witnesses as well as prosecution witnesses to testify under oath, counsel for criminal defendants and the two-witness rule. Interest in these matters lapsed and then revived after the Revolution of 1688, as a response to the Popish Plot and the treason trials of leading Whigs prior to 1688. Parliament began with bills designed to protect both felony and treason defendants, but the legislation that finally emerged in 1696 was limited to cases of treason. Those accused of felony did not gain those protections until much later. Protection for the accused was of negligible interest to sixteenth- and early seventeenth-century proponents of moderate reform. It became a significant part of the mid-seventeenth-century radical agenda and a significant issue just prior to and just after the Revolution of 1688.

Different courts had different procedures and dispensed different penalties. Neither the ecclesiastical courts nor Star Chamber could inflict the death penalty, but both employed oaths that were thought to make defendants testify against themselves. Anger about use of the *ex officio* oath was commonly expressed during the pre-Civil War period. The ecclesiastical courts used fines and a variety of shaming devices or rituals. High Commission, until it was abolished, relied on fines and physical mutilation. Admiralty used the procedure of the civil law, which included the need for two witnesses. Justices of the peace used yet a different procedure in their petty and quarter sessions and in the summary justice they increasingly exercised.

X. Rationalising the Law

One of the most frequently heard complaints throughout the whole period was the disorderly and chaotic condition of the law. Three quite different kinds of efforts were offered as remedies. The first, rationalising the statutes, had the support of both lawyers and laymen. Jacobean parliaments were most active in efforts to remove contradictory and obsolete statutes, but did not accomplish a great deal. Although replacing conflicting and obsolete statutes may not have been difficult from an intellectual point of view, it would have required the time and labour of many lawyers. Reorganising and pruning the statutes remained a frequently heard but never satisfied demand.

The second type of rationalisation, that of making the common law accessible and easier to understand, was far more difficult and complicated because most members of the legal profession did not wish the common law to become a written code. Legal professionals who attempted to reduce confusion and disorder by providing aids for the help of law students, lawyers and laymen were consistent in insisting that their digests and principles were not the law itself. Printed reports became increasingly available, but did not have the status of law. During the Elizabethan period and later, there were a number of attempts to 'methodise' the law in order to give it a rational order. These efforts should not be labelled codification. Concern with how precedents should be used appeared from time to time and became greater over time.

At the outset of the period studied, the common law consisted of the common learning of the legal profession. Its transmission, centred in the Inns of Court and the law courts, tended to be oral. Many complaints suggested that lawyers benefited from its esoteric state and its language of law French. However, the printing of law reports and other kinds of legal material began to change the transmission of education and the practice of the law. Printing made it possible for more lawyers to have access to the same legal material and was significant in making the law more uniform and predictable. Precedent, so important in later law, could not play a major role until access to the opinions of judges was readily available and was thought to have an appropriate function in legal decision-making. There were complaints about confusion caused by conflicting precedents as well as concern that relying on precedents would prevent the legal changes necessary to a changing society.

The third type of reform was the demand that the law be reduced, written in English and printed in brief form. The idea of the law simplified and codified in a pocket-sized form was desired by many mid-century radicals. What seems to have been envisioned were codes along the lines of those in early New England. This type of rationalisation was typically urged by radical reformers who were ready to scrap the common law. Its adherents sometimes referred to a 'new model' or new 'body' of law to replace the chaotic and confusing existing law.

XI. Language and the Law

A review of proposed law reform legislation and the pamphlets dealing with law reform suggests that a common vocabulary was employed throughout the period surveyed. Some words and phrases appear time after time and became part of the conventions of law reform discourse. One of the most common was 'corruption', a term with several meanings. Sometimes it was the law that was 'corrupt' or 'corrupted', which often meant deviation from an earlier better condition. In these instances 'corruptions' were to be removed. Most often, however, 'corruption' referred to the bribes, gifts, favour or other kinds of pressure directed at juries, lawyers, judges and court clerks. Those on the taking rather than the giving side were most often mentioned. There were many references to 'corrupt juries', 'corrupt judges' and corrupt court officials.[2]

Unpaid or poorly paid legal officials were typical of early modern governments and payments of various kinds were often expected for legal services. The trial of Sir Francis Bacon for corruption suggests both the evil of corruption and the claim that taking gifts and various payments were not bribes and did not interfere with judicial impartiality. The most frequently mentioned remedy for judicial 'corruption' was a salaried judiciary. Although salaried court officials were sometimes

[2] Criticism of courtiers often referred to corrupt morals.

mentioned by reformers, they were not mentioned in connection with jurors, justices of the peace and only very occasionally lawyers.

Other frequently used terms were 'abuses', 'mischiefs', 'vexatious' lawsuits, 'inconveniences' and 'fraudulent' conveyances. It is not clear whether terms such as 'mischiefs' or 'inconveniences' had a well-understood meaning or whether they were used to characterise any disliked practice. Hostility to attorneys is often expressed in words such as 'pettifoggers' or 'vermin'. Sometimes they were characterised as locusts or caterpillars that devastated the land. Despite the wish of some reformers to abolish the entire legal profession, the upper part of the legal profession – that is, counsellors or barristers – were not often described using this language. The word 'greed' was most frequently associated with them. When judges were treated positively they were 'learned' and 'impartial'. When criticised, they were 'partial' or 'corrupt'. The concept of an 'independent' judiciary was not part of legal discourse. Judges were part of the executive apparatus and were often expected to perform non-judicial tasks. Over and over again, we hear that judges were to 'interpret' but not 'make' the law. Law-making was assumed to be the province of parliament. Those supporting proposals for improvement often used the language of 'reform' or 'reformation', terms most often applied to desired changes in religious or moral practice.

Both moderate and radical law reformers made use of the same agricultural metaphors, albeit in different ways. Radicals used the term 'root and branch', a phrase frequently found in Scripture, to refer to major change, most famously in the 1640 Root and Branch petition to abolish episcopacy. Moderates repeatedly insisted that they wished only to 'prune' abuses or unnecessary growth, but not 'uproot' the entire 'plant' or 'tree'. Moderate reformers also referred to weeding the garden of noxious weeds, cleansing the rust off a still-excellent product or cleansing streams to restore river channels to their earlier purity. They sometimes spoke of removing a defective superstructure from the law's sound foundation.

Moderate reformers emphatically proclaimed the common law to be the best in the world. However, this glowing view was typically followed by a statement that even the best sometimes developed accretions that should be removed in order to restore them back to their pristine state. Reform often meant restoration, not innovation. 'Amendment' was also common in moderate reform discourse. Radical reformers were more likely to speak of a 'new model' of law.

Styles of presentation were modified according to time and place. Prior to the 1640s, moderates in parliament could be enthusiastic about reform. After 1640, they typically adopted a more defensive stance that made them appear to have changed their views of reform. After 1660, moderate reformers were anxious to distinguish themselves from the Civil War and Interregnum radicals, using very negative language emphasising their low social class, ignorance, religious fanaticism and willingness to bring the law into chaos.

A different issue relating to the language of the law occurred when legal terminology no longer fitted legal practice. The distinction between a felony and a non-felony, sometimes labelled a misdemeanour, provides a striking example.

The death penalty was required for crimes labelled a felony, but not for other offences. Thefts became felonies when they reached the threshold of 12 pence, an amount that remained unchanged despite the enormous change in value of money over the centuries. One begins to hear of 'small felonies' or 'lesser felonies' that did not deserve the death penalty. In practice, the distinction led juries to wholesale evasion of the law by reducing the value of stolen goods to 11 pence regardless of their actual value or by substituting 'attempt' to the otherwise felony charge. The early modern notion of 'trespass' is significantly different from modern usage. However, the term was not part of the reform discourse. Legal categories made a tremendous difference in outcomes because felonious and non-felonious crimes were tried in different courts with different legal procedures. For most of the early modern period, those charged with a felony were permitted neither counsel nor witnesses who testified under oath, though these defendant protections were not forbidden in non-felony cases or in the ecclesiastical courts and non-common law courts. Some moderate reformers of the Civil War and Interregnum years supported allowing defence witnesses to have counsel. In a related matter, we noticed that when certain offences were transferred from the church courts or Star Chamber to the common law courts, offences that had previously not incurred capital punishment now did so. However, there was no comment on the fact that changes in court venue increased the possibility of capital punishment.

In some instances, it was the language of the law rather than the practice of the law that changed. An example is to be found in the instruction judges gave to juries in criminal trials. Judges instructed jurors to reach verdicts on the basis of a 'satisfied conscience', a concept derived from casuistry, 'moral certainty', and later 'conscience and understanding' or 'understanding'. By the late eighteenth century, the 'beyond reasonable doubt' language would come into use. All these phrases meant the same thing – the highest level of certainty possible in 'matters of fact'. The change in terminology was not the work of reformers.[3]

The language of the law itself was a prominent issue. Early humanist reformers wished to replace law French with Latin or English. However, the demand for Latin was short-lived. Most proposals emphasised the need for English on the grounds that law French was incomprehensible or because it was the language of the hated Normans. Many but not all lawyers disagreed, arguing that law French provided an agreed-upon set of terms that made the law clear and certain. Some moderates were sympathetic to the use of English in the courts and in legal literature.

Legal language became a major issue during the revolutionary era. Legislation during the Interregnum made English the language of the courts and the law.

[3] Although the beyond reasonable doubt language became the predominant standard, 'satisfied conscience' and 'moral certainty' remained in use. 'Moral certainty' continued to be used long after its meaning was no longer understood. See Barbara J Shapiro, *'Beyond Reasonable Doubt' and 'Probable Cause': Historical Perspectives on the Anglo American Law of Evidence* (Berkeley, University of California Press, 1991). See also Barbara J Shapiro, '"Beyond Reasonable Doubt": The Neglected Eighteenth-Century Context,' (2014) 8 *Law and Humanities* 9.

Many legal works were translated into English at that time. When the Restoration Parliament repudiated all legislation enacted between the death of Charles I and the restoration of the monarchy in 1660, English as the language of the law was swept away. Demands for English were heard occasionally after 1660, but were not a featured item in parliament. Legislation making English the language of Acts of Parliament and the courts of justice was enacted in 1731 with little discussion. Its justification was familiar. As the statute indicated, English must be used because 'many and great mischiefs do frequently happen … from the proceedings in the courts of justice being in an unknown language'. Standard handwriting replaced the 'court hand', which few could decipher and confusing abbreviations were abolished.[4]

XII. Law Reform and the English Past

Radical and moderate reformers understood the history of England differently, and those differences shaped their view of the common law, the legal profession, legal institutions and acceptable approaches to law reform. Radicals favoured the restoration of a somewhat mythical Saxon past, while moderates emphasised legal continuity. Radicals, many of whom were influenced by the Levellers, saw the Norman Conquest as marking a sharp division between praiseworthy Saxon law and institutions and the imposition of the Norman Yoke. The Normans brought with them the evils of feudalism and a tyrannical monarchy, as well as the common law and the legal profession. Radicals were adamant about eliminating a law incomprehensible to the people. Many wished to restore pre-Conquest law which was thought to have been brief, clear and written in English. The codification of the much-lauded King Edward the Confessor was frequently invoked, and local juries and local justice, thought to characterise the Saxon past, should replace the justice provided by the centralised royal courts with their lawyers and judges.

While moderate reformers recognised that the Norman Conquest introduced much that was new, they emphasised continuity rather than a sharp break in legal culture in 1066. English law was the cumulative wisdom of many generations, not an oppressive law imposed by the Normans. They recognised that there had been changes in the law and many referred to Danish and Saxon predecessors. They did not associate the Norman kings, the aristocracy and the feudal law that emerged from the Norman Conquest with tyranny. The common law and the legal profession

[4] 4 Geo II c 26. It has been suggested that the legislation of 1731 may have been related to Union with Scotland; Peter M Teitsma, *Legal Language* (Chicago, University of Chicago Press, 1999); Ruth Morris, 'Great Mischiefs: An Historical Looked at Language Legislation in Great Britain' in D Kibbe (ed), *Language, Legislation and Linguistic Rights* (Amsterdam, John Benjamins Publishing Company, 1996) 32–54.

that emerged over time was a praiseworthy rather than a malignant growth. Moderate reformers were divided on the question of whether English should replace law French. Some supported the use of English in the courts and engaged in efforts to simplify and clarify the law; some did not. Moderates also looked to Edward the Confessor, but used his example to support the notion of kings as compilers and rationalisers of the law. James I and Justinian, like Edward, are often treated as model law reformers.

Some moderates insisted that the common law did not change, while others recognised that it did. Both emphasised continuity and treated that continuity as desirable. Moderate reformers writing during and after the revolutionary decades made a great effort to distance themselves from the radicals, characterising them as ignorant, hasty, wild and wishing to dismantle the existing social order. Moderates showed no interest in modifying current social arrangements and distinctions.

XIII. Comments and Speculation

The remaining section of the chapter examines a number of relevant but unanswerable or only partially answerable questions that emerge from my account of English law reform. Some are unique to the period studied, while others may also be relevant for those interested in legal change or legal systems more generally. This section in some instances strays from the historical to the general and more speculative issues.

The first is the question of how satisfied or dissatisfied the English were with their laws and legal institutions. The question is worth some thought since we know that most, if not all, legal systems are subject to complaints about excessive cost, long delays, greedy lawyers and less than impartial judges. Is the presence of such complaints alone sufficient evidence to indicate overwhelming dissatisfaction? Do the complaints that issued from parliament and the press reveal that the laws and the legal institutions functioned adequately or that they were in desperate need of major repair? I suggest that moderate reformers fall mostly into the first category and that this was the dominant strand of law reform at least through the mid-eighteenth century. Parliament was the place where that criticism was primarily expressed. The Crown's interest in reform was considerable during the sixteenth and early seventeenth centuries, but diminished over time. However much the judges were sympathetic to modest improvements, few were vocal advocates of change. The exceptions were the Lord Chancellors and Lord Keepers. A judicial ideology that emphasised continuity and insisted that judges did not make the law meant that the judiciary on whole did not encourage or support major change. Yet quite a few tried to reform their own courts. Can we label them satisfied or dissatisfied? Moderate reformers who wished to improve an existing system were generally satisfied with the institutions themselves. There appears to have been a compatibility of reform with a reluctance to make substantial changes.[5]

Radical reformers, whose existence was largely limited to the revolutionary decades, were anxious to eradicate an unacceptable system 'root and branch'. Their intense dissatisfaction was expressed primarily in print, petitions and to some extent in the New Model Army. As for the population at large, there is insufficient evidence to say much about its satisfaction or dissatisfaction. Some no doubt purchased, read and discussed the reform publications, both radical and moderate; others probably did not. In either case, we have little or no information about their response.

The enormous fluctuations in the use of legal institutions, something that most earlier historians of law reform were unaware of, complicates the issue of dissatisfaction and satisfaction. We have now become aware of the very large increase in the number of people from different social classes who engaged in litigation during the period 1580–1680, more than at any time in England's history. This great increase must have put great pressure on the courts and thus increased the delays of which there were so often complaints. Despite the expansion of Chancery and the addition of the conciliar courts, the legal system proved insufficient to handle the increased litigation in what was considered a timely matter. Increased participation might suggest either increased confidence in the legal system or that the vastly increased contact with courts and lawyers generated increased dissatisfaction.

High levels of participation began to decline in about 1640, then more sharply about 1680, and dropped off precipitously during the eighteenth century. Although it has been suggested that the decline was the result of increased lawyer fees, other conditions may also have been at work. A large proportion of the population engaged in credit transactions that were the mainstay of court business. It is likely that the increased supply of coinage made transactions easier, reducing the need to deal with the courts. Later, debt settlement may also have been eased with the increased use of bills of exchange or Bank of England notes. The absence of the services once provided by the conciliar courts may also help explain of the decline. The decline that began in around 1640 may be explained by the disruptions of the Civil War and its aftermath. There is a correlation between the growth in the number using the courts and the increased interest of parliament in law reform, but the relationship is unclear because the number of those people using the courts dropped off sharply while parliamentary reform measures continued and law reform publications declined.

Complaints of the excessive costs of litigation were a constant over the entire period. It must be pointed out that such complaints are found in many, if not all,

[5] For a discussion of moderate and radical law reform and the role of lawyers in the late eighteenth and early nineteenth century, see Michael Lobban, '"Old Wine in New Bottles": The Concept and Practice of Law Reform 1780–1830' in Joanna Innis and Arthur Burns (eds), *Rethinking the Age of Reform: Britain 1780–1850* (Cambridge, Cambridge University Press, 2003) 114–36.

legal systems and are still with us. How can one determine whether legal costs were or are excessive? Access to justice in the early modern period was clearly shaped by the ability to pay lawyers and court officials. Although litigation was expensive, it nevertheless proved possible for very large numbers of people to pay for it. Many were willing and able to increase their legal expenses by moving their cases from one court to another. Lawyers were and continue to be charged with extracting overly large fees from their clients, but it is unclear how one might determine what were or are appropriate fees.

If it was expensive for litigants, the English legal system was inexpensive for the government. There were only 12 judges. The cost to the government was low even after judges became salaried. Although increasing the number of judges might have eased delays, that option was not considered. Court officials were supported by user fees and other payments frequently labelled 'corruption'. Payment in 'gifts' and other forms of 'corruption' would continue until the government paid its bureaucrats and public officials.

Nor was the cost of local justice a significant expense for the government. The cost of assizes was borne by local communities. Justices of the peace were unpaid, as were the grand and petty juries that were a mainstay of English justice. Plaintiffs, defendants, witnesses and jurors complained of the cost to them in terms of time and income lost. Jurors often refused to appear. Government expenditures on the justice system remained very low compared to most European countries. Who should pay for what legal services remains an issue for societies concerned with access to justice.

The centrality of juries in the English legal system is often noted. Misbehaving juries were punishable by Star Chamber until its abolition. Juries were increasingly freed from central control. When Vaughan's decision in Bushel's case determined that judges were not to control jury verdicts, and juries could not be fined, institutional control of juries disappeared. Although juries, at least in theory, were immune from any outside pressure, they were often said to be dominated by judges. Throughout the early modern period, jurors were criticised for lack of education, economic status and the pressure on them from bribery or social and economic superiors. In civil cases, damage judgments could be set aside, but jurors in criminal cases were answerable to no one. Juries had become largely answerable to no one and were becoming what is often called a 'black box'.

Another difficult-to-answer question involves the low rate of law reform success. Both contemporaries and later historians frequently attributed failure to lawyer opposition. Lawyers certainly opposed reforms that reduced their income, but lawyer MPs were also deeply involved in drafting and arguing on behalf of reform bills and statute consolidation. Many moderate law reformers were lawyers, and Lord Chancellors were active spokesmen for reform. Recalcitrant lawyers cannot be a sufficient answer.[6]

[6] For a discussion of lawyers and reform failure, see Blair Worden, *The Rump Parliament 1648–1653* (Cambridge, Cambridge University Press, 1974) 108–17. Donald Veall attributed the failure to the

I suggest that the institutional weakness of parliament that made the completion of legislation so difficult must be taken into account. The number of bills completed by parliament was remarkably few throughout the period. This meant that law reform legislation was lost, along with other kinds of legislation. Parliaments, before the Revolution of 1688, were not regular parts of the government. They were often suddenly called, suddenly prorogued and suddenly adjourned. There were also considerable stretches of time when parliament did not meet at all. It is all too easy to forget that parliaments were held intermittently and were typically called to meet some financial or other emergency. And when they were called, law reform was rarely a high-priority item. Moderate law reform was a recurrent theme in early modern parliaments, but not an urgently sought-after goal. Parliaments met more frequently after 1688 and sat for longer, but continued to have a relatively poor record of completing legislation. The continuing lack of success in completing legislation helps to explain the failure of many reform measures.[7]

Parliament itself recognised that it was not an effective institution for developing law reform proposals, and from time to time it appointed committees or commissions composed of lawyers and non-lawyers to investigate and prepare legislation. The early Stuart era marked the high point in the creation of committees dealing with law and court reform issues. The Rump Parliament's Hale Commission, which produced the most complete programme of reform for parliament, came to nothing when the Rump was forcibly dismissed and replaced by the Barebones Parliament. William Sheppard's *England's Balme*, commissioned by Oliver Cromwell, was the work of a single person and was ignored after the end of the Protectorate.

The appropriate role and status of judges is difficult to define. This role in early modern England was quite different from the present one. During much of the early modern period, judges performed administrative and legislative as well as judicial functions and were often leading political figures as well. That combination is an uncomfortable one, at least for Americans, who typically think in terms of Montesquieu's three distinct branches of government and see judiciaries as more or less independent branches of government largely uncontrolled by the executive or legislature. Early modern judges were not independent of the Crown or the Lord Protector and did not speak of independence from them. A good judge was thought to be learned and unbiased rather than independent.

Now, as in the distant past, there are occasions when judges have become unpopular. During the pre-revolutionary era, judges were sometime criticised for supporting the Crown rather than 'the law'. What that law was, however, was not always clear, especially during the reigns of the early Stuarts, when the judges were quite sympathetic to the Crown's version of the law. If judges were to adhere to the

insufficient will of those in authority; Donald Veall, *The Popular Movement for Law Reform 1640–1660* (Oxford, Clarendon Press, 1970) 239; see also 225–26.

[7] For a comparative treatment of the role of legislation and instruments of justice, see Padoa Schioppa, *Legislation and Justice* (Oxford, Clarendon Press, 1997) 103–22.

law, how might they act when the law itself was contested? The clash of loyalties was very great at the time of the trial of Charles I, which many believed to be unlawful, and again during the Protectorate, when judges became reluctant to adopt legal procedures that did not conform to traditional legal practice. Judges were reluctant to use the Protector's Chancery ordinance because it lacked parliamentary approval. They felt it necessary to resign or to continue using the traditional legal procedures. Trouble was likely to occur when judges and/or their supporters believed that governments, monarchical or otherwise, were not obeying the law.

A different type of judicial issue arose when parliaments became particularly hostile to particular judicial opinions. The most extreme example occurred in 1640–41, when Parliament sought to impeach the judges on charges of treason for their legal opinions in the ship money case. When judicial decisions led to divisive politics, the role and status of judges became part of the controversy, and this continues to this day in many countries.

Since there were only 12 common law judges at any one time, the same number as had existed for several hundred years, their dockets overflowed and the progress of cases through their courts was slow. It became even slower as the number of litigants expanded. It is therefore puzzling that reformers did not consider increasing the number of judges. One can only speculate as to whether an increase in the number of the common law judges might have alleviated the problem of long delays. How many judges and how many courts are 'enough'?

Similar questions can be raised in connection with the assizes. The number of days and the time that judges spent at the assizes judging cases, like the number of judges, differed little from the medieval era, despite the enormous increase in legal business and the decay of local courts. On some occasions, when there were insufficient judges to man all the circuits, highly respected lawyers were recruited to serve as temporary judges. However, there were no suggestions of expanding the number of assize judges, despite the complaints about rushed or unfinished cases as the judge moved on to the next group of trials or to the next assize location. Historians have often noted that criminal trials were dispatched especially rapidly. However, modifying the assizes so as to better meet current needs was on neither the moderate nor the radical agenda.

Given the recent scholarly interest in state building, we should at least raise the question of whether and how England's legal system of the early modern period fits into that process. Medieval historians have often emphasised the role of the common law and the common law courts in medieval state building. The efforts of early modern governments to gain control of outlying parts of the country by expanding the reach of the law should also be considered part of that process.[8]

[8] Michael Braddick, *State Formation in England c 1550–1700* (Cambridge, Cambridge University Press, 2000); Paul Brand, 'The Formation of the English Legal System, 1150–1400' in Schioppa (n 7) 103–22; Clive Holmes, 'Legal Instruments of Power and the State in Early Modern England' in Schioppa (n 7) 262–90.

We have seen the process at work in the activities of the Council of the North and the Council of Wales. Wales was successfully incorporated into England's legal and political system; the north took somewhat longer. Efforts to incorporate Scotland and Ireland might also be considered when considering the question of state building. The unsuccessful Jacobean proposal for Union foundered over the unification of the laws of Scotland and England. When political union was achieved in 1707, it was a political union that retained two distinct laws and legal institutions. Scotland became a part of Great Britain, not part of England. One might also consider England's long-term efforts to impose English legal institutions on Ireland as a failed effort at state building. Was England's relation to its American and Caribbean colonies a success or failure in the context of state building? The growth of the Empire and its relationship to various kinds of local law makes the questions even more complicated.

The question of state building segues into questions regarding centralisation in the legal system. How much centralisation of political and legal institutions is necessary to achieve a unified state or to prevent state dissolution? Tension between the centre and the local was a continuing one in early modern England. Noble control over the localities was gradually brought under control. The addition of the conciliar courts was a centralising development, but those courts lasted only until 1640–41.

There were both localising and centralising features of the English legal system. The Crown was obviously a centralising institution. Parliament was both a local and central institution. It spoke for the whole country and much but not all of its legislation covered the entire country, yet its members were mindful of local issues and often promoted local interests. Although appointments and dismissals of justices of the peace were in the hands of the Crown and its advisors, the unpaid justices were and remained local in their mindset. Over time, the justices of the peace experienced increased duties and less supervision. Though responsible for administering a good deal of the law, they never became Crown officials.

The common law and its judges covered the entire country and thus were centralising institutions, but jury trials were local. Grand juries were composed of local dignitaries and on some occasions used petitions or addresses to influence parliament to act on their behalf. Vocal spokesmen for reducing central law and institutions were to be found in the 1640s and 1650s. Local judges and local courts were featured in Leveller manifestoes and those of their allies, leading to fears of 'cantonisation' and dissolution of an existing law for the whole country.

Discussion of the mid-seventeenth-century English revolution quite naturally leads to questions about the relationship between political revolution and legal change. Should we expect revolutions to be accompanied by major changes in the law and legal institutions? England may have experienced a revolution, but, aside from the king, the ruling elite was not dislodged from power. After the abolition of the conciliar courts, the Long Parliament did not push for major changes in the legal system. Though the Protectorate government supported legal reform, it did not propose reforms that were as drastic as the abolition of the conciliar courts. After the abolition of the conciliar courts, only the Barebones Parliament among the numerous parliaments wished to transform the legal system. Those who actually held power during the revolutionary years did not wish to greatly alter the existing law or the legal system. Those who advocated radical legal change never became major power-holders, with the possible exception of some members of the New Model Army. One therefore might ask how revolutionary were the governments of revolutionary England? What degree of change merits the label revolution? Does it require replacement of the ruling class or only of the ruler? Or does it require a major reshaping of the law and legal institutions?

Another issue that is difficult to deal with involves how to access the role and impact of the polemical publications that appeared in such large numbers during the 1640s and 1650s. Merely counting them yields some information about what ideas circulated, but tells us little about how influential those ideas were or how many people read or were even aware of the publications.[9] Contemporaries probably saw or heard about some radical proposals, but how many each person might have been aware of is unclear. Were radical publications successful in gaining adherents or did they turn readers away? We know that radical publications had some impact because parliaments expressed worry about the radical threat of overturning traditional institutions and the social hierarchy. Although the newsbooks of the revolutionary era have been well studied by literary historians and parliamentary historians, they have been insufficiently explored for information about the availability of information on law reform. We know little about the response of the larger public to the publications of the radical or moderate reformers and even less about the vast majority who never read about law reform, and who may or may not have paid much attention to the publications they did read. The problem, of course, is not unique to revolutionary-era publications. The same or similar issues arise for intellectual and cultural historians engaged in assessing the impact or influence of individual or groups of published works and for other scholars attempting to determine public opinion. Political scientists and others who are engaged in efforts to determine modern public opinion at a given moment in time, but public opinion and the reasons for changes in public opinion often remain elusive.

As we have noted earlier, crime control in early modern England has been characterised as a combination of harsh penalties and a wide range of discretion in its execution. Should we conclude that the English were ambivalent or held contradictory views? It is possible that they were satisfied with the combination of harsh laws and local discretion. Competing approaches to crime control, of course, are to be found in many polities and there continue to be debates on how best to deal with criminal offenders. What alternatives are available to societies that are unwilling or unable to support police or prisons? Are prisons viable when local

[9] The numerous studies of Jason Peacey provide the best information on this subject.

and/or central governments are neither willing nor able to provide the necessary resources for housing and feeding prisoners?

English parliaments and publicists were frequently concerned with problems associated with creditors and debtors. Imprisonment for debt was often criticised. Periodically emptying the prisons of poor debtors did little to solve the problem. One cannot help but wonder if there were consciously ignored alternatives, since several European countries managed without imprisonment for debt.

This study suggests that law reform must take into account how the various proposed reforms fit into the legal system as a whole. Looking at reform publications alone is insufficient. Looking at parliament alone is insufficient. It is necessary to include the positive, negative or neutral stance of the Crown and the Privy Council, jurisdictional competition that underlay a good deal of reform interest, the creation of new courts and the decline in old courts and the number of people seeking to use the legal system. It must take into account the roles of the Lord Chancellors, judges and the legal profession in promoting or opposing reform. It must also look beyond the letter of the laws and take into account whether or not they were executed. The exercise of discretion existed throughout the legal system and we have seen it practised by prosecutors, plaintiffs, defendants, grand juries, juries and judges.

In brief summary, then, those I have labelled moderate reformers voiced a considerable repertoire of changes. This included a wide range of complaints and proposals concerning the cost, efficiency and structure of courts, and the composition and faults of juries. The legal profession, including judges and justices of the peace, attracted scrutiny. There was a great deal of concern in relation to fraud, especially in land transactions and occasional pleas for a system of land registration. The intersection of law and religion yielded debates about sanctuaries, an established church, toleration, tithes, wills and probate and oaths. Creditor–debtor conflicts, bankruptcy, imprisonment for debt and prison conditions were all issues in the early modern period. The reach of the criminal law and the severity or lack thereof, habeas corpus, rationalisation of the statutes, the production of systematised legal texts and reports of court decisions received considerable attention, particularly from judges and the large contingent of lawyers in parliament. There was much praise of the common law in general, defences of the common law combined with attacks on particular legal rules and doctrines. There was generally agreement that judges were to follow not make law, law-making being reserved for parliament.

This repertoire, with fluctuations over time as to which particulars were most at issue, was in continuous play from the beginning to the end of the period under study here. Of course, those who favoured particular legal changes saw them then and see them now as reforms, while those in opposition saw them as anything but. That the reform proposals discussed at the beginning of the period were still under debate at the end would seem to indicate that very few changes were actually achieved.

Although political trials, mostly for treason, should not themselves be treated as reform, criticism of what were thought to be unreasonable or unfair trials with a strong political context did stimulate discussion. Often highlighted in these critiques were the oaths for defendants and defence witnesses, the number of required witnesses for conviction, counsel for defendants as well as the prosecution, and a right to see a copy of the indictment. The use of special tribunals, often labelled 'high courts of justice', rather than jury trials was also questioned from time to time, as were the definitions of treason and seditious libel. Though discussion was sporadic, often following in the wake of prominent treason trials, the issues recurred and may be considered part of the reform agenda. Such issues were most likely to be explored during such trials or in their immediate aftermath. With the exception of the late seventeenth-century trials which resulted in the Treason Act of 1696, they were not a significant part of the early modern moderate reform agenda.

Why did the reform proposals result in so few changes? Various answers can be offered to this question. Most obviously, the parliament centred-process of law-making rarely produced actual reforms because of parliament's institutional weakness for passing any kind of statutes. The patriotic attachment to the common law undoubtedly played some role in the reluctance to support major legal reform. The legal profession, including both judges and lawyers, had an enormous self-interest in the stability of traditional legal learning and practice, and had an influential voice in public affairs. Certainly many contemporaries and then later historians believed that greed and self-interest led them to thwart law reform efforts. The reform movement began long before what we habitually think of as the revolutionary era of English history and lasted long afterwards. The reform agenda before, during and after constantly raised the same issues and suggested the same solutions, clear proof that most reform initiatives were only satisfied after long periods in which they failed or never succeeded at all. Reform initiative often required parliamentary legislation, and parliament had great difficulty in completing most legislation most of the time.

Unlike the long, continuous agenda of what I have called 'moderate reformers', the radical law reform movement was prevalent only from 1643 to 1660. It was expressed primarily in pamphlets, petitions and the army rather than in parliament. Many of its adherents purported to seek a return to the simple law of pre-Norman times, sweeping away the common law, common lawyers and the Westminster courts in favour of local justice, self-representation by the parties and, especially among the Levellers, special protections for defendants. There should be a short, easy-to-understand code imposing Scripturally derived criminal penalties. It sought to abolish tithes and to establish religious toleration. The radical reformers were also especially active in promoting the end to imprisonment for debt and in providing protections for defendants in trials for treason and felony. The radical movement was unsuccessful, although for a time it added variety and confusion to a crowded reform agenda.

Historians tend to be more attracted to tracing change than continuities. One might ask why bother to provide a lengthy account of a largely unsuccessful movement. All periods of time are composed of a mixture of both change and continuity. This study has attempted to show the importance of the latter as well as the former in understanding early modern English political and legal culture. While legal systems are more or less comfortable with change, continuity, stability, and certainty are essential parts of a successful legal system.

Like most historical studies, this one leaves a number of important questions unresolved. Some of these are specific to early modern England; others may be relevant to other legal studies. It is to be hoped that pointing to some of the difficult-to-deal-with interpretive issues, along with my account of early modern English law reform, will lead to discussion of these and similar issues among historians and non-historians interested in the nature of legal reform, legal change, state building and legal systems in other times and other places.

INDEX